al · Danbi Original · Danbi Original · Danbi Original · Danbi Original · Danbi Original · Da

HISSING

vol.2

Kang EunYoung

ice Kunion

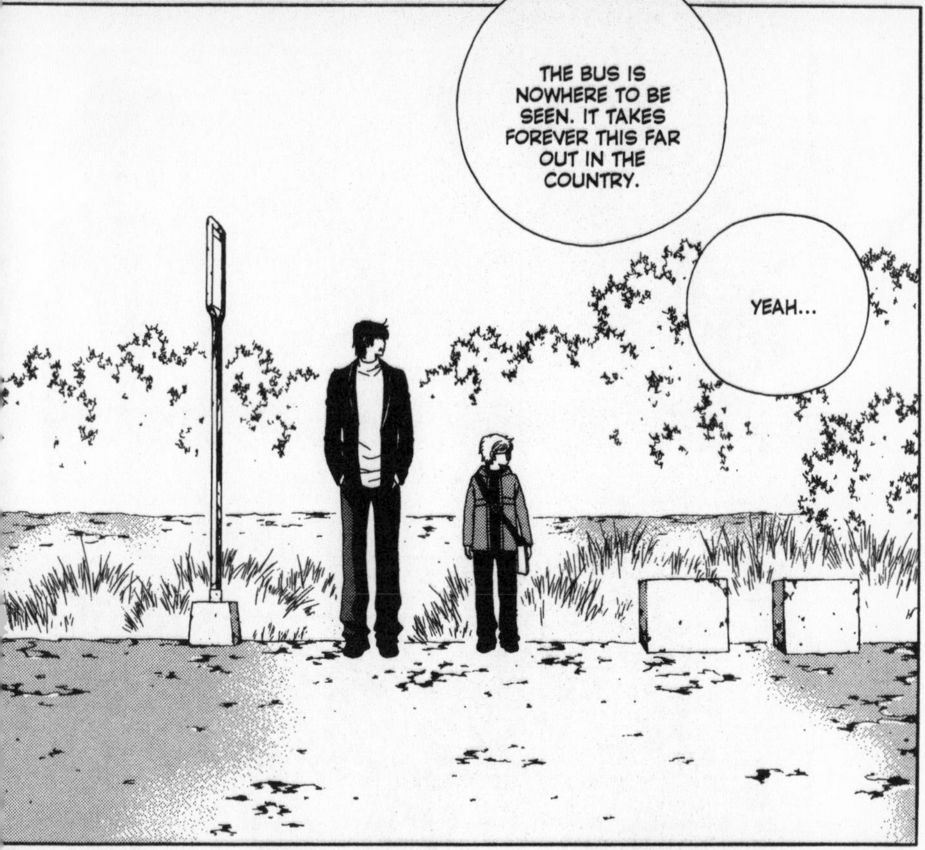
THE BUS IS NOWHERE TO BE SEEN. IT TAKES FOREVER THIS FAR OUT IN THE COUNTRY.
YEAH...

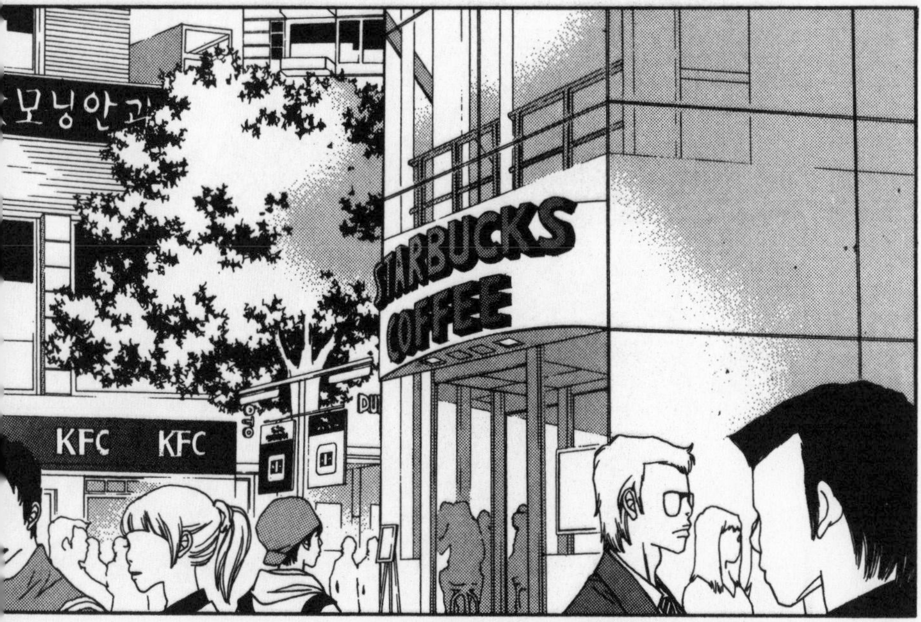
COFFEE
KFC
KFC

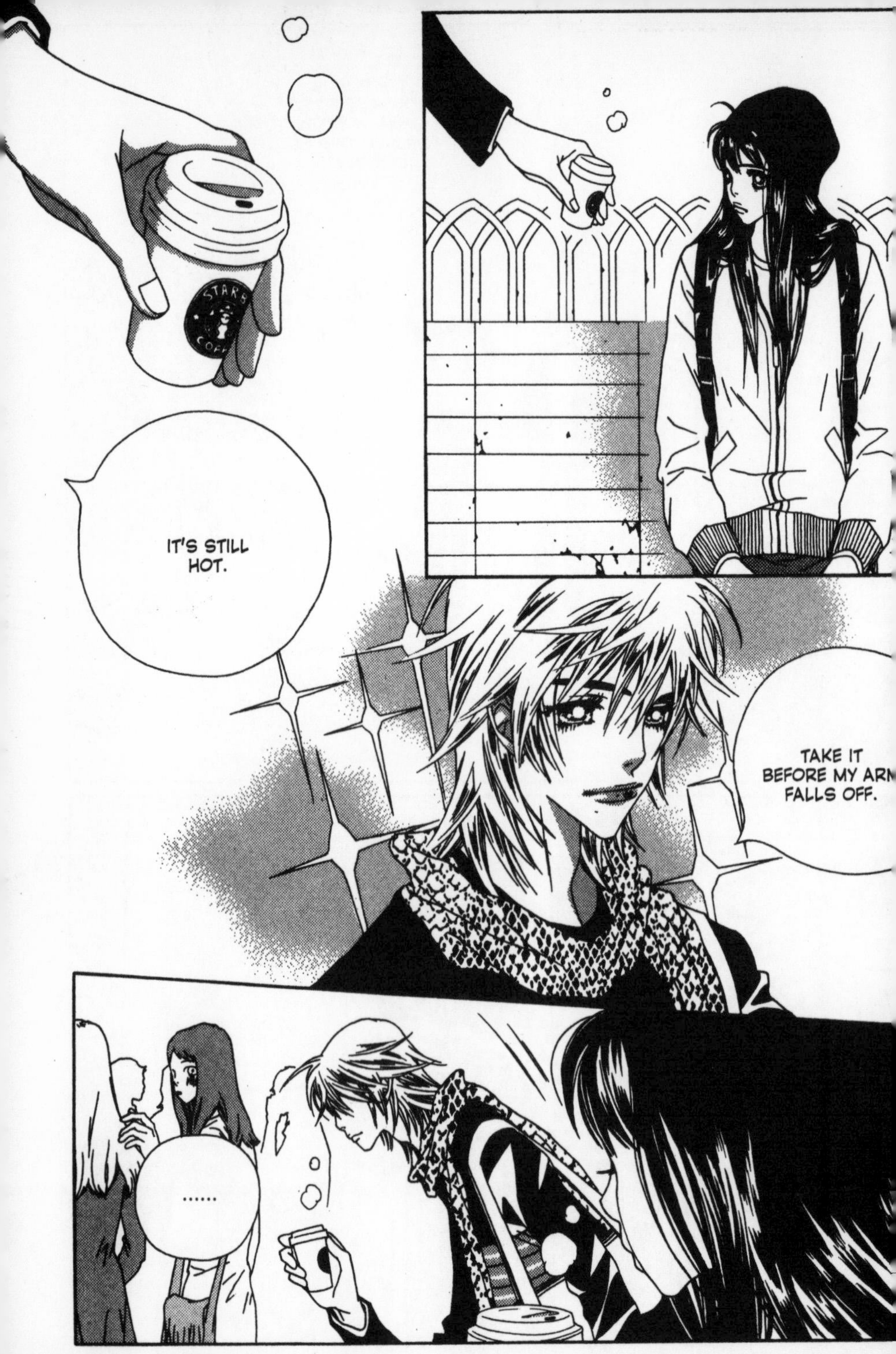
IT'S STILL HOT.
TAKE IT BEFORE MY ARM FALLS OFF.
......

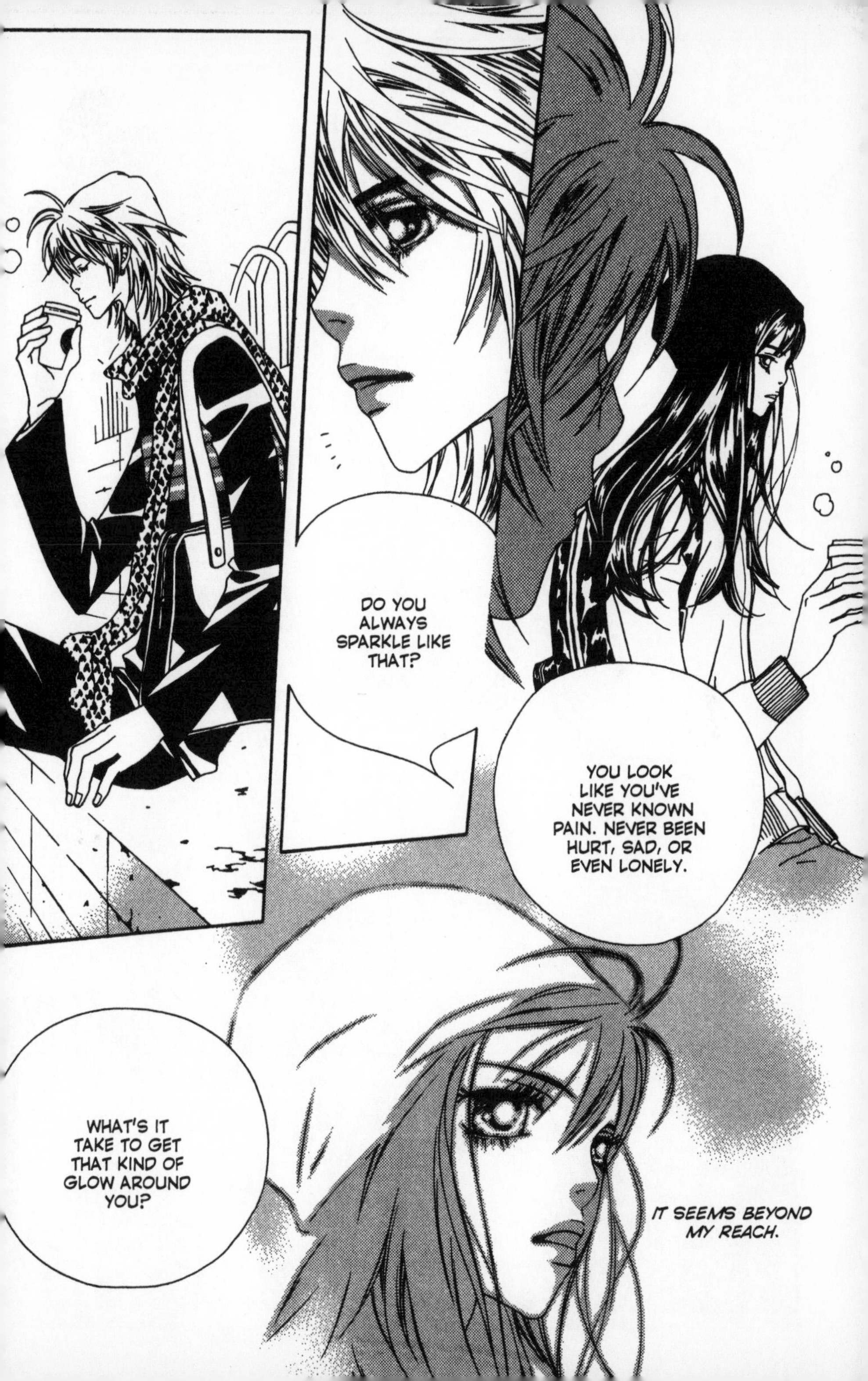
DO YOU ALWAYS SPARKLE LIKE THAT?
YOU LOOK LIKE YOU'VE NEVER KNOWN PAIN. NEVER BEEN HURT, SAD, OR EVEN LONELY.
WHAT'S IT TAKE TO GET THAT KIND OF GLOW AROUND YOU?
IT SEEMS BEYOND MY REACH.

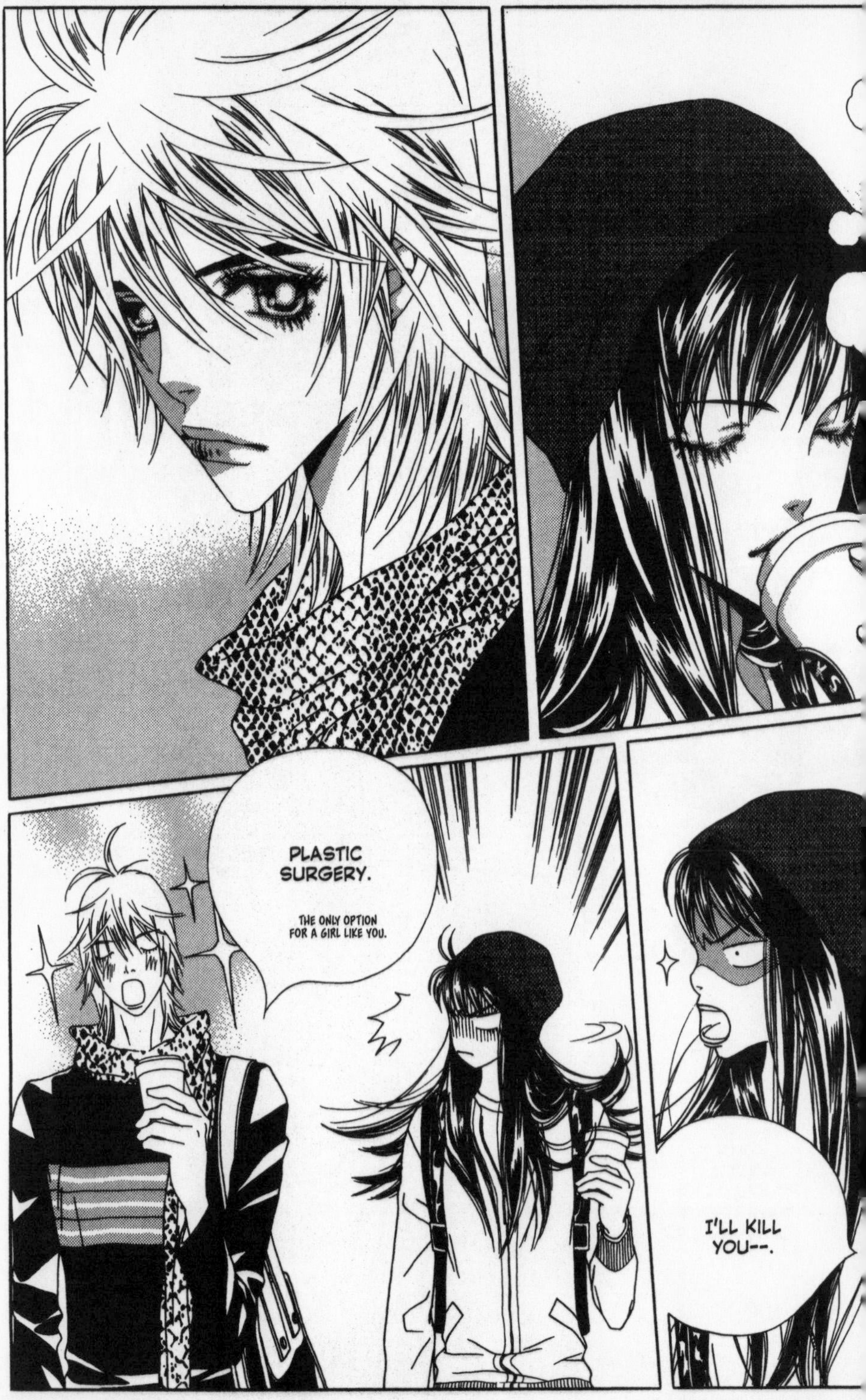
PLASTIC SURGERY.
THE ONLY OPTION FOR A GIRL LIKE YOU.
I'LL KILL YOU--.

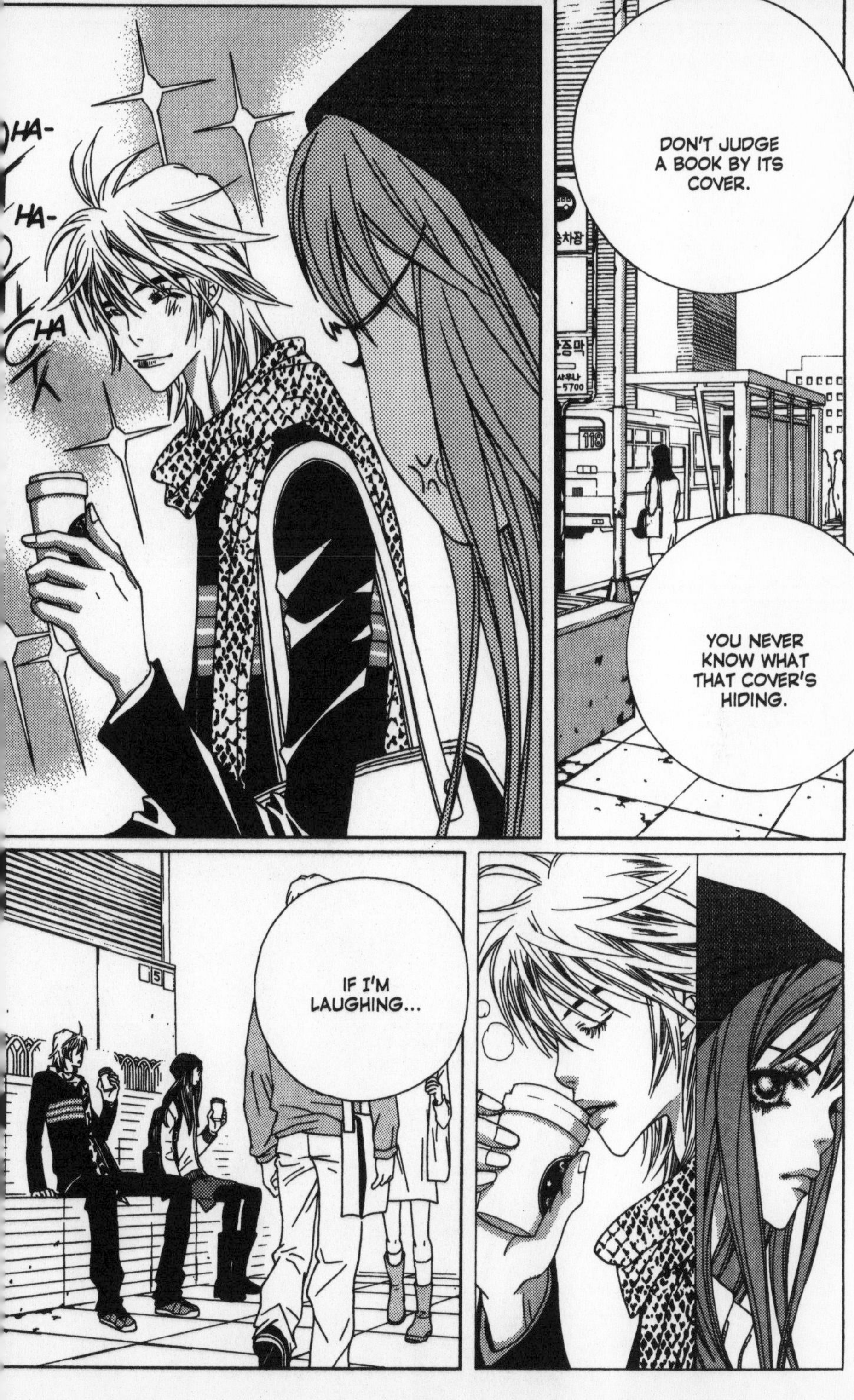
HA-
HA-
CHA
DON'T JUDGE A BOOK BY ITS COVER.
YOU NEVER KNOW WHAT THAT COVER'S HIDING.
IF I'M LAUGHING...

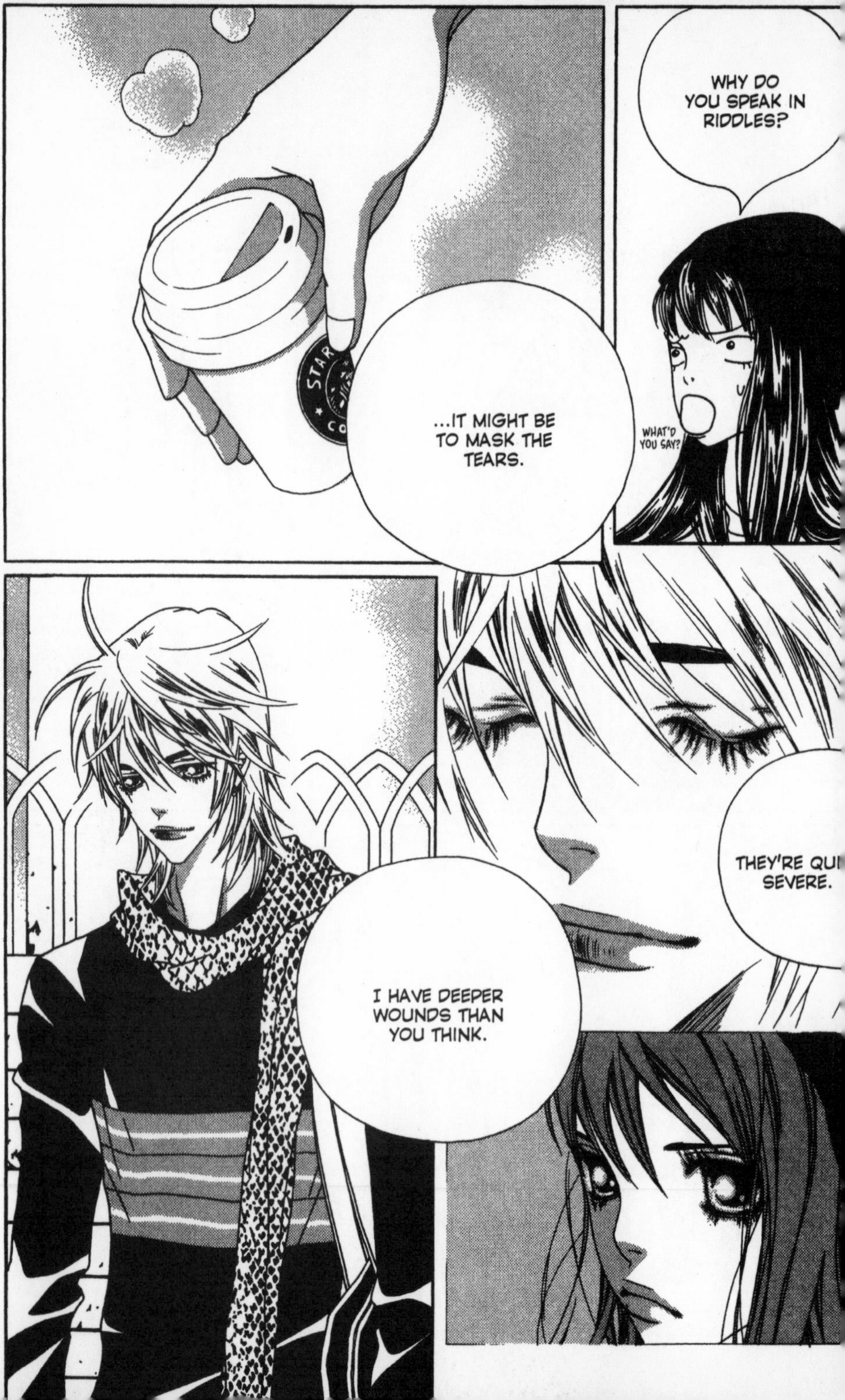
...IT MIGHT BE TO MASK THE TEARS.
WHY DO YOU SPEAK IN RIDDLES?
WHAT'D YOU SAY?
I HAVE DEEPER WOUNDS THAN YOU THINK.
THEY'RE QUI
SEVERE.

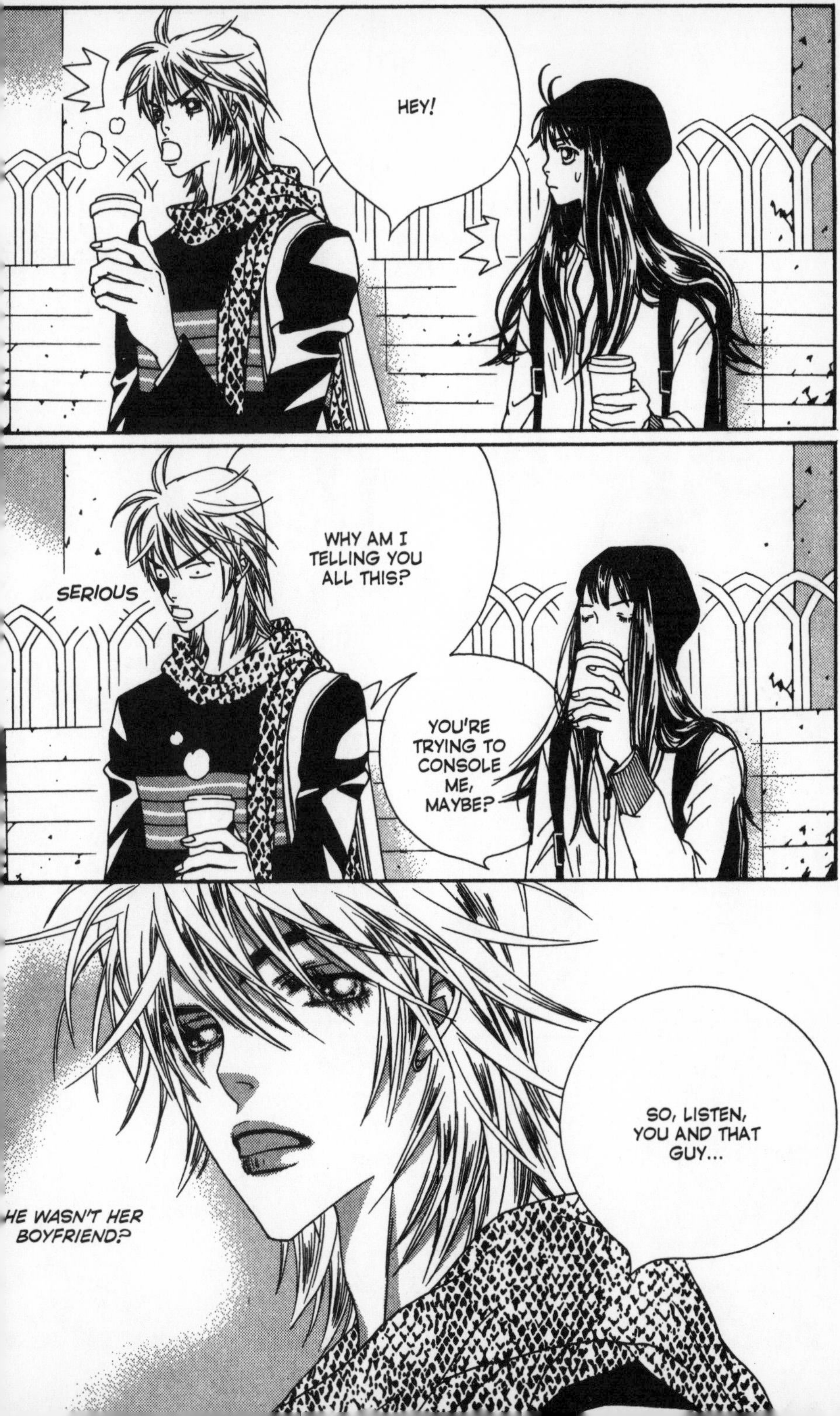
HEY!
SERIOUS
WHY AM I TELLING YOU ALL THIS?
YOU'RE TRYING TO CONSOLE ME, MAYBE?
HE WASN'T HER BOYFRIEND?
SO, LISTEN, YOU AND THAT GUY...

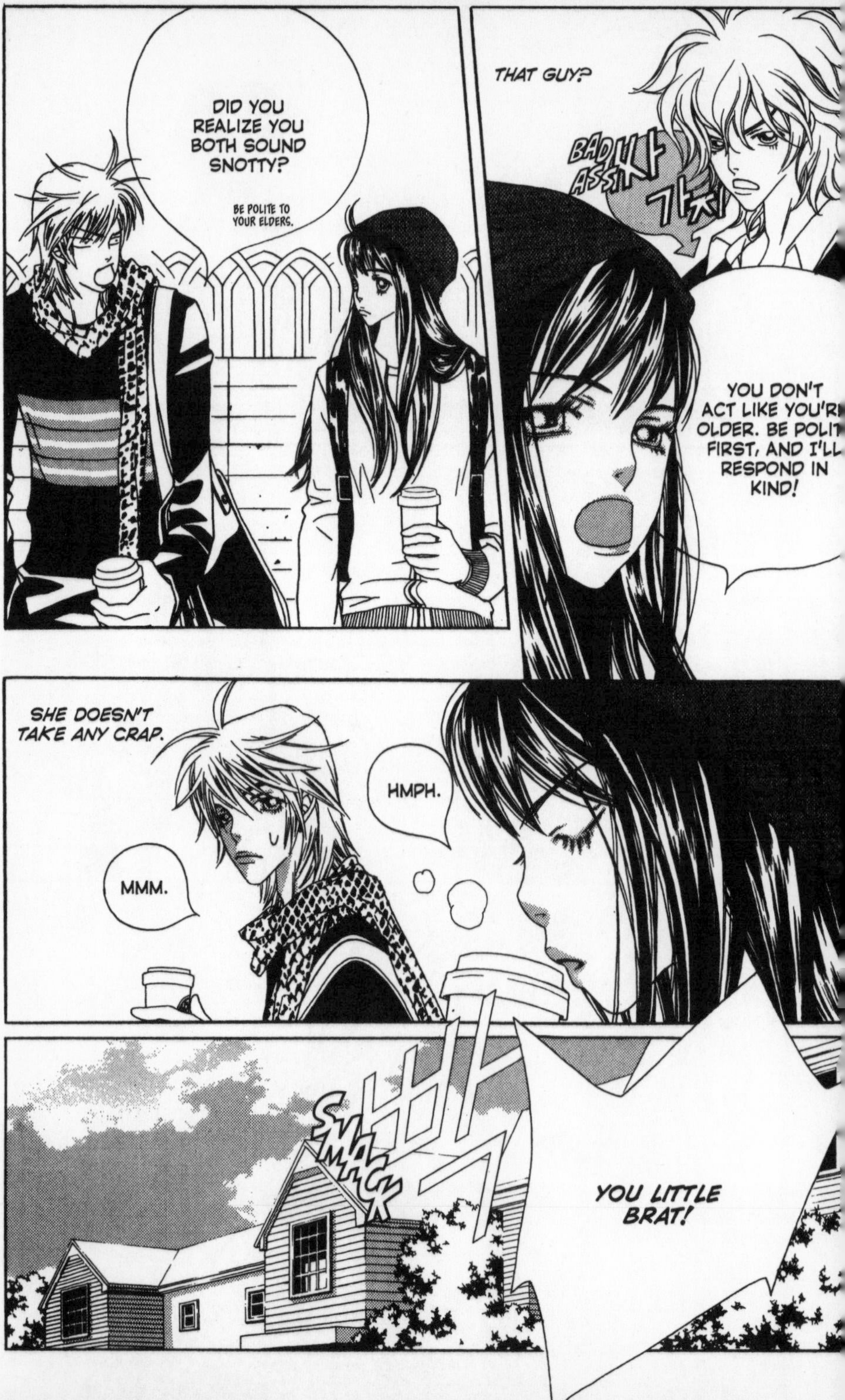
DID YOU REALIZE YOU BOTH SOUND SNOTTY?
BE POLITE TO YOUR ELDERS.
THAT GUY?
BAD ASS
YOU DON'T ACT LIKE YOU'R OLDER. BE POLIT FIRST, AND I'LL RESPOND IN KIND!
SHE DOESN'T TAKE ANY CRAP.
HMPH.
MMM.
SMACK
YOU LITTLE BRAT!

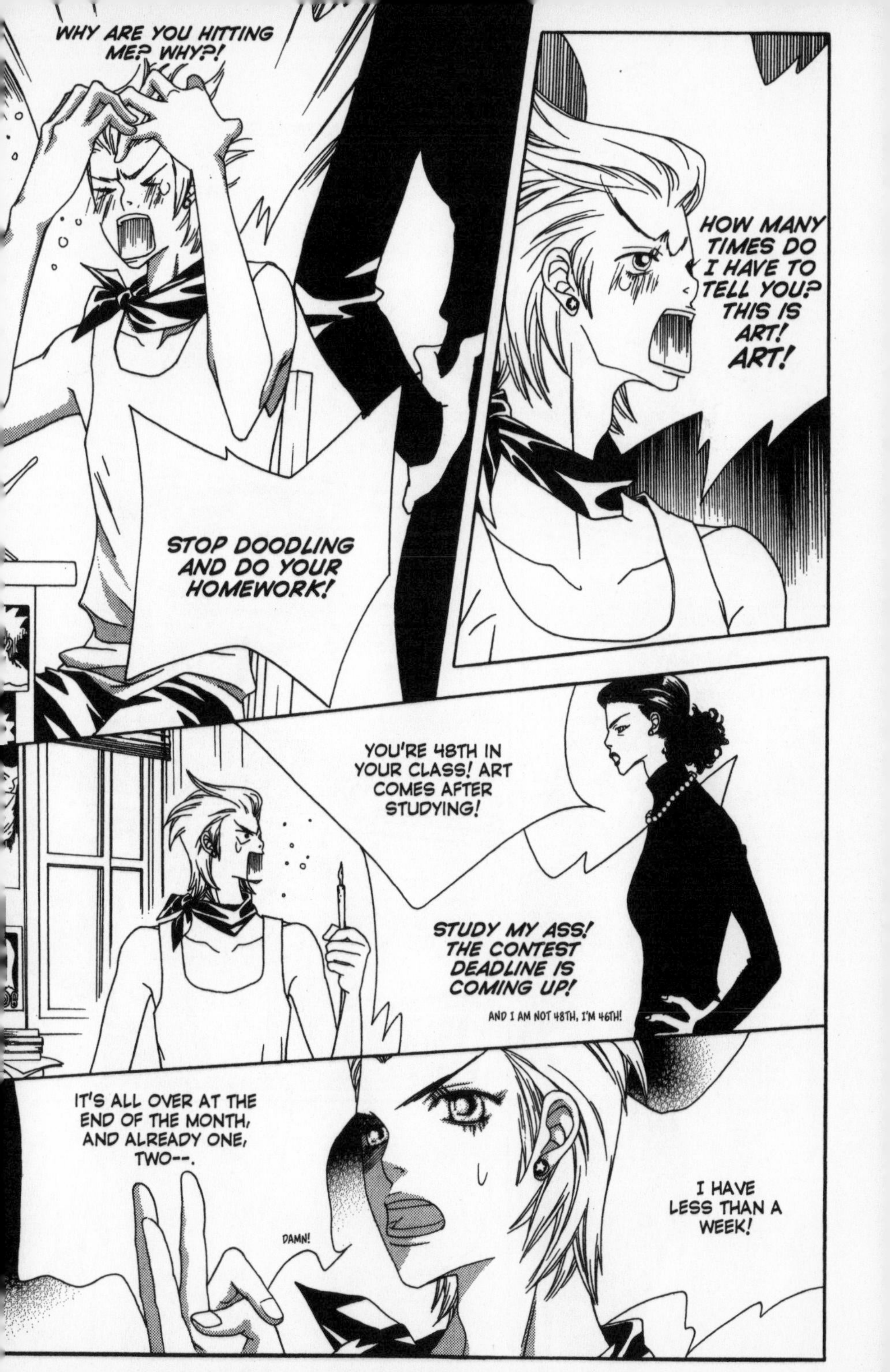
WHY ARE YOU HITTING ME? WHY?!
STOP DOODLING AND DO YOUR HOMEWORK!
HOW MANY TIMES DO I HAVE TO TELL YOU? THIS IS ART! ART!
YOU'RE 48TH IN YOUR CLASS! ART COMES AFTER STUDYING!
STUDY MY ASS! THE CONTEST DEADLINE IS COMING UP!
AND I AM NOT 48TH, I'M 46TH!
IT'S ALL OVER AT THE END OF THE MONTH, AND ALREADY ONE, TWO--.
DAMN!
I HAVE LESS THAN A WEEK!

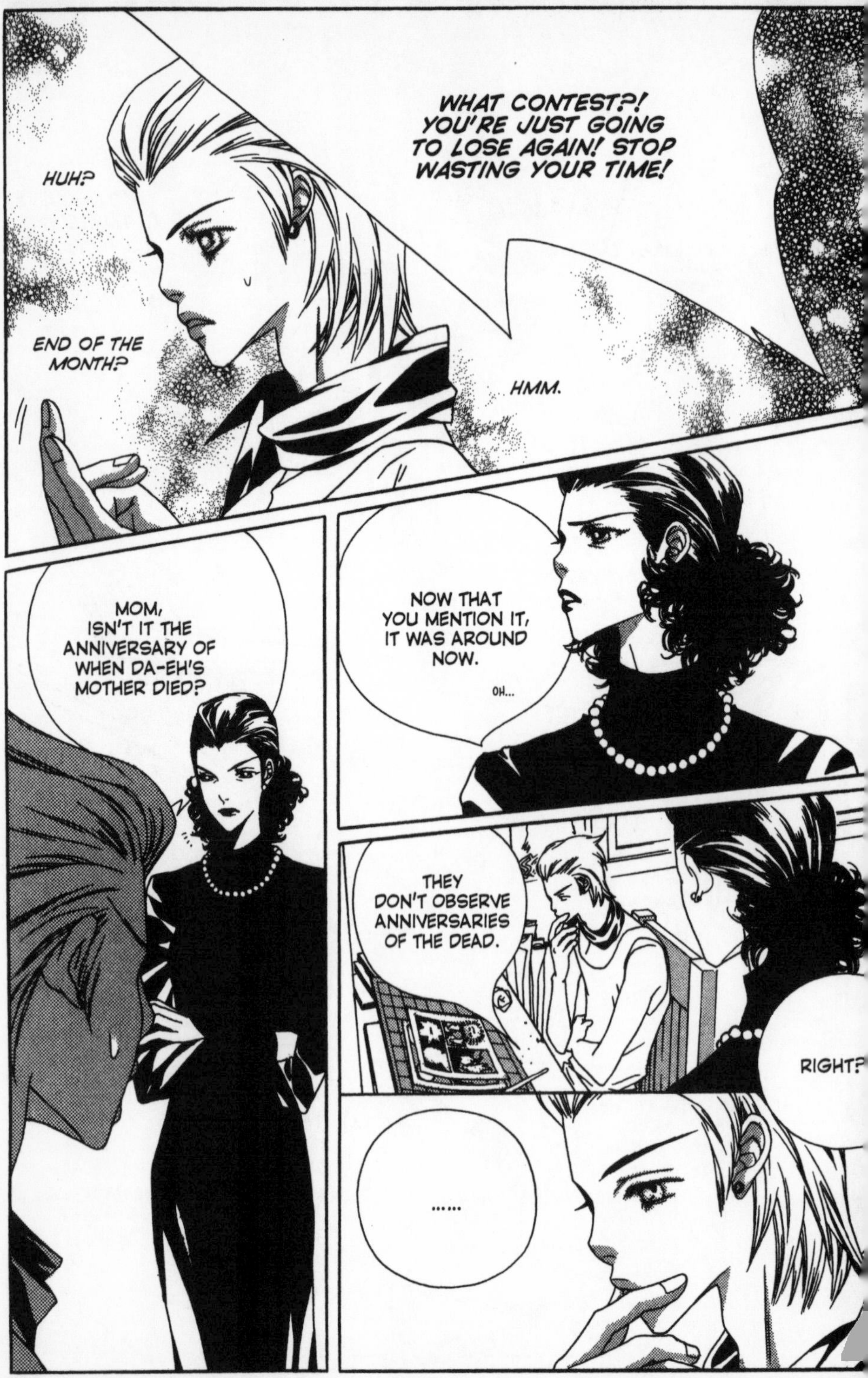
HUH?
END OF THE MONTH?
WHAT CONTEST?! YOU'RE JUST GOING TO LOSE AGAIN! STOP WASTING YOUR TIME!
HMM.
MOM, ISN'T IT THE ANNIVERSARY OF WHEN DA-EH'S MOTHER DIED?
NOW THAT YOU MENTION IT, IT WAS AROUND NOW.
OH...
THEY DON'T OBSERVE ANNIVERSARIES OF THE DEAD.
RIGHT?
......

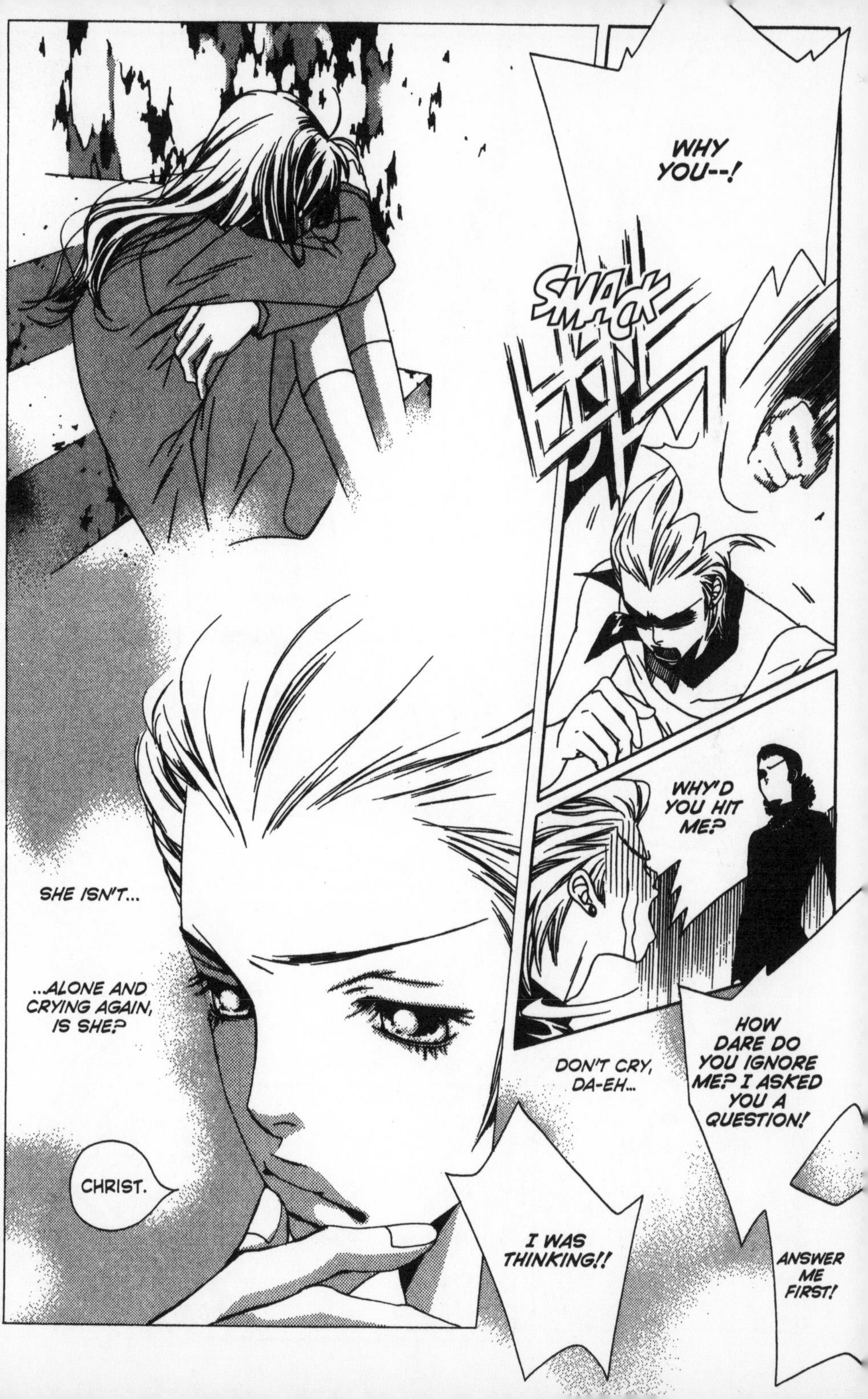
SHE ISN'T...
...ALONE AND CRYING AGAIN, IS SHE?
CHRIST.
WHY YOU--!
SMACK
WHY'D YOU HIT ME?
DON'T CRY, DA-EH...
HOW DARE DO YOU IGNORE ME? I ASKED YOU A QUESTION!
I WAS THINKING!!
ANSWER ME FIRST!

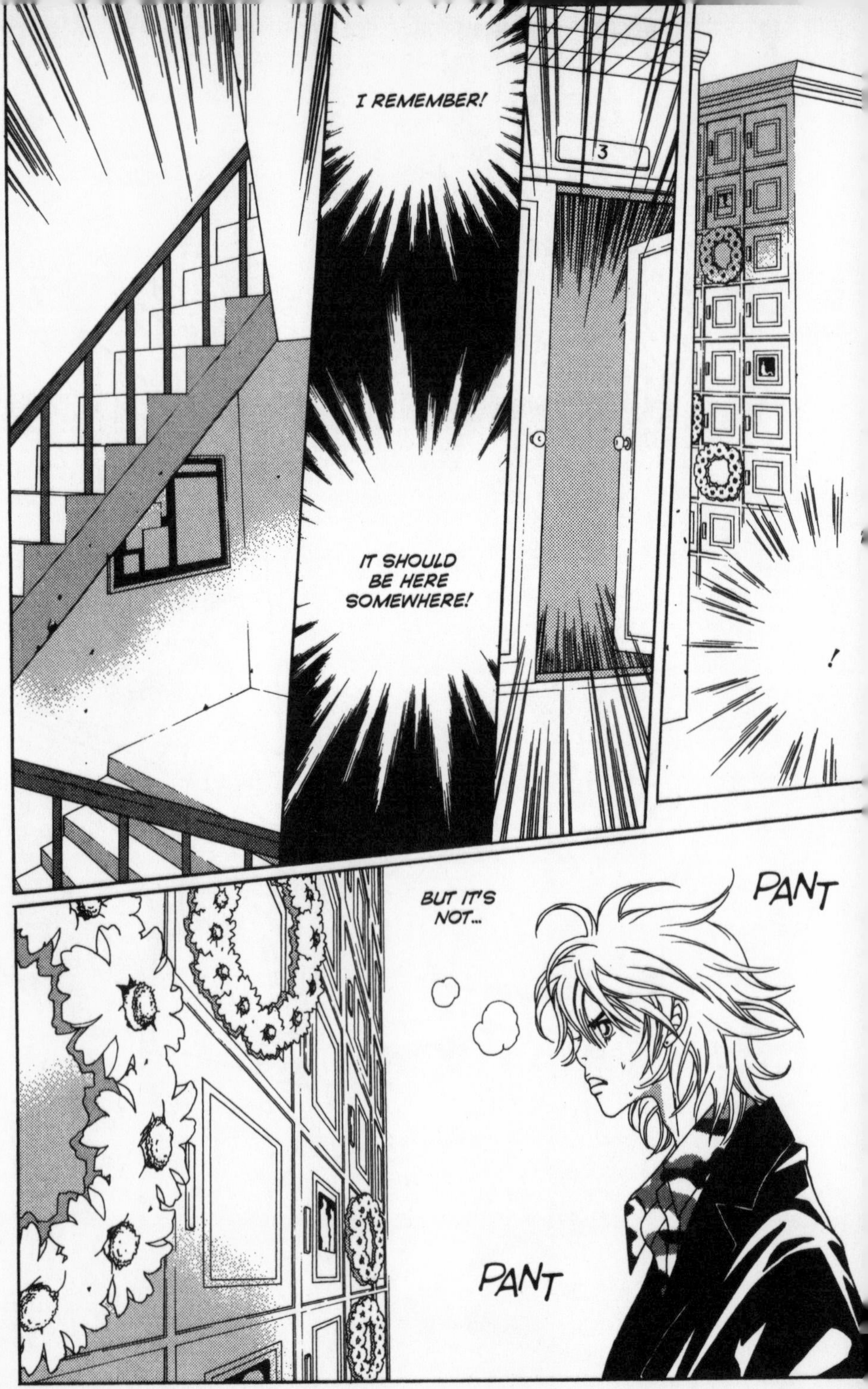
I REMEMBER!
IT SHOULD BE HERE SOMEWHERE!
!
BUT IT'S NOT...
PANT
PANT

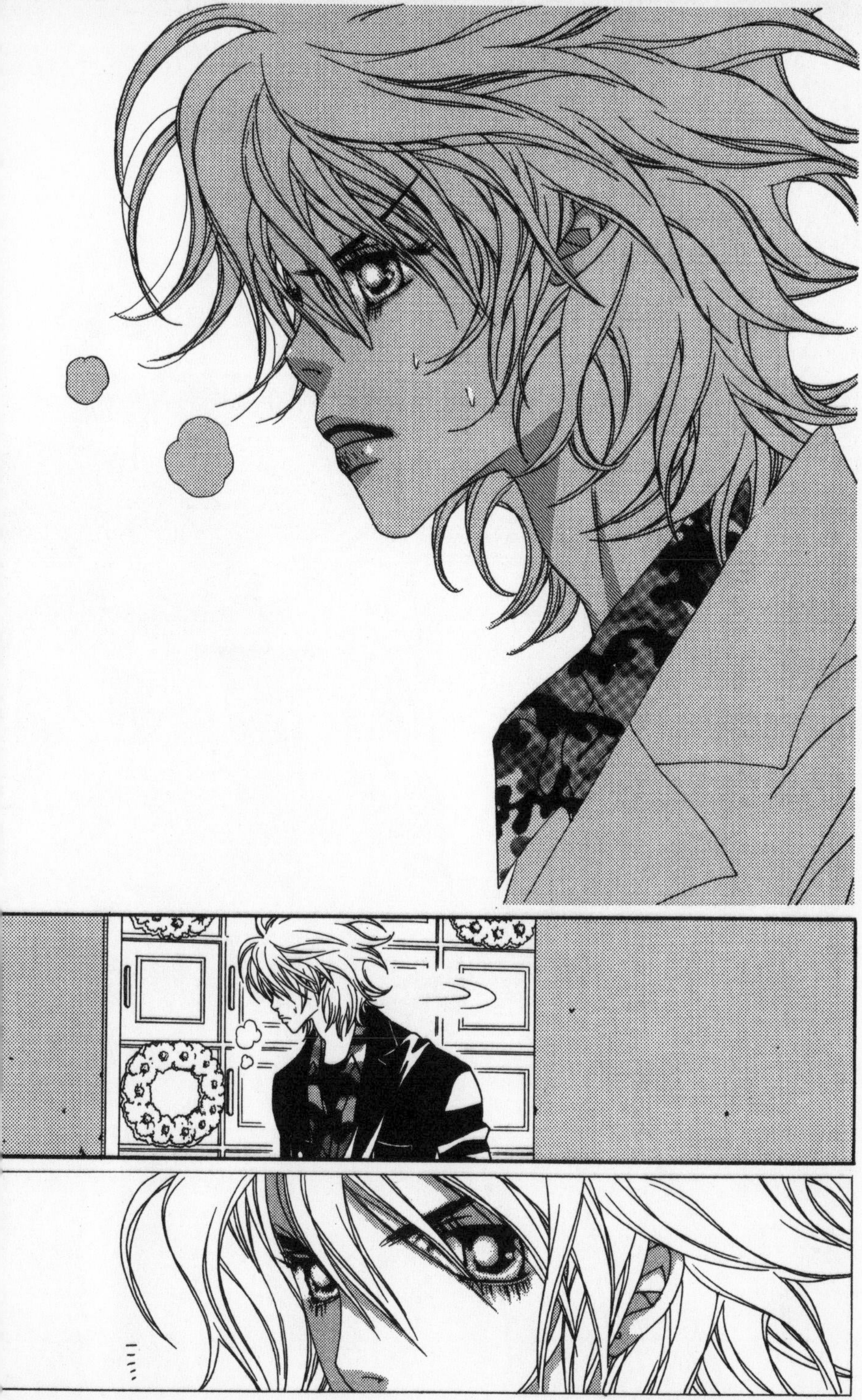

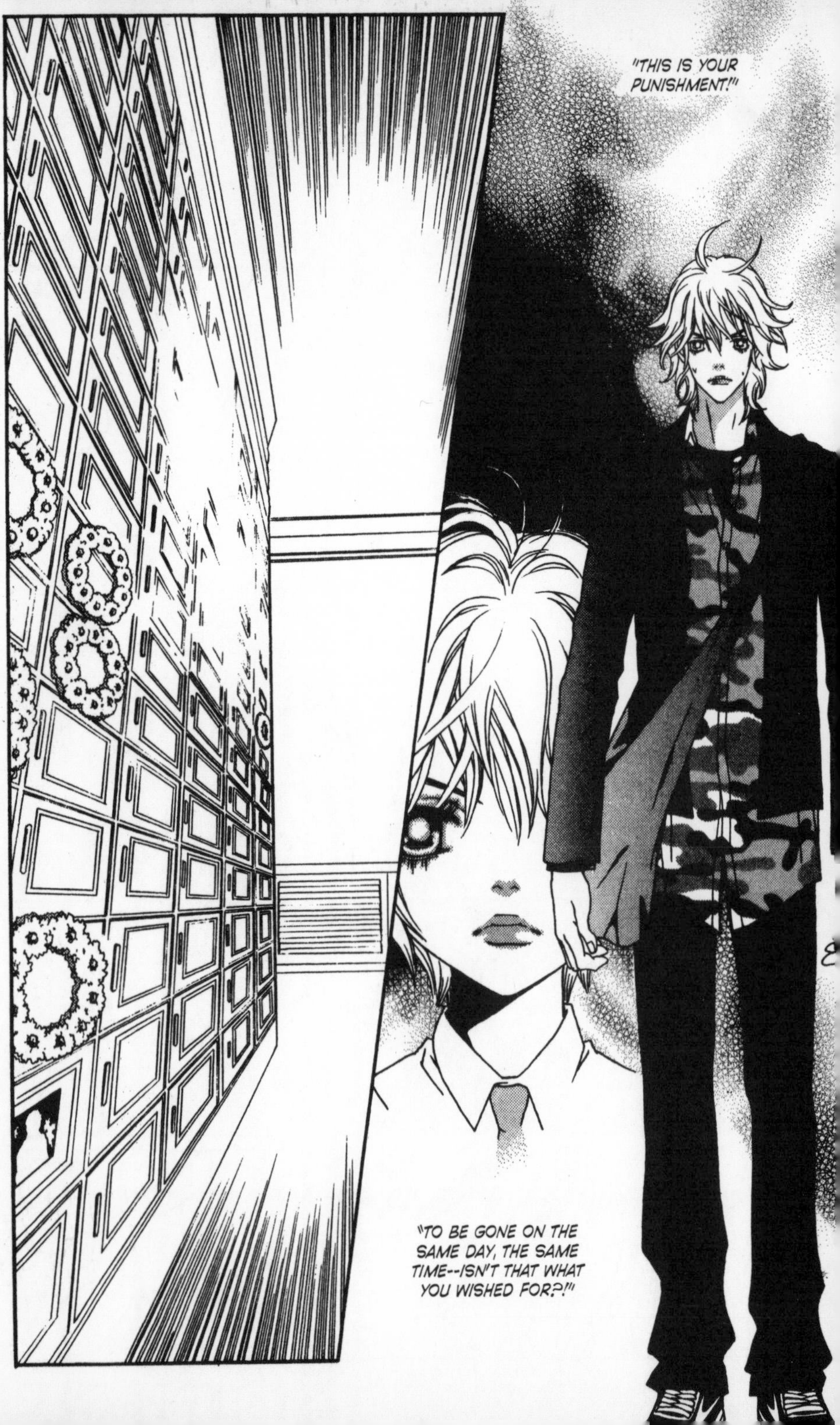
"THIS IS YOUR PUNISHMENT!"
"TO BE GONE ON THE SAME DAY, THE SAME TIME--ISN'T THAT WHAT YOU WISHED FOR?!"

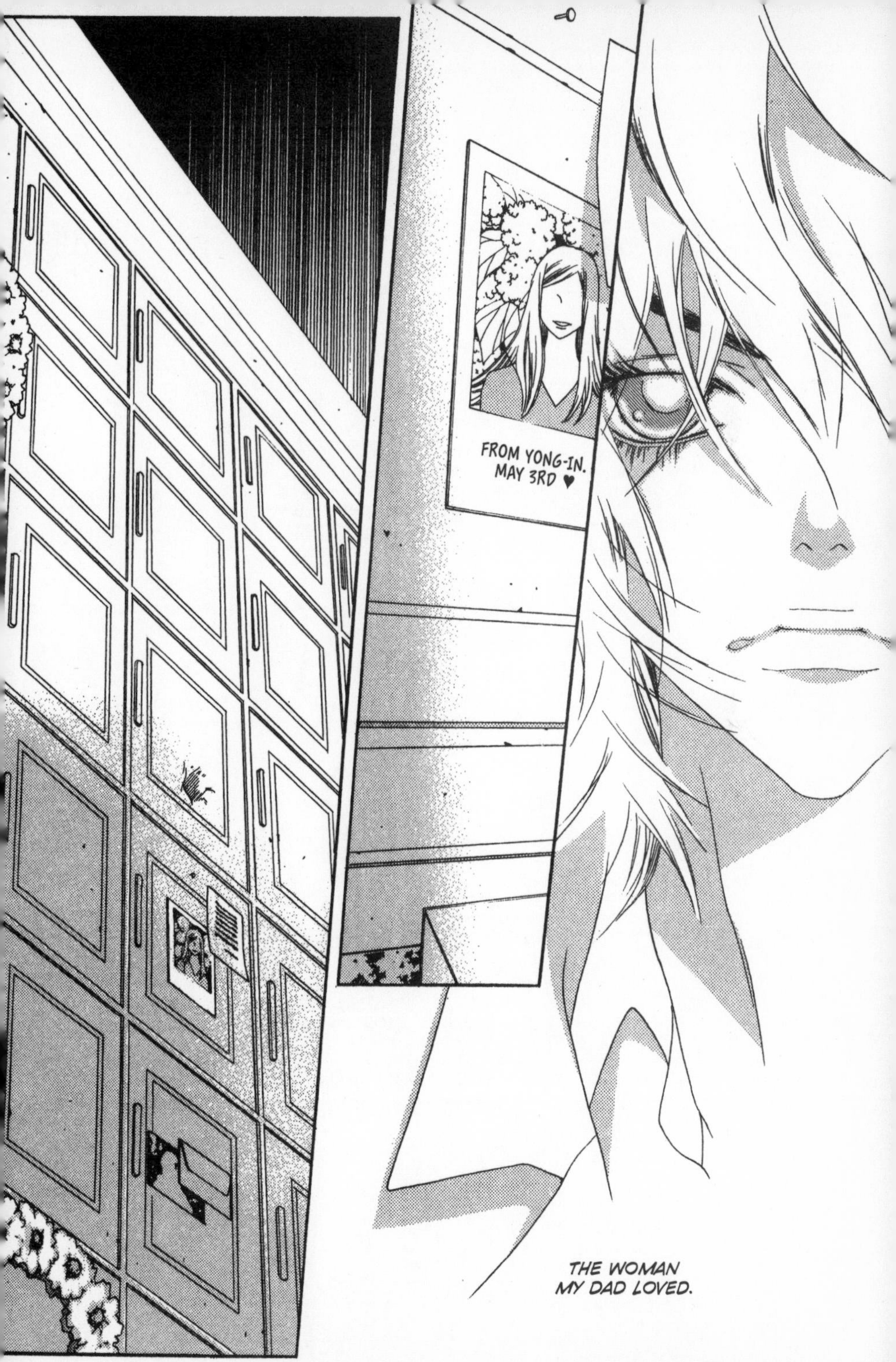
FROM YONG-IN.
MAY 3RD ♥
THE WOMAN
MY DAD LOVED.

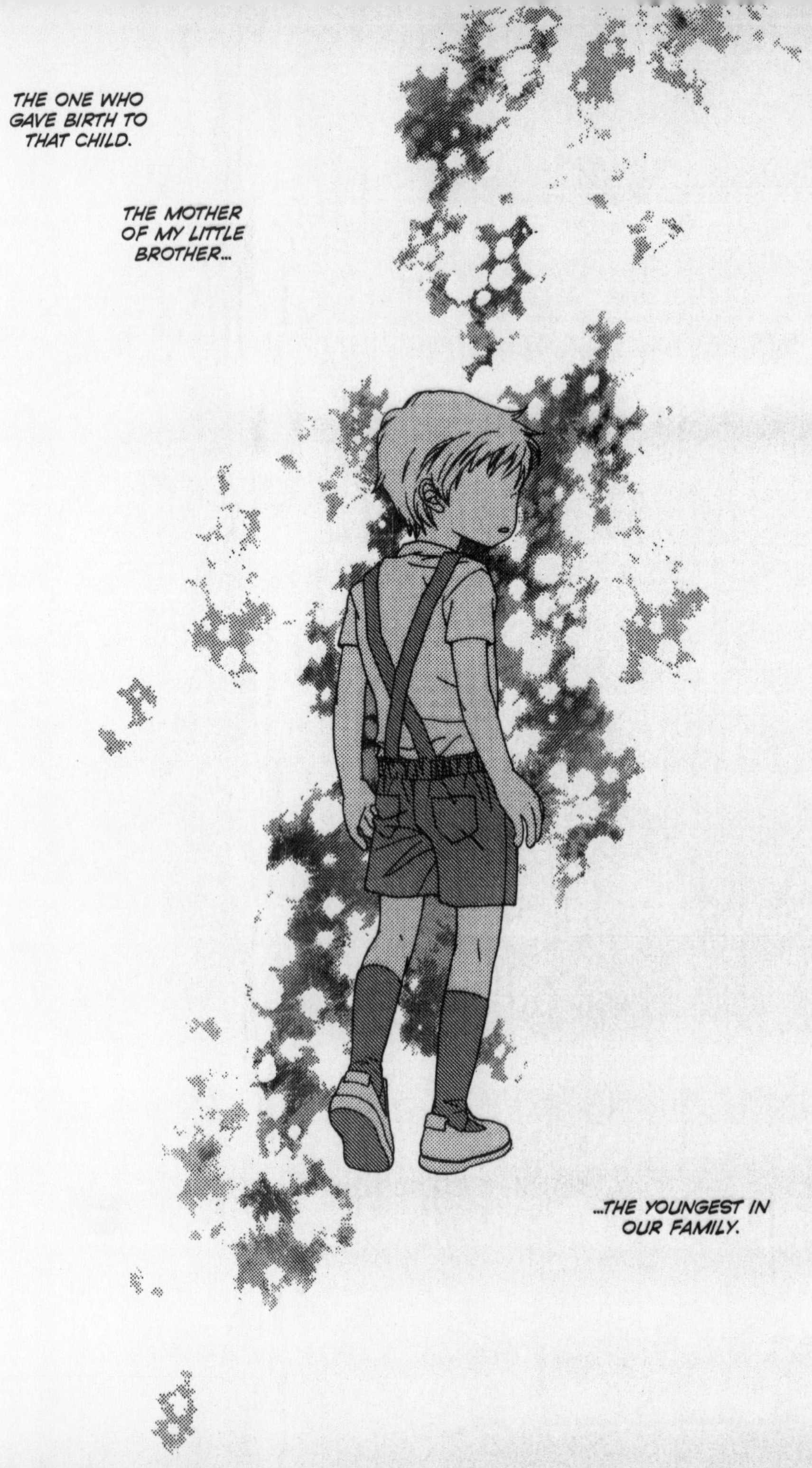
THE ONE WHO GAVE BIRTH TO THAT CHILD.
THE MOTHER OF MY LITTLE BROTHER...
...THE YOUNGEST IN OUR FAMILY.

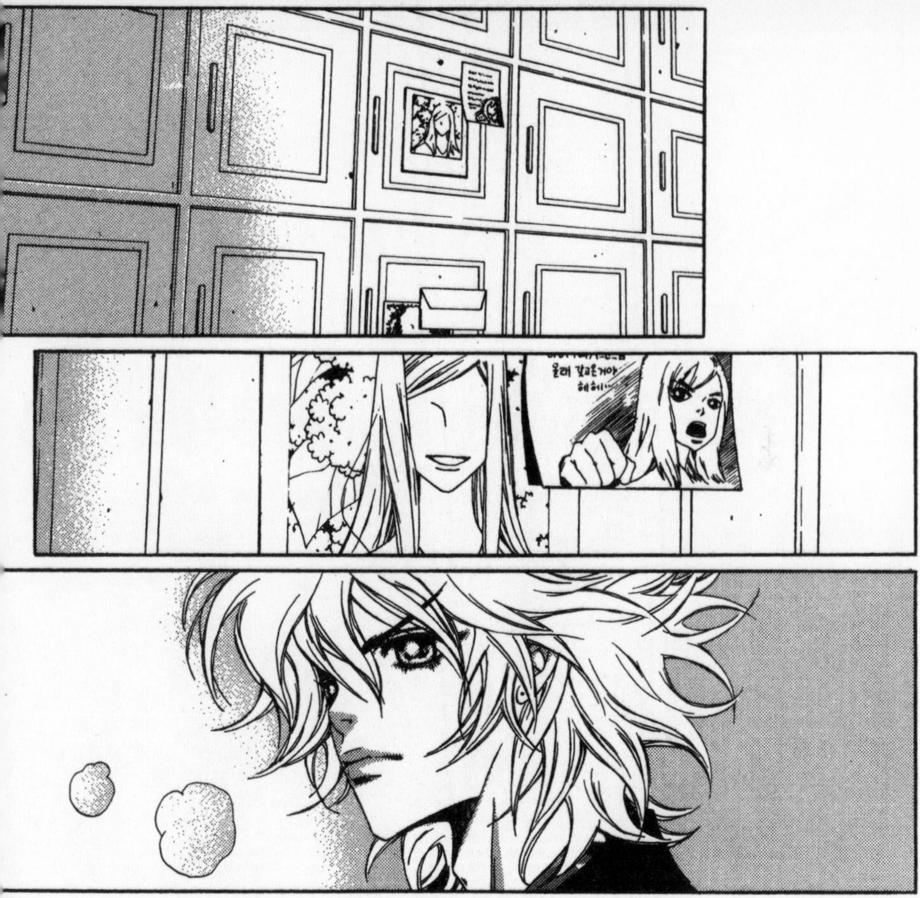
몰래 갖고온거야
헤헤…

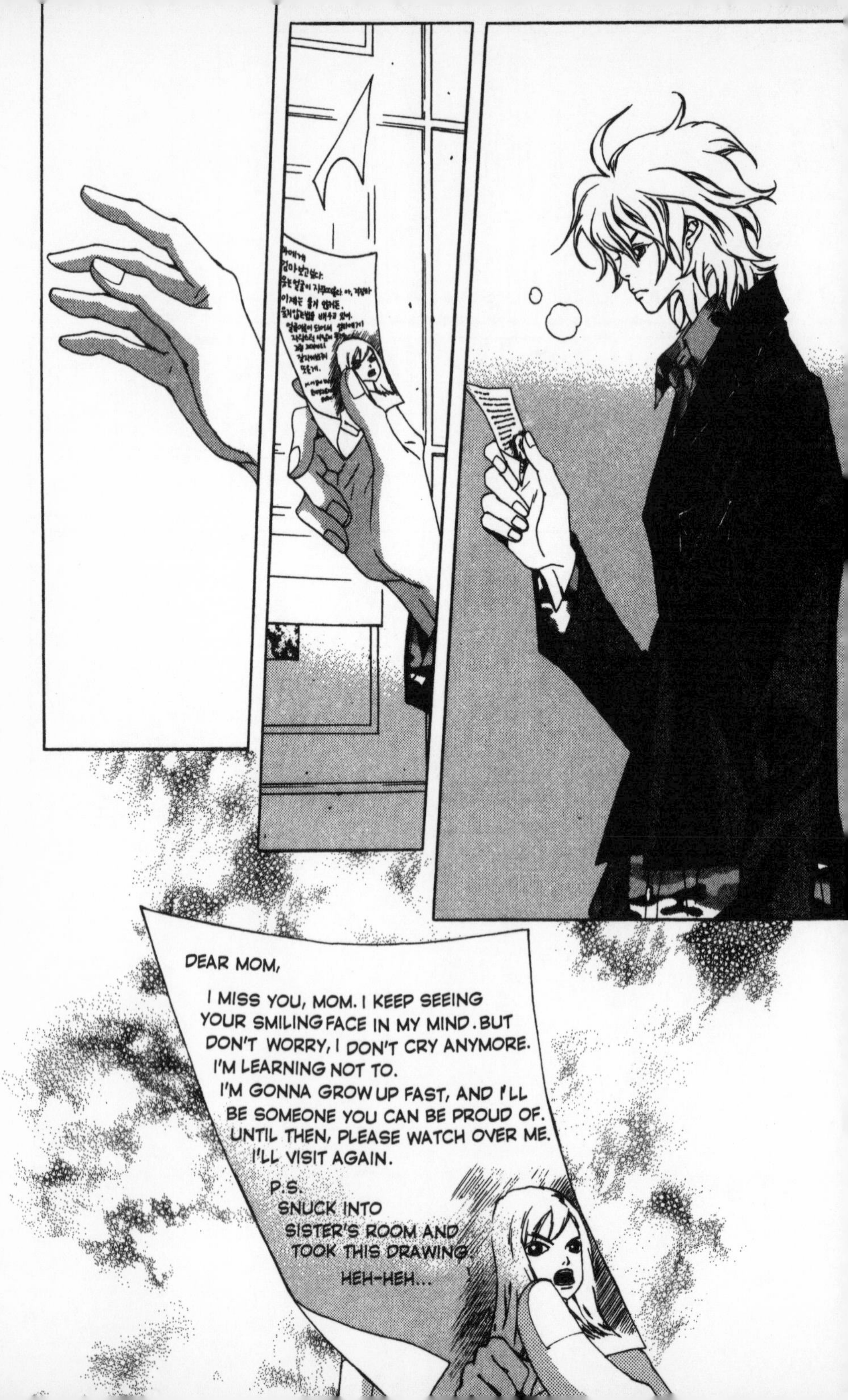
DEAR MOM,
I MISS YOU, MOM. I KEEP SEEING YOUR SMILING FACE IN MY MIND. BUT DON'T WORRY, I DON'T CRY ANYMORE. I'M LEARNING NOT TO.
I'M GONNA GROW UP FAST, AND I'LL BE SOMEONE YOU CAN BE PROUD OF. UNTIL THEN, PLEASE WATCH OVER ME. I'LL VISIT AGAIN.
P.S.
SNUCK INTO SISTER'S ROOM AND TOOK THIS DRAWING.
HEH-HEH...

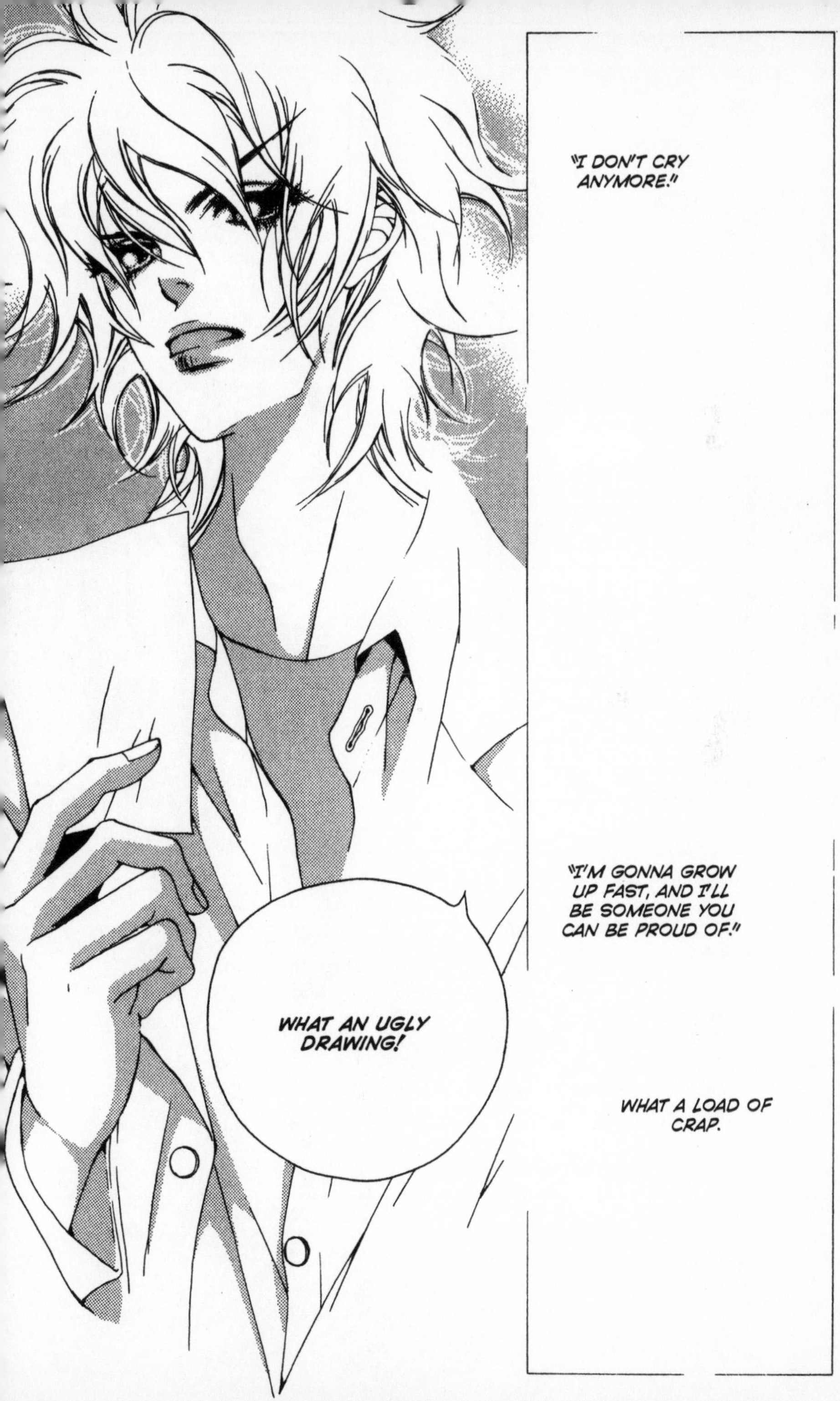
WHAT AN UGLY DRAWING!
"I DON'T CRY ANYMORE."
"I'M GONNA GROW UP FAST, AND I'LL BE SOMEONE YOU CAN BE PROUD OF."
WHAT A LOAD OF CRAP.

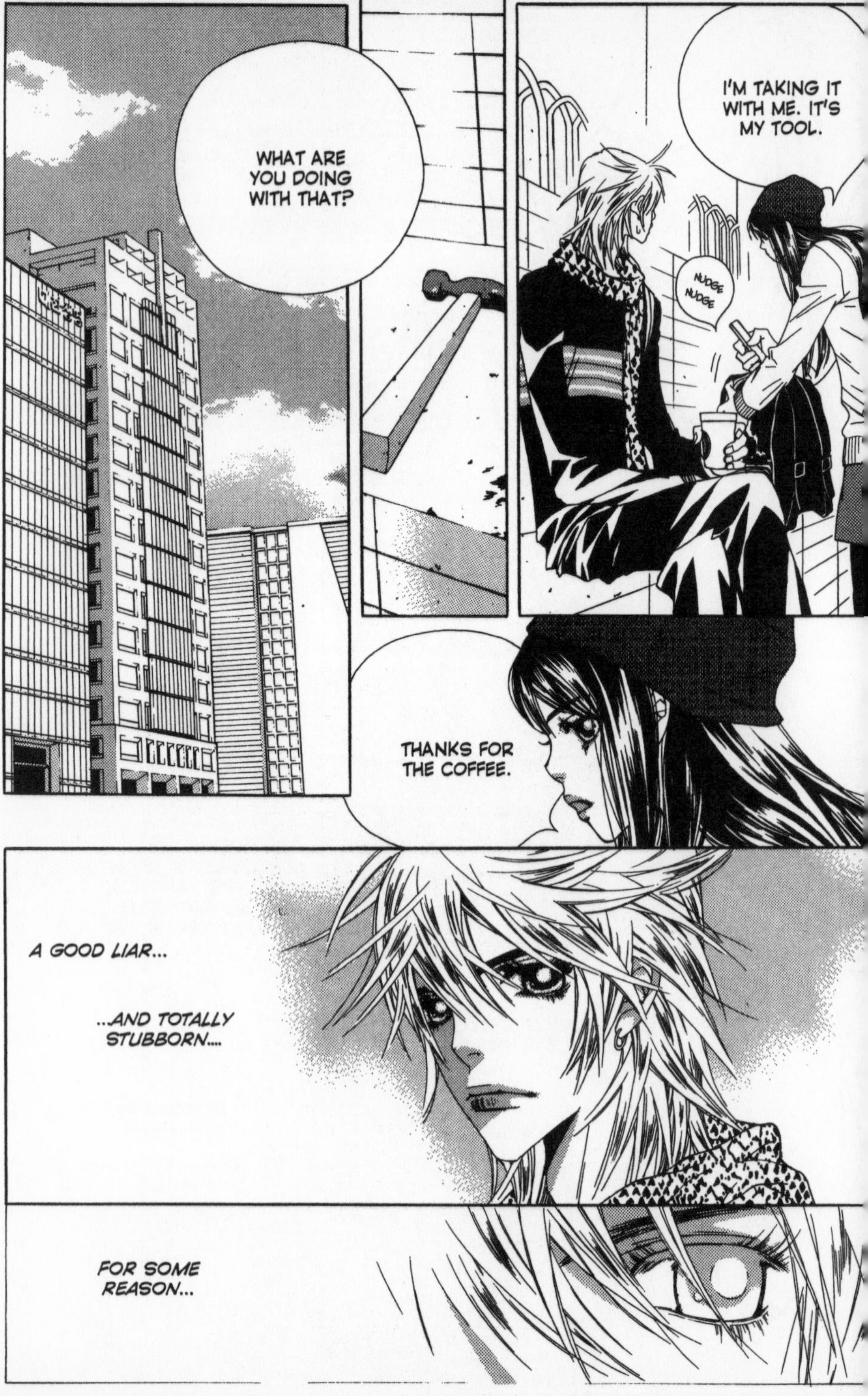
WHAT ARE YOU DOING WITH THAT?
I'M TAKING IT WITH ME. IT'S MY TOOL.
NUDGE NUDGE
THANKS FOR THE COFFEE.
A GOOD LIAR...
...AND TOTALLY STUBBORN....
FOR SOME REASON...

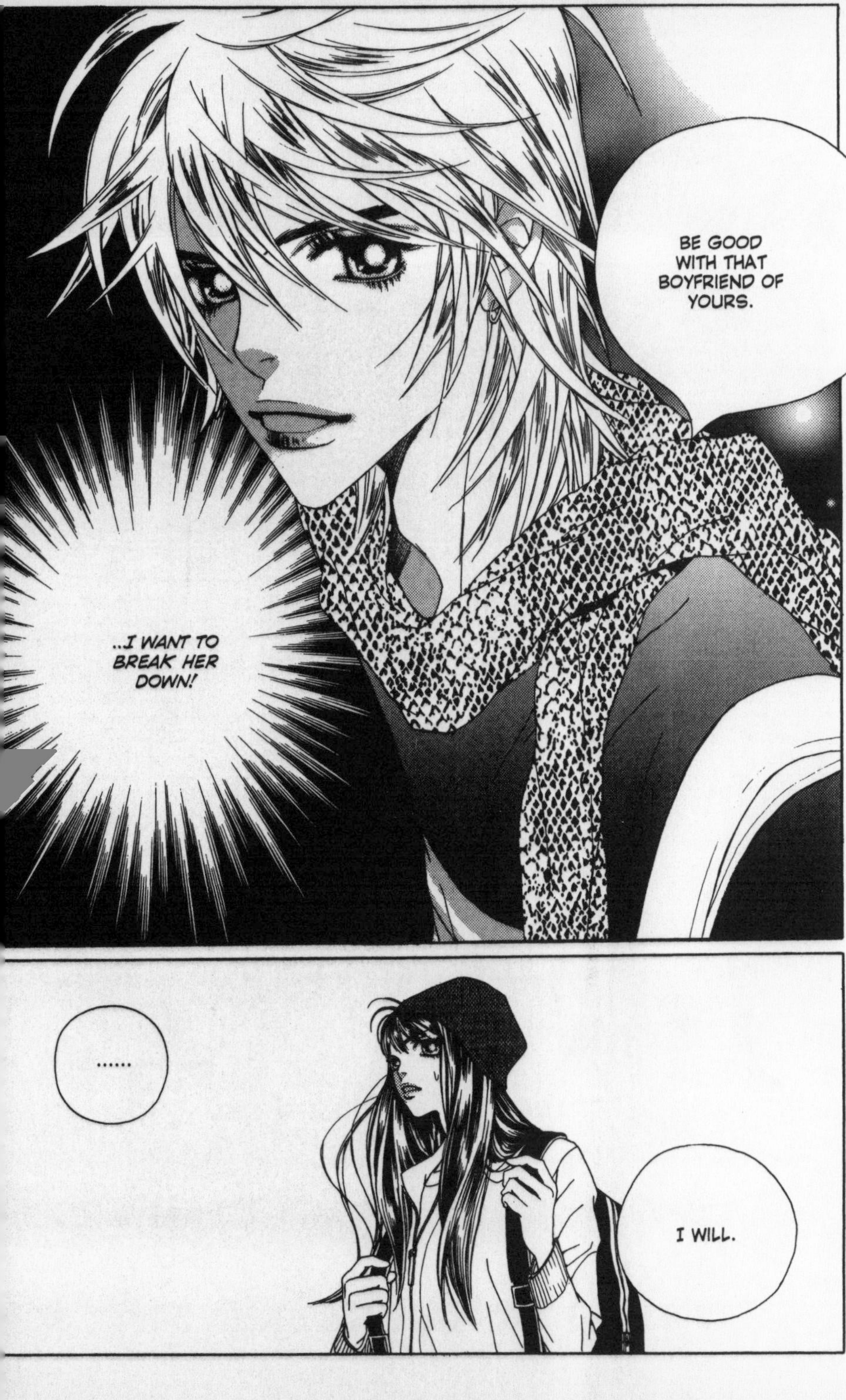
...I WANT TO BREAK HER DOWN!
BE GOOD WITH THAT BOYFRIEND OF YOURS.
......
I WILL.

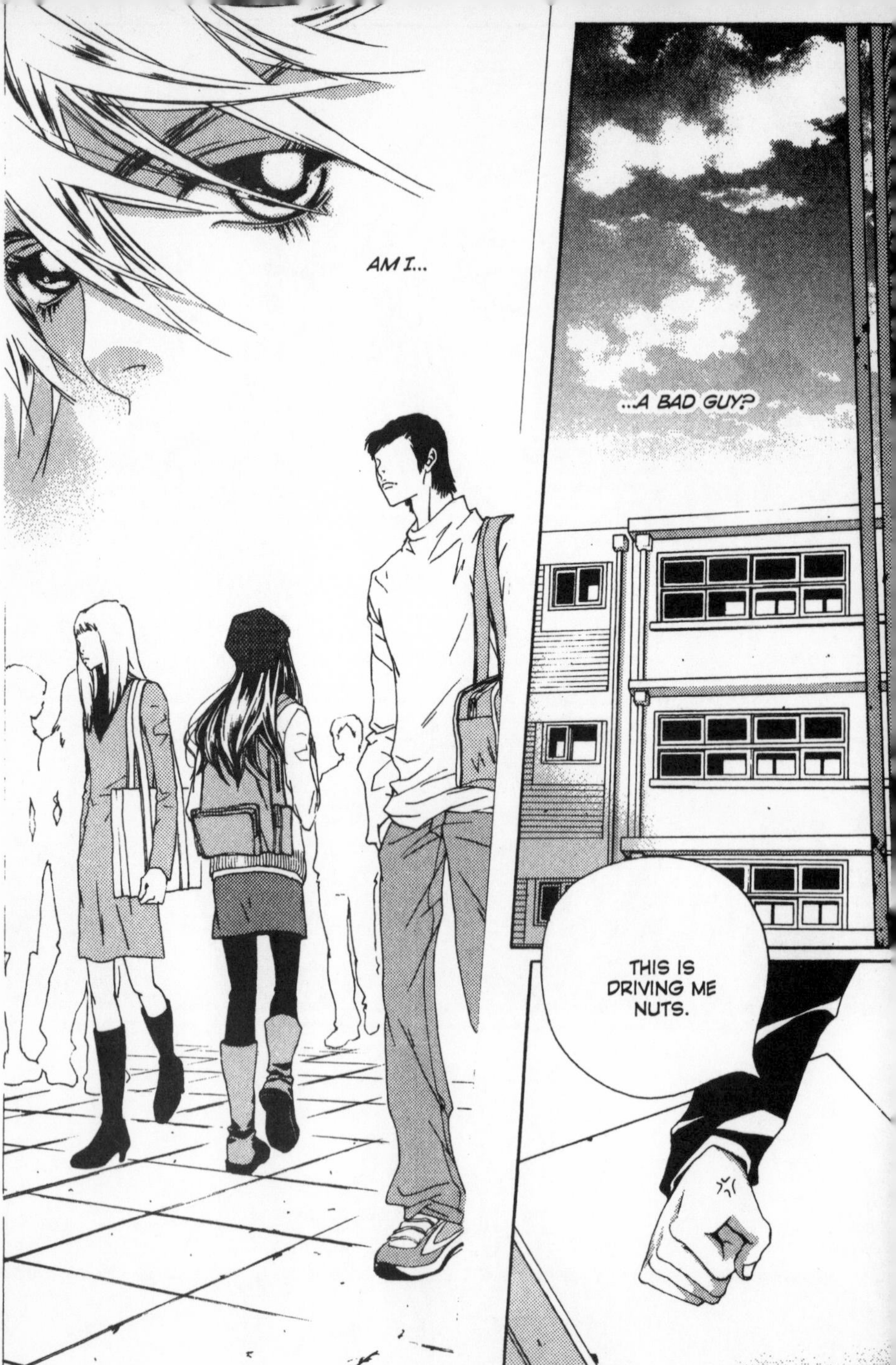
AM I...
...A BAD GUY?
THIS IS DRIVING ME NUTS.

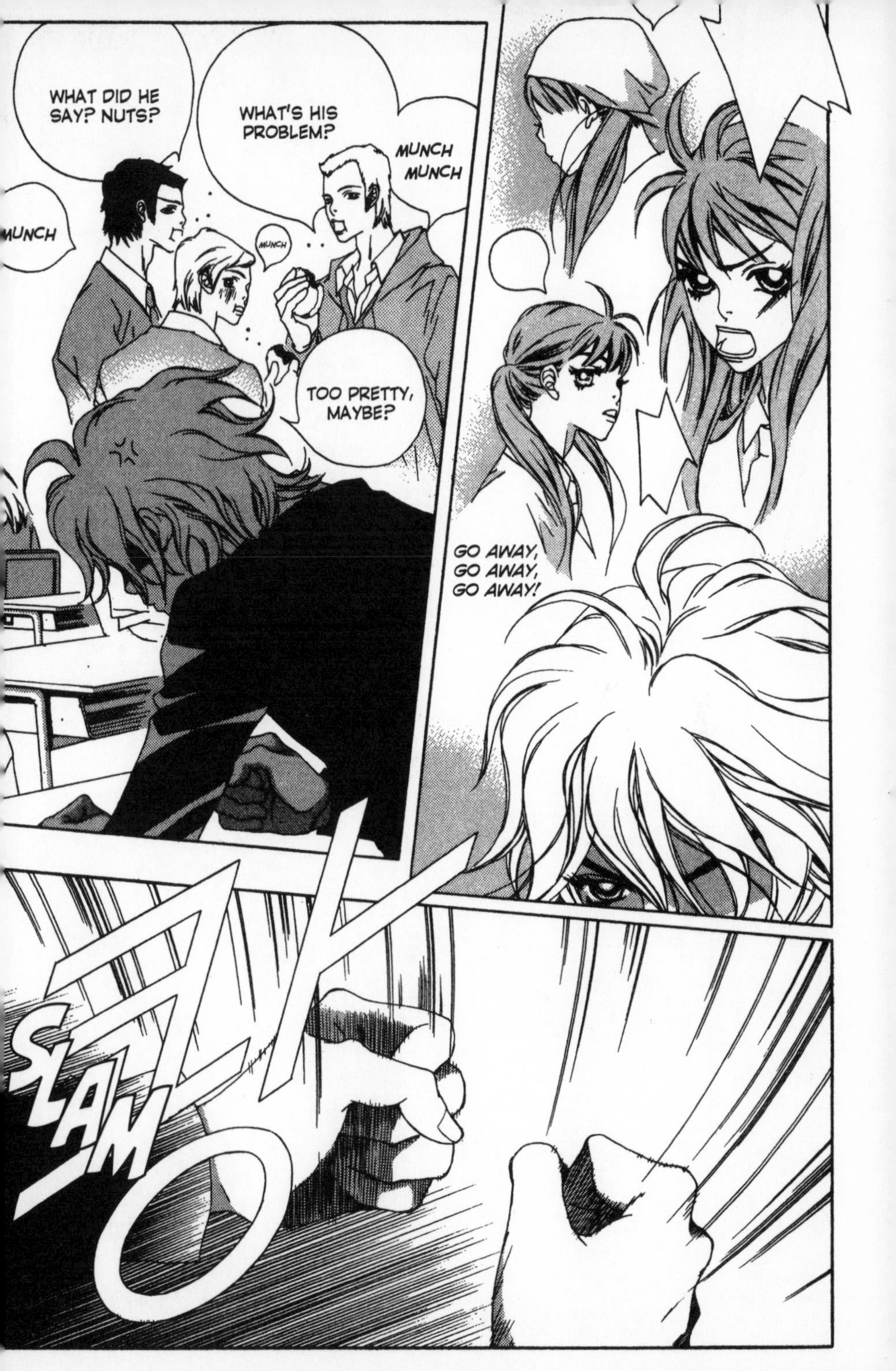
WHAT DID HE SAY? NUTS?
WHAT'S HIS PROBLEM?
MUNCH MUNCH
MUNCH
MUNCH
TOO PRETTY, MAYBE?
GO AWAY, GO AWAY, GO AWAY!
SLAM

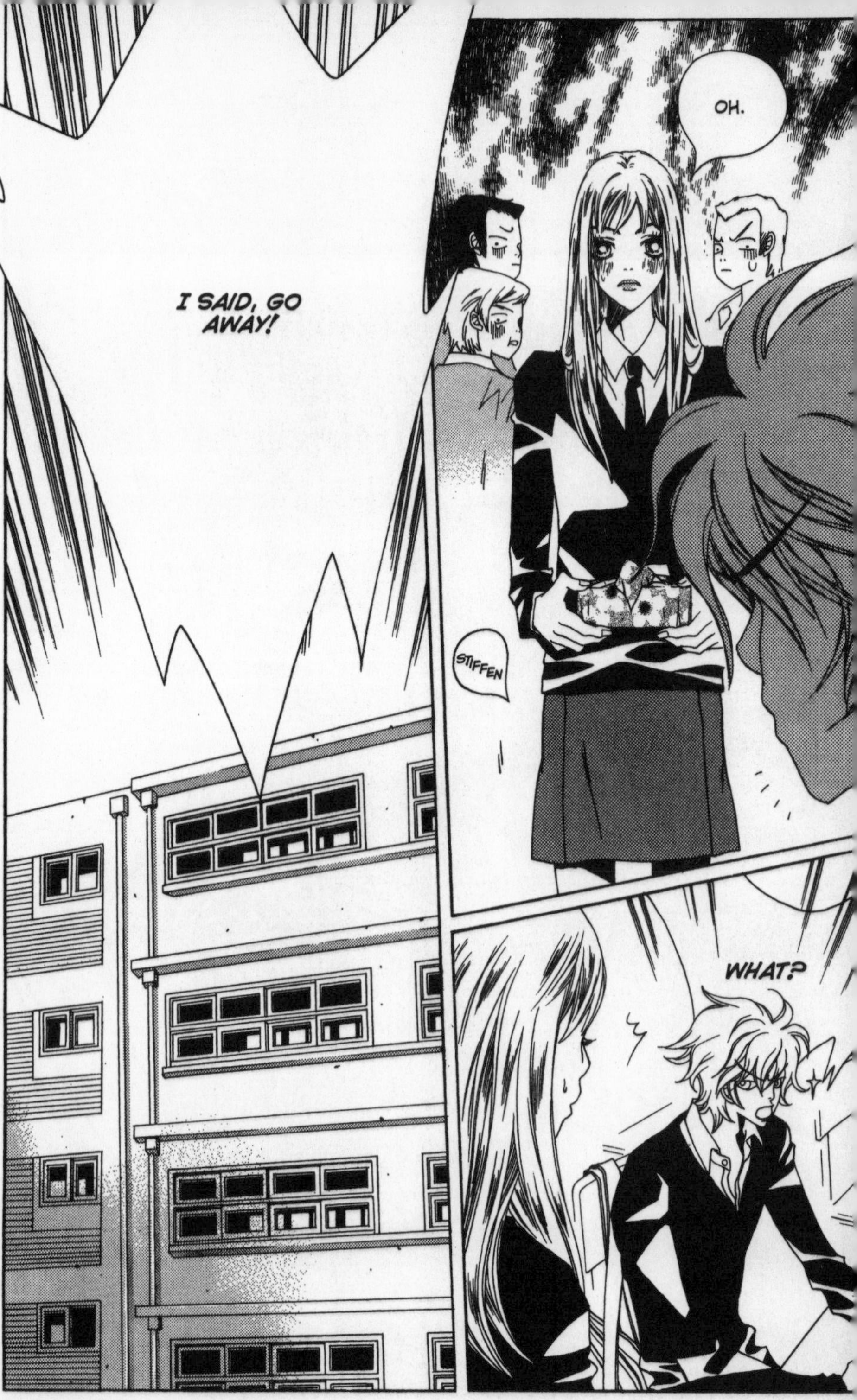
I SAID, GO AWAY!
OH.
STIFFEN
WHAT?

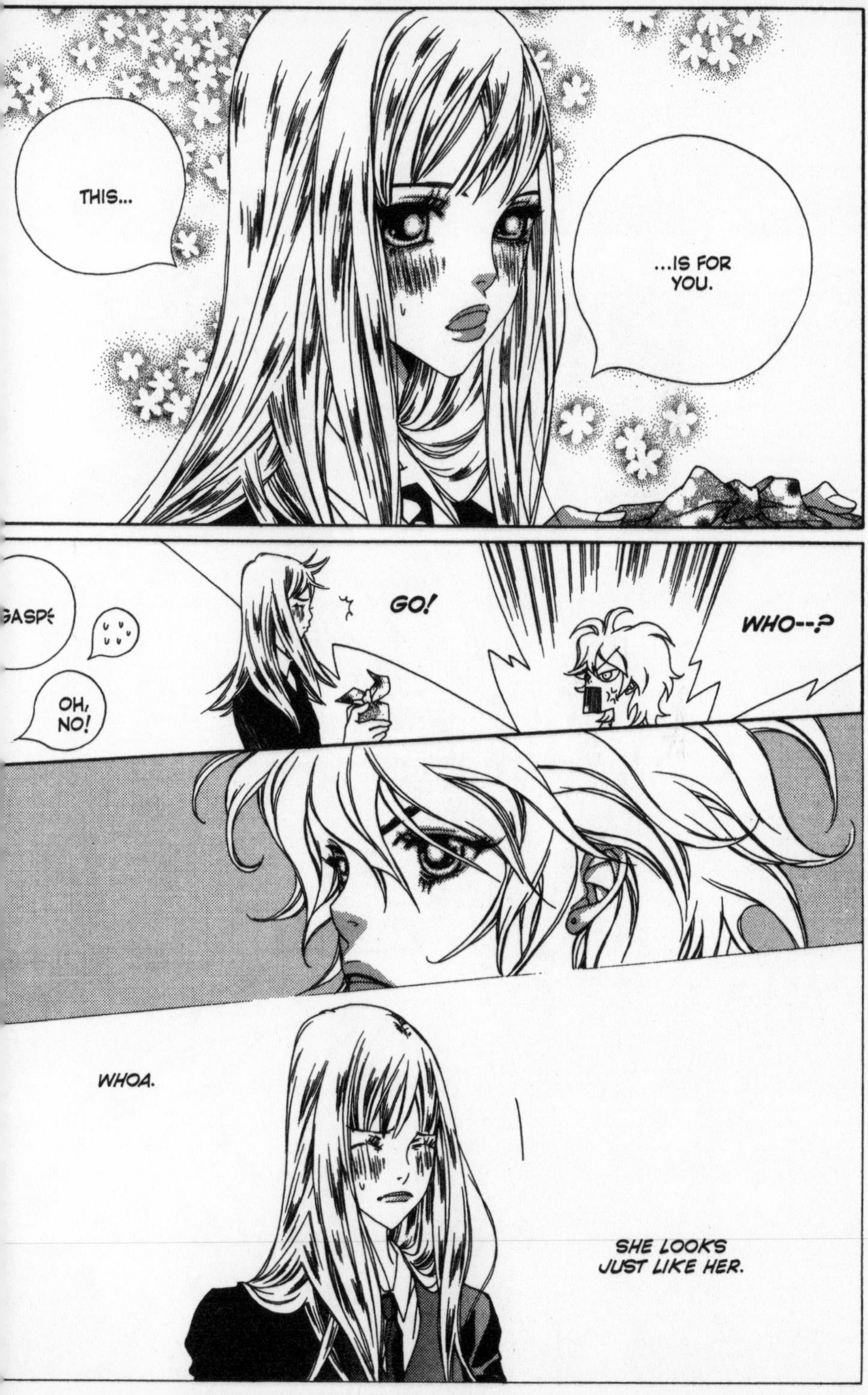
THIS...
...IS FOR YOU.
GASP
OH, NO!
GO!
WHO--?
WHOA.
SHE LOOKS JUST LIKE HER.

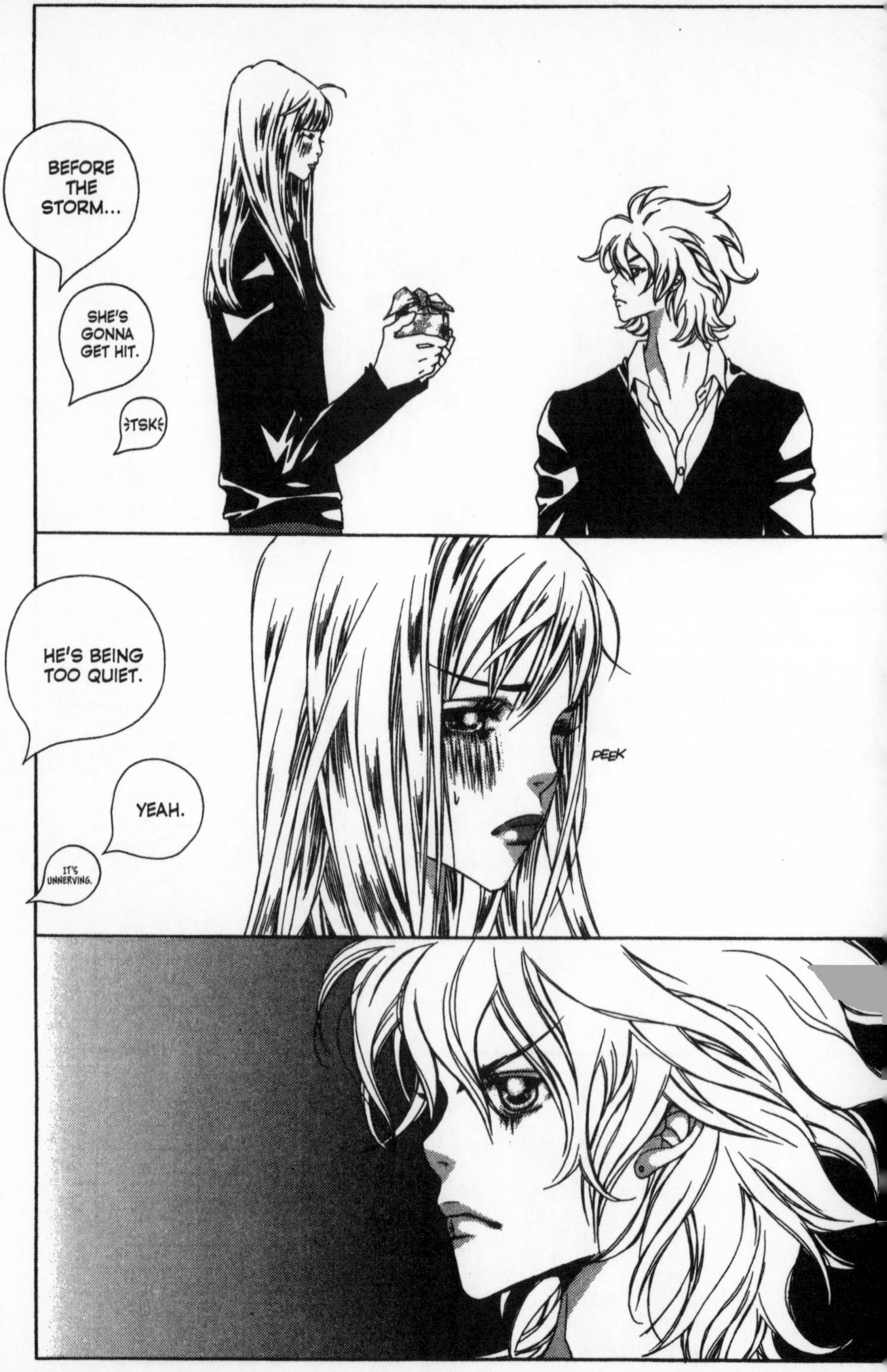
BEFORE THE STORM...
SHE'S GONNA GET HIT.
TSK
HE'S BEING TOO QUIET.
YEAH.
IT'S UNNERVING.
PEEK

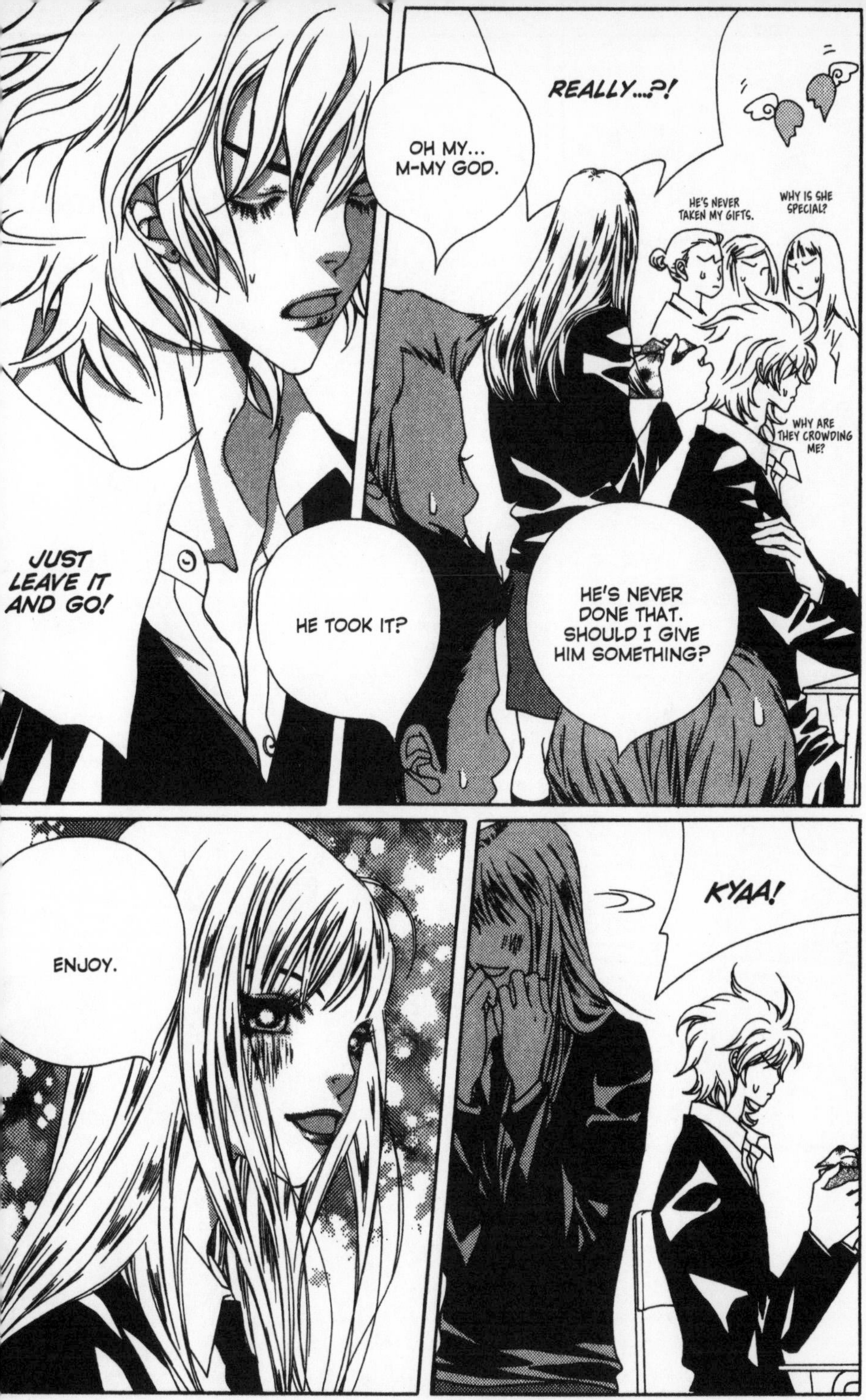
JUST LEAVE IT AND GO!
OH MY... M-MY GOD.
REALLY...?!
HE'S NEVER TAKEN MY GIFTS.
WHY IS SHE SPECIAL?
WHY ARE THEY CROWDING ME?
HE TOOK IT?
HE'S NEVER DONE THAT. SHOULD I GIVE HIM SOMETHING?
ENJOY.
KYAA!

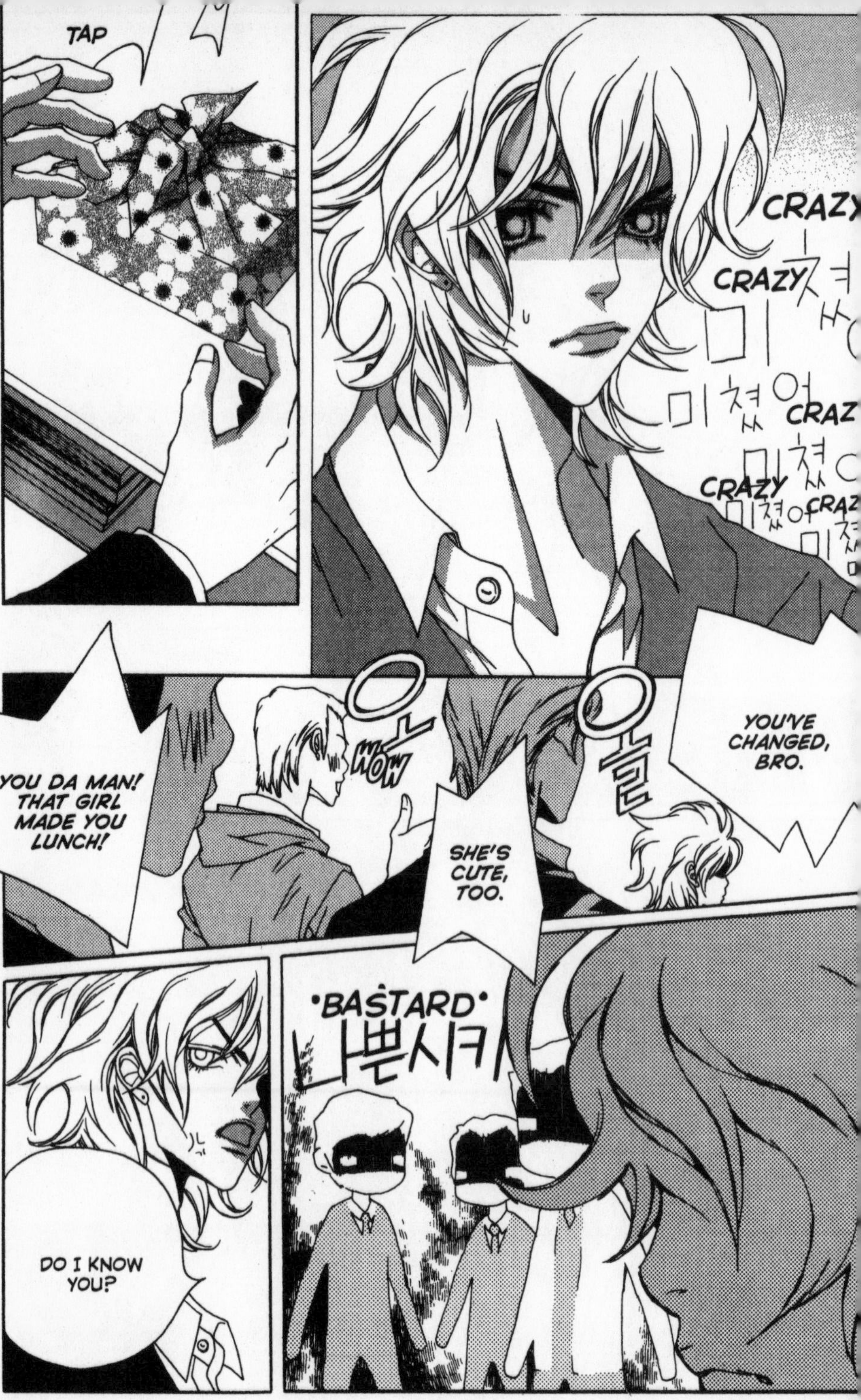
TAP
CRAZY
CRAZY
미쳤어
CRAZ
CRAZY
YOU DA MAN! THAT GIRL MADE YOU LUNCH!
WOW
SHE'S CUTE, TOO.
YOU'VE CHANGED, BRO.
DO I KNOW YOU?
•BASTARD•

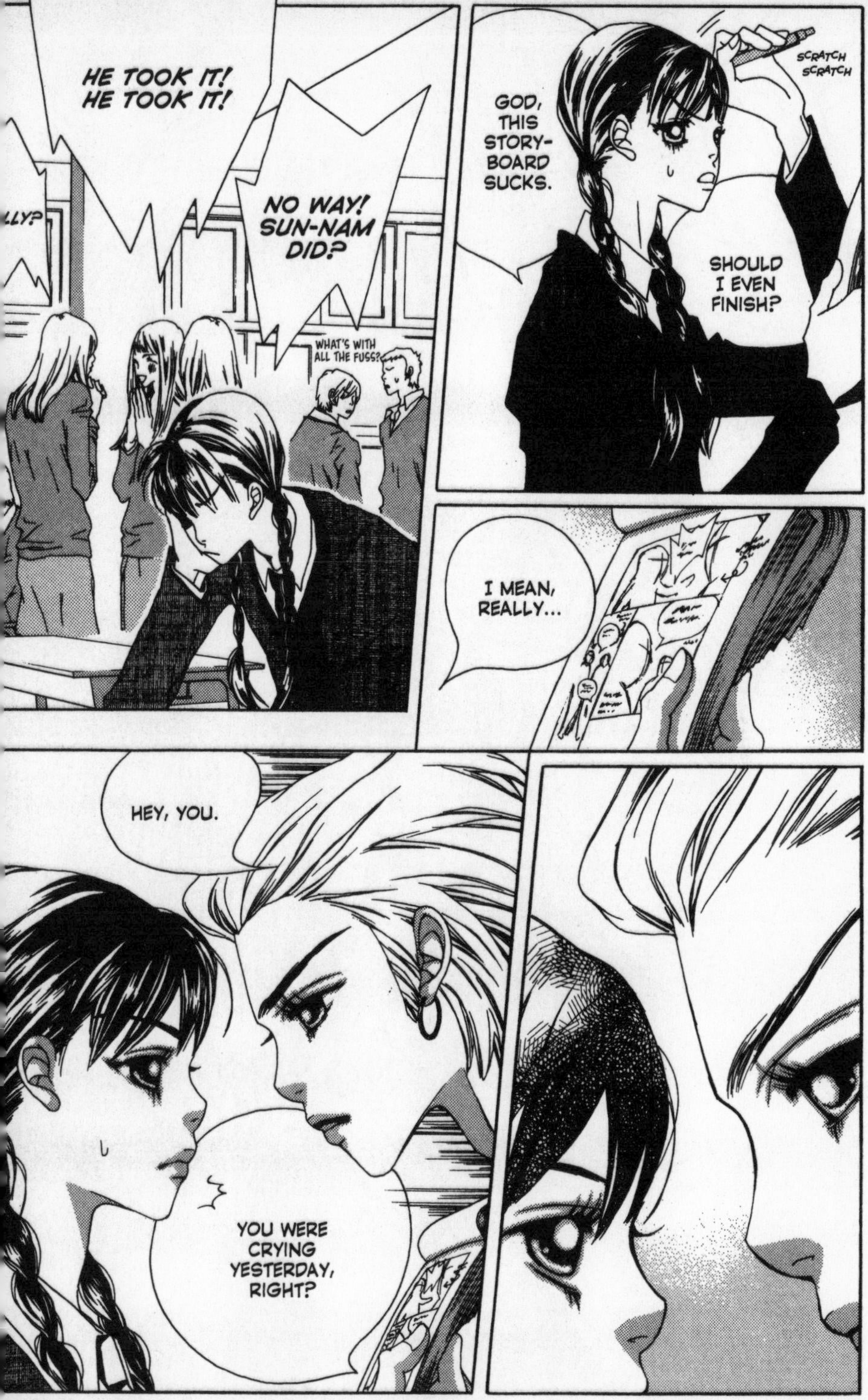
HE TOOK IT! HE TOOK IT!
LLY?
NO WAY! SUN-NAM DID?
WHAT'S WITH ALL THE FUSS?
GOD, THIS STORY-BOARD SUCKS.
SCRATCH SCRATCH
SHOULD I EVEN FINISH?
I MEAN, REALLY...
HEY, YOU.
YOU WERE CRYING YESTERDAY, RIGHT?

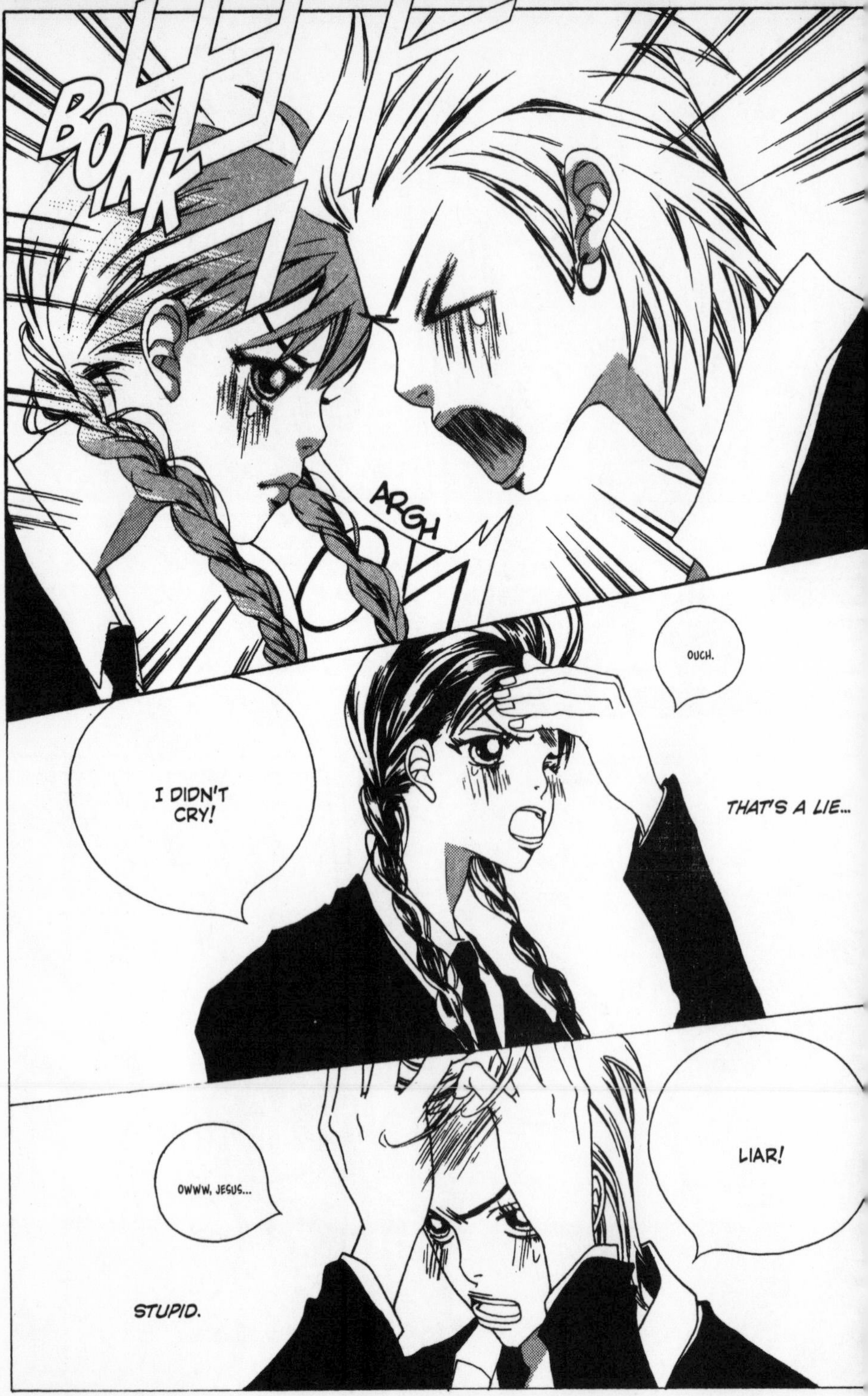
BONK
ARGH
OUCH.
I DIDN'T CRY!
THAT'S A LIE...
OWWW, JESUS...
LIAR!
STUPID.

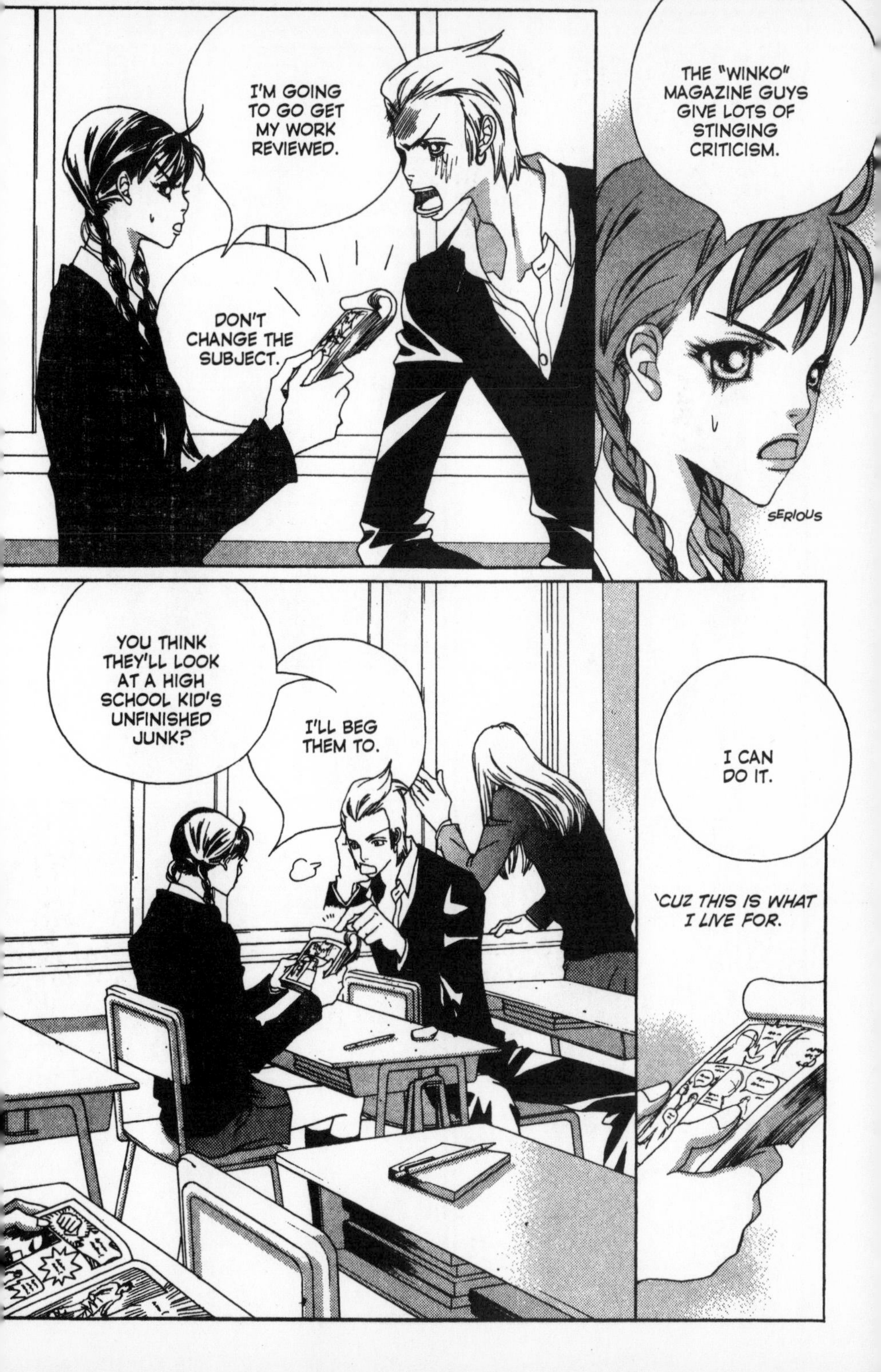
I'M GOING TO GO GET MY WORK REVIEWED.
DON'T CHANGE THE SUBJECT.
THE "WINKO" MAGAZINE GUYS GIVE LOTS OF STINGING CRITICISM.
SERIOUS
YOU THINK THEY'LL LOOK AT A HIGH SCHOOL KID'S UNFINISHED JUNK?
I'LL BEG THEM TO.
I CAN DO IT.
'CUZ THIS IS WHAT I LIVE FOR.

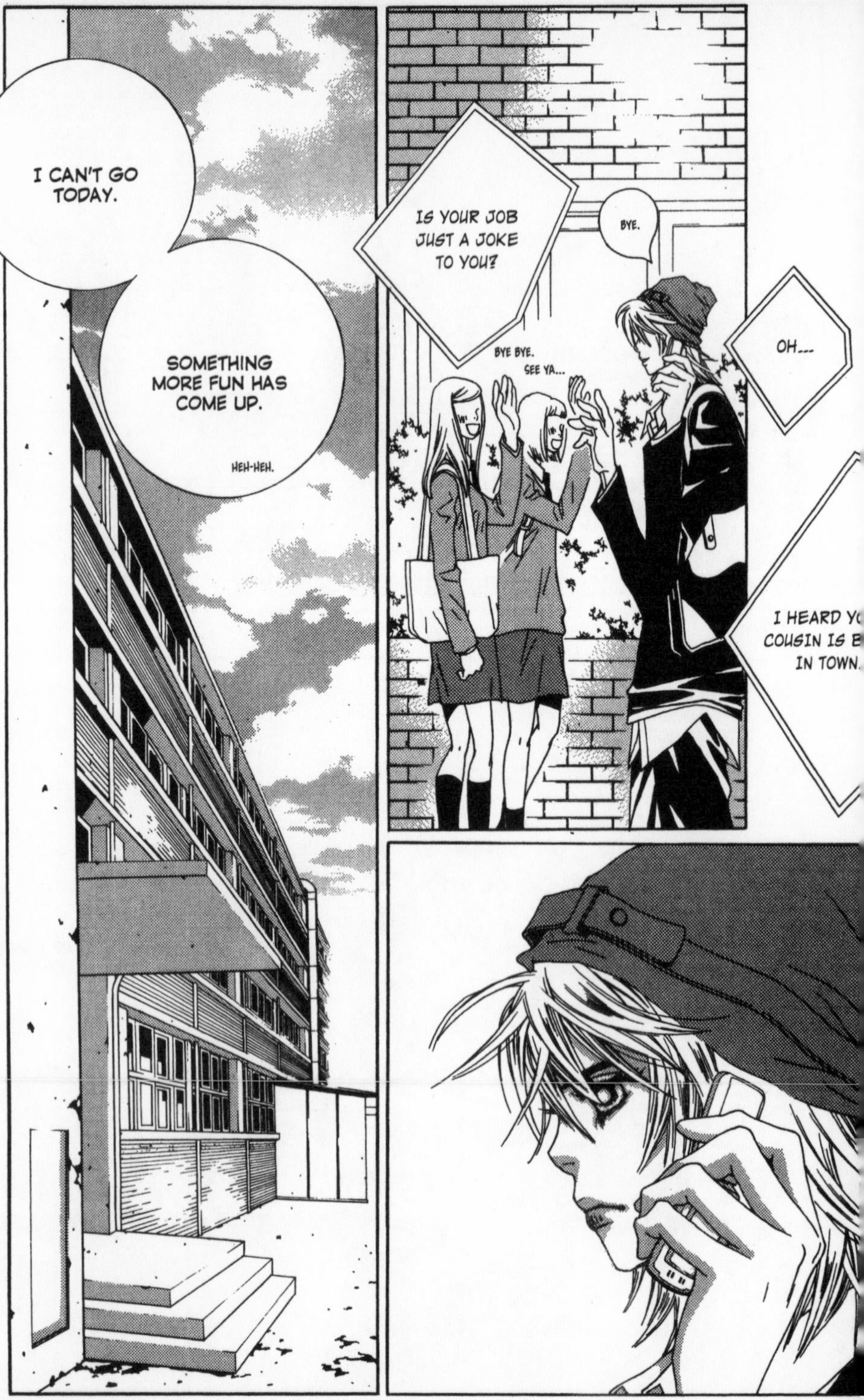
I CAN'T GO TODAY.
SOMETHING MORE FUN HAS COME UP.
HEH-HEH.
IS YOUR JOB JUST A JOKE TO YOU?
BYE.
BYE BYE.
SEE YA...
OH...
I HEARD YO COUSIN IS B IN TOWN.

A-JUN?

OLD WOUNDS
REOPEN.

RE YOU
STENING,
A-JUN?

HEY?

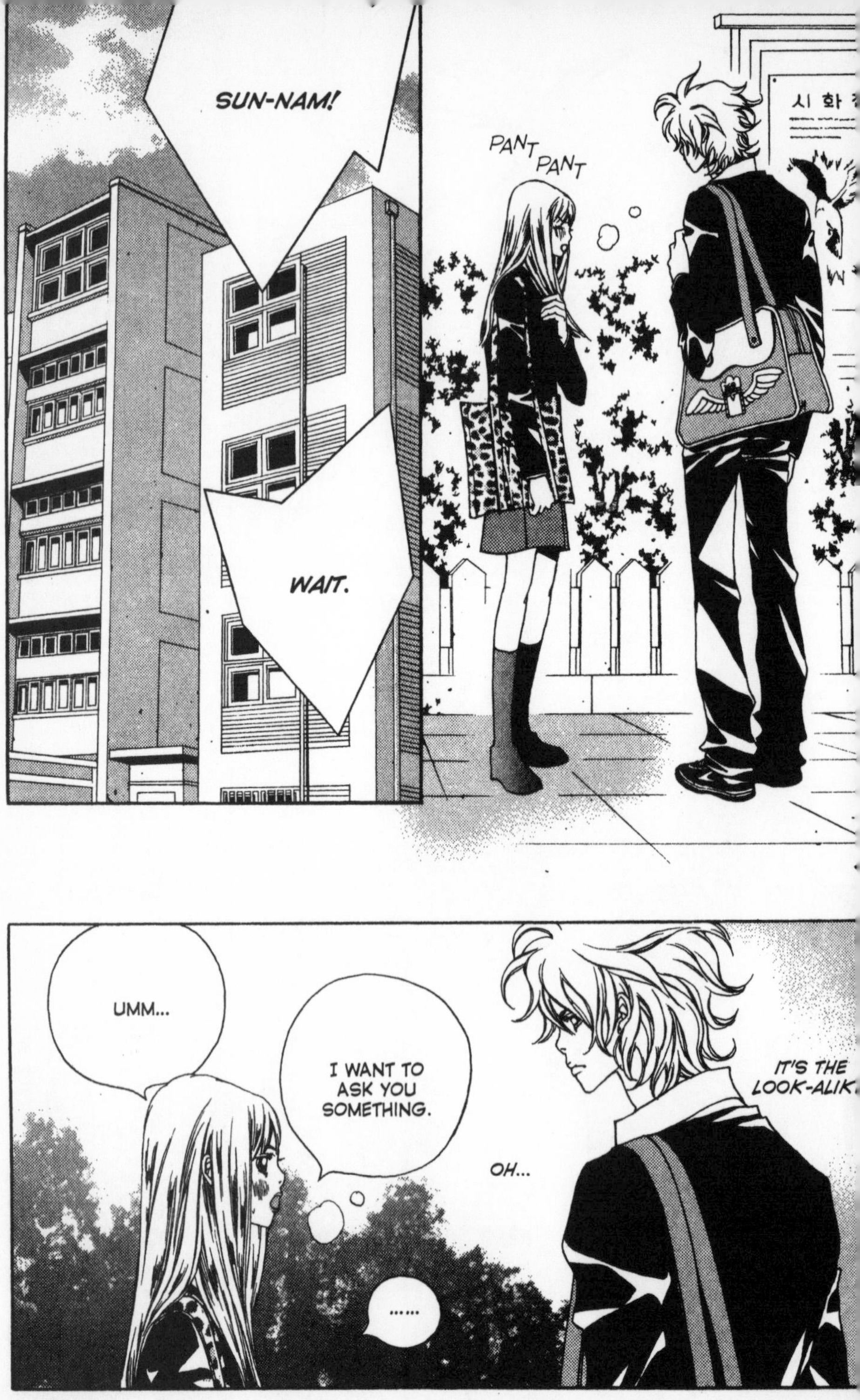
SUN-NAM!
WAIT.
PANT PANT
UMM...
I WANT TO ASK YOU SOMETHING.
OH...
......
IT'S THE LOOK-ALIK

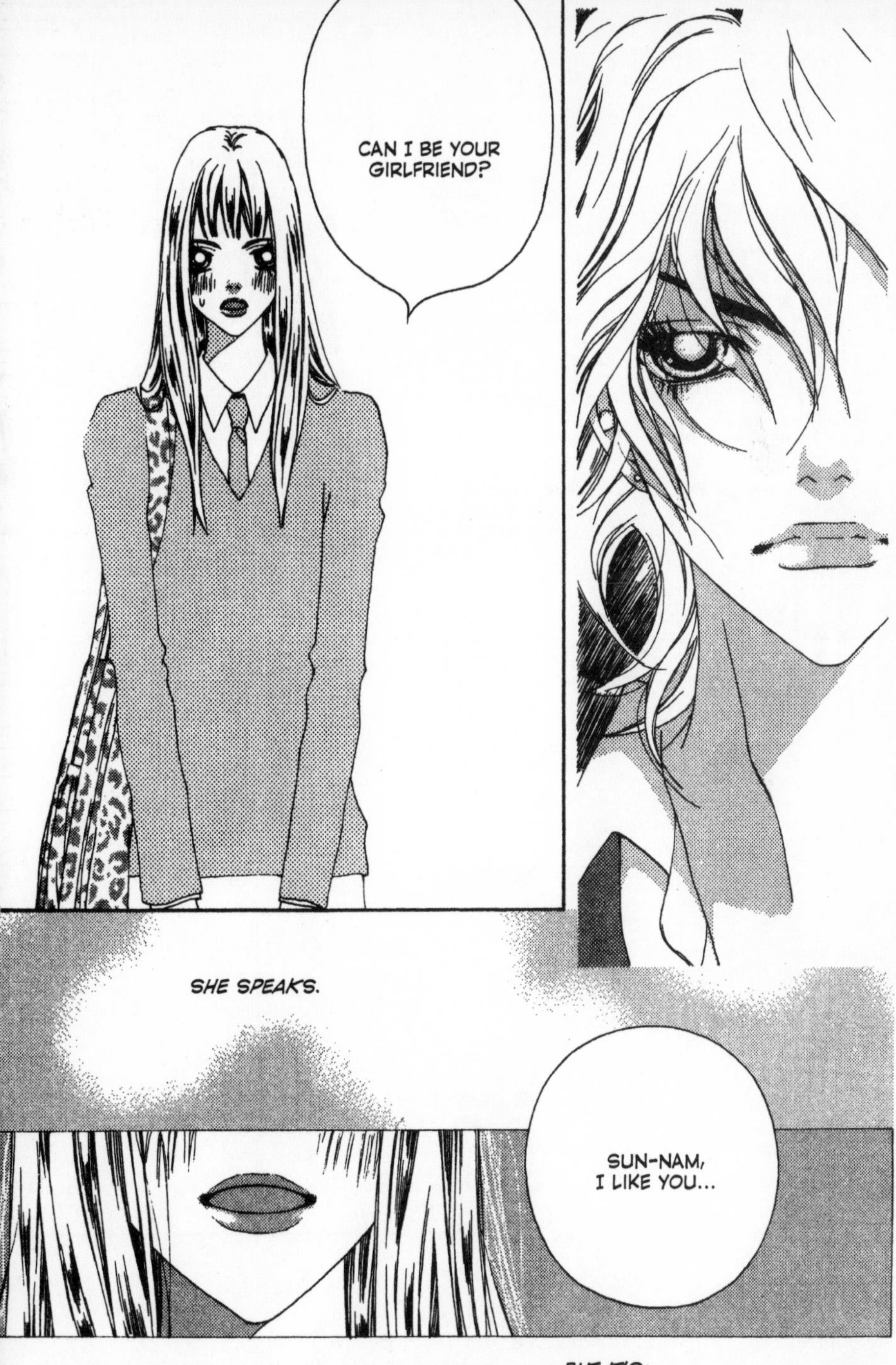
CAN I BE YOUR GIRLFRIEND?
SHE SPEAKS.
SUN-NAM, I LIKE YOU...
BUT IT'S NOT HER.

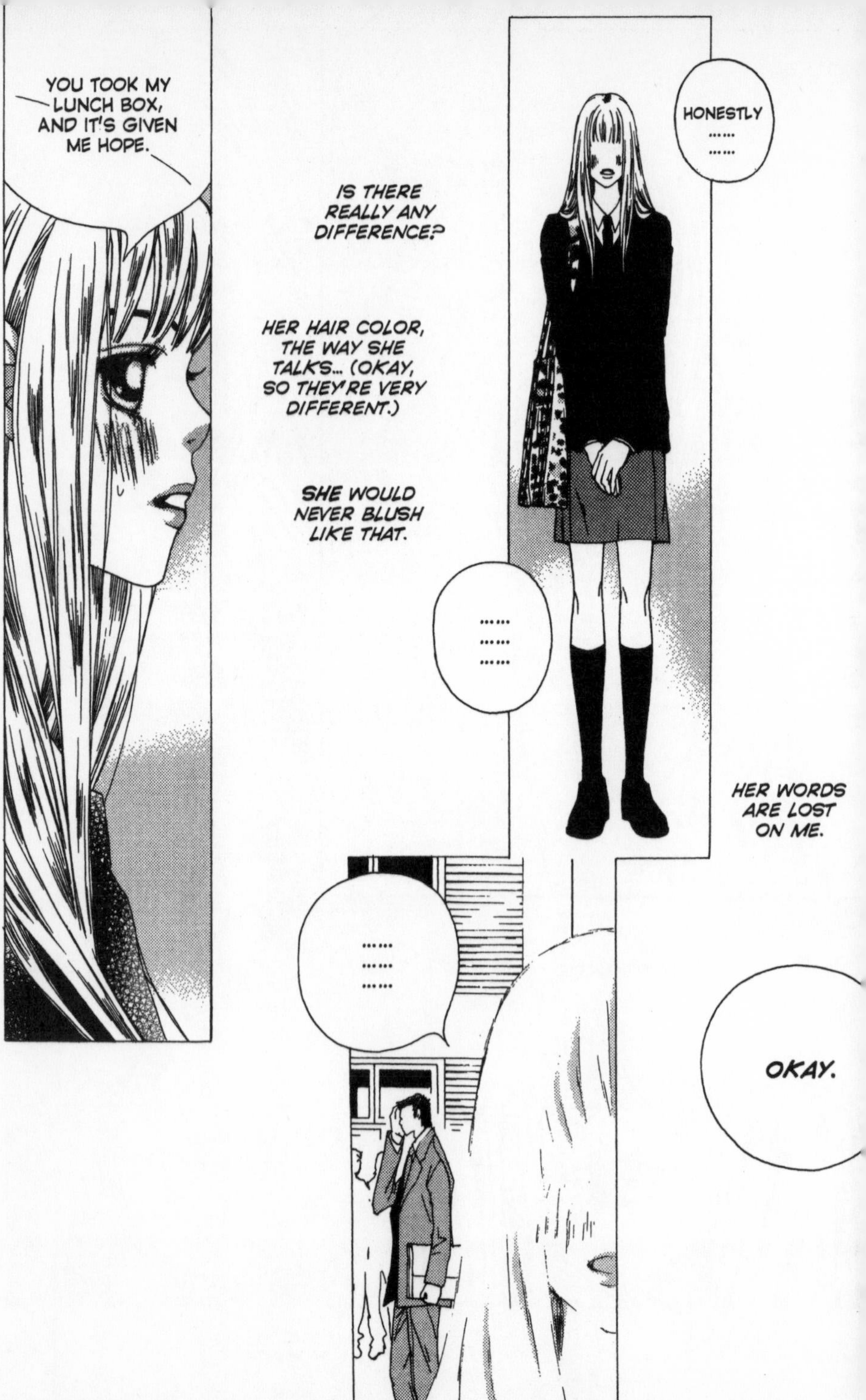
YOU TOOK MY LUNCH BOX, AND IT'S GIVEN ME HOPE.
IS THERE REALLY ANY DIFFERENCE?
HER HAIR COLOR, THE WAY SHE TALKS... (OKAY, SO THEY'RE VERY DIFFERENT.)
SHE WOULD NEVER BLUSH LIKE THAT.
HONESTLY ....
....
HER WORDS ARE LOST ON ME.
....
OKAY.

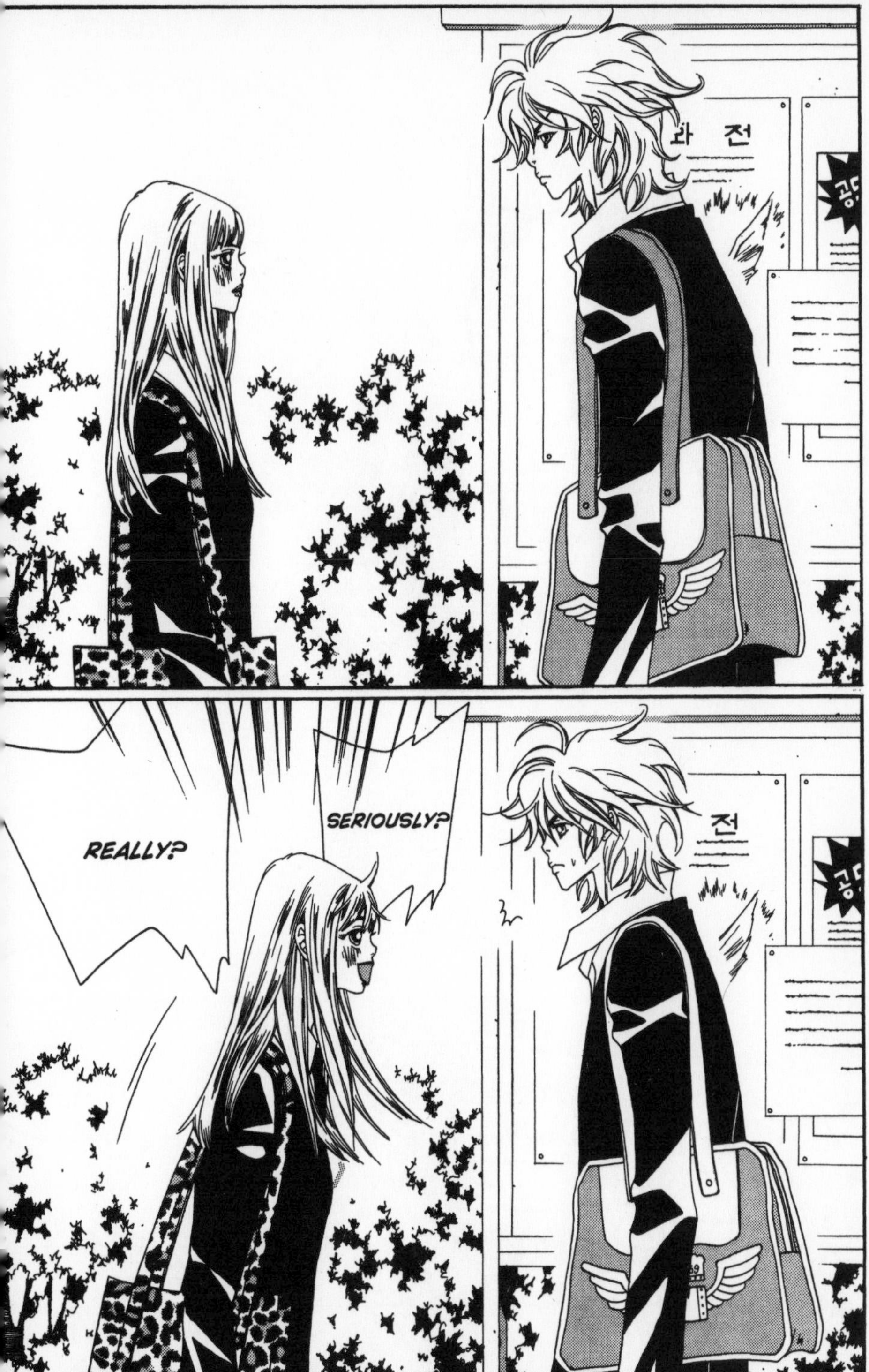
REALLY?
SERIOUSLY?

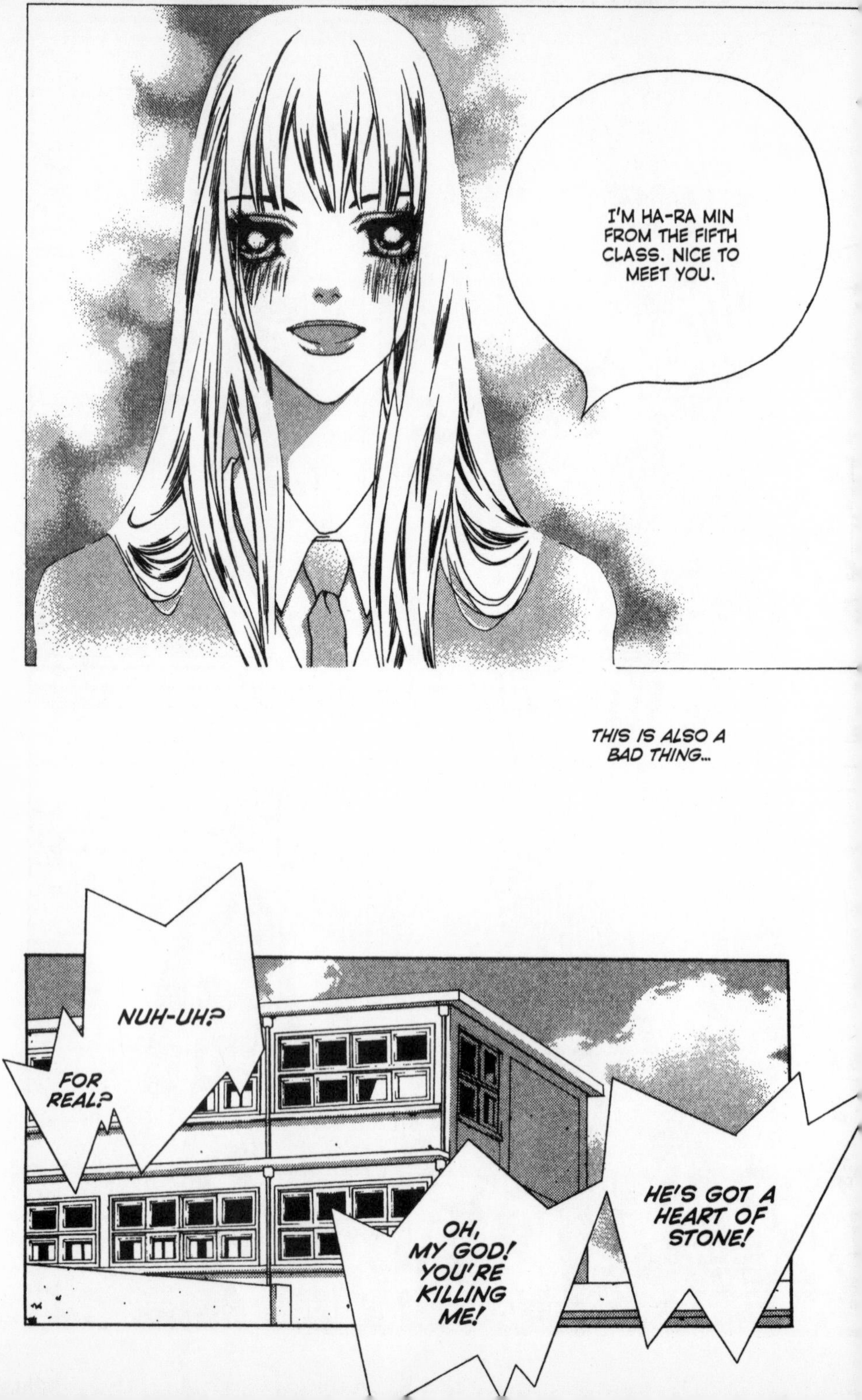
I'M HA-RA MIN FROM THE FIFTH CLASS. NICE TO MEET YOU.
THIS IS ALSO A BAD THING...
NUH-UH?
FOR REAL?
OH, MY GOD! YOU'RE KILLING ME!
HE'S GOT A HEART OF STONE!

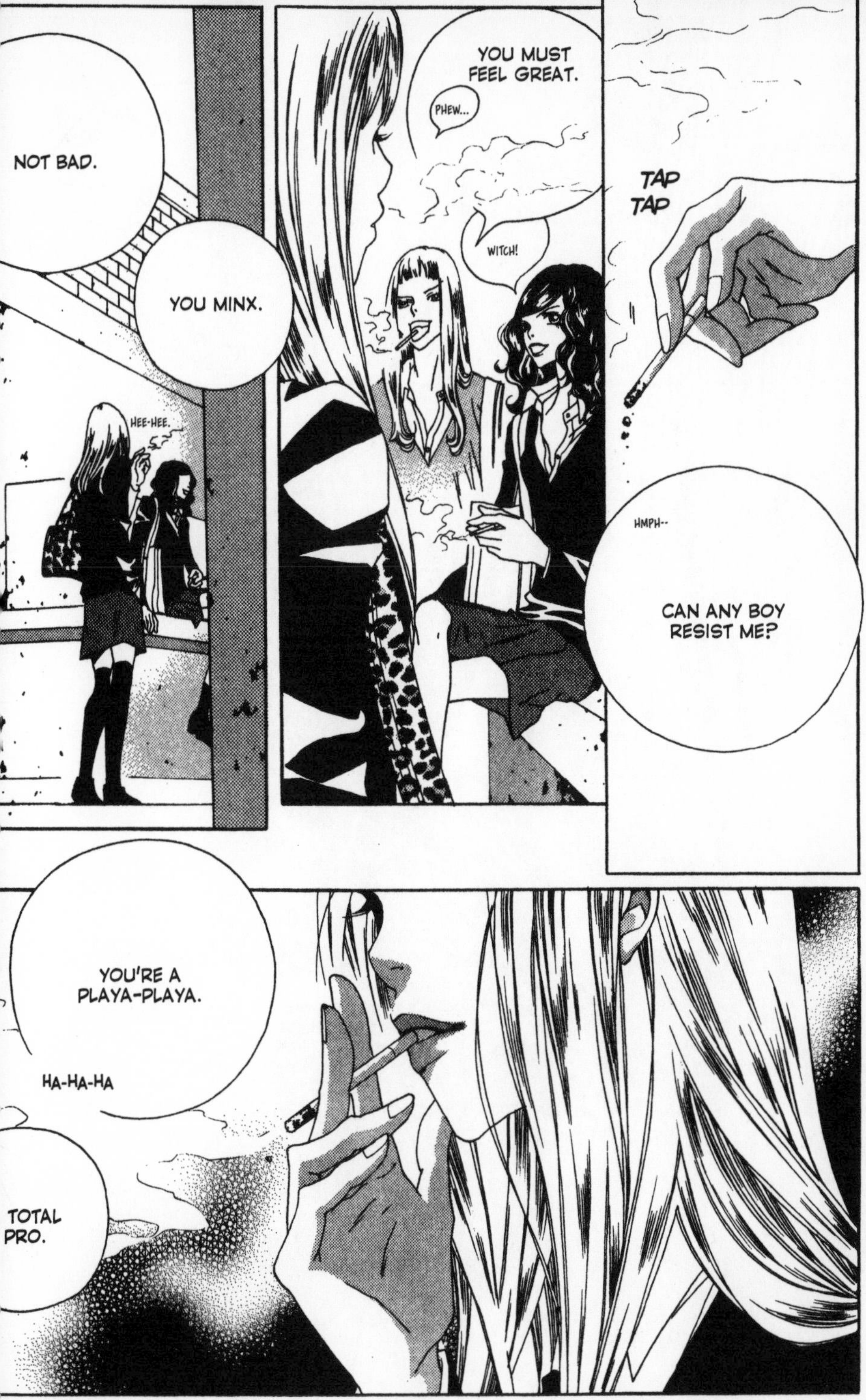
NOT BAD.
YOU MINX.
HEE-HEE.
YOU MUST FEEL GREAT.
PHEW...
WITCH!
TAP TAP
HMPH--
CAN ANY BOY RESIST ME?
YOU'RE A PLAYA-PLAYA.
HA-HA-HA
TOTAL PRO.

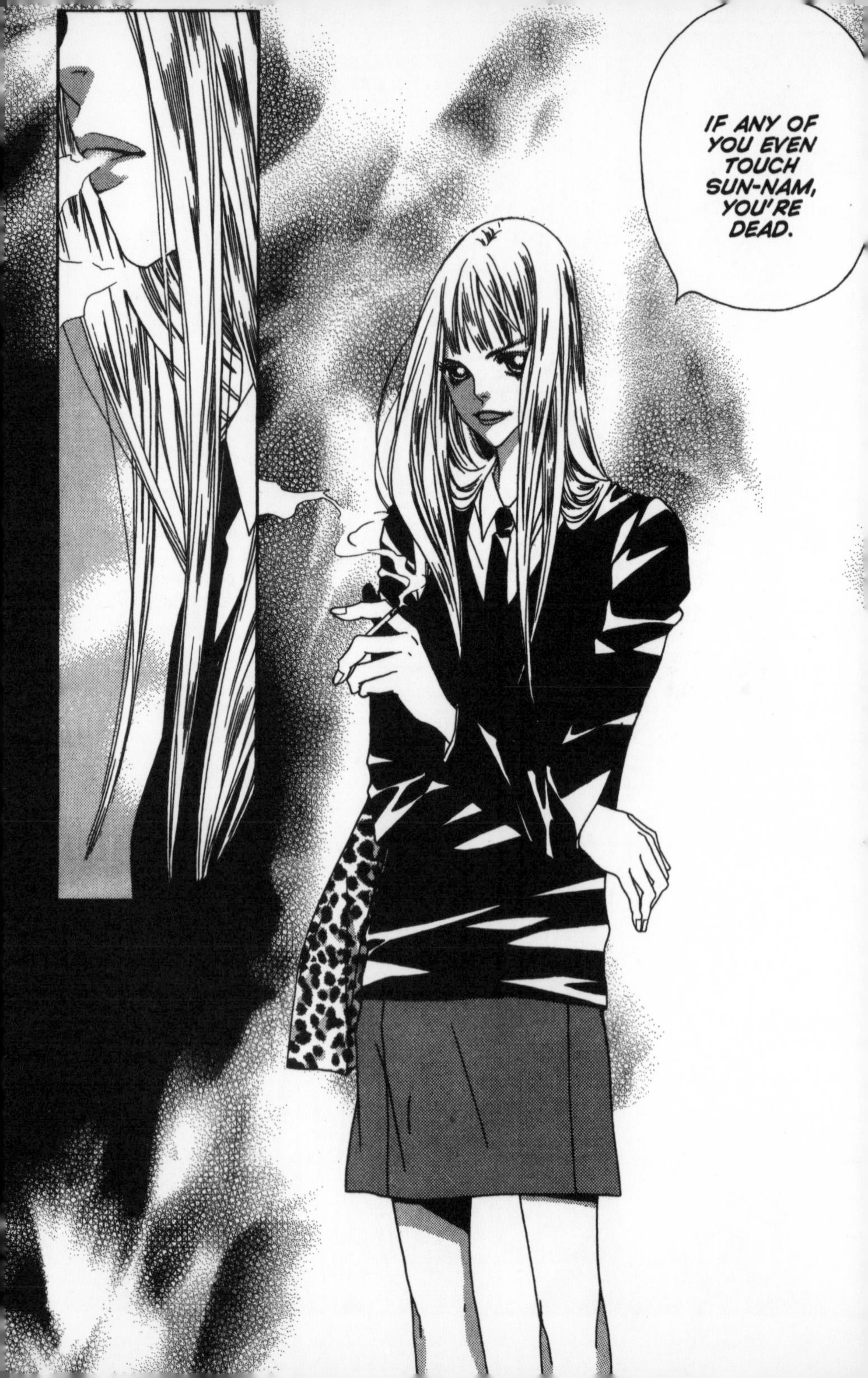
IF ANY OF YOU EVEN TOUCH SUN-NAM, YOU'RE DEAD.

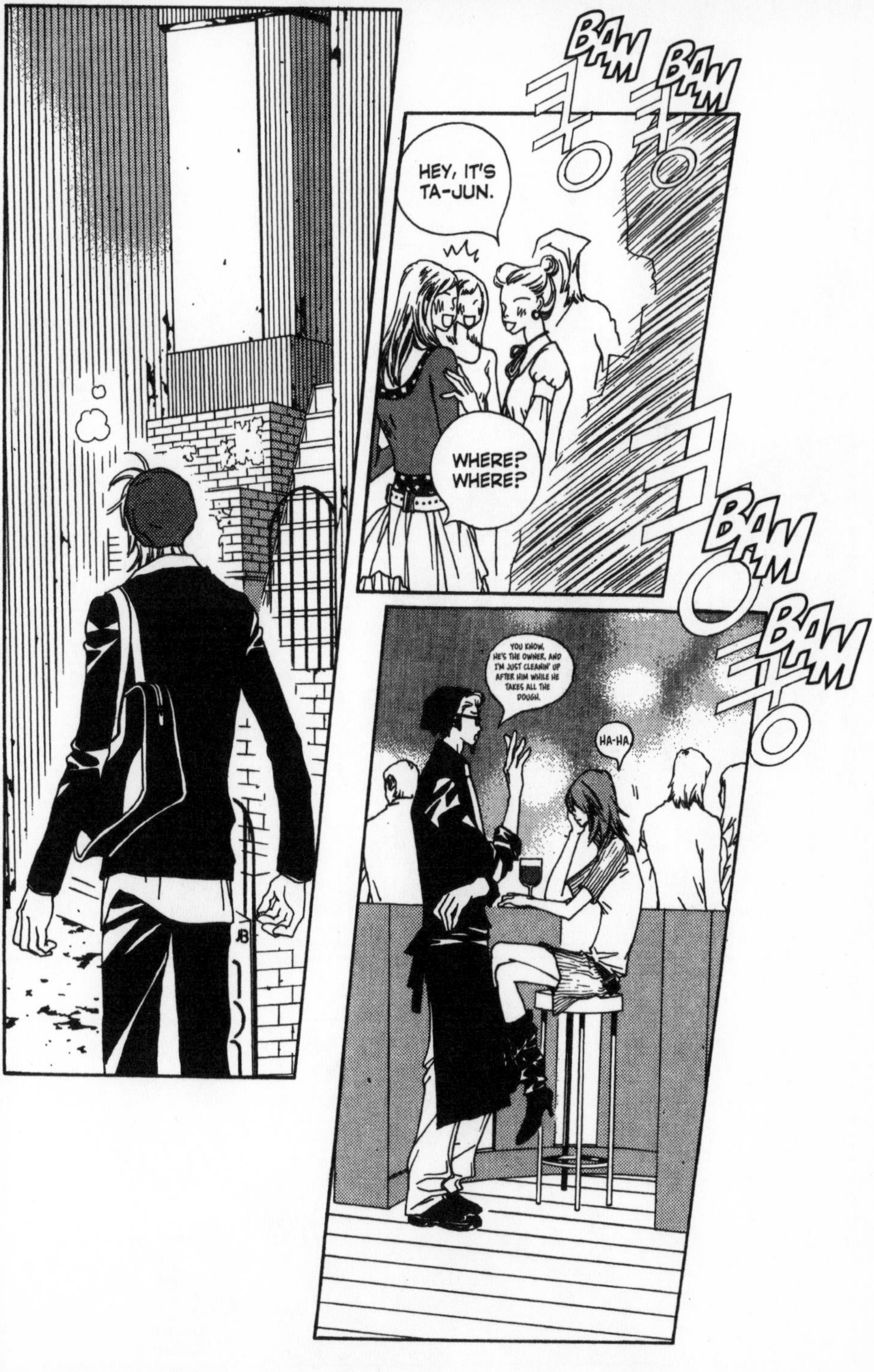
BAM
BAM
HEY, IT'S TA-JUN.
WHERE? WHERE?
BAM
BAM
YOU KNOW, HE'S THE OWNER, AND I'M JUST CLEANIN' UP AFTER HIM WHILE HE TAKES ALL THE DOUGH.
HA-HA

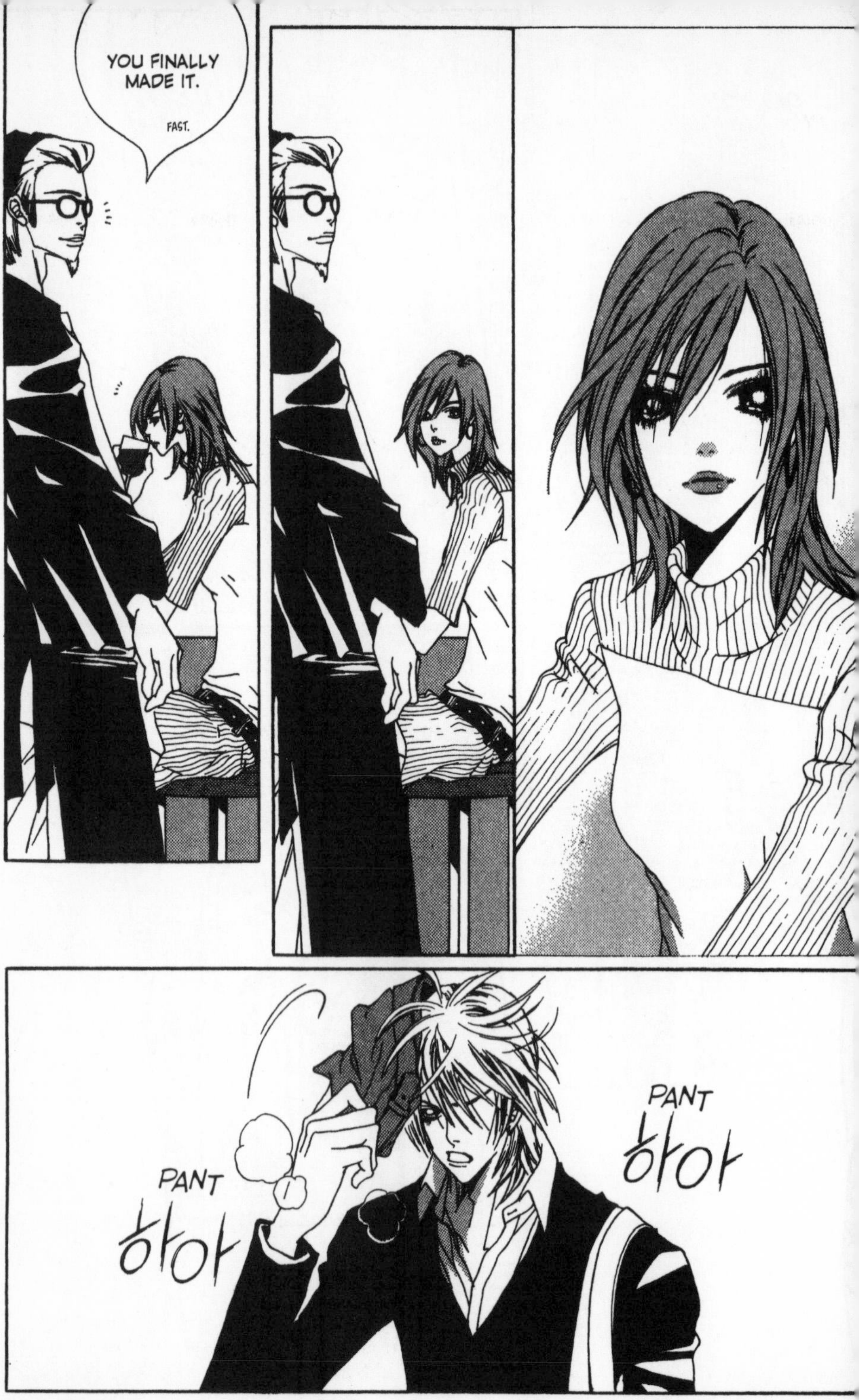
YOU FINALLY MADE IT.
FAST.
PANT
하아
PANT
하아

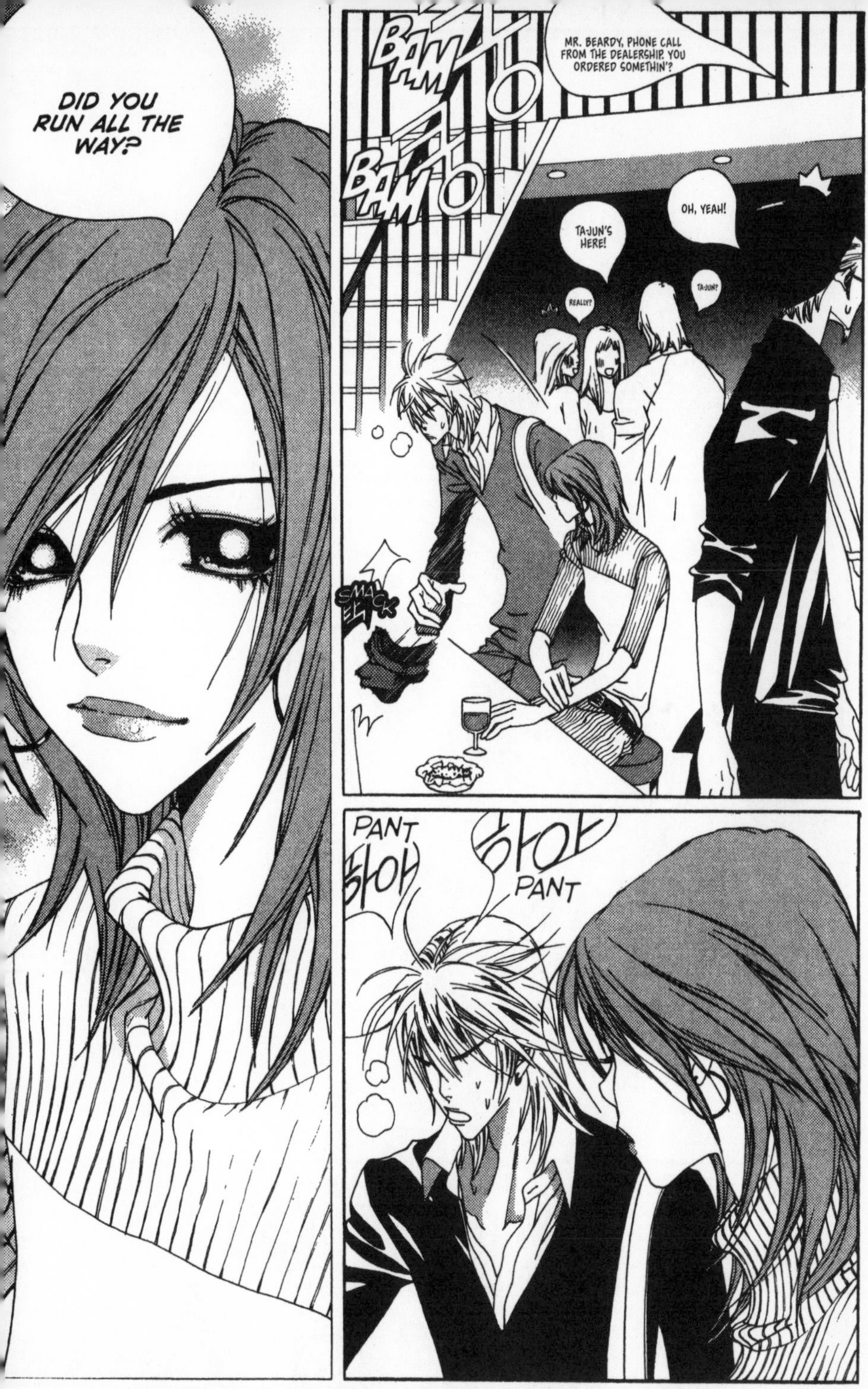
DID YOU RUN ALL THE WAY?
BAM
BAM
MR. BEARDY, PHONE CALL FROM THE DEALERSHIP. YOU ORDERED SOMETHIN'?
TA-JUN'S HERE!
OH, YEAH!
REALLY?
TA-JUN?
SMACK
PANT
하아
하아
PANT

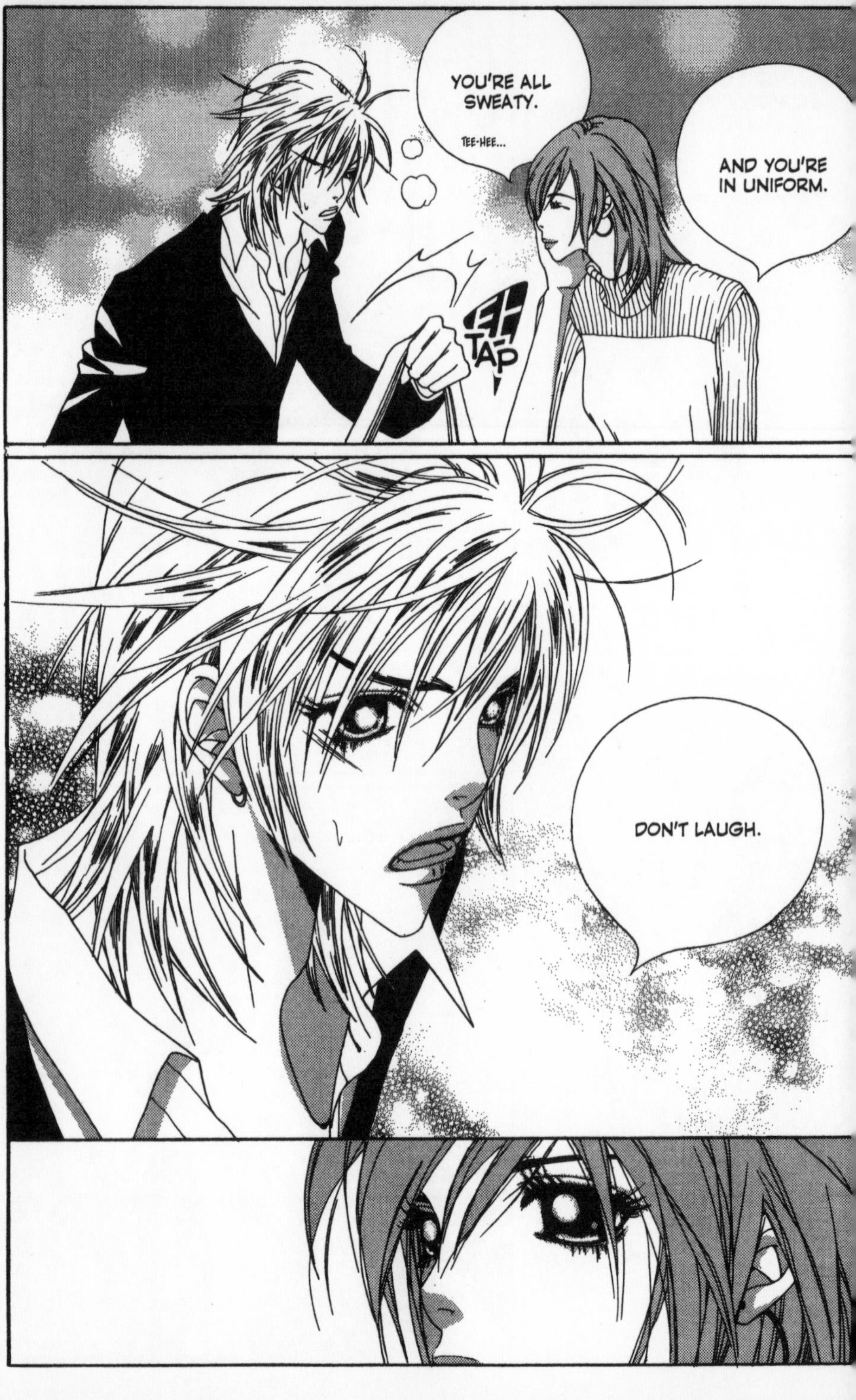
YOU'RE ALL SWEATY.
TEE-HEE...
AND YOU'RE IN UNIFORM.
TAP
DON'T LAUGH.

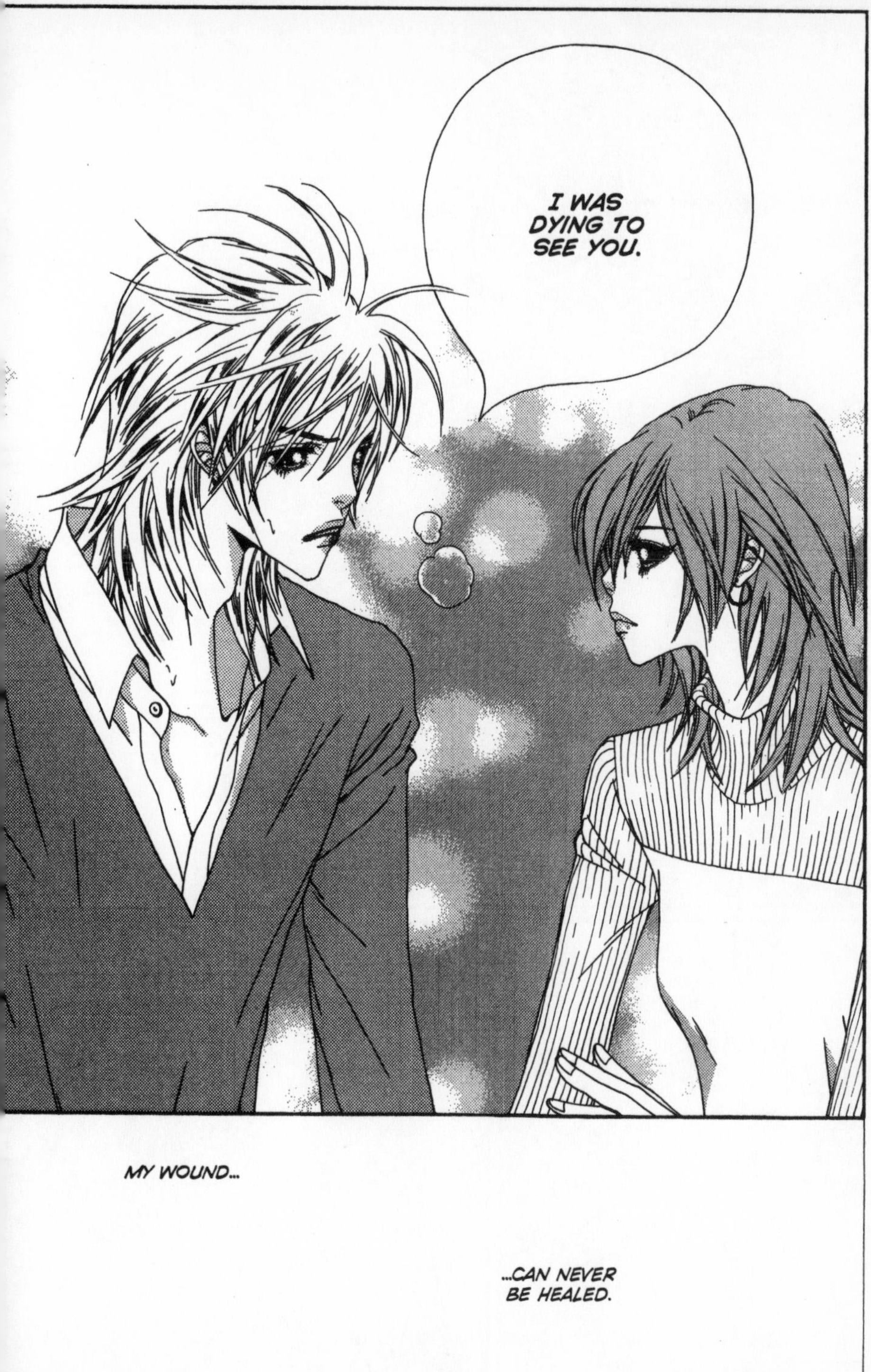
I WAS DYING TO SEE YOU.
MY WOUND...
...CAN NEVER BE HEALED.

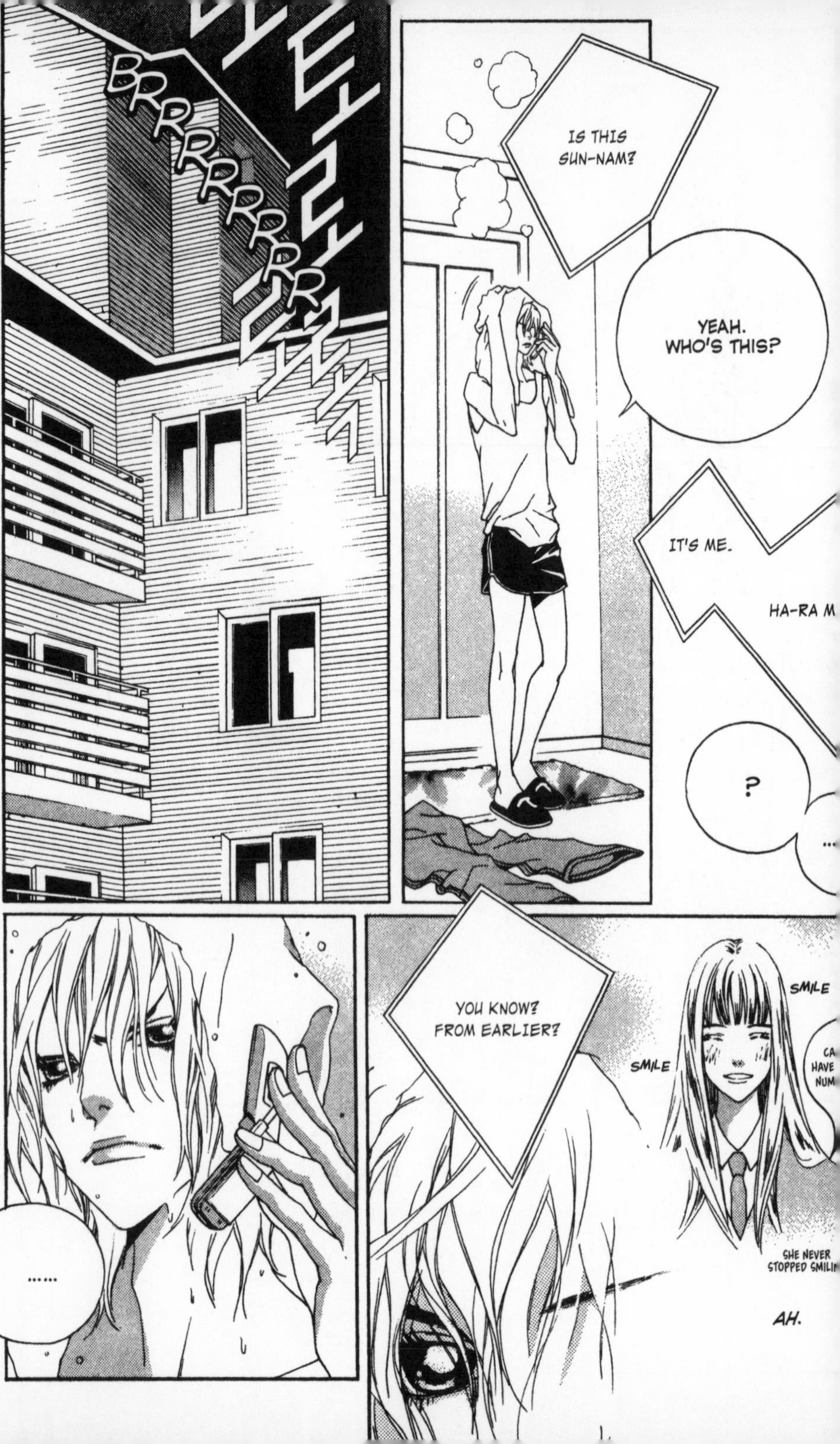
BRRRRRRRR
IS THIS SUN-NAM?
YEAH. WHO'S THIS?
IT'S ME.
HA-RA M
?
...
......
YOU KNOW? FROM EARLIER?
SMILE
SMILE
CA
HAVE
NUM
SHE NEVER STOPPED SMILI
AH.

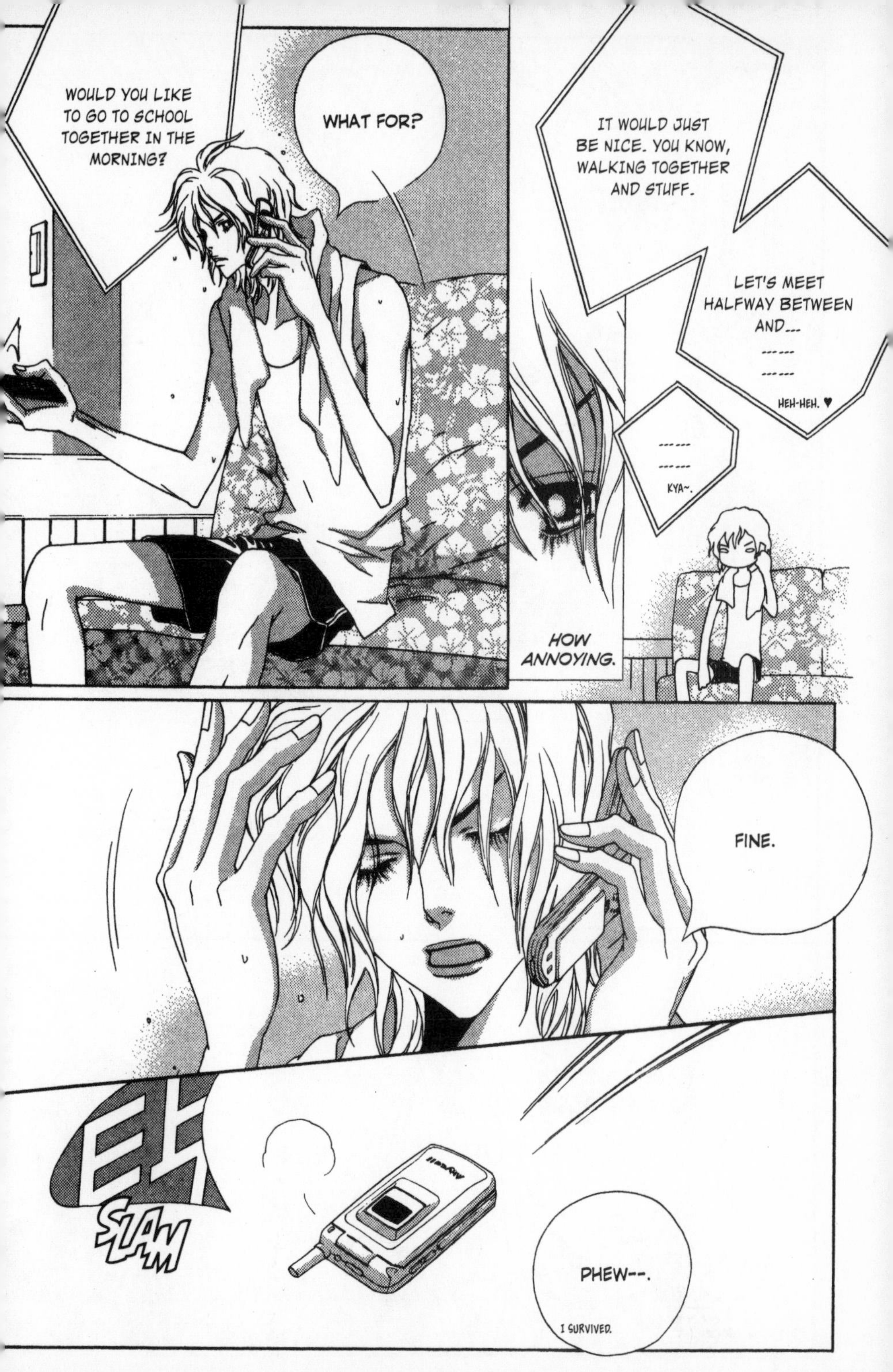
WOULD YOU LIKE TO GO TO SCHOOL TOGETHER IN THE MORNING?
WHAT FOR?
IT WOULD JUST BE NICE. YOU KNOW, WALKING TOGETHER AND STUFF.
LET'S MEET HALFWAY BETWEEN AND... ------ ------
HEH-HEH. ♥
------ ------
KYA~.
HOW ANNOYING.
FINE.
SLAM
PHEW--.
I SURVIVED.

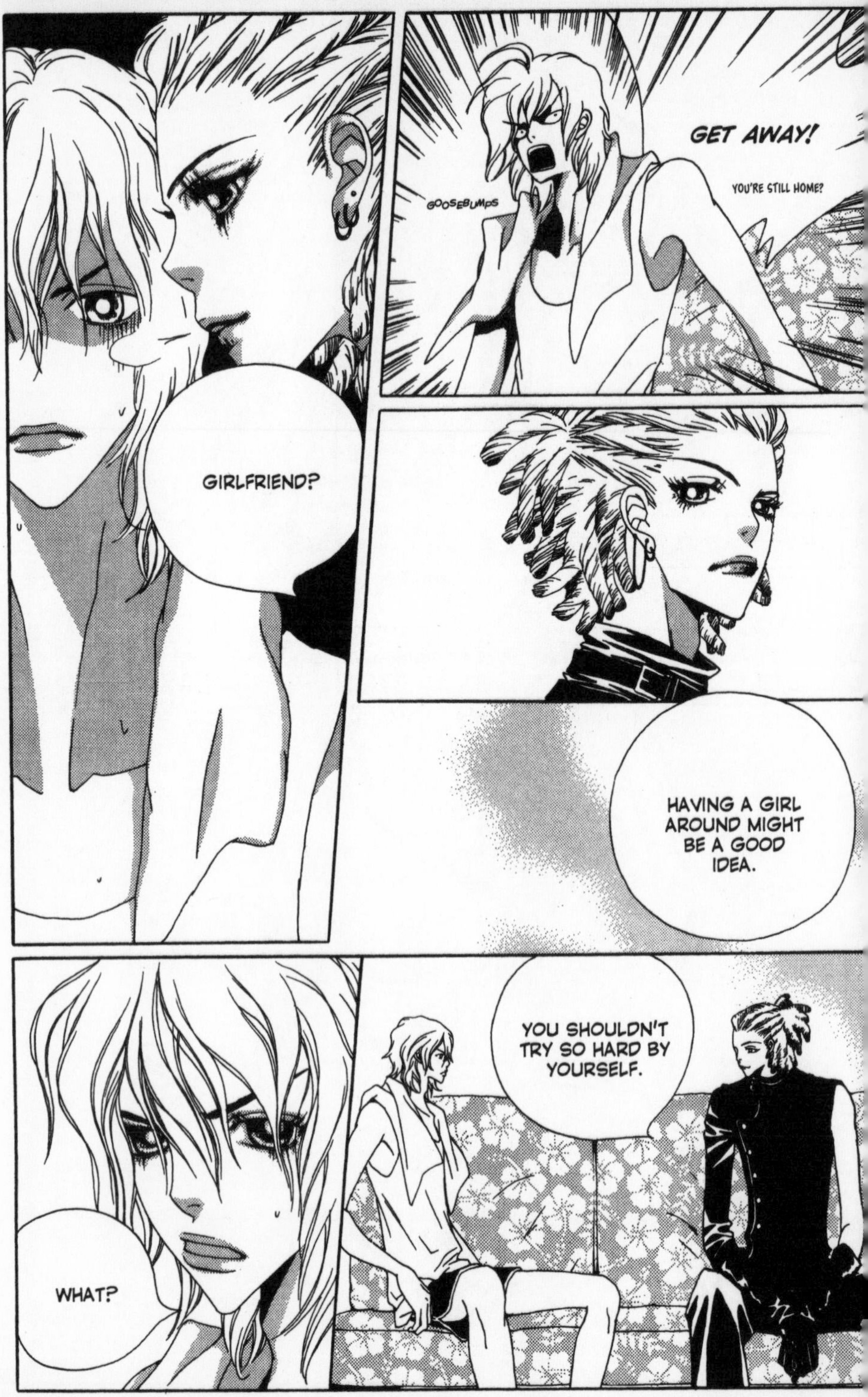
GIRLFRIEND?
GOOSEBUMPS
GET AWAY!
YOU'RE STILL HOME?
HAVING A GIRL AROUND MIGHT BE A GOOD IDEA.
WHAT?
YOU SHOULDN'T TRY SO HARD BY YOURSELF.

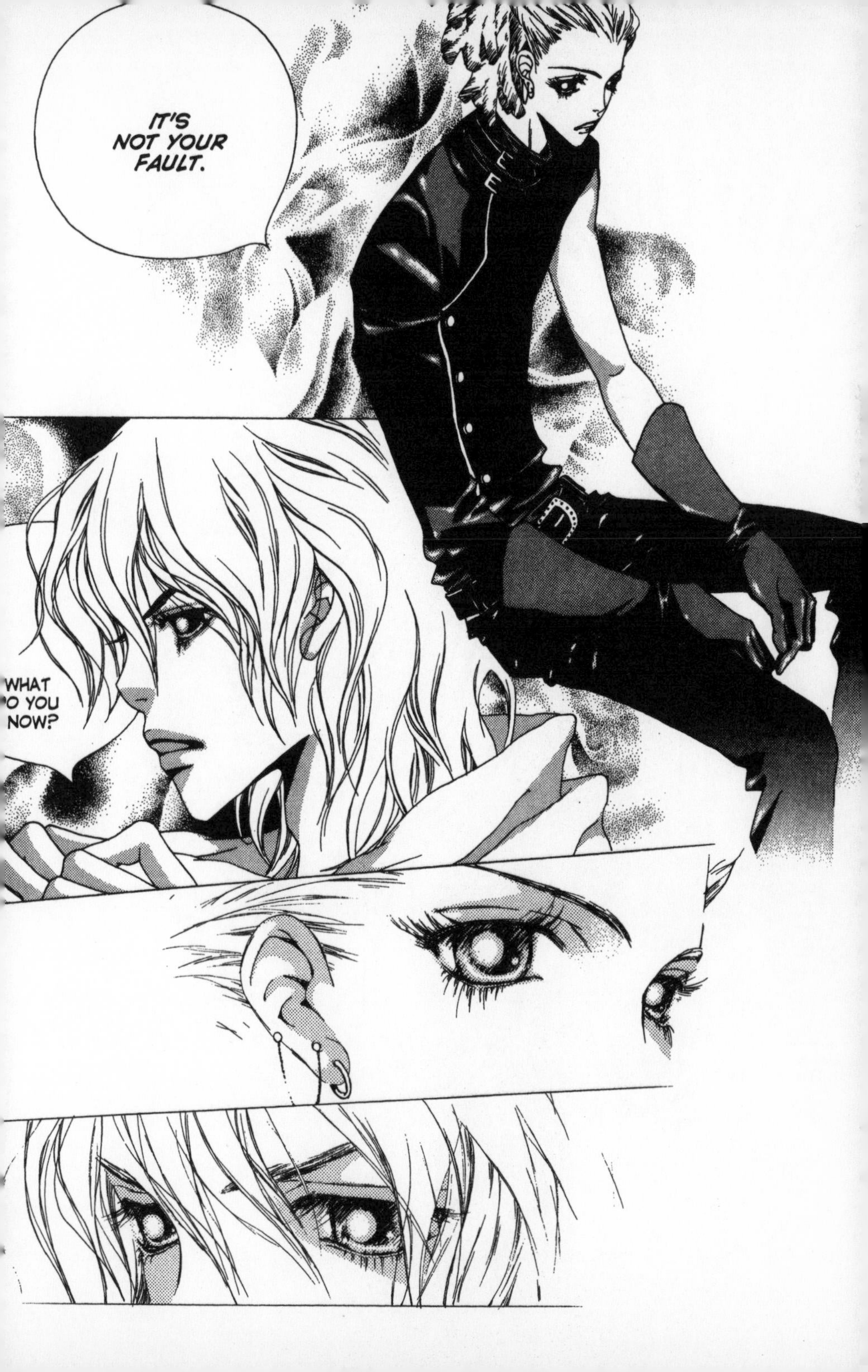
IT'S NOT YOUR FAULT.
WHAT
O YOU
NOW?

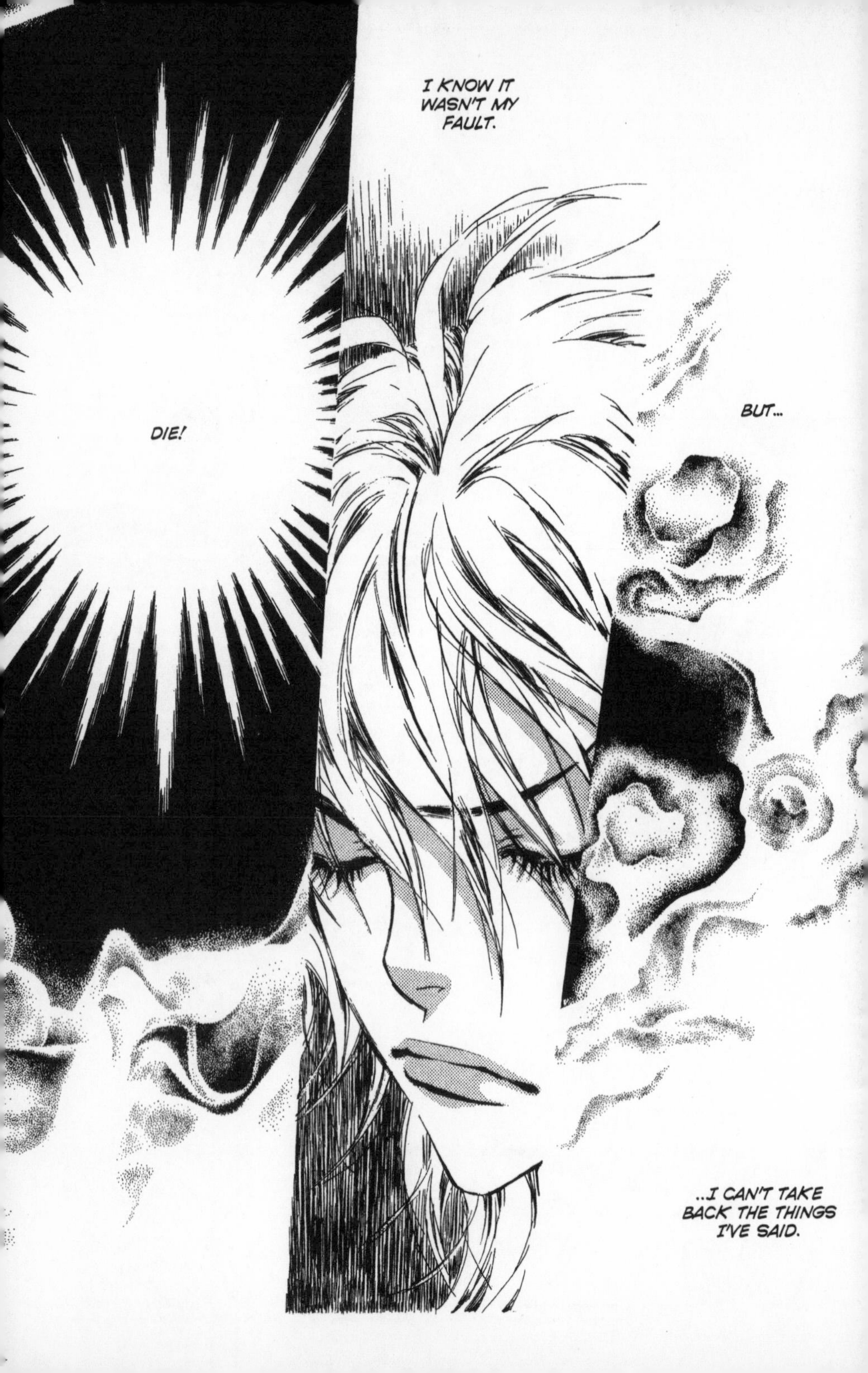
DIE!
I KNOW IT WASN'T MY FAULT.
BUT...
...I CAN'T TAKE BACK THE THINGS I'VE SAID.

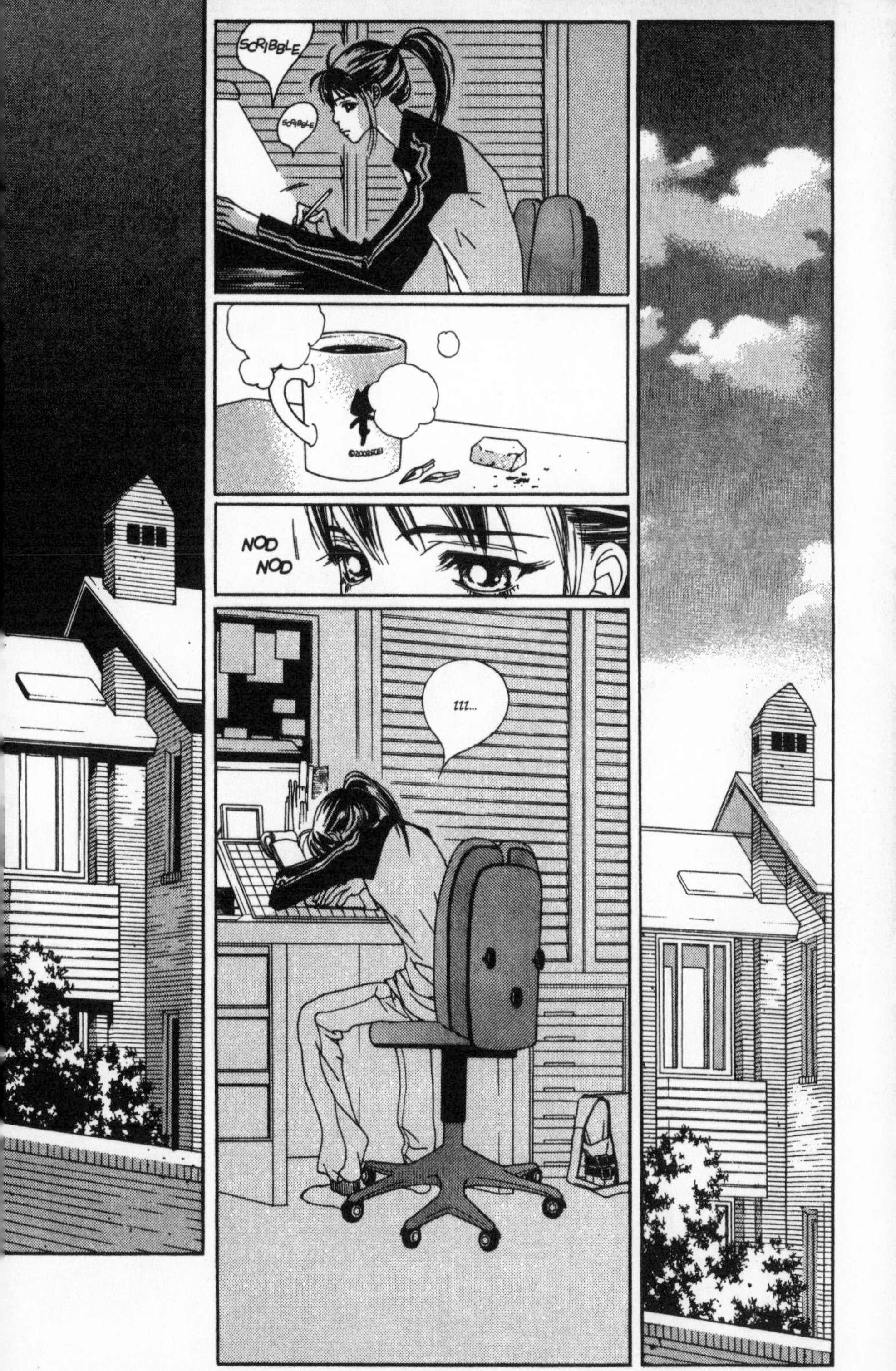
SCRIBBLE
SCRIBBLE
NOD
NOD
zzz...

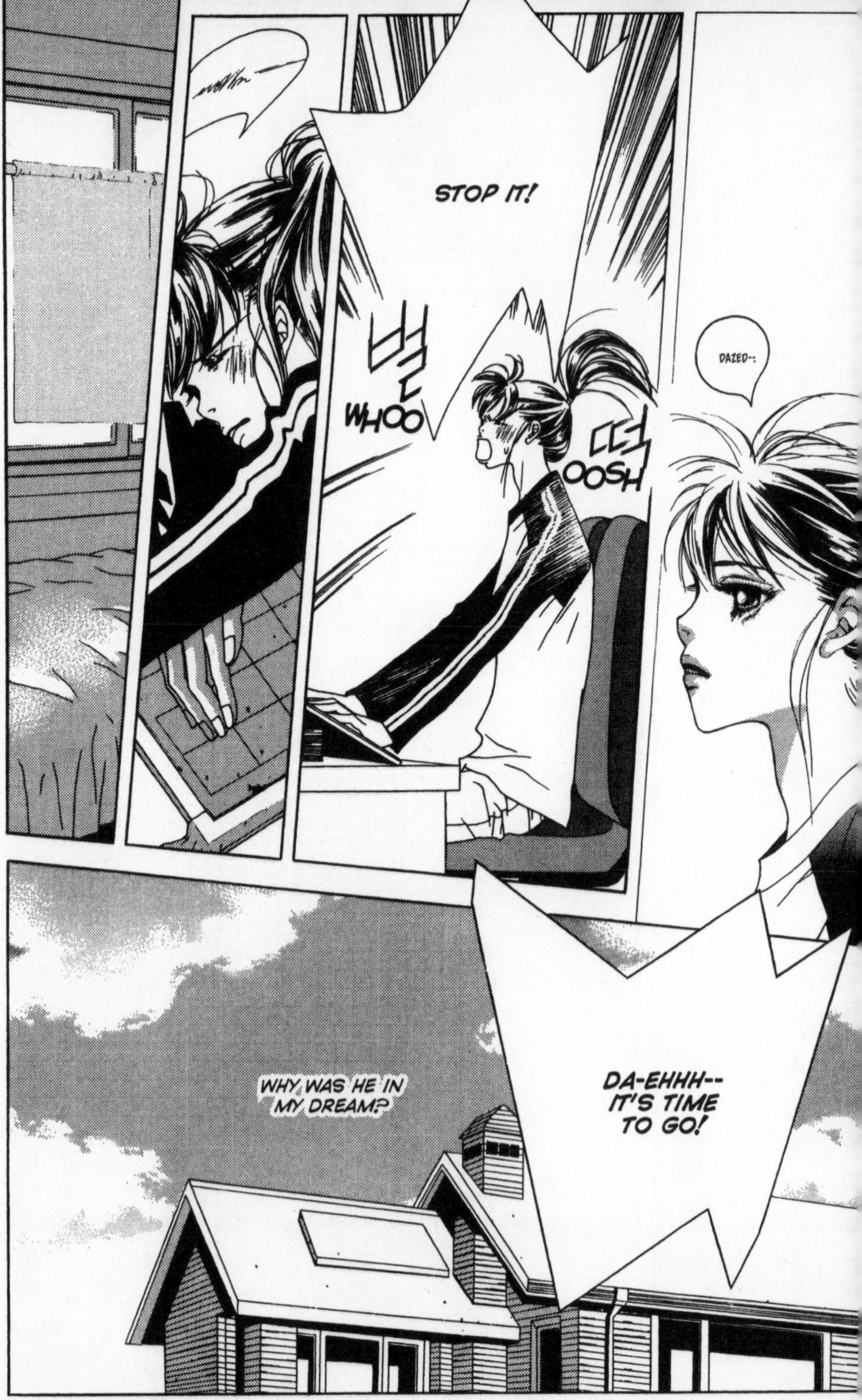
STOP IT!
WHOO
OOSH
DAZED--;
WHY WAS HE IN MY DREAM?
DA-EHHH-- IT'S TIME TO GO!

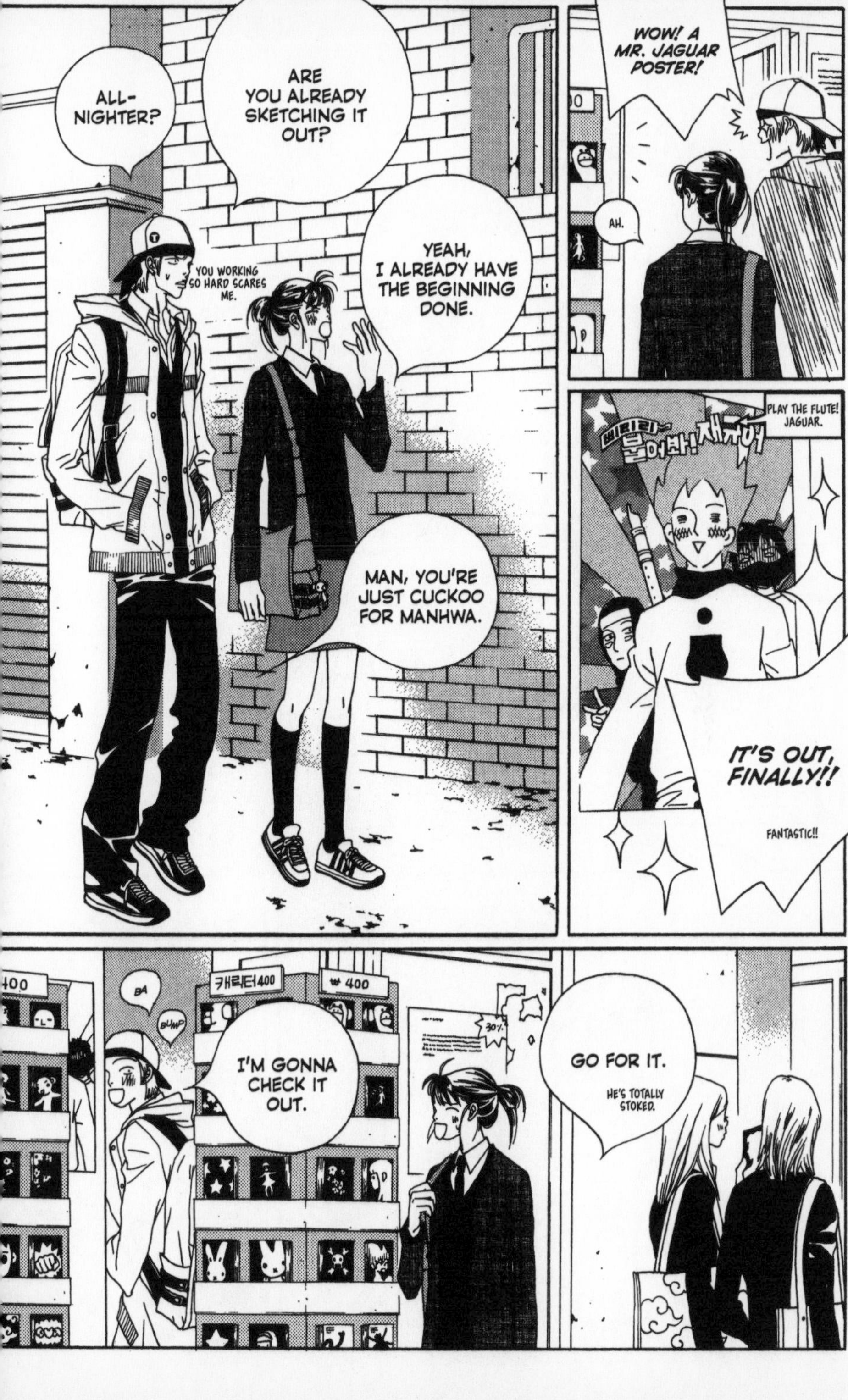
ALL-NIGHTER?
ARE YOU ALREADY SKETCHING IT OUT?
YOU WORKING SO HARD SCARES ME.
YEAH, I ALREADY HAVE THE BEGINNING DONE.
MAN, YOU'RE JUST CUCKOO FOR MANHWA.
WOW! A MR. JAGUAR POSTER!
AH.
삐리리~ 불어봐! 재규어
PLAY THE FLUTE! JAGUAR.
IT'S OUT, FINALLY!!
FANTASTIC!!
BA
BUMP
캐릭터400
₩400
I'M GONNA CHECK IT OUT.
30%
GO FOR IT.
HE'S TOTALLY STOKED.

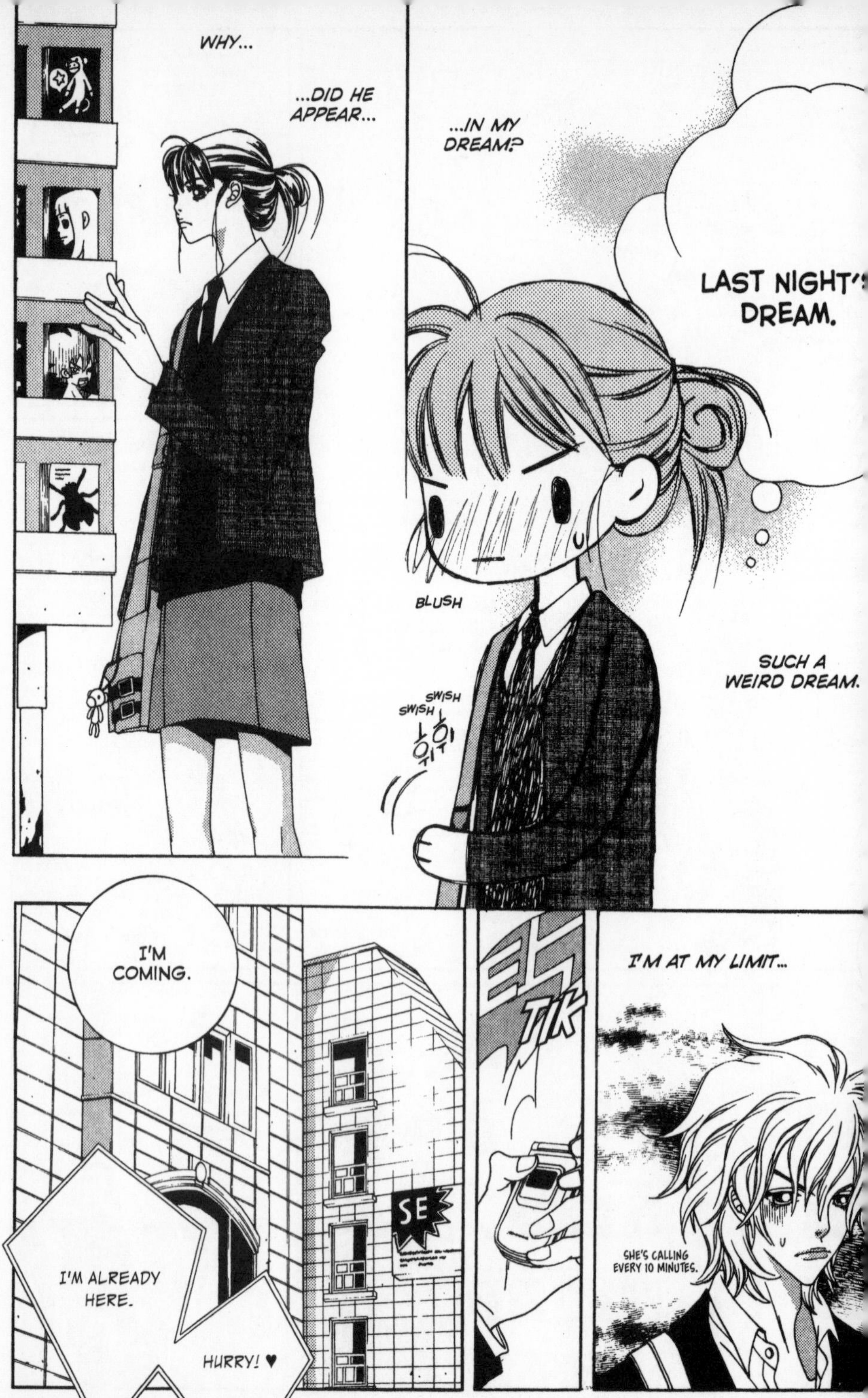
WHY...
...DID HE APPEAR...
...IN MY DREAM?
LAST NIGHT'S DREAM.
BLUSH
SUCH A WEIRD DREAM.
SWISH SWISH
I'M COMING.
I'M ALREADY HERE.
HURRY! ♥
SE
TIK
I'M AT MY LIMIT...
SHE'S CALLING EVERY 10 MINUTES.

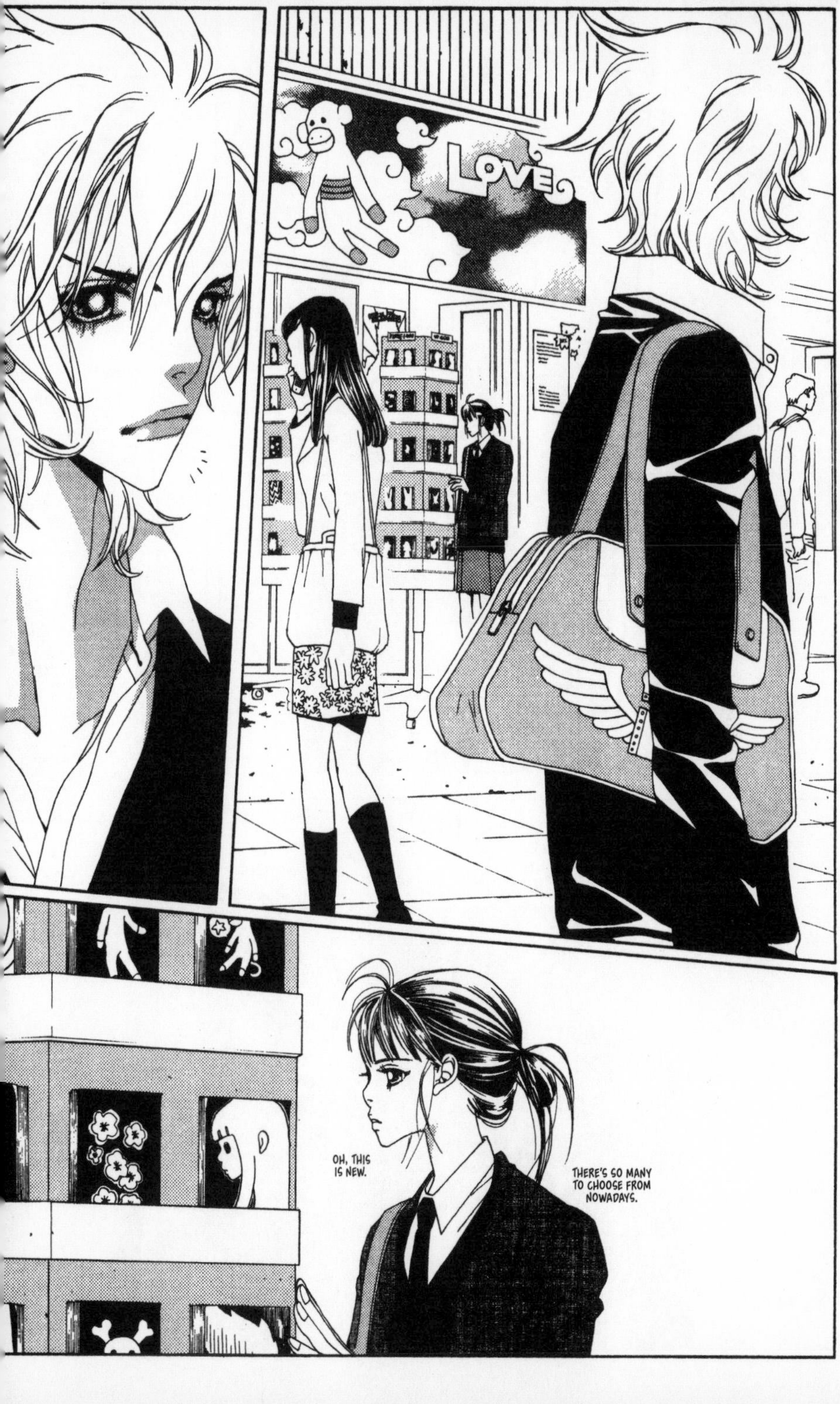
LOVE
OH, THIS IS NEW.
THERE'S SO MANY TO CHOOSE FROM NOWADAYS.

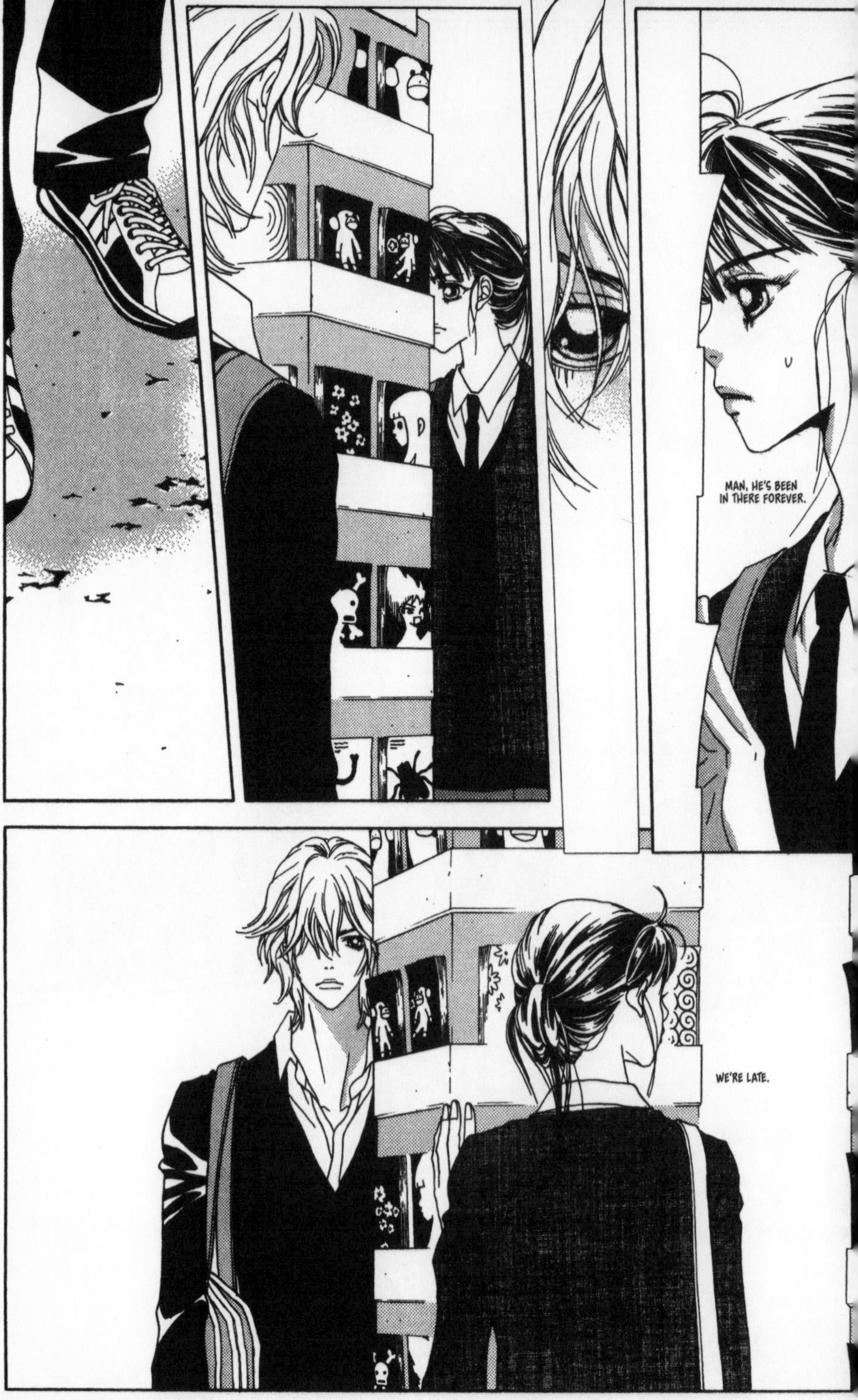
MAN, HE'S BEEN IN THERE FOREVER.
WE'RE LATE.

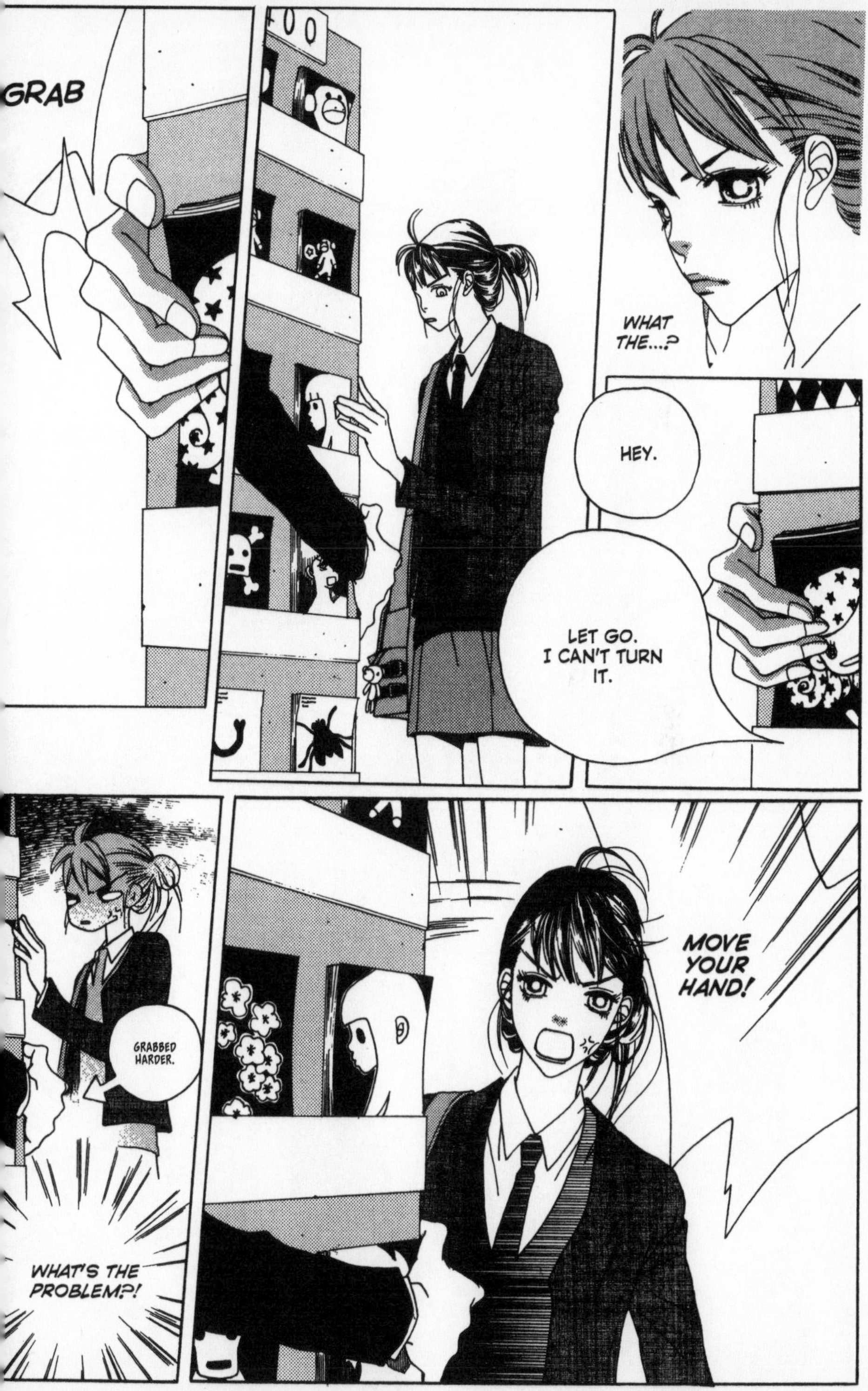
GRAB
WHAT THE...?
HEY.
LET GO. I CAN'T TURN IT.
GRABBED HARDER.
WHAT'S THE PROBLEM?!
MOVE YOUR HAND!

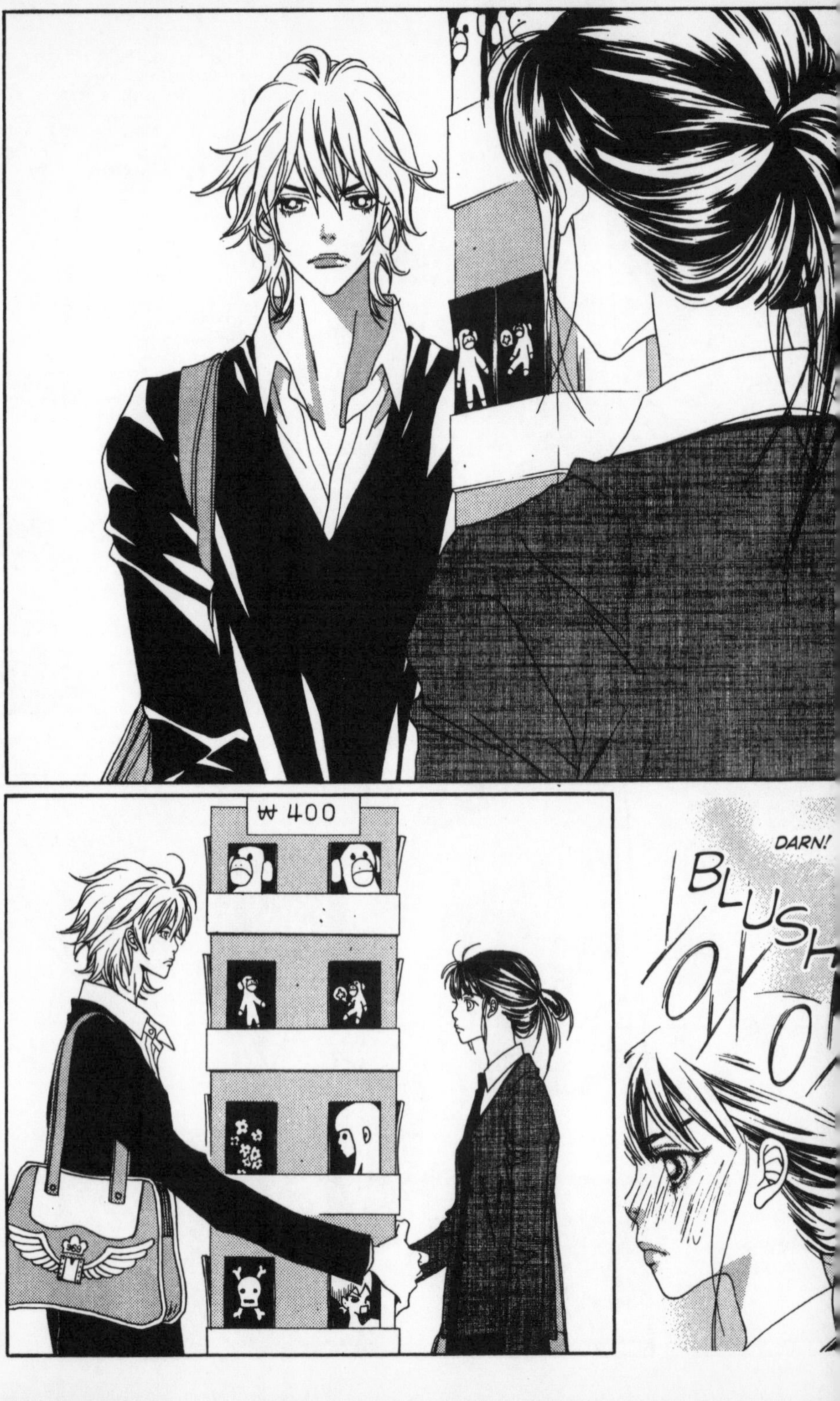
₩ 400
DARN!
BLUSH

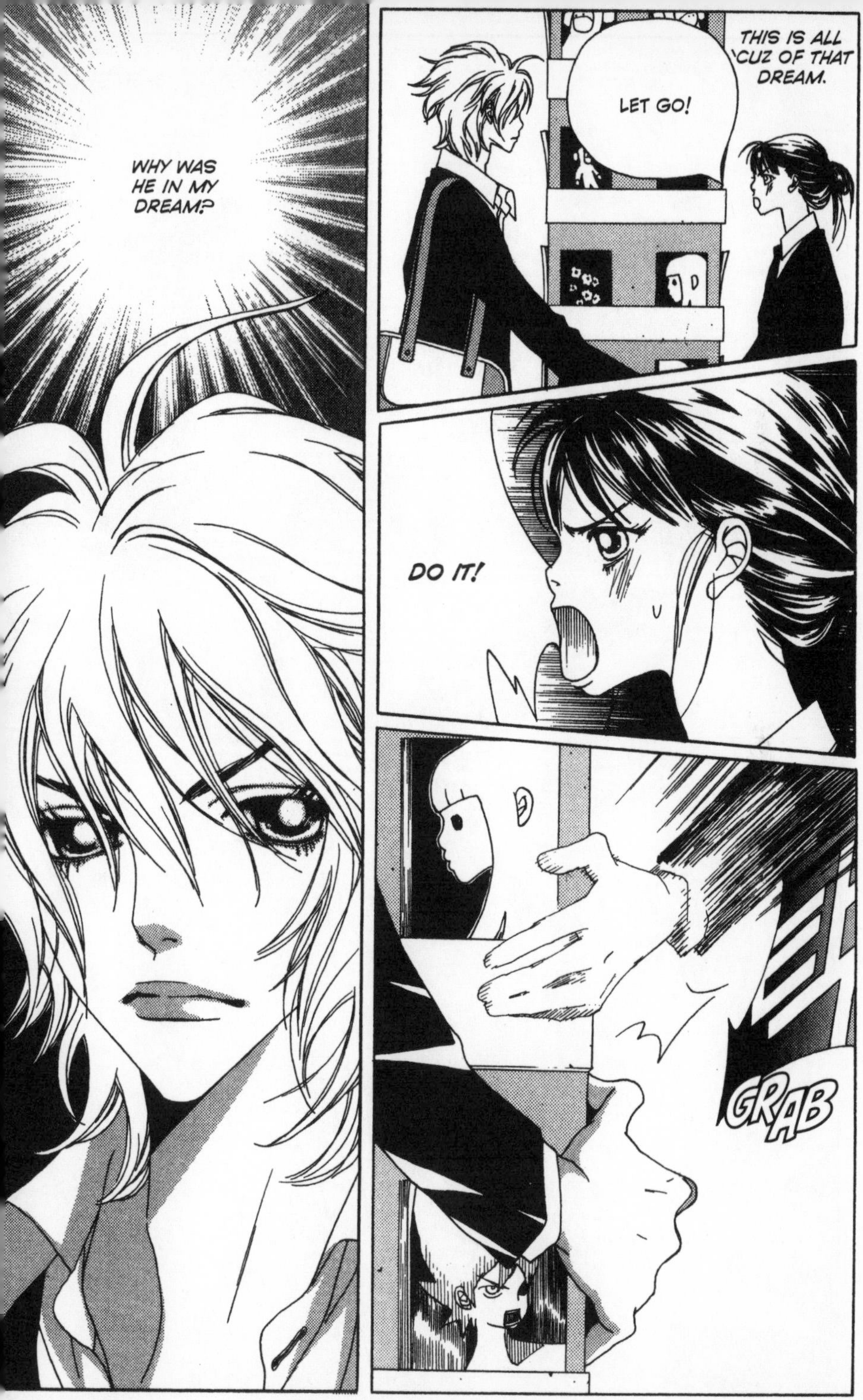
WHY WAS HE IN MY DREAM?
THIS IS ALL 'CUZ OF THAT DREAM.
LET GO!
DO IT!
GRAB

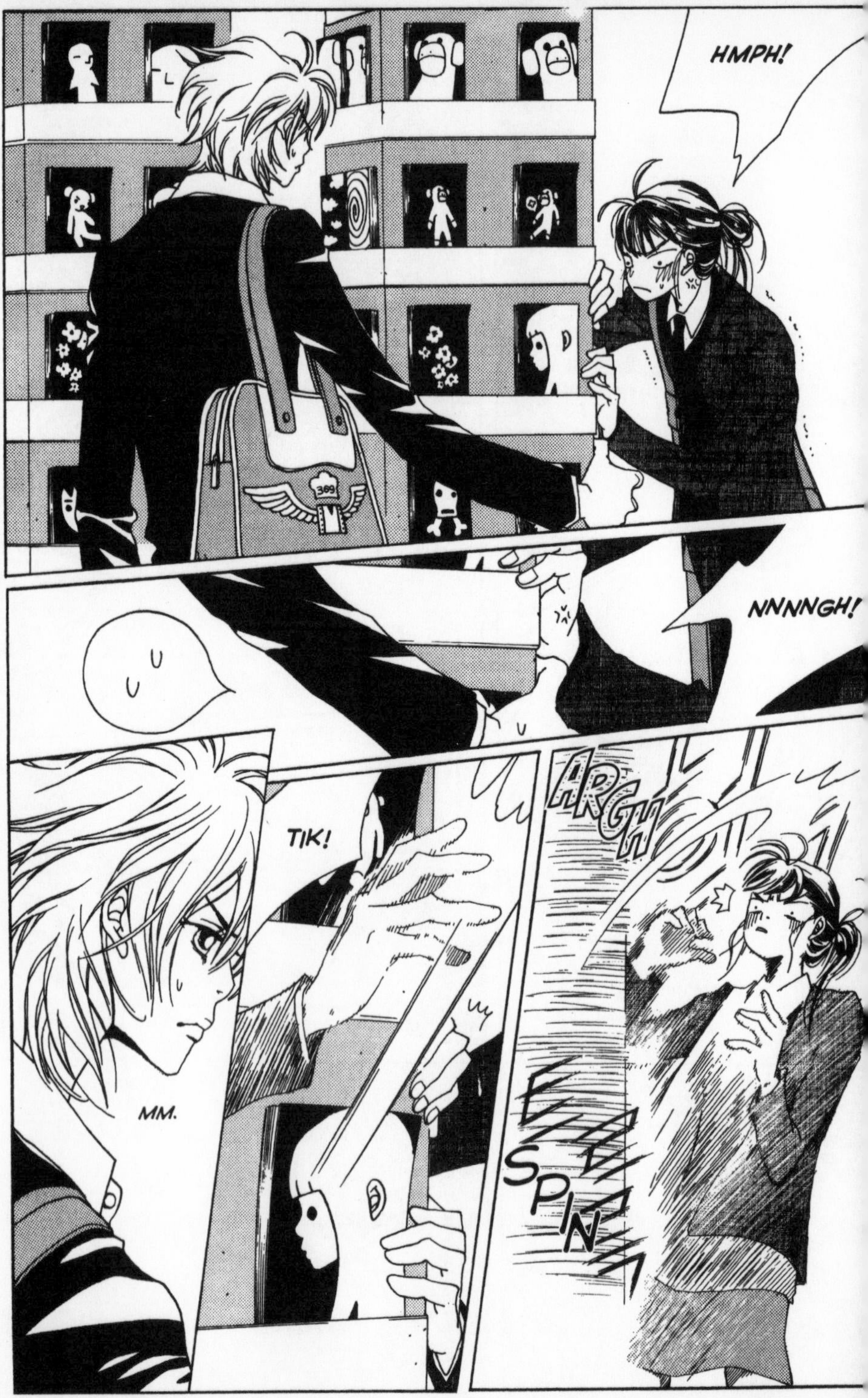
HMPH!
NNNNGH!
TIK!
MM.
ARGH
SPIN

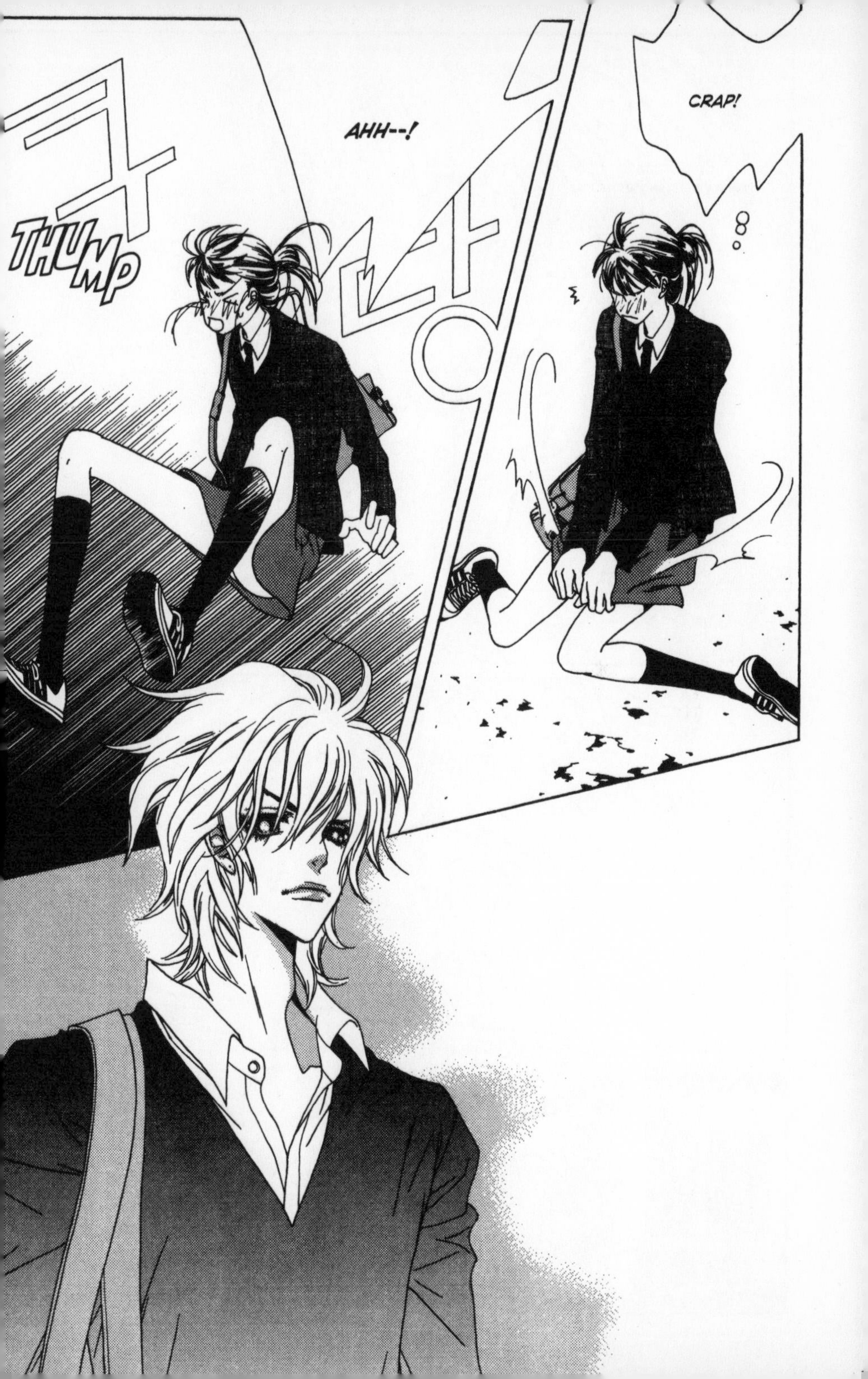
THUMP
AHH--!
CRAP!

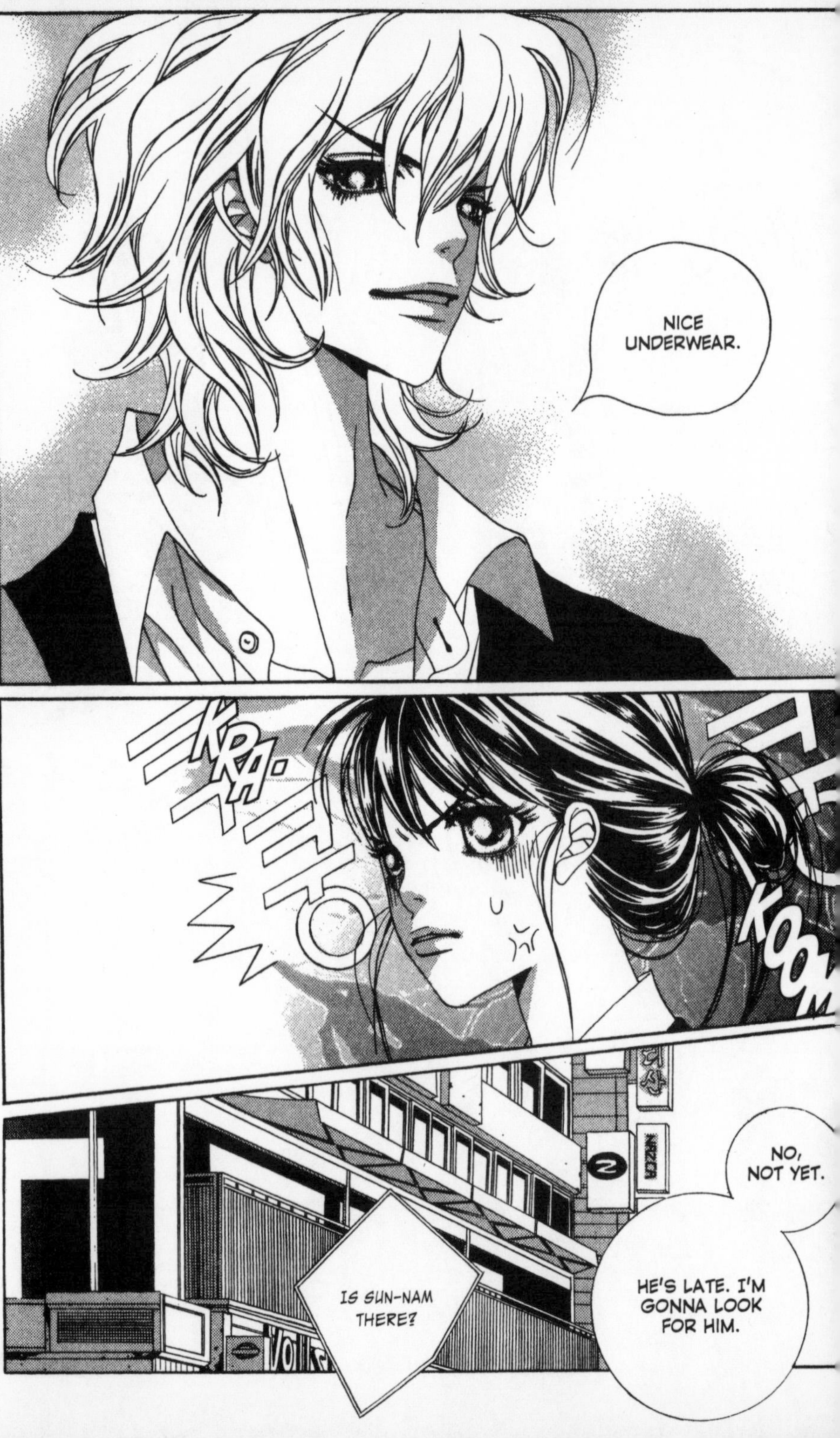
NICE UNDERWEAR.
KRA-
KOOM
IS SUN-NAM THERE?
NO, NOT YET.
HE'S LATE. I'M GONNA LOOK FOR HIM.

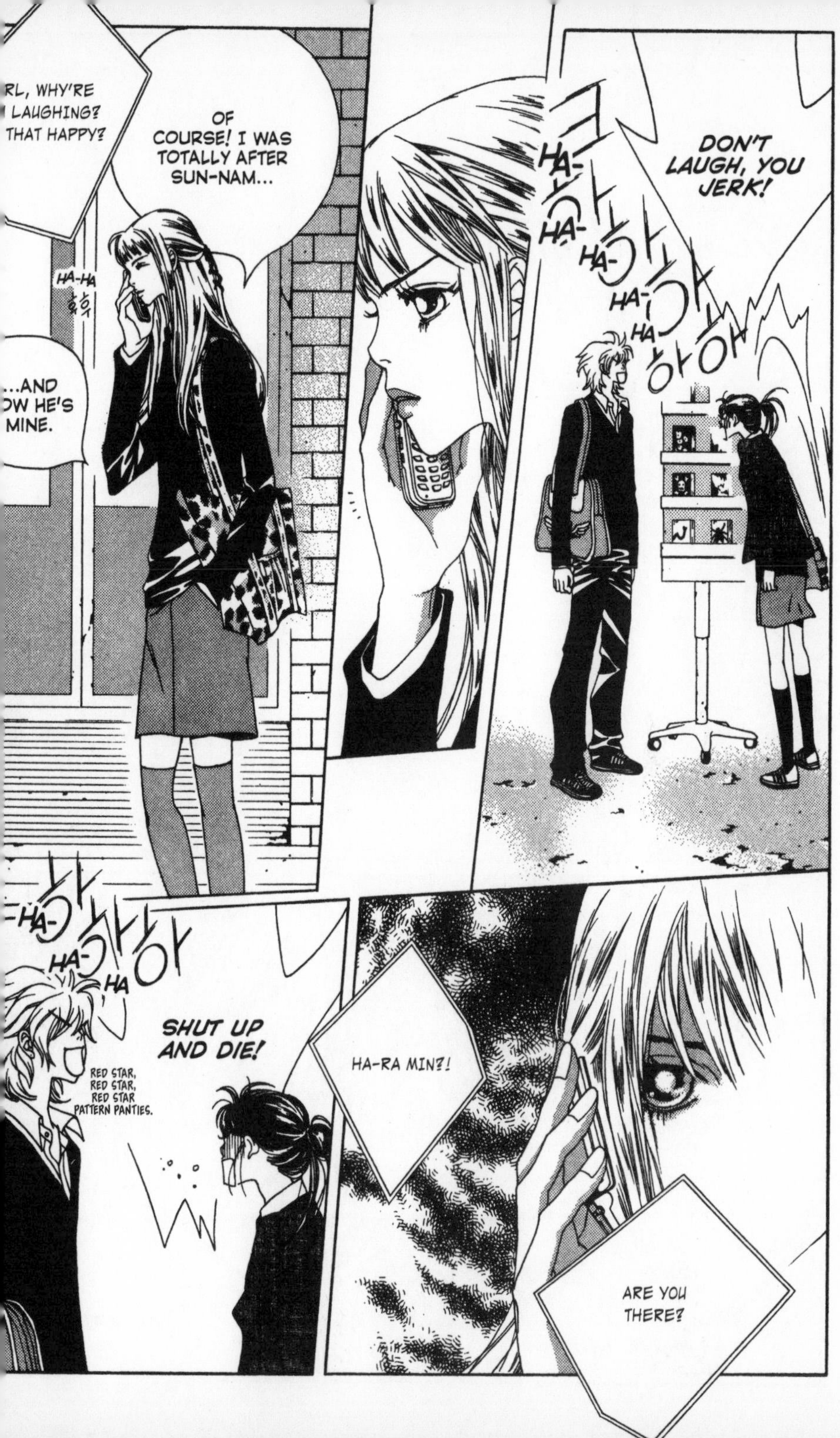
RL, WHY'RE
LAUGHING?
THAT HAPPY?
OF COURSE! I WAS TOTALLY AFTER SUN-NAM...
HA-HA
...AND
OW HE'S
MINE.
HA-HA-HA-HA-HA
DON'T LAUGH, YOU JERK!
HA-HA-HA
SHUT UP AND DIE!
RED STAR, RED STAR, RED STAR PATTERN PANTIES.
HA-RA MIN?!
ARE YOU THERE?

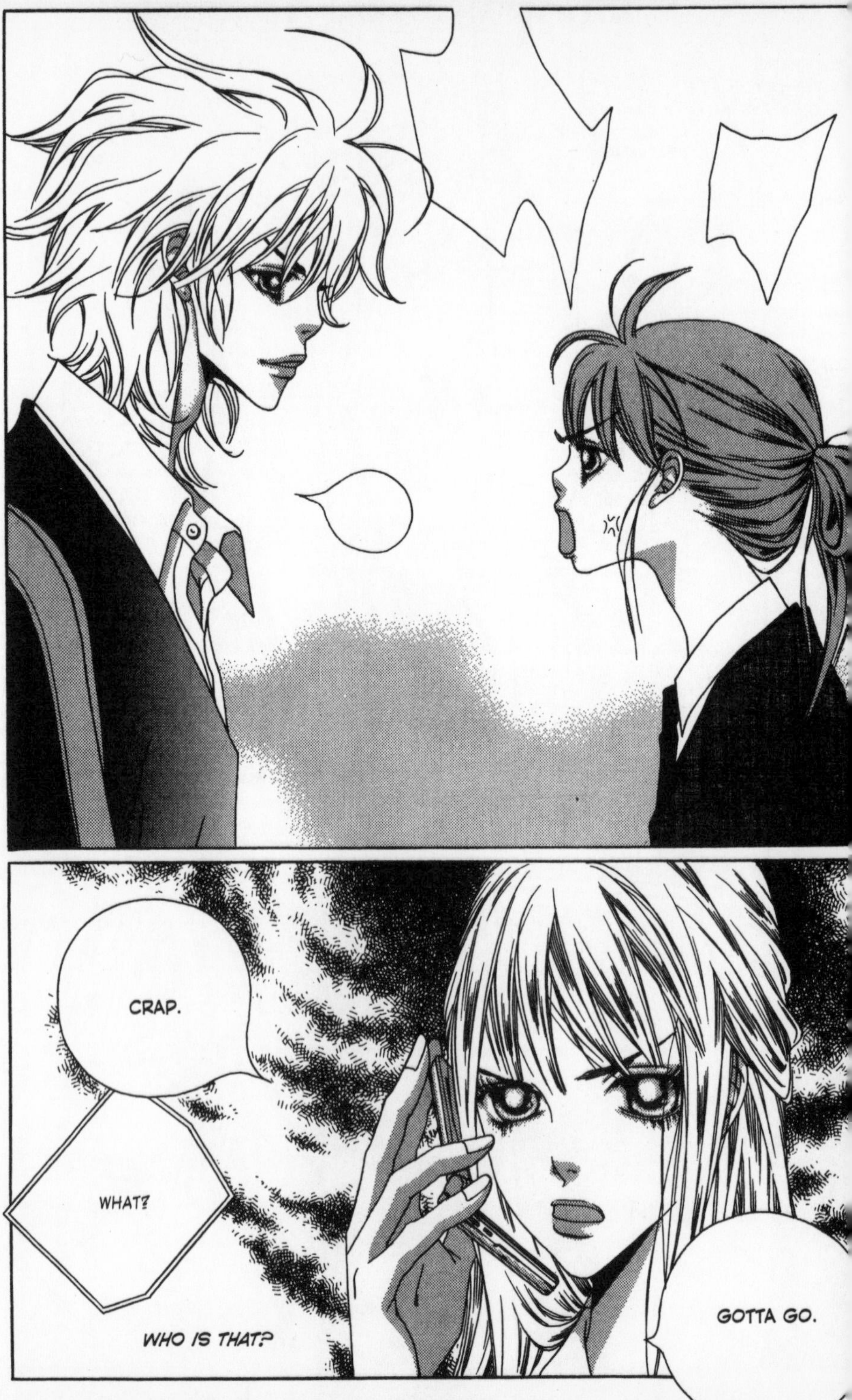
CRAP.
WHAT?
WHO IS THAT?
GOTTA GO.

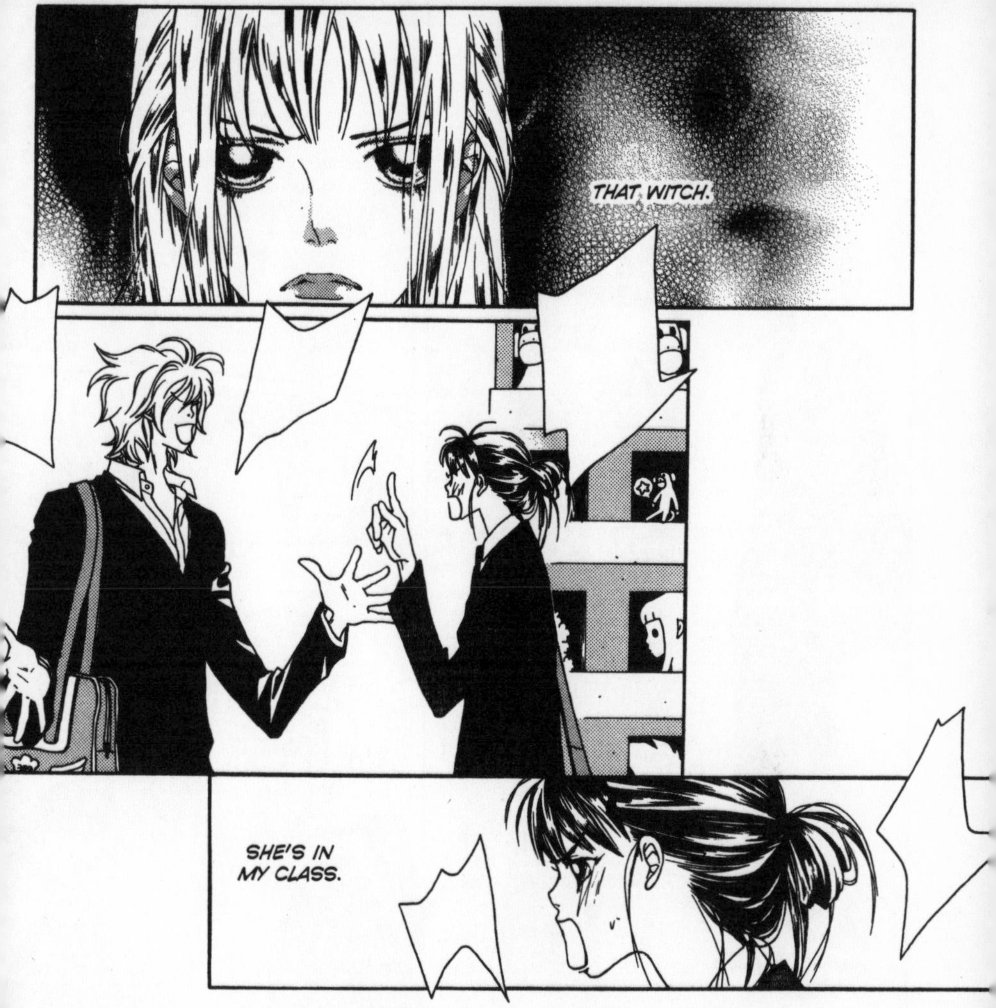
THAT WITCH.
SHE'S IN MY CLASS.

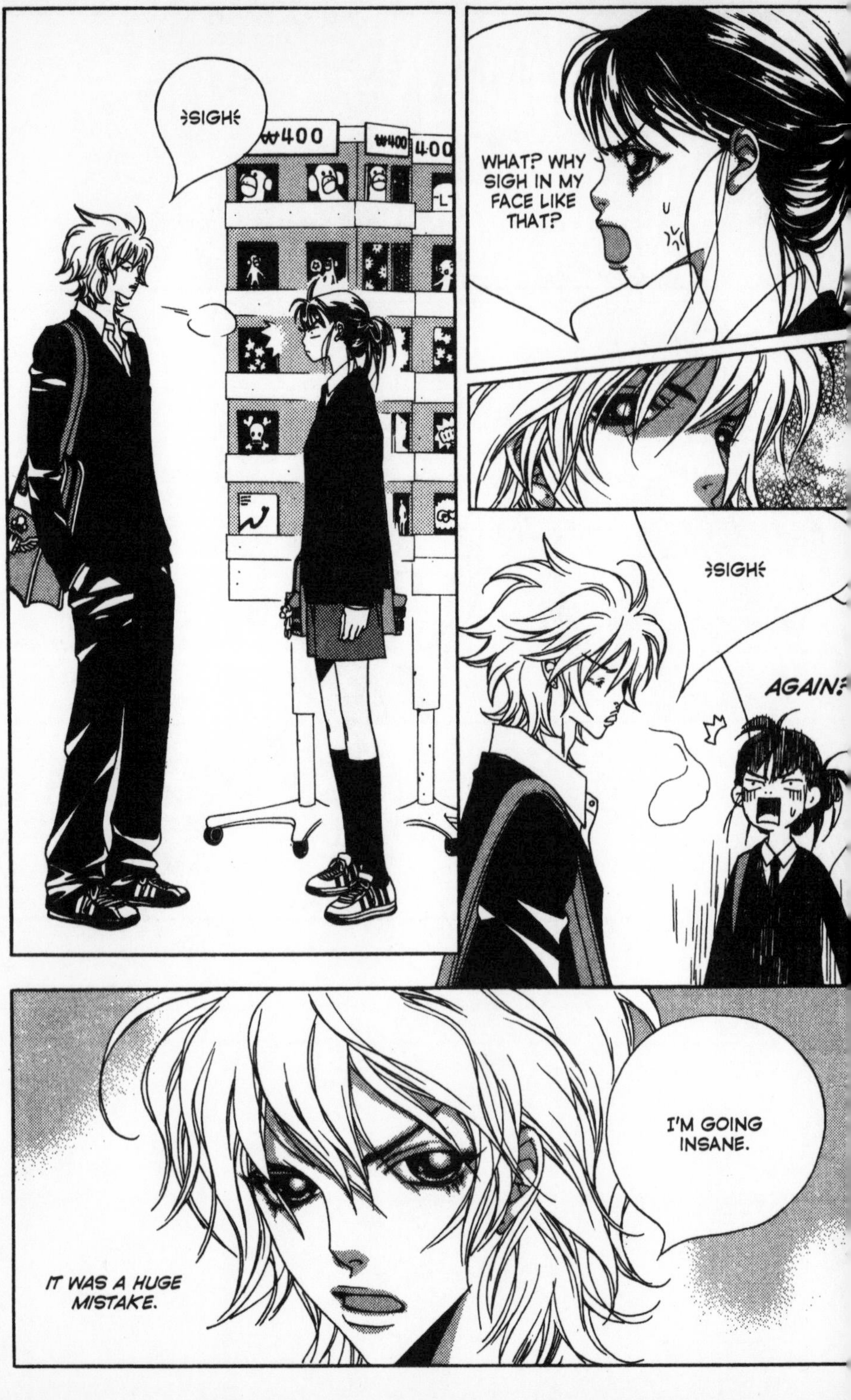

SIGH
₩400
₩400
400
WHAT? WHY SIGH IN MY FACE LIKE THAT?
SIGH
AGAIN!?
I'M GOING INSANE.
IT WAS A HUGE MISTAKE.

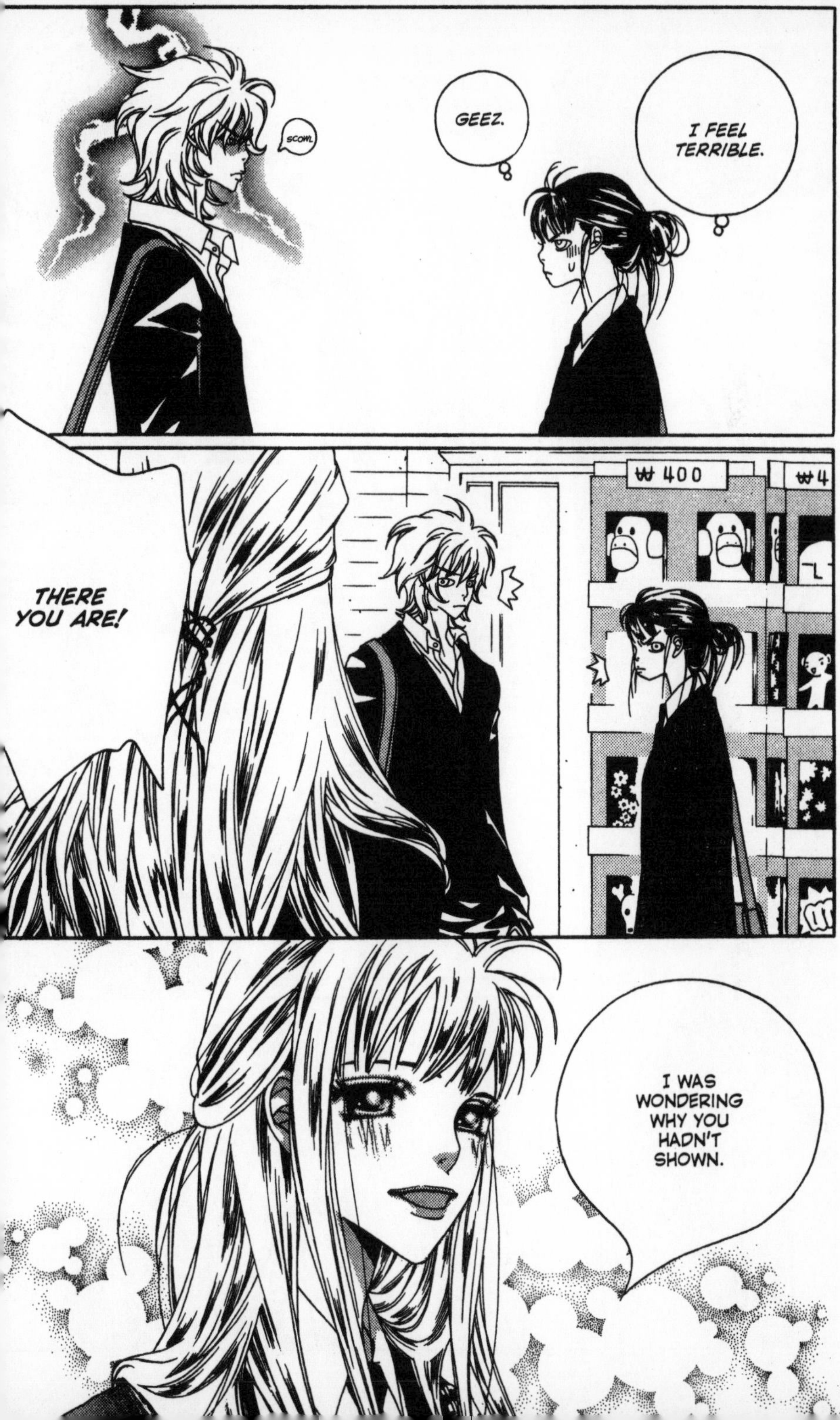
SCOWL
GEEZ.
I FEEL TERRIBLE.
₩400
THERE YOU ARE!
I WAS WONDERING WHY YOU HADN'T SHOWN.

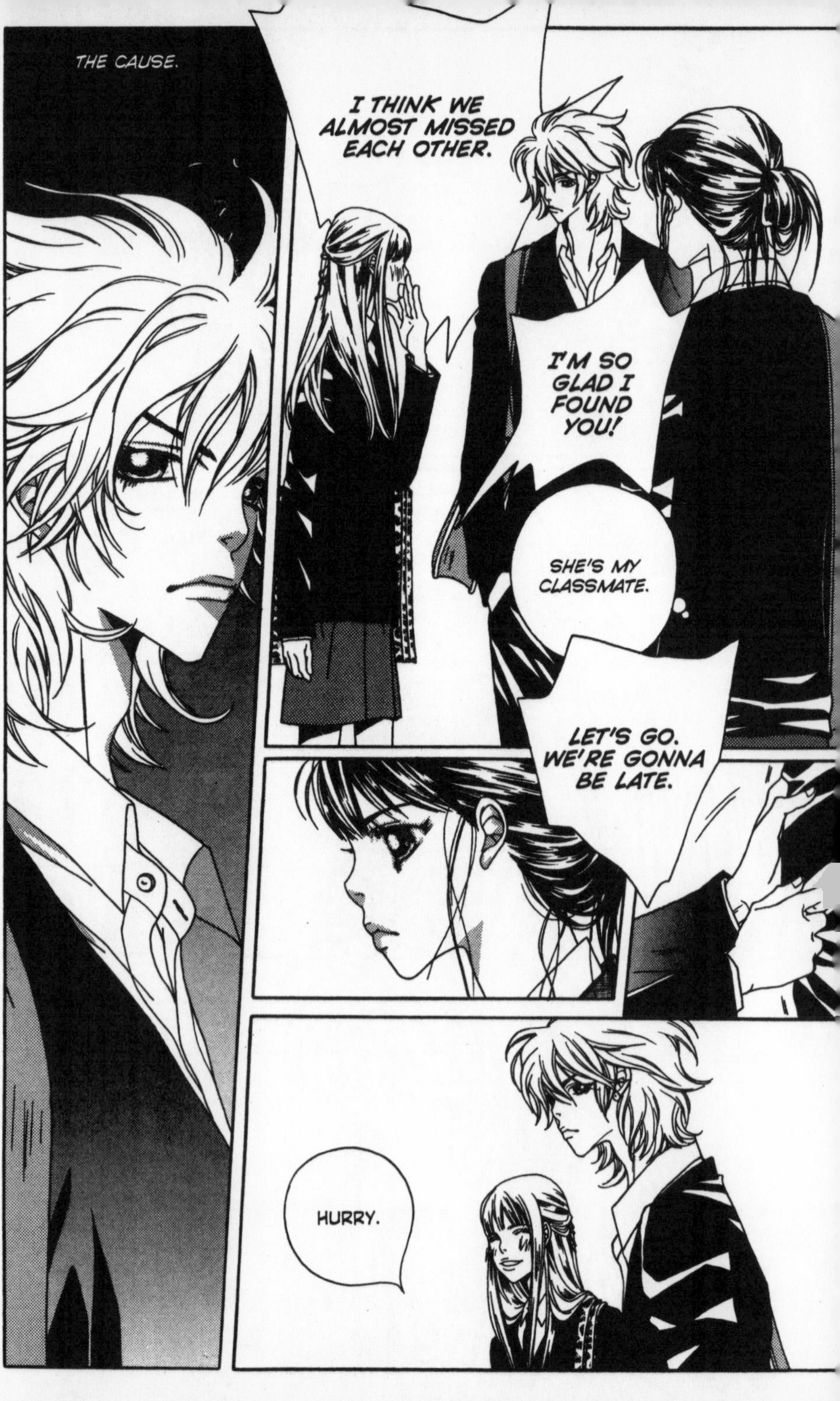
THE CAUSE.
I THINK WE ALMOST MISSED EACH OTHER.
I'M SO GLAD I FOUND YOU!
SHE'S MY CLASSMATE.
LET'S GO. WE'RE GONNA BE LATE.
HURRY.

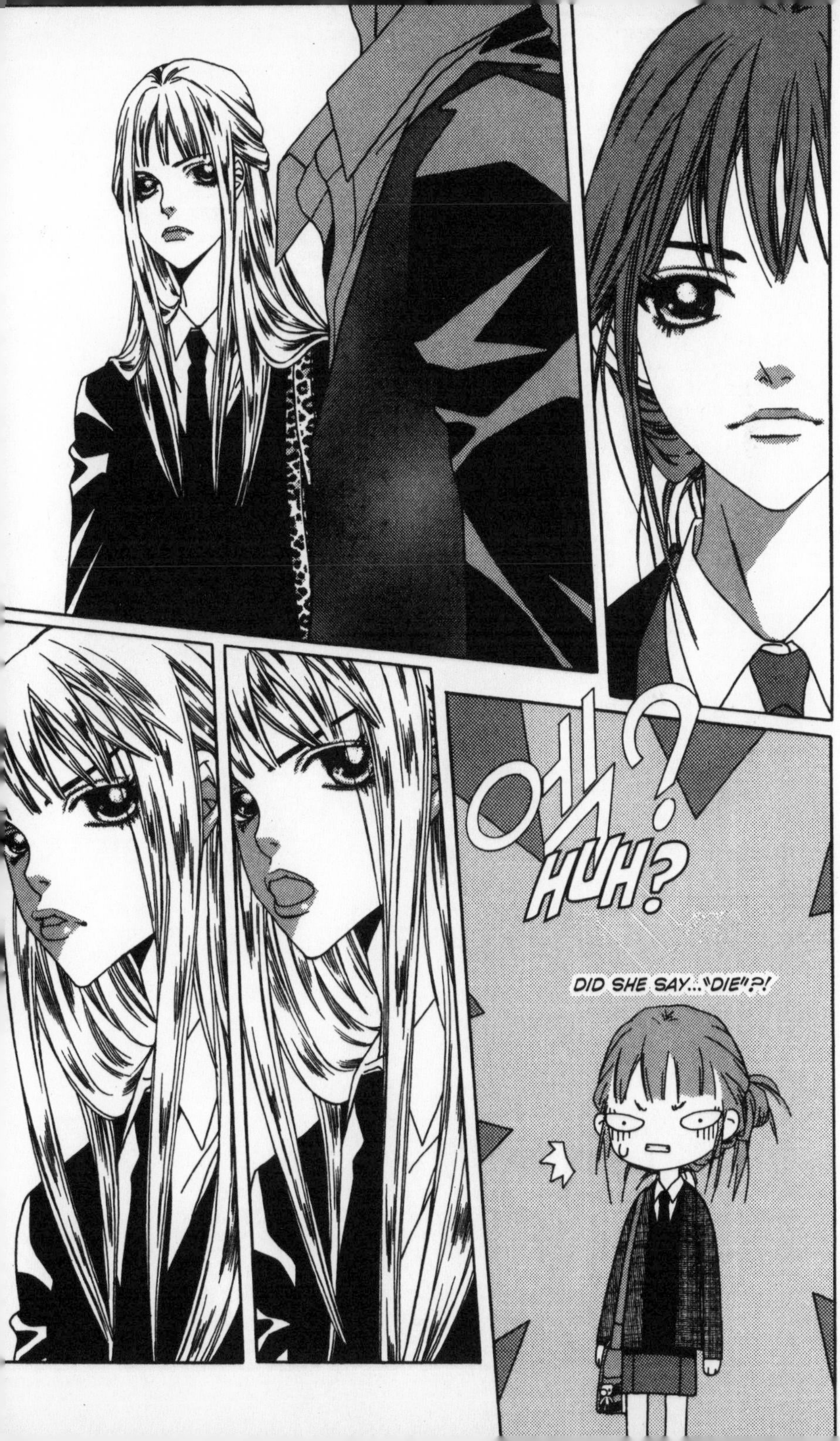
HUH?
DID SHE SAY..."DIE"?!

I WAS HALF AN HOUR EARLY.

WHY?

ANXIOUS TO SEE YOU.

GEEZ.

DON'T LET THAT DREAM GET TO YOU, DA-EH.

HE'S STILL THE SAME JERK.

NOTHING ELSE.

SMILE

YOU BOUGHT ALL THESE?

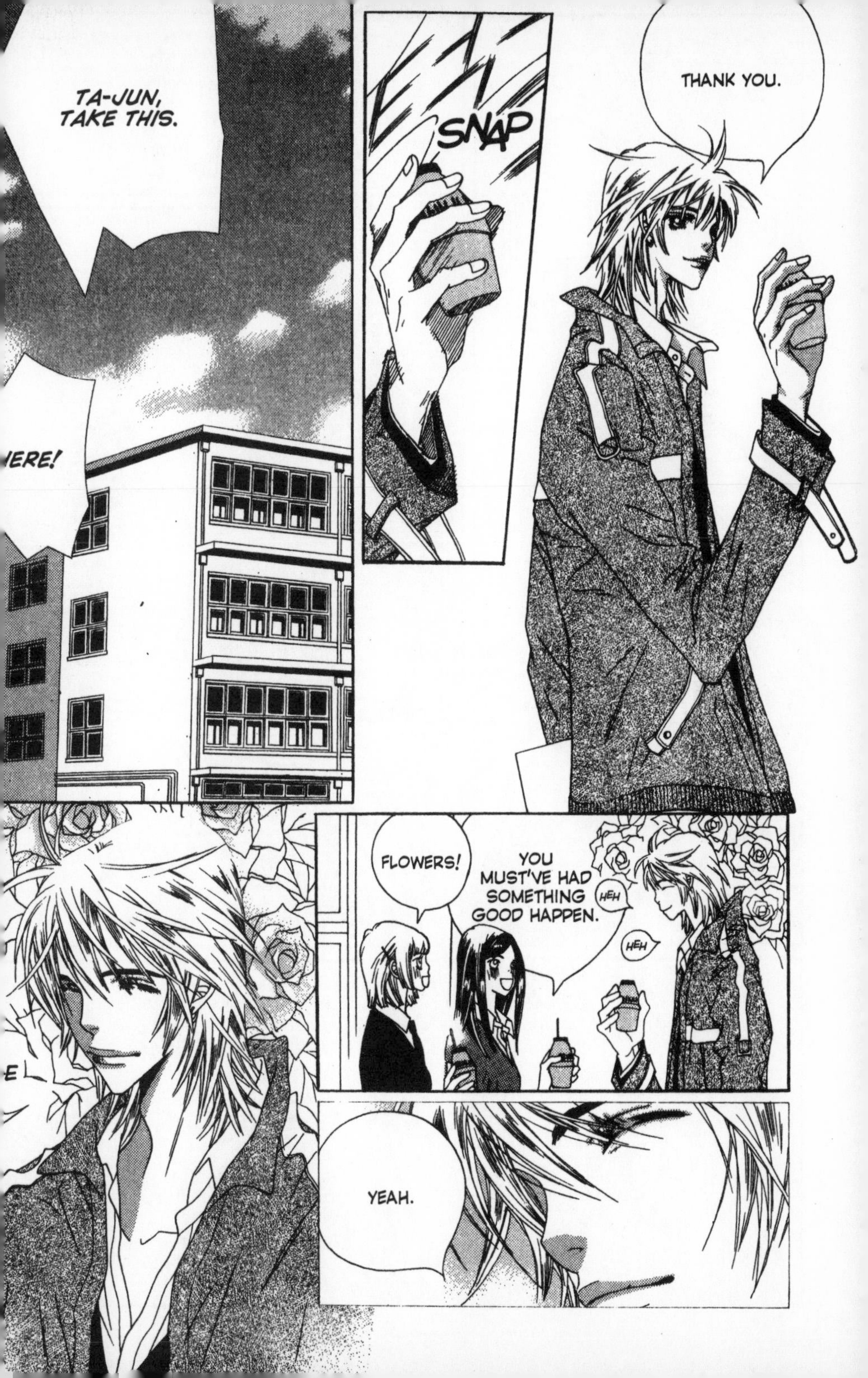
TA-JUN, TAKE THIS.
ERE!
SNAP
THANK YOU.
E
FLOWERS!
YOU MUST'VE HAD SOMETHING GOOD HAPPEN.
HEH
HEH
YEAH.

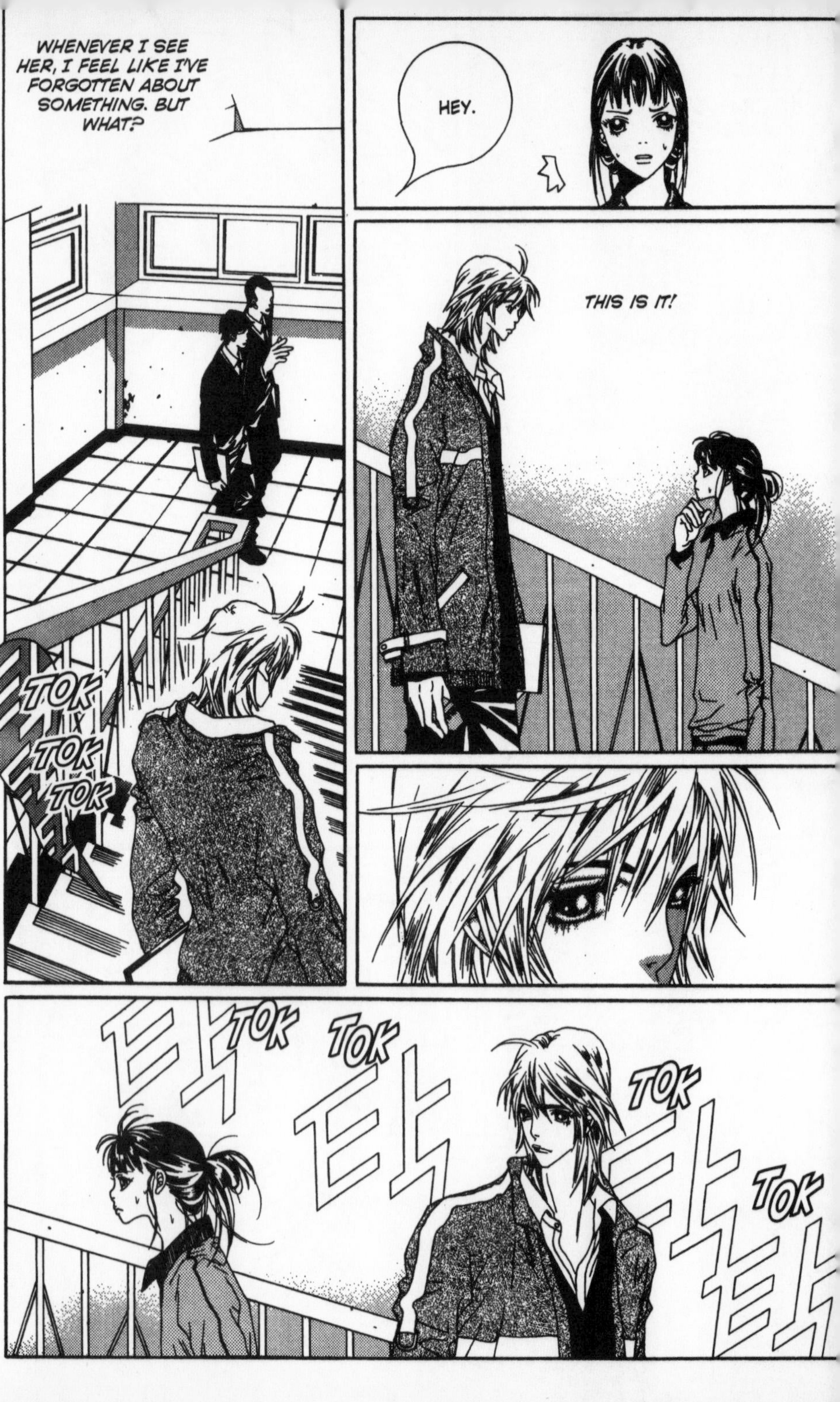
WHENEVER I SEE HER, I FEEL LIKE I'VE FORGOTTEN ABOUT SOMETHING. BUT WHAT?
TOK
TOK
TOK
HEY.
THIS IS IT!
TOK
TOK
TOK
TOK

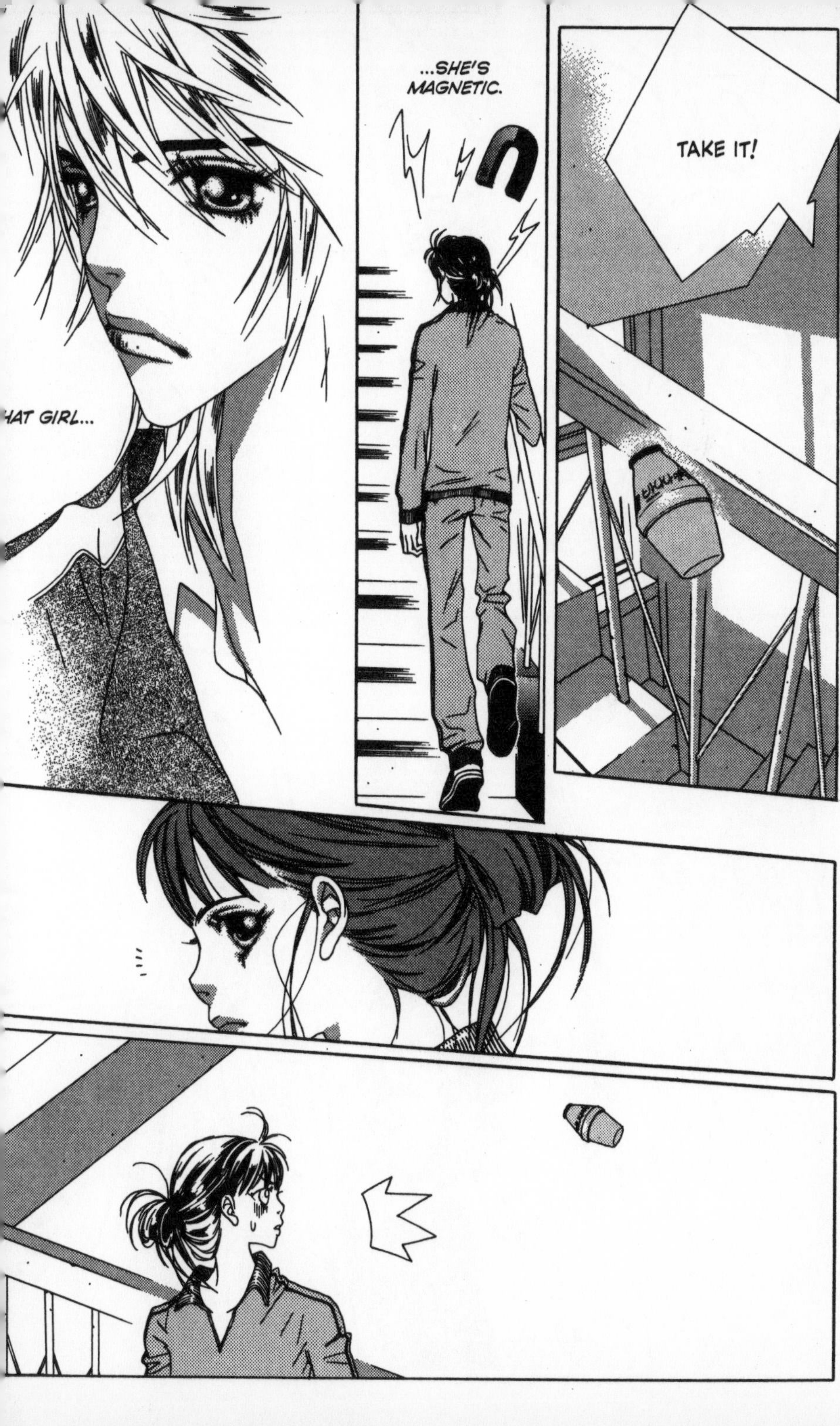
HAT GIRL...
...SHE'S MAGNETIC.
TAKE IT!

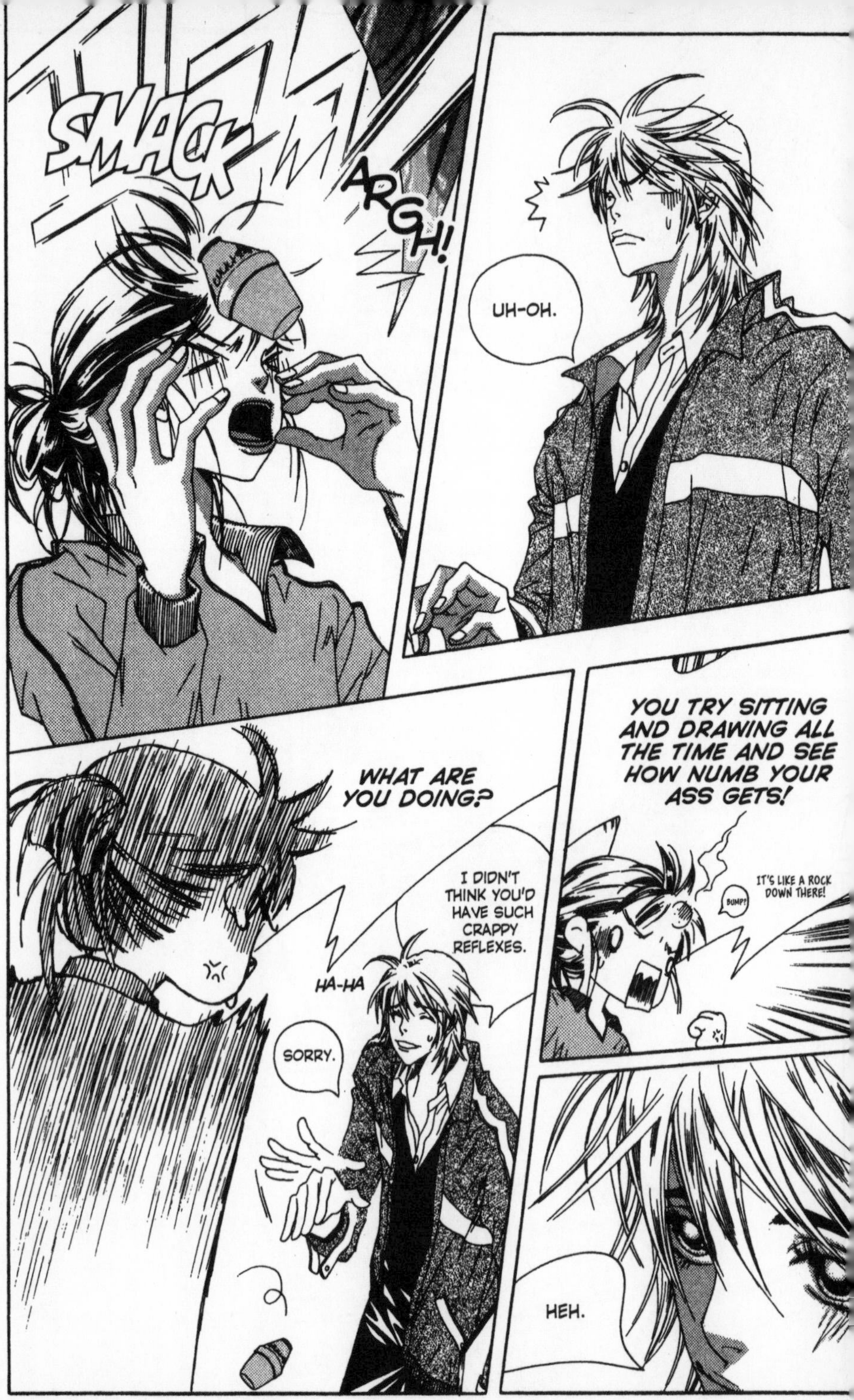
SMACK
ARGH!
UH-OH.
WHAT ARE YOU DOING?
I DIDN'T THINK YOU'D HAVE SUCH CRAPPY REFLEXES.
HA-HA
SORRY.
YOU TRY SITTING AND DRAWING ALL THE TIME AND SEE HOW NUMB YOUR ASS GETS!
BUMP?
IT'S LIKE A ROCK DOWN THERE!
HEH.

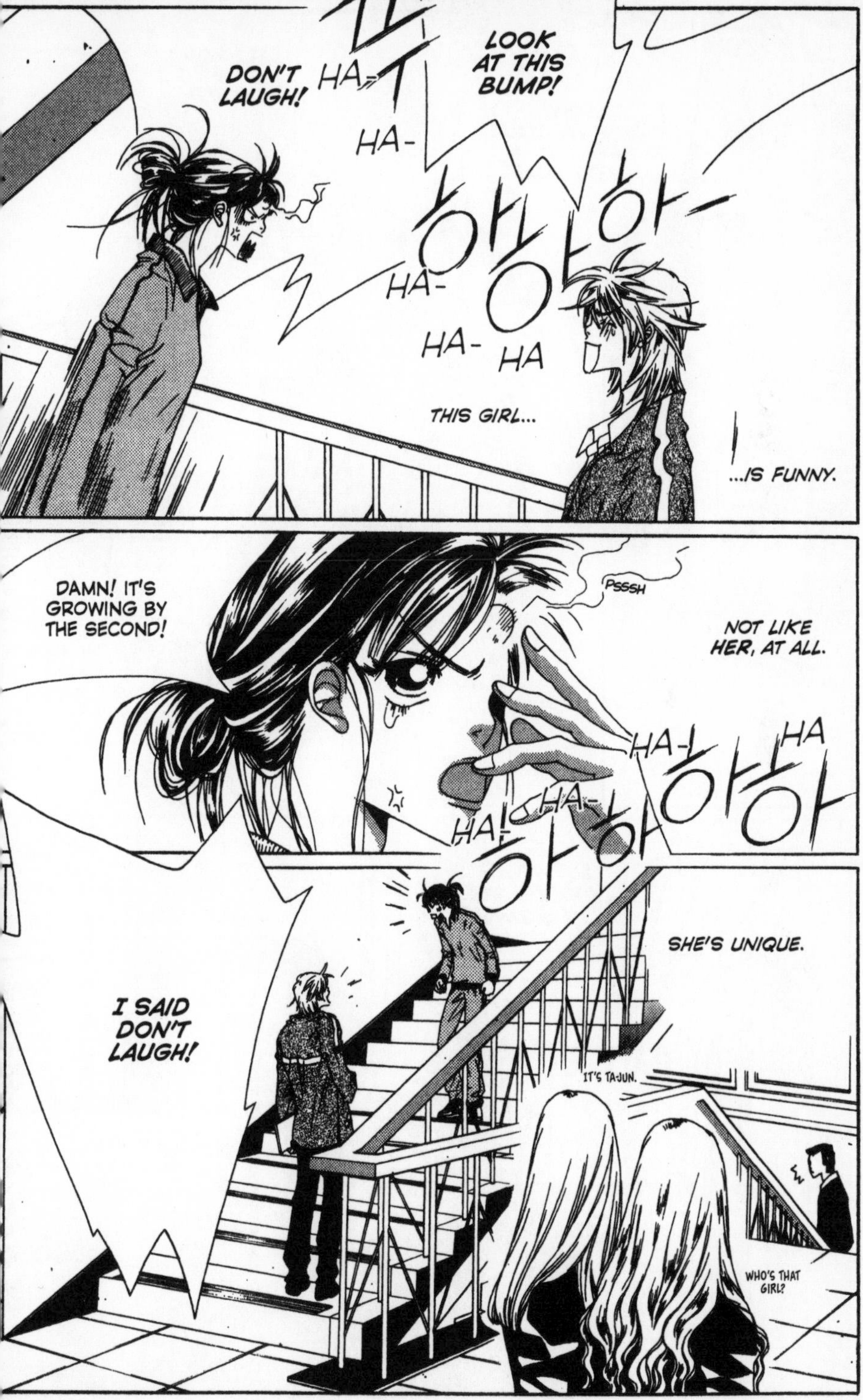
DON'T LAUGH!
HA- HA- HA- HA- HA
LOOK AT THIS BUMP!
THIS GIRL...
...IS FUNNY.
DAMN! IT'S GROWING BY THE SECOND!
PSSSH
NOT LIKE HER, AT ALL.
HA- HA HA-HA!
I SAID DON'T LAUGH!
SHE'S UNIQUE.
IT'S TA-JUN.
WHO'S THAT GIRL?

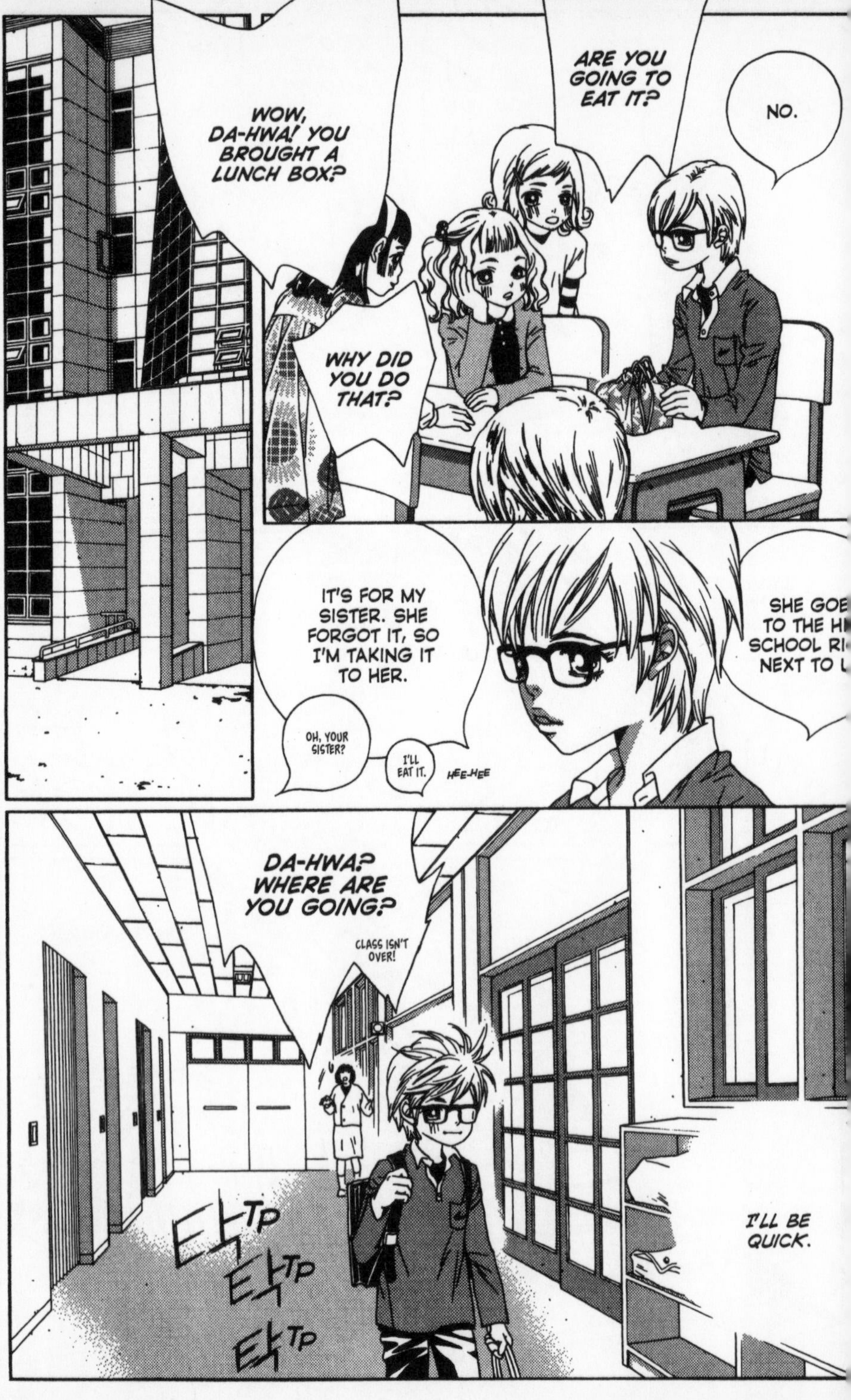
WOW, DA-HWA! YOU BROUGHT A LUNCH BOX?
ARE YOU GOING TO EAT IT?
NO.
WHY DID YOU DO THAT?
IT'S FOR MY SISTER. SHE FORGOT IT, SO I'M TAKING IT TO HER.
OH, YOUR SISTER?
I'LL EAT IT.
HEE-HEE
SHE GOE
TO THE H
SCHOOL RI
NEXT TO U
DA-HWA? WHERE ARE YOU GOING?
CLASS ISN'T OVER!
탁 TP
탁 TP
탁 TP
I'LL BE QUICK.

탁TP
탁TP
탁TP
HEH-HEH.
HEY, KID...?
탁TP
TP
탁

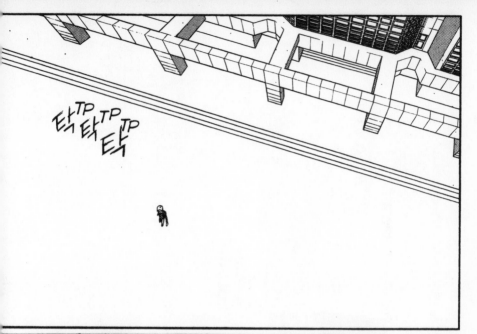

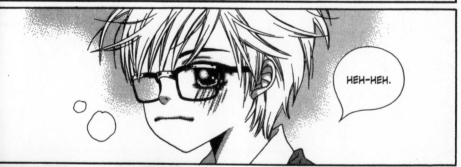

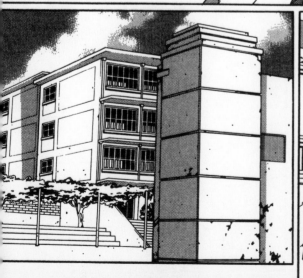

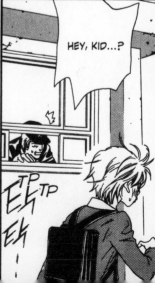

HEY, LOOK AT THE SQUIRT.

GOOD

WHERE'S HER CLASS?

IT'S TOO BIG.

UM YEA

ARE YOU LOST, KID? YOU WANT BIG BROTHER TO HELP?

CUTE KID

NO!

NO, THANK YOU!

ZOOM

HUH?

THEY THINK I'M LYING.

I TOLD THEM W WERE GOING TOGETHER...

...BUT THEY STILL DON'T BELIEVE ME...HA-HA...... THEN...... ......

HA-HA.

SHE'S SO NOISY.

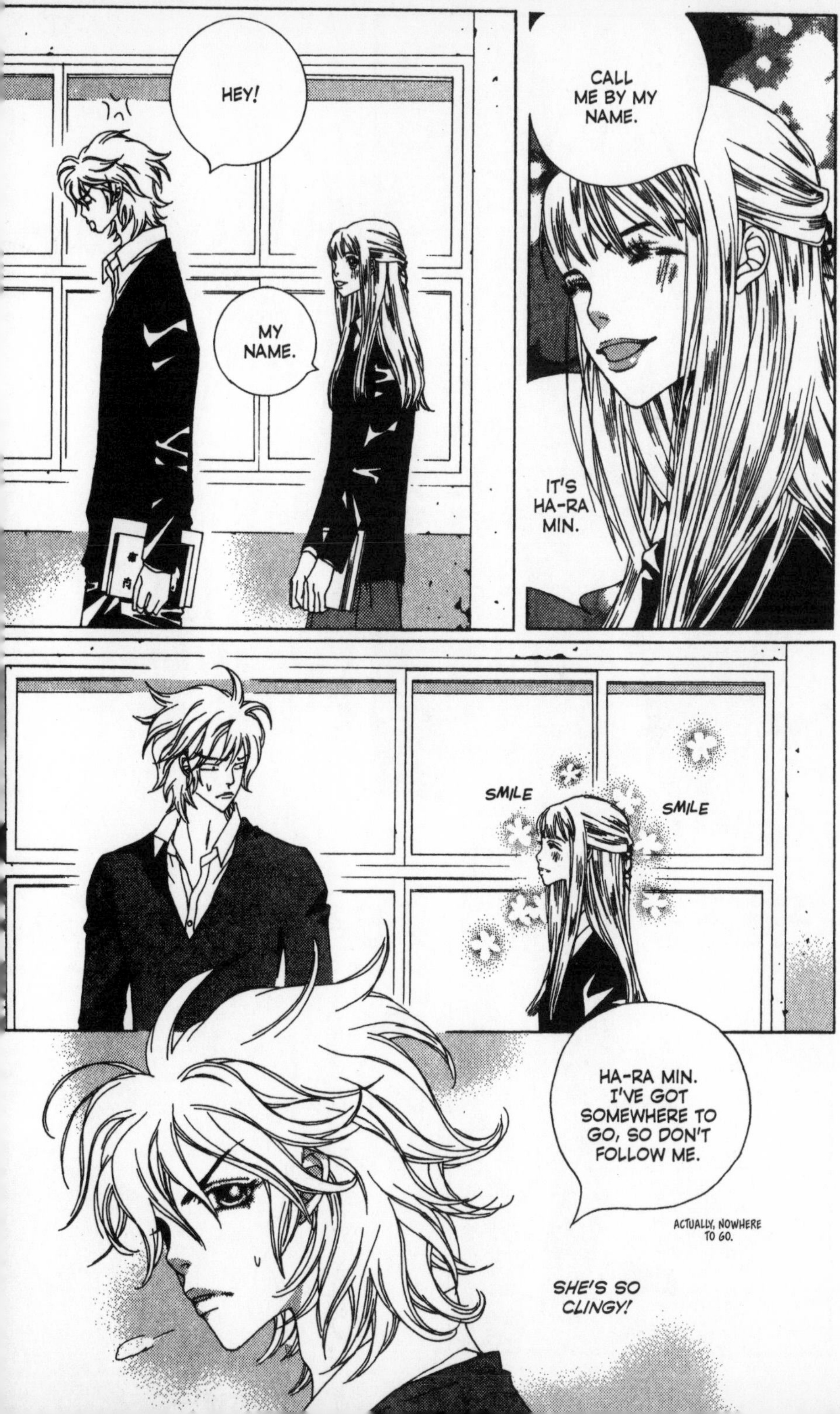
HEY!
MY NAME.
CALL ME BY MY NAME.
IT'S HA-RA MIN.
SMILE
SMILE
HA-RA MIN. I'VE GOT SOMEWHERE TO GO, SO DON'T FOLLOW ME.
ACTUALLY, NOWHERE TO GO.
SHE'S SO CLINGY!

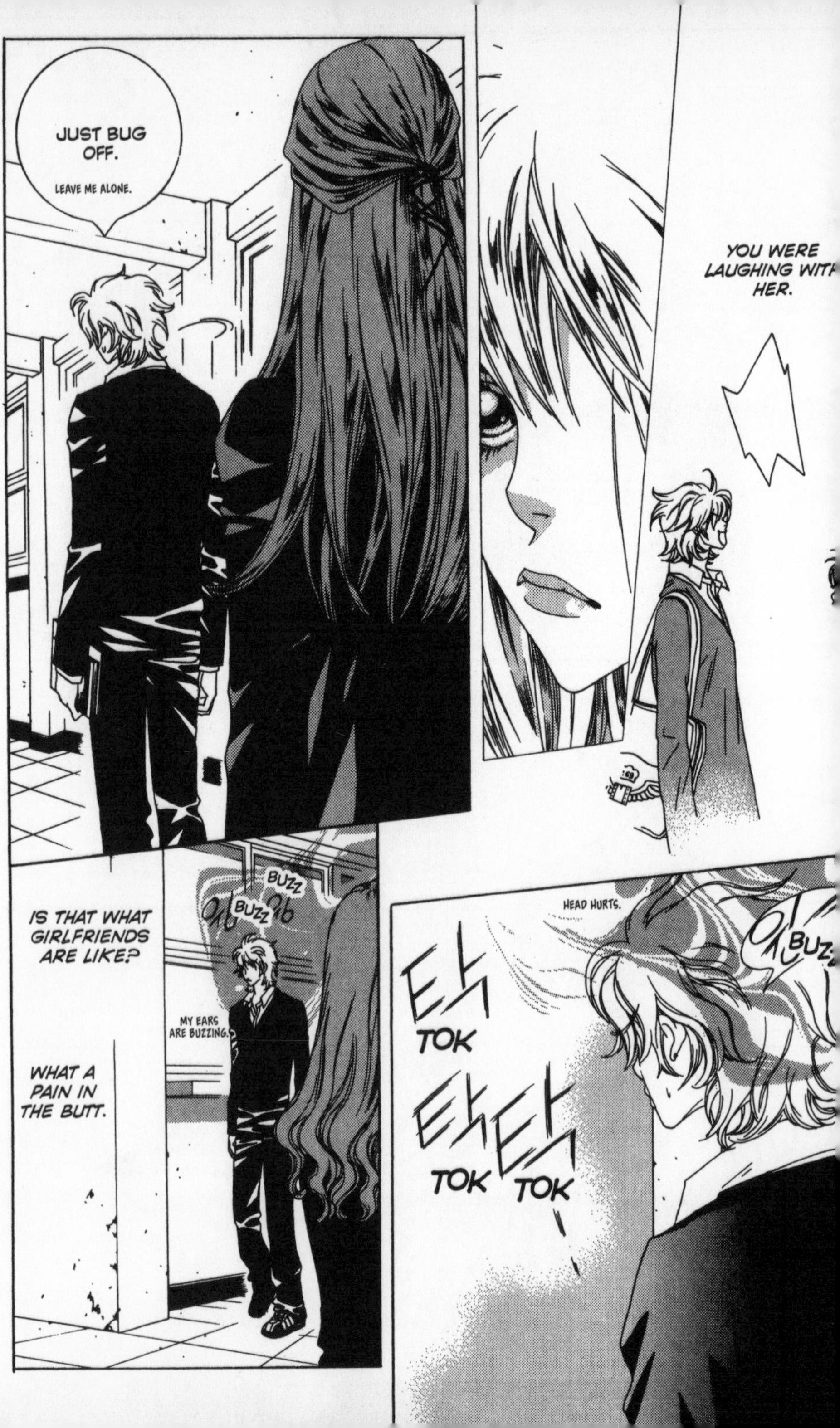
JUST BUG OFF.
LEAVE ME ALONE.
YOU WERE LAUGHING WITH HER.
IS THAT WHAT GIRLFRIENDS ARE LIKE?
BUZZ
BUZZ
MY EARS ARE BUZZING.
WHAT A PAIN IN THE BUTT.
HEAD HURTS.
BUZZ
TOK
TOK
TOK

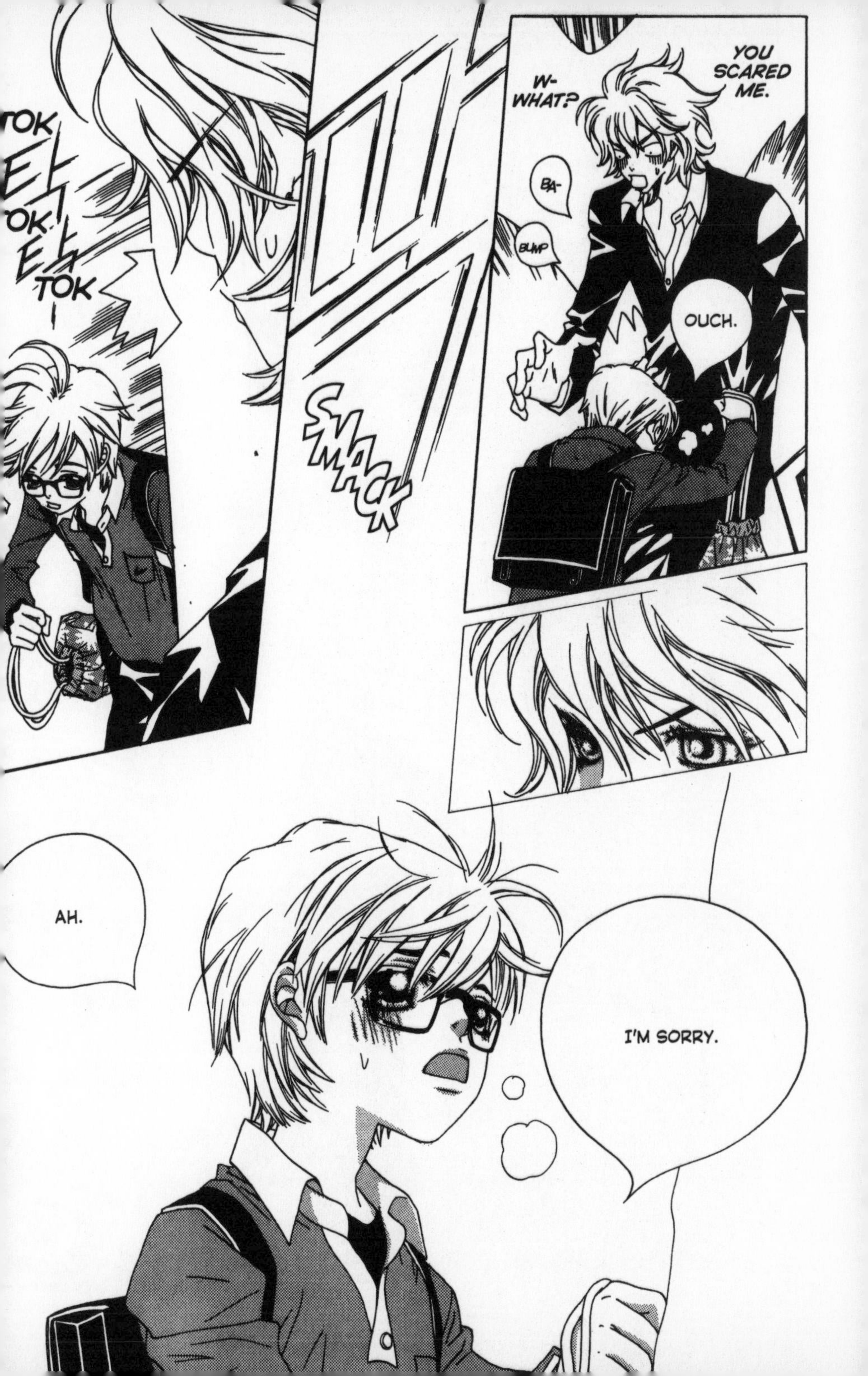
TOK
TOK
TOK
SMACK
W-WHAT?
YOU SCARED ME.
BA-
BUMP
OUCH.
AH.
I'M SORRY.

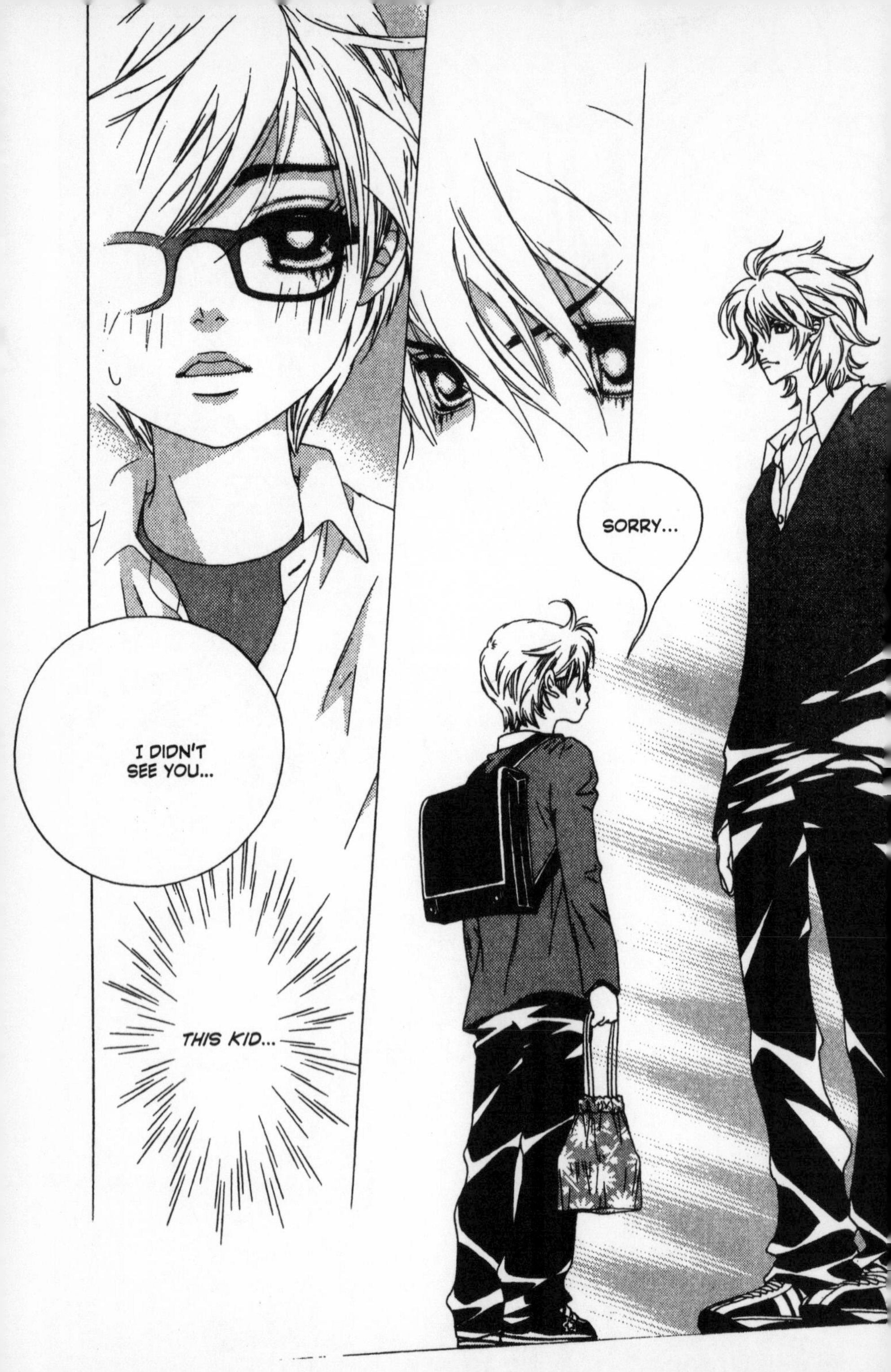
I DIDN'T SEE YOU...
THIS KID...
SORRY...

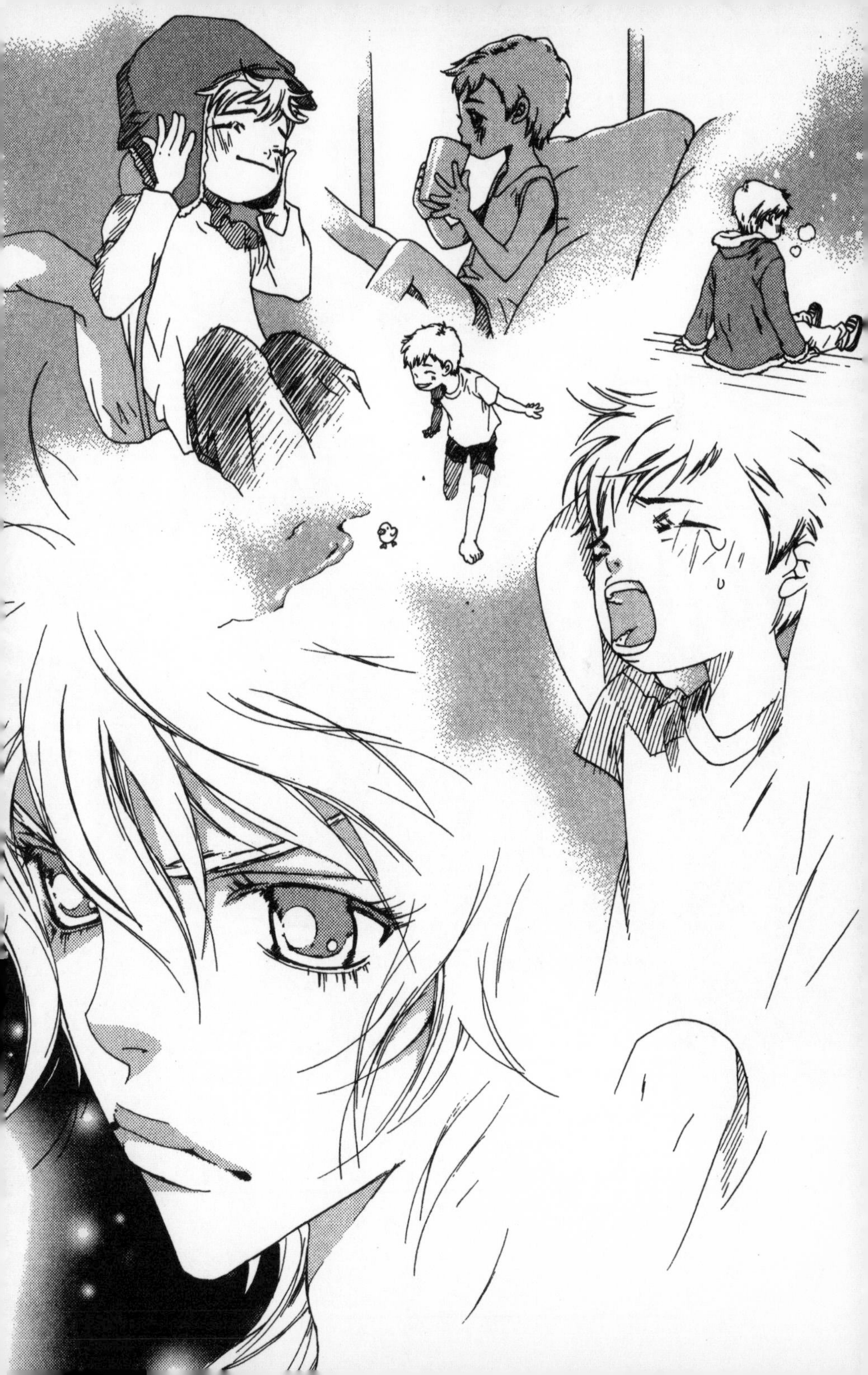

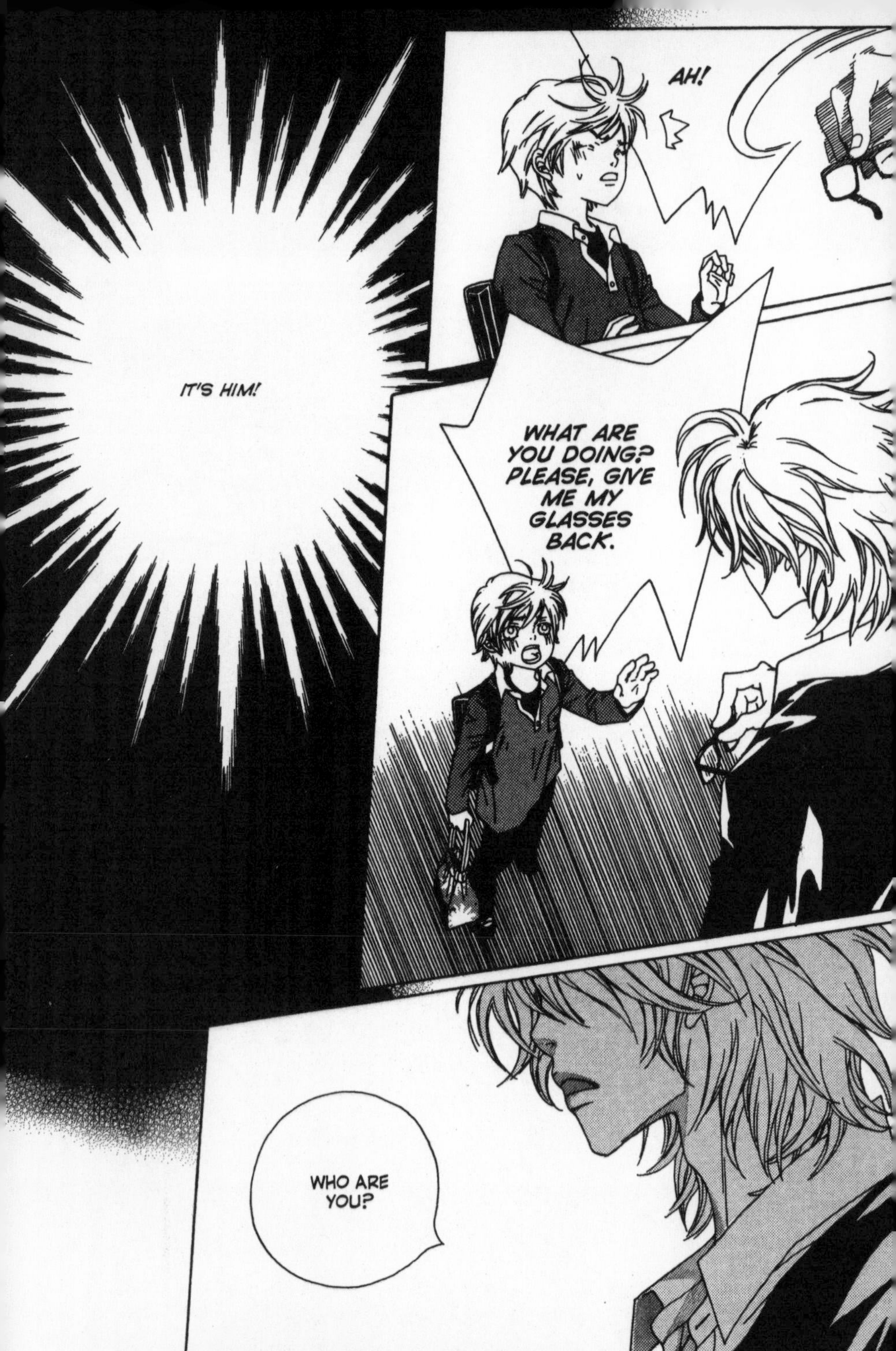
IT'S HIM!
AH!
WHAT ARE YOU DOING? PLEASE, GIVE ME MY GLASSES BACK.
WHO ARE YOU?

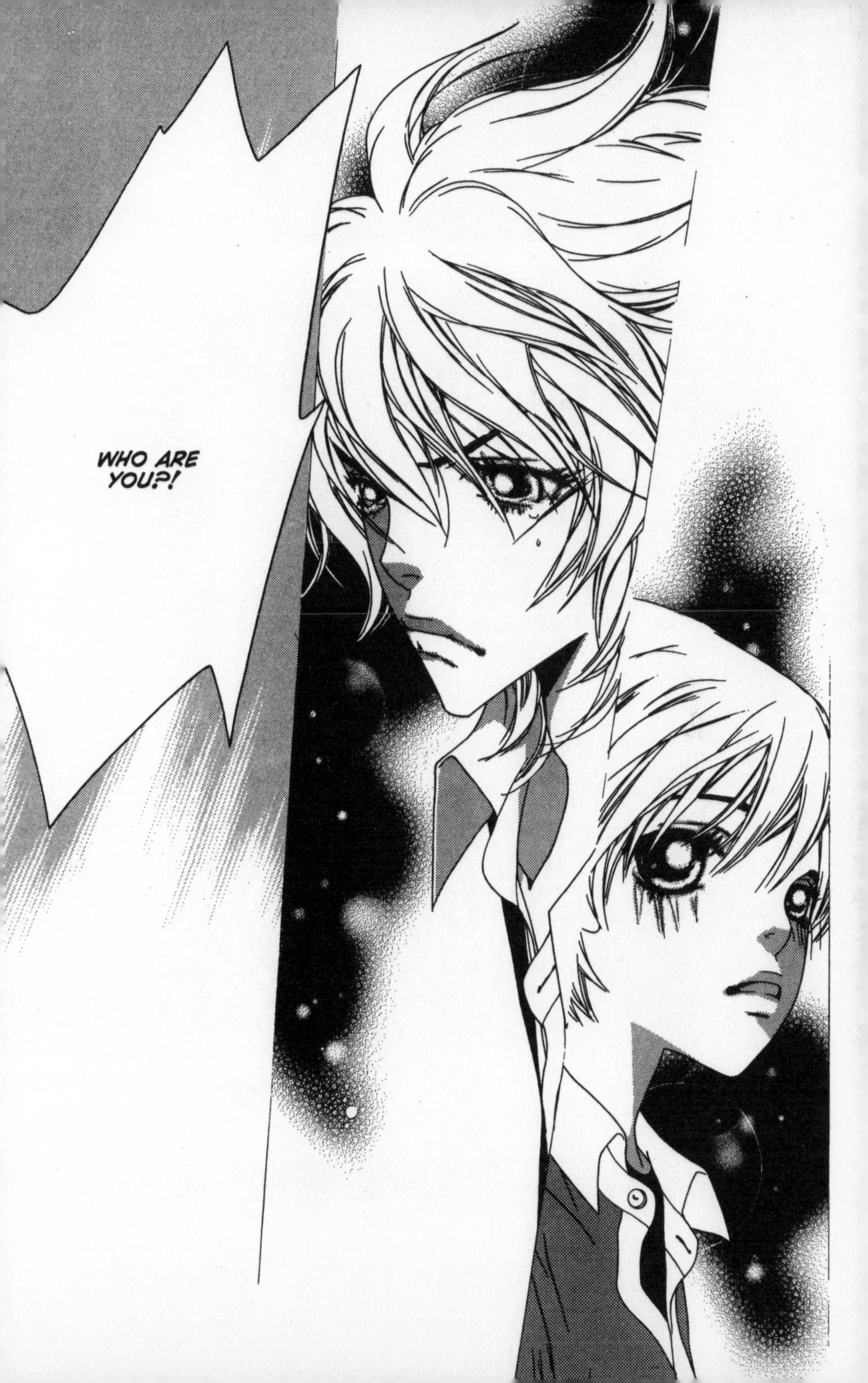
WHO ARE
YOU?!

I'M SURE...

I REMEMBER
THOSE EYES.

BUT...

..I DON'T
KNOW THESE
TEARS.

..I RECOGNIZE
HIS EYES.

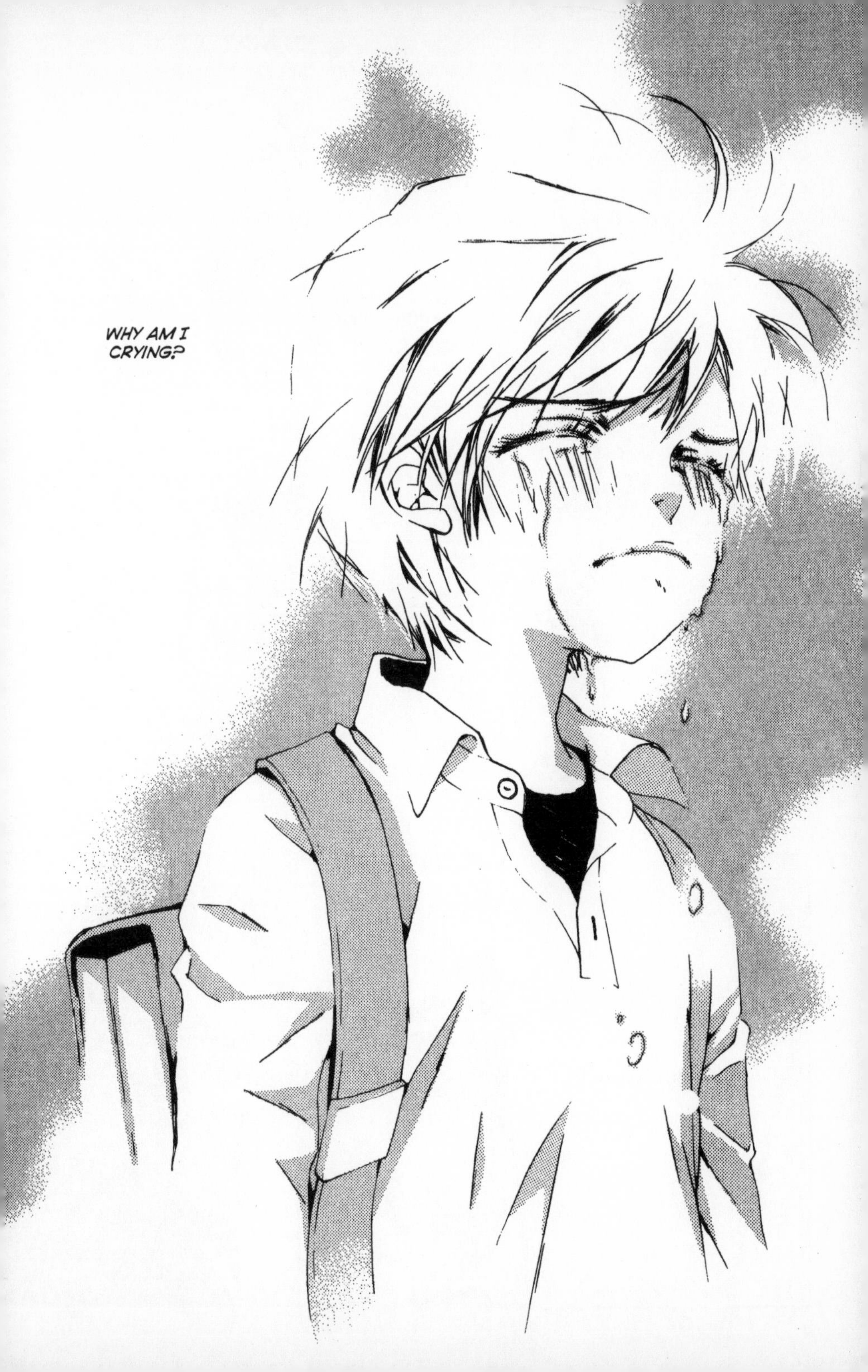
WHY AM I CRYING?

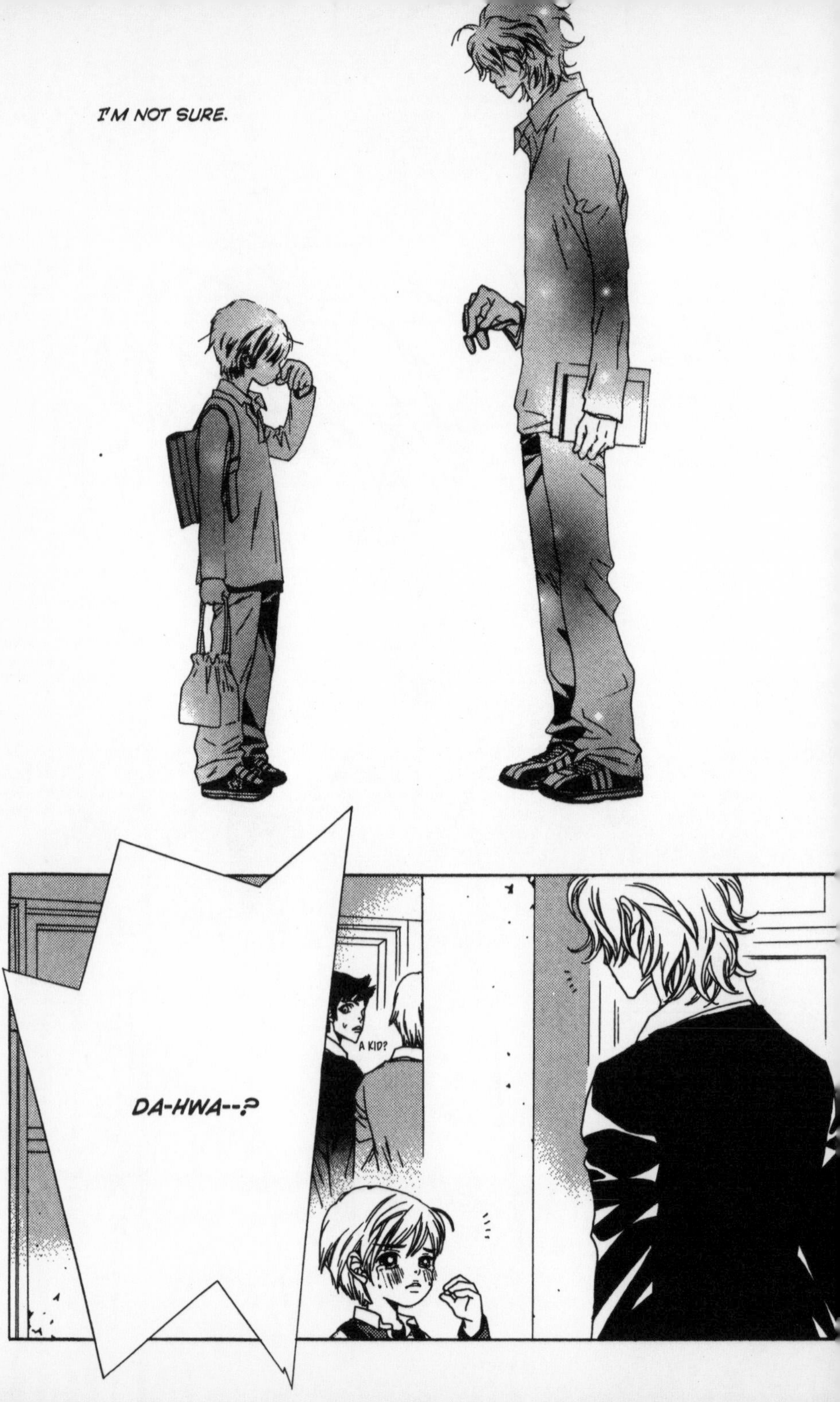
I'M NOT SURE.
DA-HWA--?
A KID?

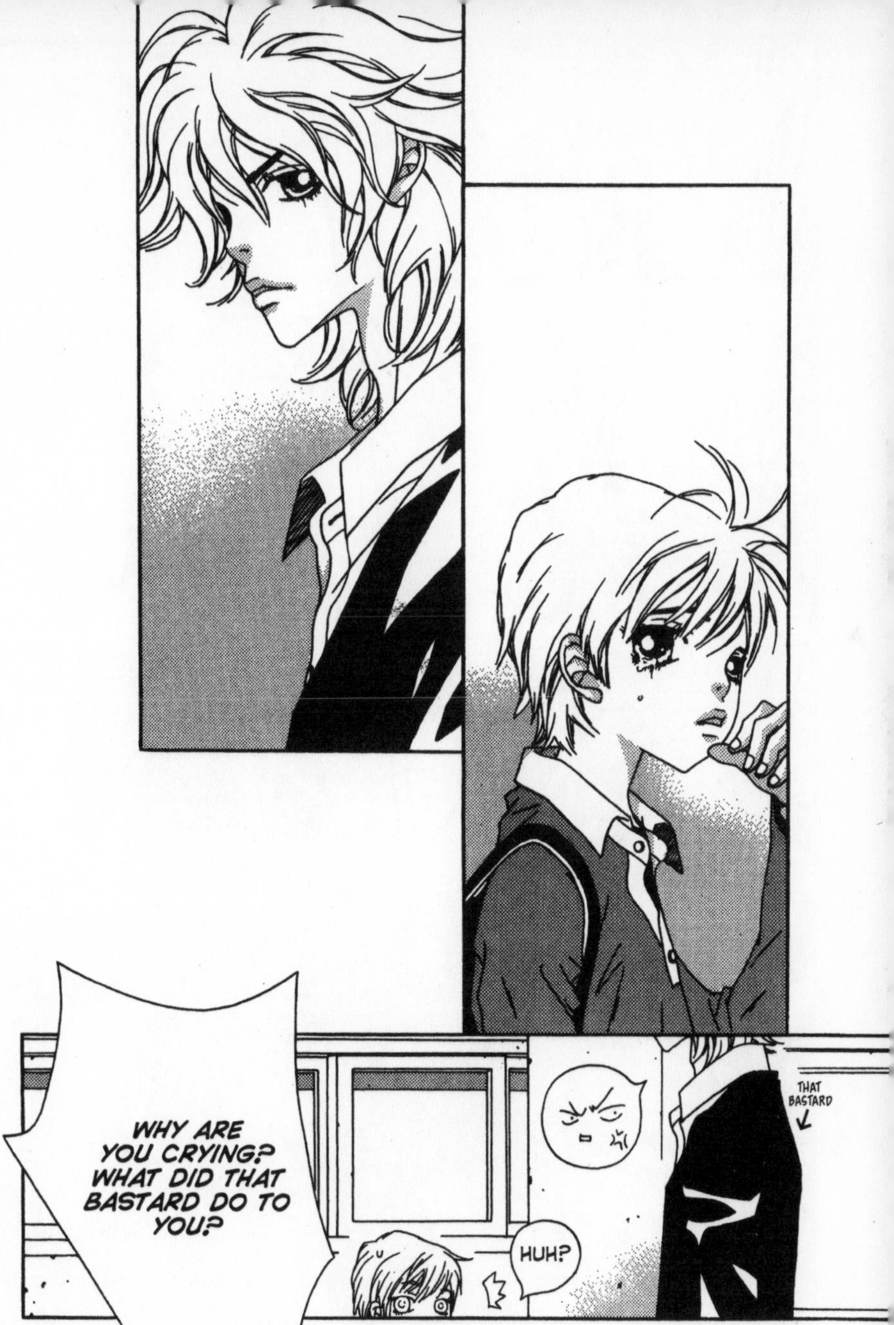
WHY ARE YOU CRYING? WHAT DID THAT BASTARD DO TO YOU?
HUH?
THAT BASTARD

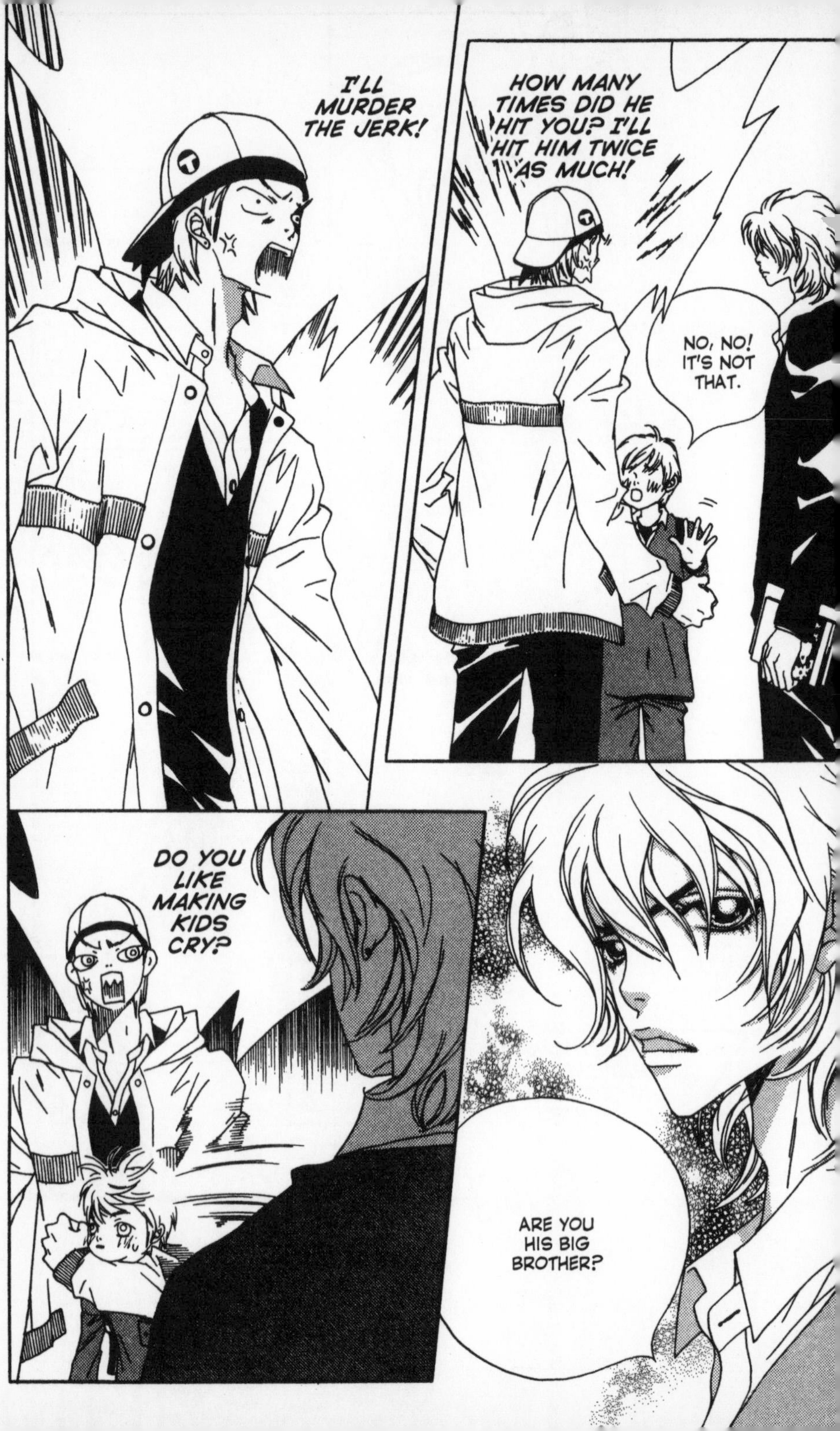
I'LL MURDER THE JERK!
HOW MANY TIMES DID HE HIT YOU? I'LL HIT HIM TWICE AS MUCH!
NO, NO! IT'S NOT THAT.
DO YOU LIKE MAKING KIDS CRY?
ARE YOU HIS BIG BROTHER?

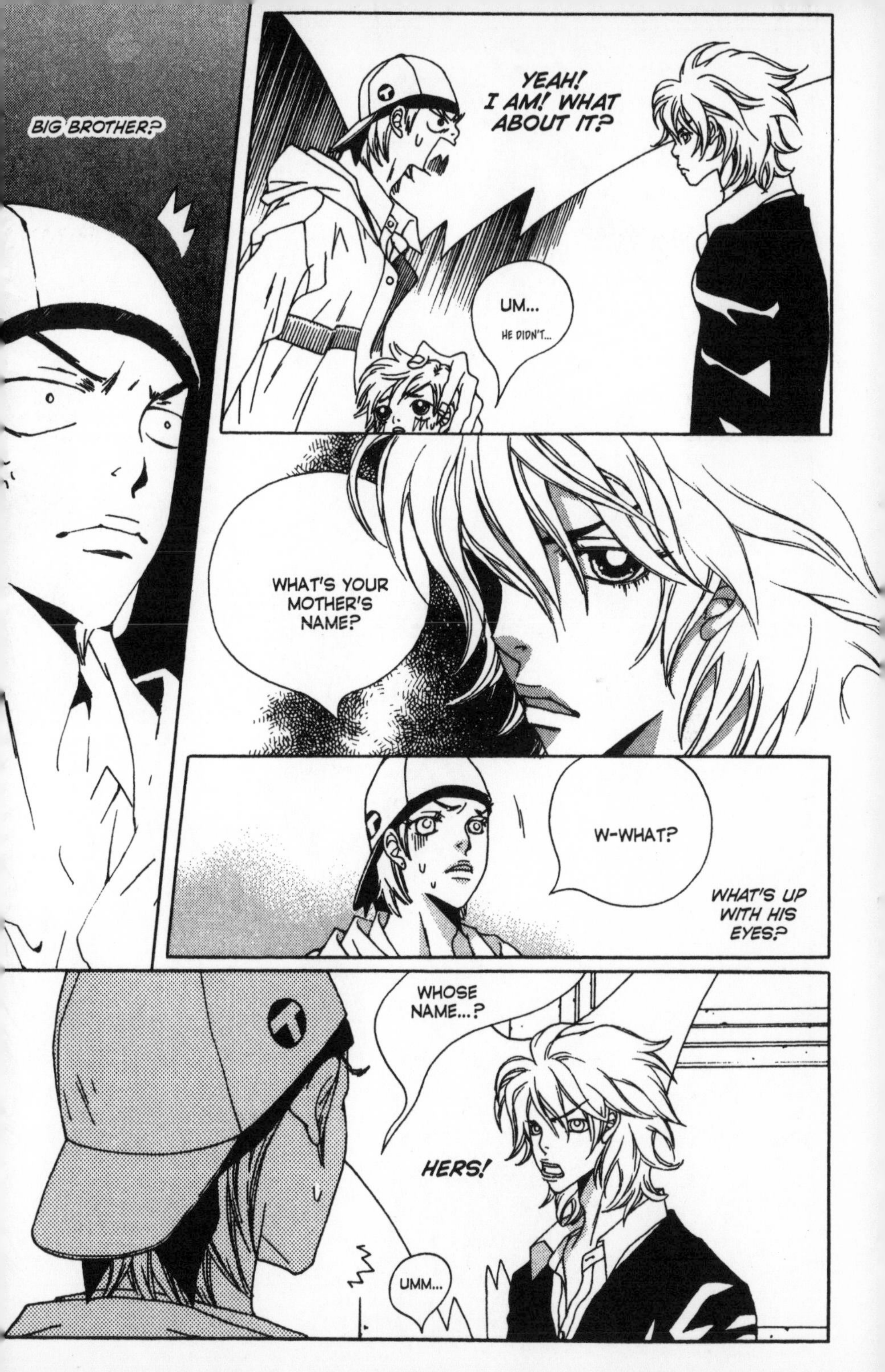
BIG BROTHER?
YEAH! I AM! WHAT ABOUT IT?
UM...
HE DIDN'T...
WHAT'S YOUR MOTHER'S NAME?
W-WHAT?
WHAT'S UP WITH HIS EYES?
WHOSE NAME...?
HERS!
UMM...

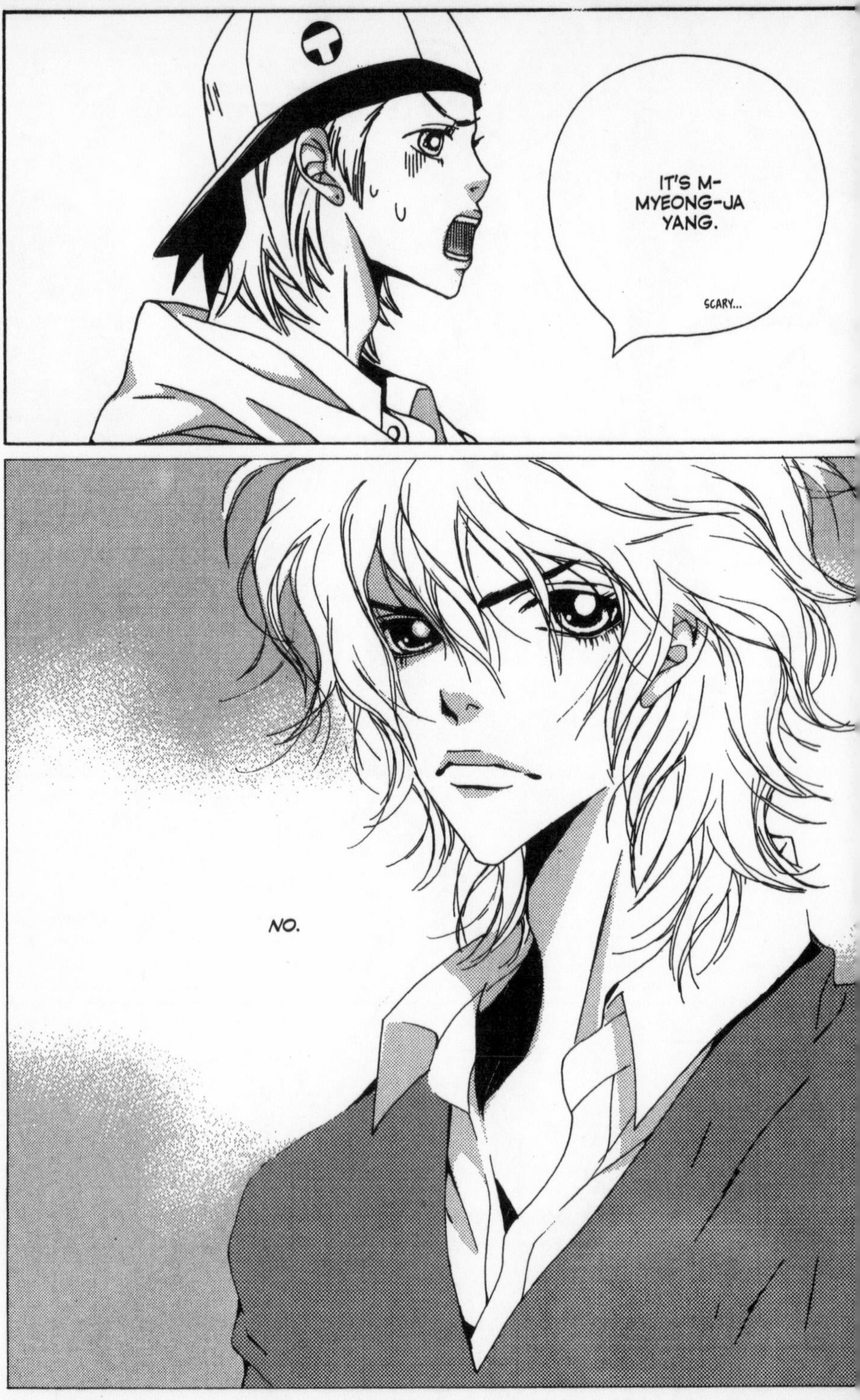
IT'S M-MYEONG-JA YANG.
SCARY...
NO.

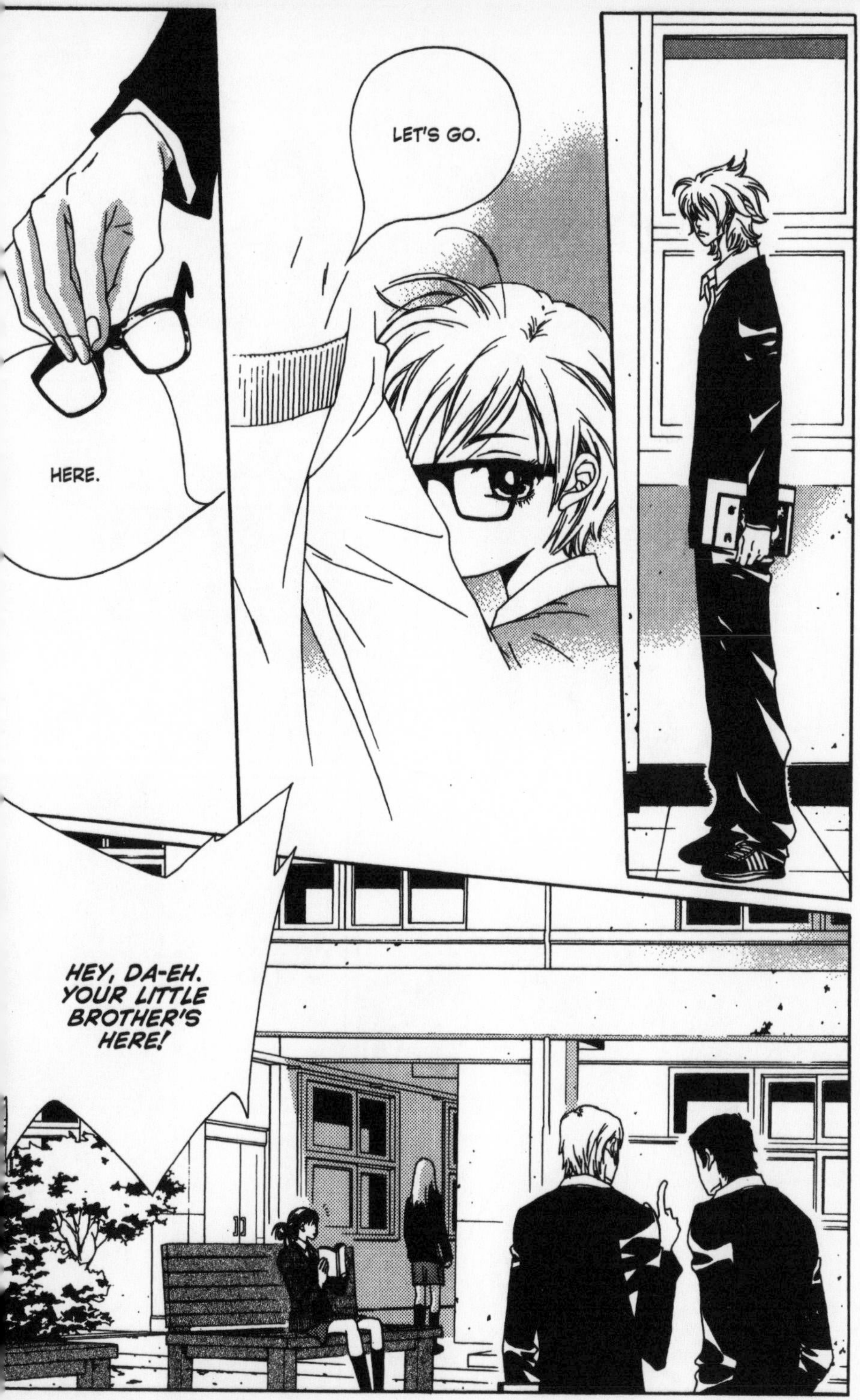
HERE.
LET'S GO.
HEY, DA-EH. YOUR LITTLE BROTHER'S HERE!

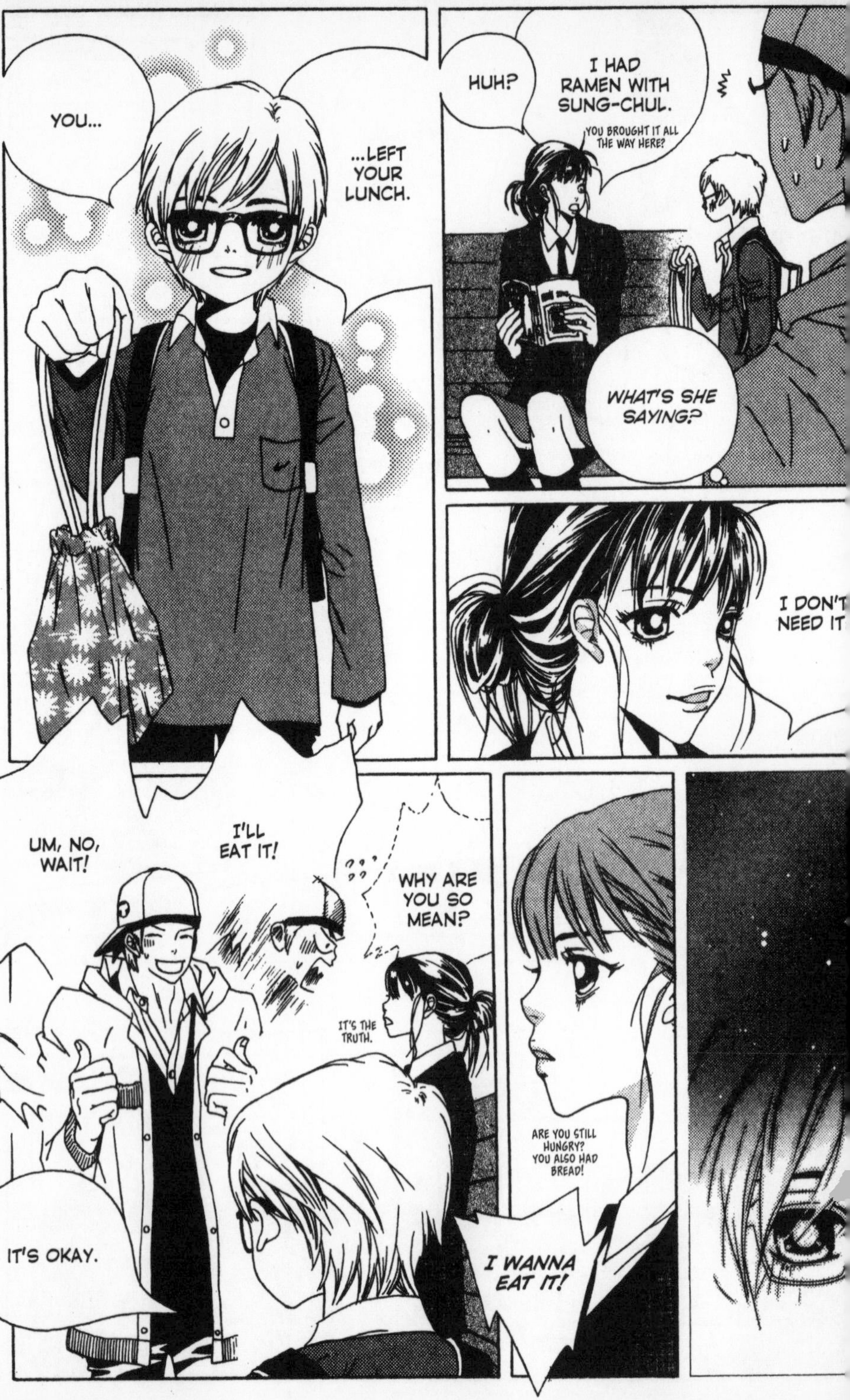

YOU...
...LEFT YOUR LUNCH.
HUH?
I HAD RAMEN WITH SUNG-CHUL.
YOU BROUGHT IT ALL THE WAY HERE?
WHAT'S SHE SAYING?
I DON'T NEED IT
UM, NO, WAIT!
I'LL EAT IT!
WHY ARE YOU SO MEAN?
IT'S THE TRUTH.
IT'S OKAY.
ARE YOU STILL HUNGRY? YOU ALSO HAD BREAD!
I WANNA EAT IT!

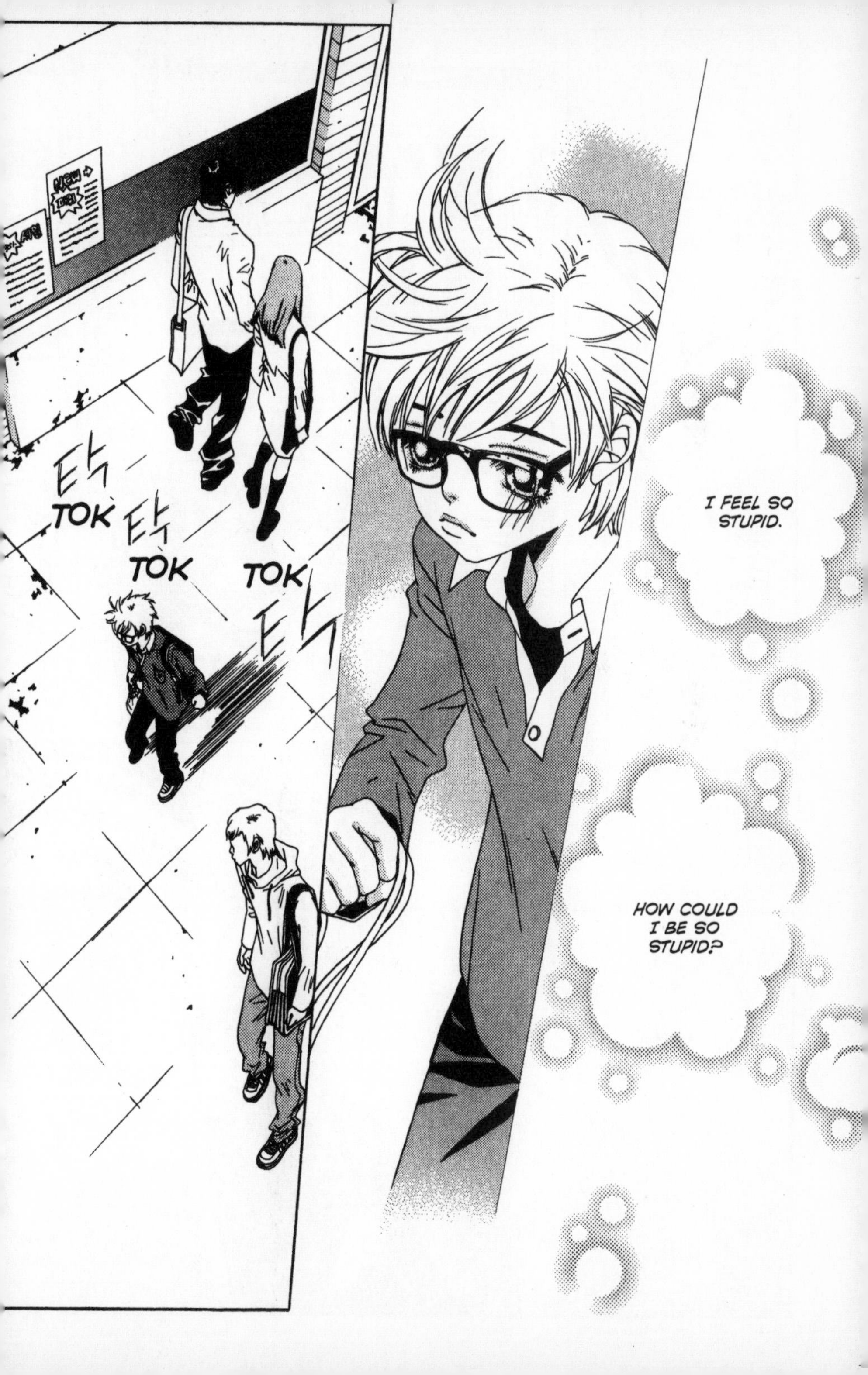
탁
TOK
탁
TOK
TOK
탁
I FEEL SO STUPID.
HOW COULD I BE SO STUPID?

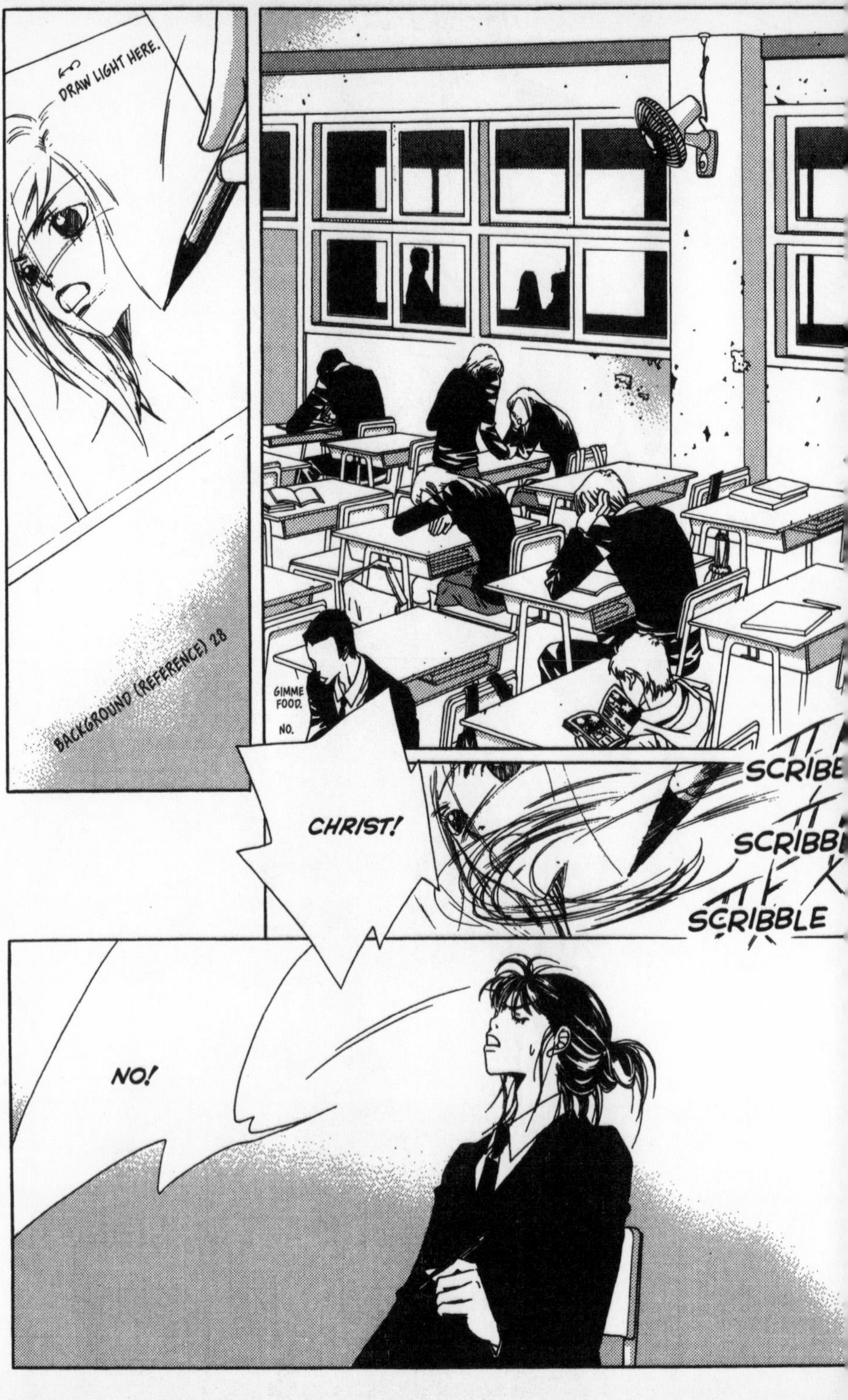
DRAW LIGHT HERE.
BACKGROUND (REFERENCE) 28
GIMME FOOD.
NO.
CHRIST!
SCRIBBLE
NO!

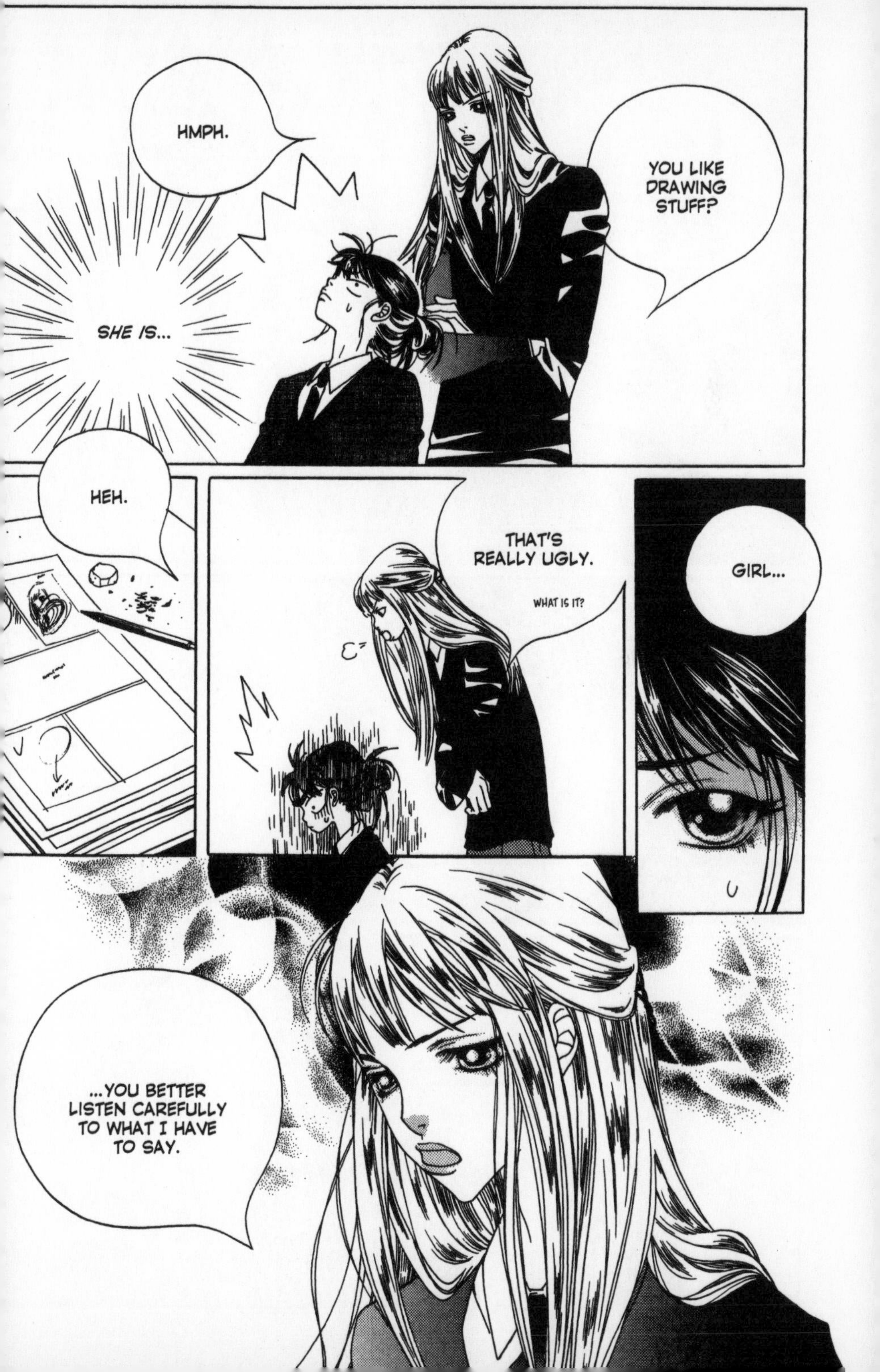
HMPH.
YOU LIKE DRAWING STUFF?
SHE IS...
HEH.
THAT'S REALLY UGLY.
WHAT IS IT?
GIRL...
...YOU BETTER LISTEN CAREFULLY TO WHAT I HAVE TO SAY.

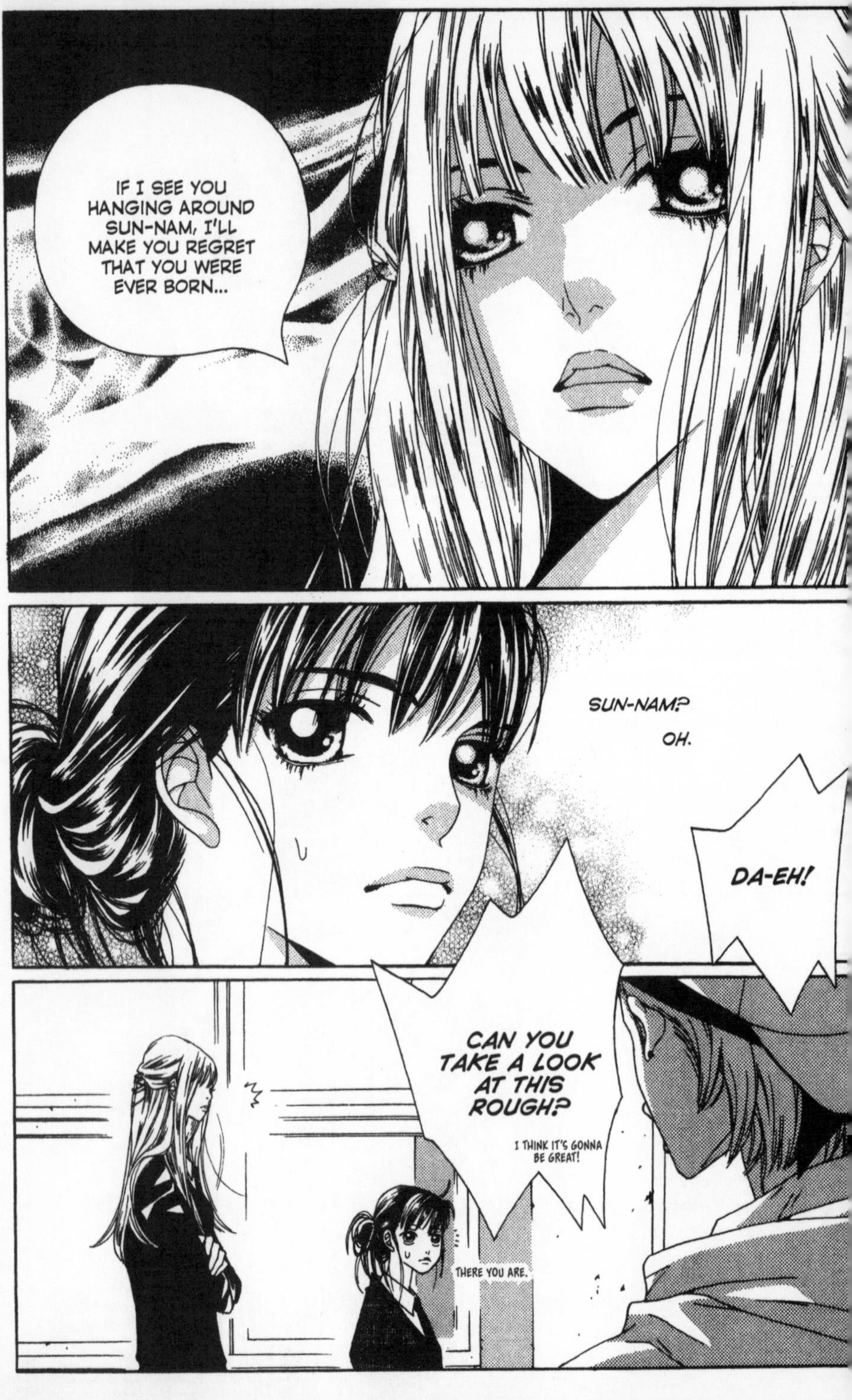
IF I SEE YOU HANGING AROUND SUN-NAM, I'LL MAKE YOU REGRET THAT YOU WERE EVER BORN...
SUN-NAM?
OH.
DA-EH!
CAN YOU TAKE A LOOK AT THIS ROUGH?
I THINK IT'S GONNA BE GREAT!
THERE YOU ARE.

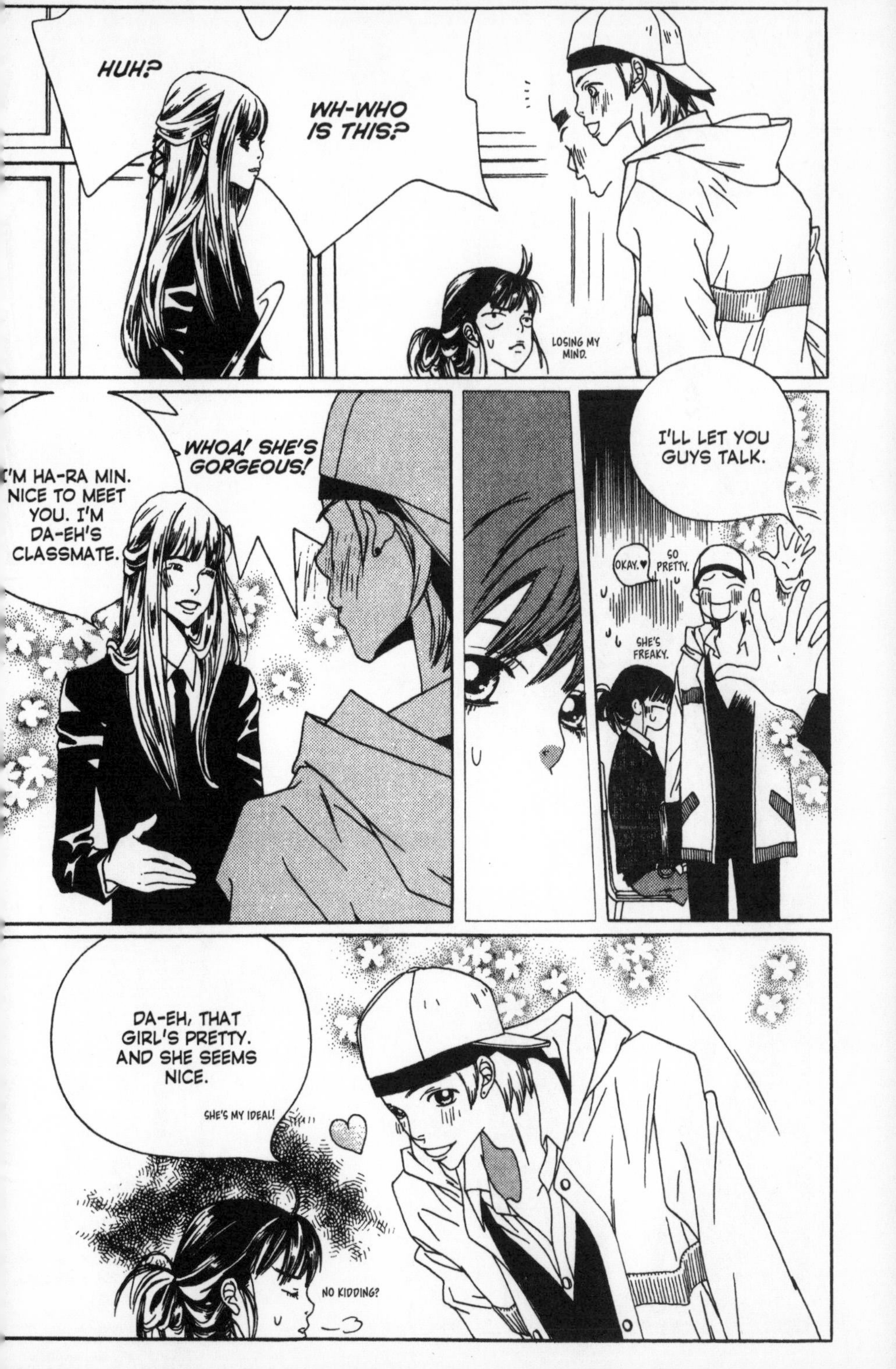
HUH?
WH-WHO IS THIS?
LOSING MY MIND.
I'M HA-RA MIN. NICE TO MEET YOU. I'M DA-EH'S CLASSMATE.
WHOA! SHE'S GORGEOUS!
I'LL LET YOU GUYS TALK.
OKAY.♥
SO PRETTY.
SHE'S FREAKY.
DA-EH, THAT GIRL'S PRETTY. AND SHE SEEMS NICE.
SHE'S MY IDEAL!
NO KIDDING?

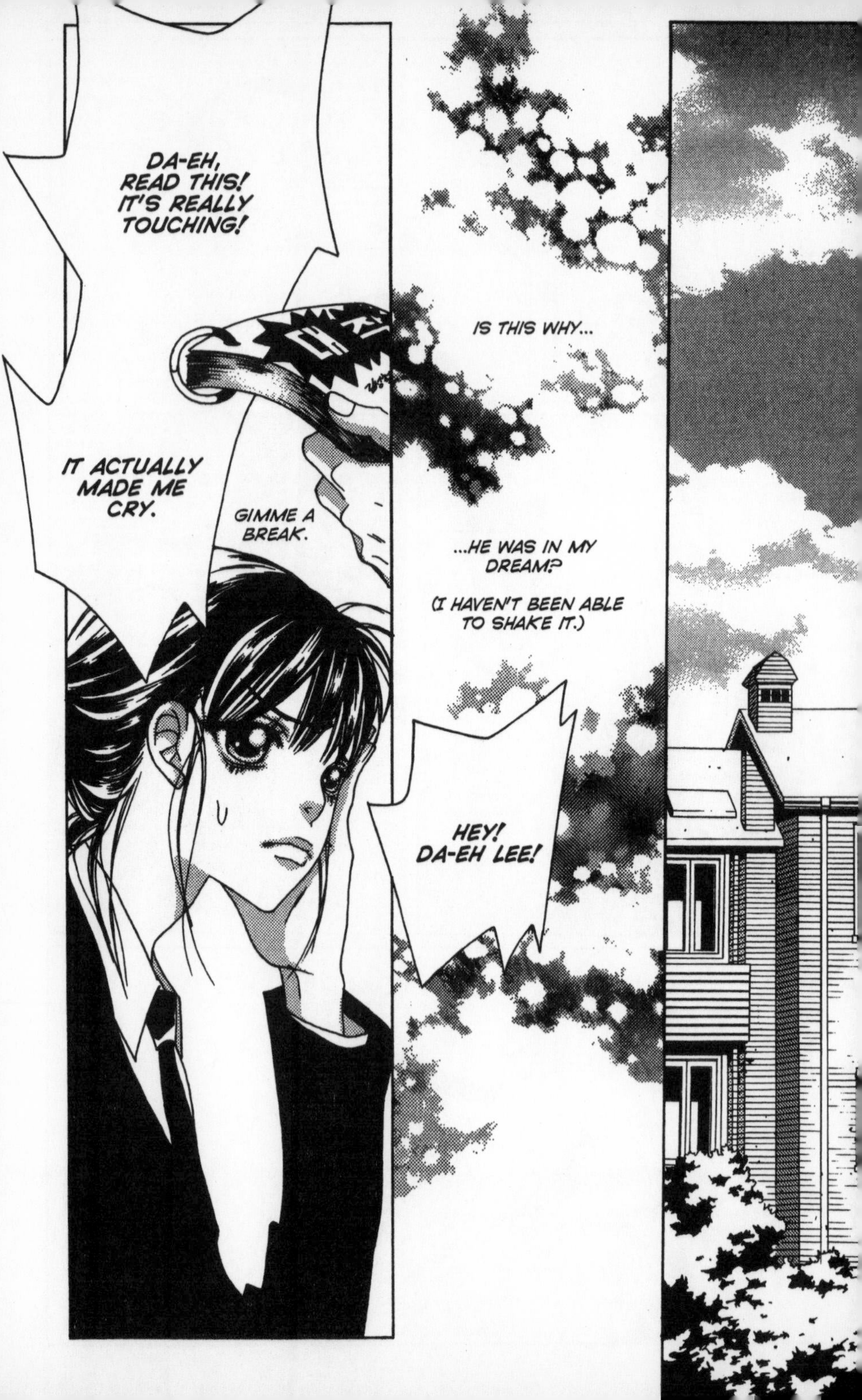
DA-EH, READ THIS! IT'S REALLY TOUCHING!
IT ACTUALLY MADE ME CRY.
GIMME A BREAK.
IS THIS WHY...
...HE WAS IN MY DREAM?
(I HAVEN'T BEEN ABLE TO SHAKE IT.)
HEY! DA-EH LEE!

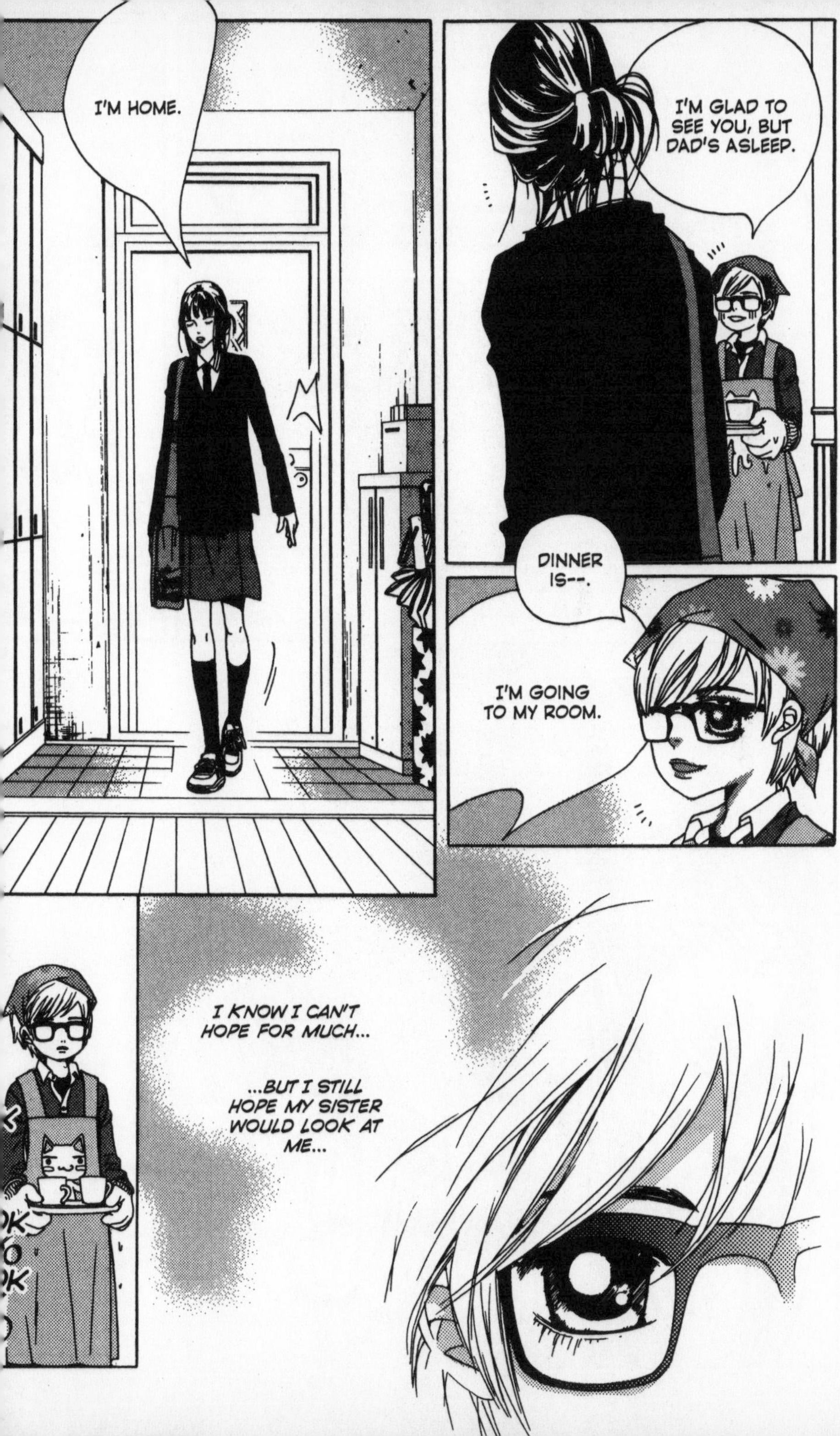
I'M HOME.
I'M GLAD TO SEE YOU, BUT DAD'S ASLEEP.
DINNER IS--.
I'M GOING TO MY ROOM.
I KNOW I CAN'T HOPE FOR MUCH...
...BUT I STILL HOPE MY SISTER WOULD LOOK AT ME...

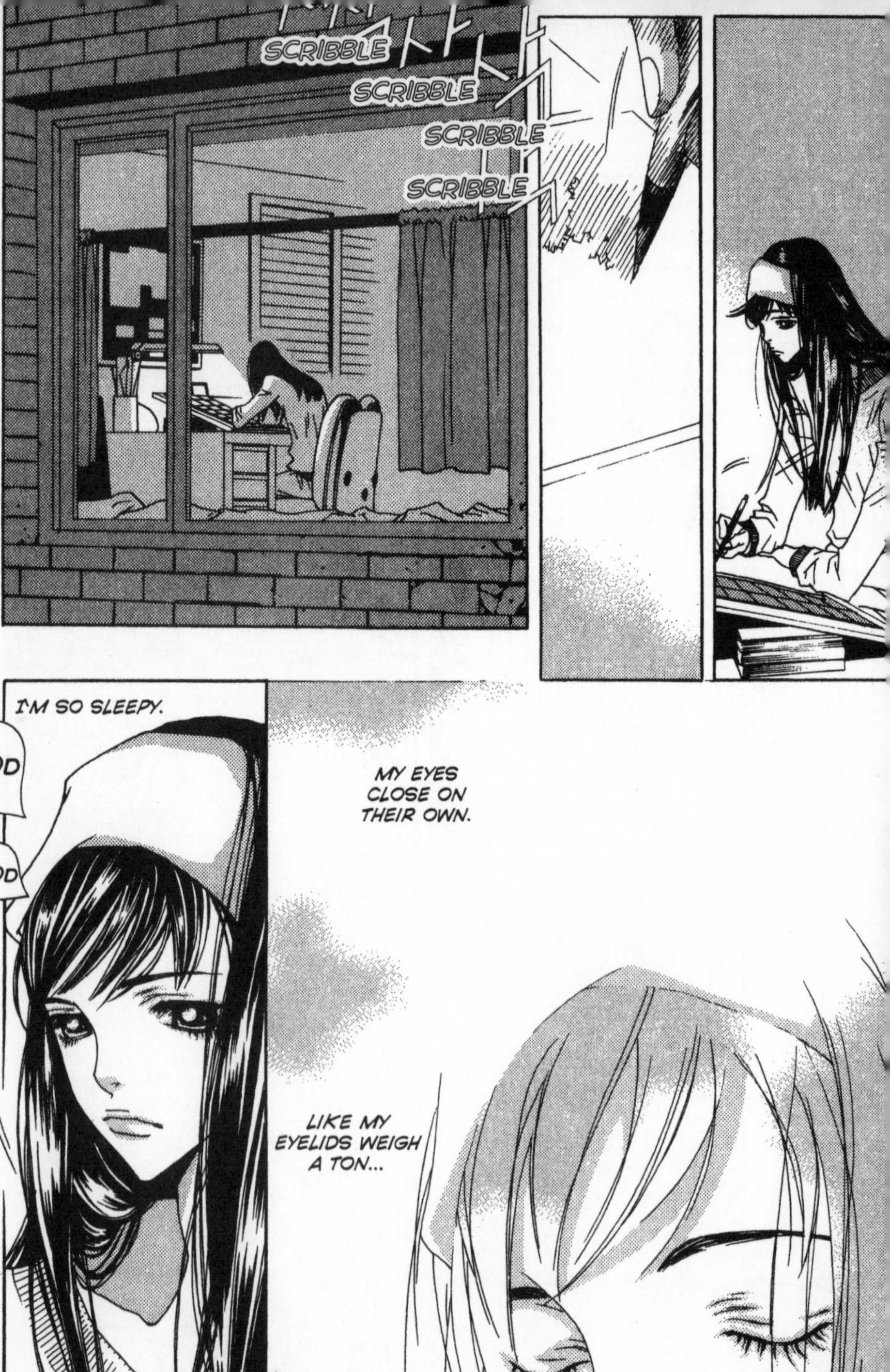
SCRIBBLE
SCRIBBLE
SCRIBBLE
SCRIBBLE
I'M SO SLEEPY.
NOD
NOD
MY EYES CLOSE ON THEIR OWN.
LIKE MY EYELIDS WEIGH A TON...

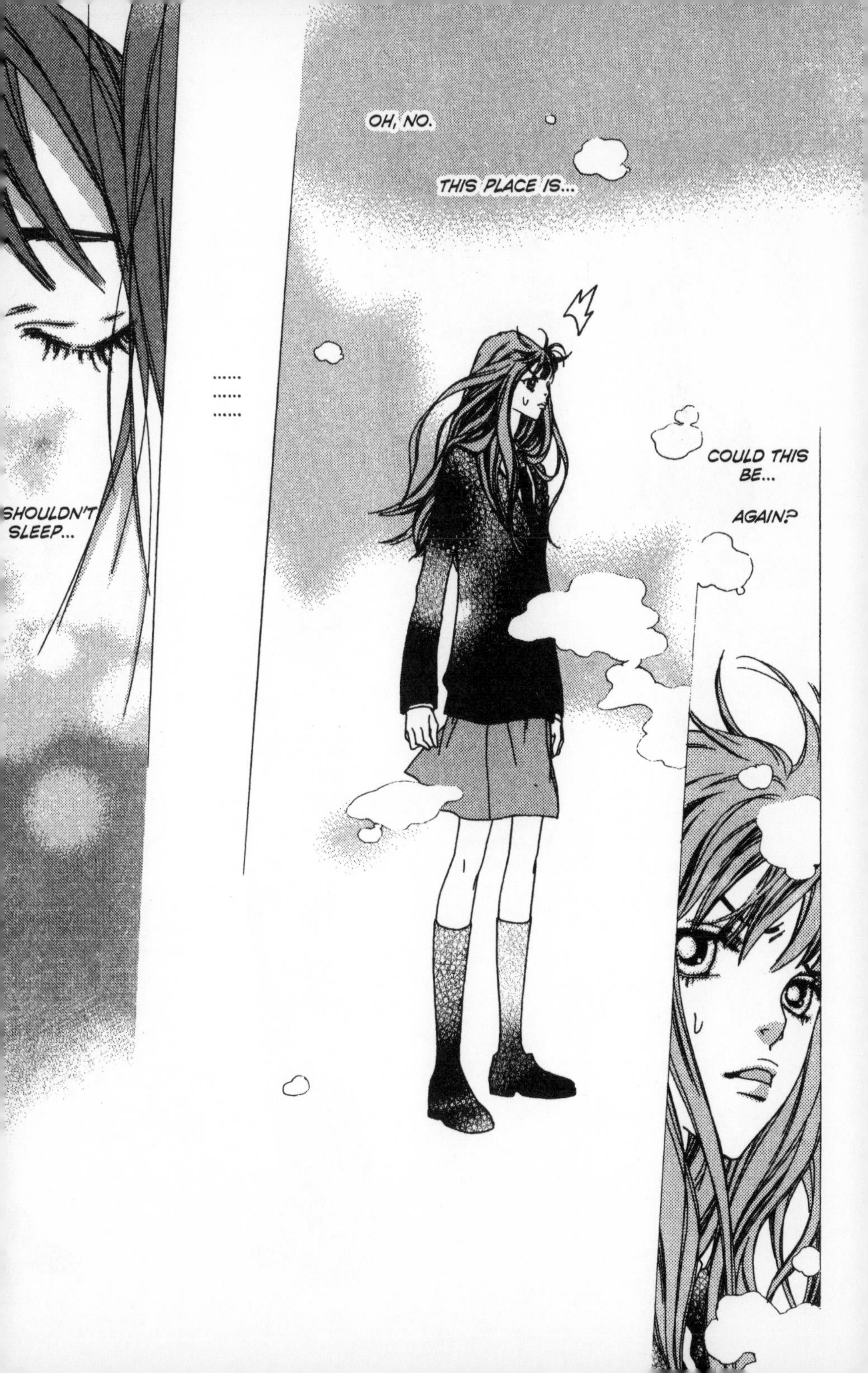

SHOULDN'T SLEEP...
......
......
......
OH, NO.
THIS PLACE IS...
COULD THIS BE...
AGAIN?

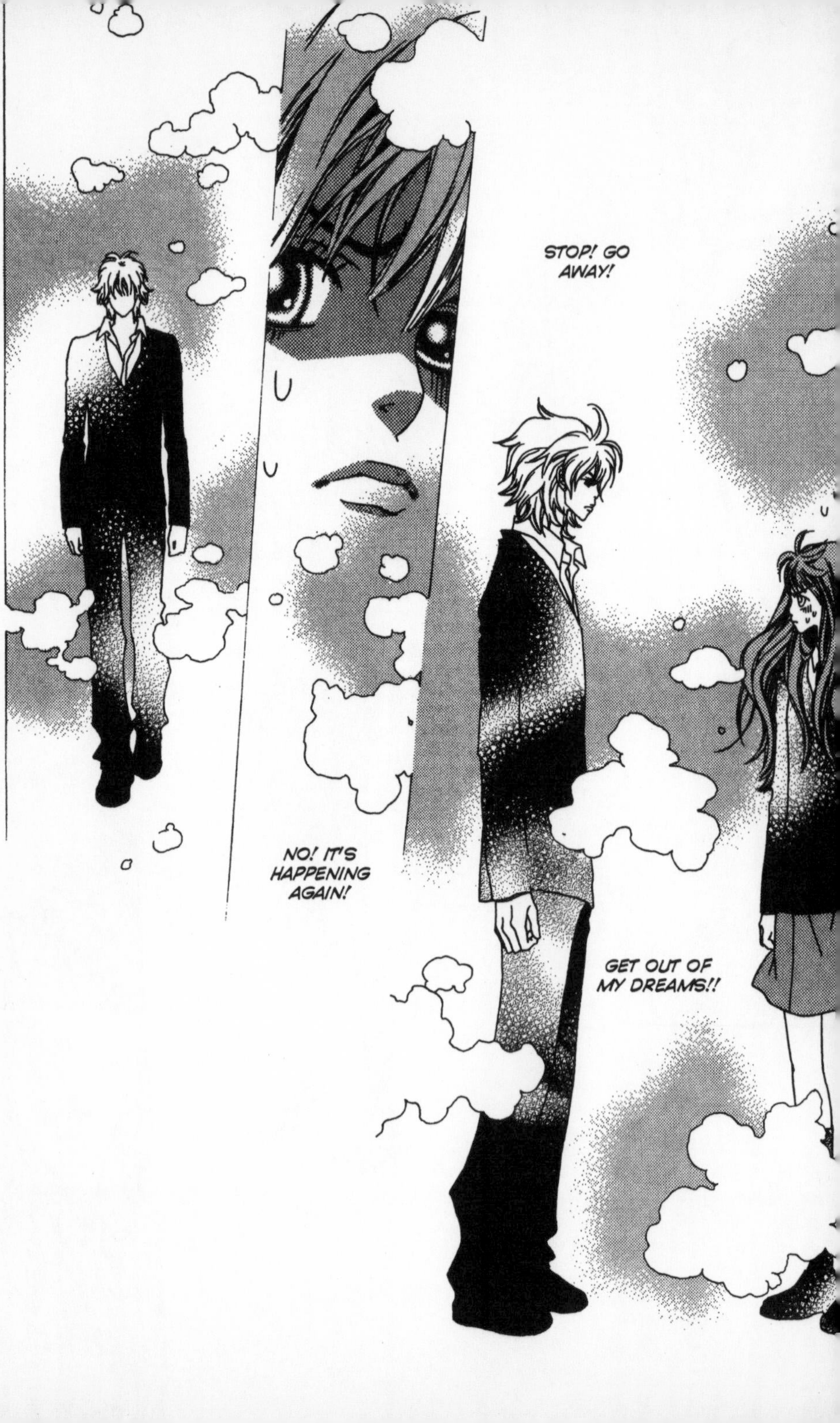
NO! IT'S HAPPENING AGAIN!
STOP! GO AWAY!
GET OUT OF MY DREAMS!!

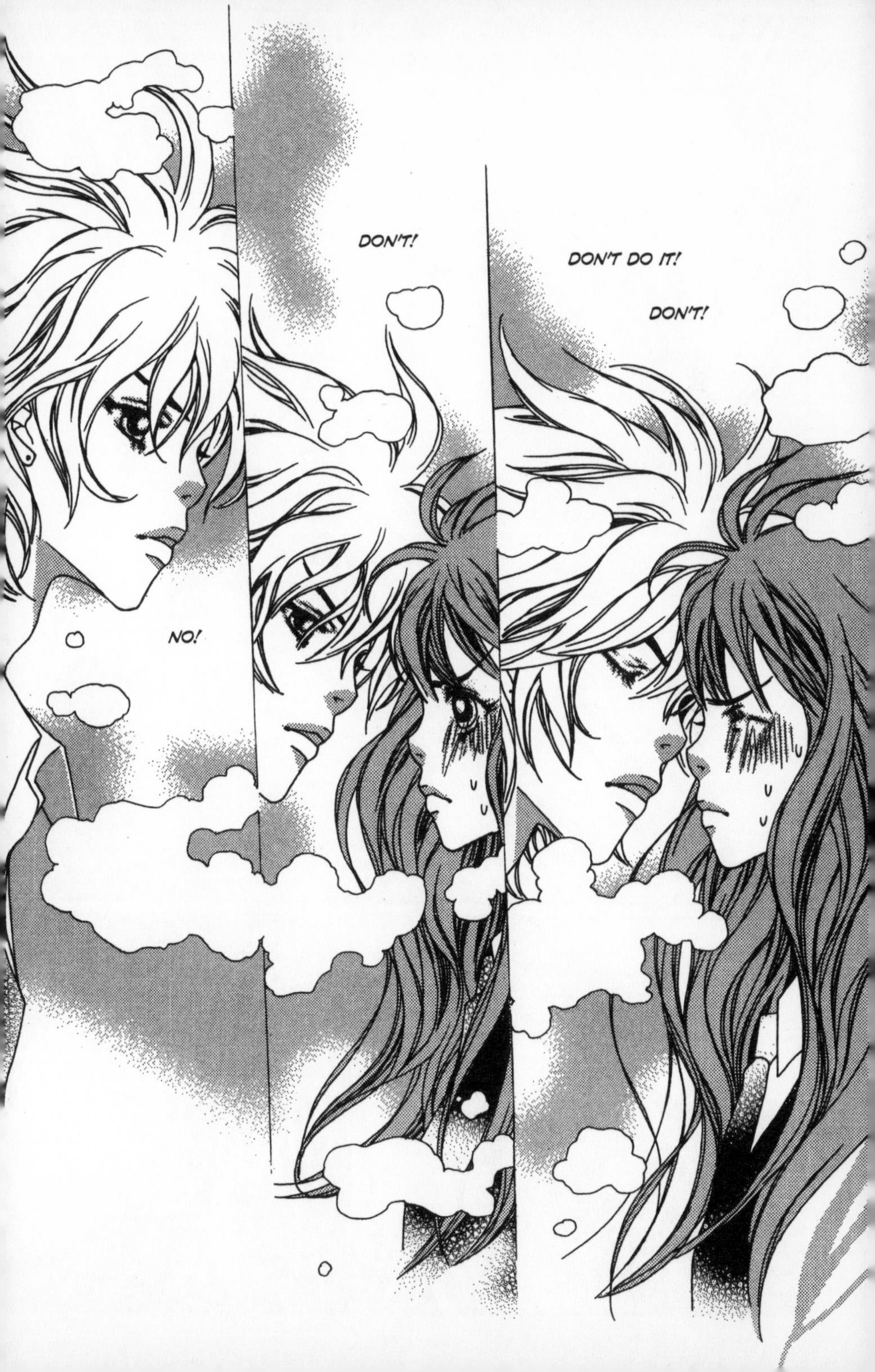
NO!
DON'T!
DON'T DO IT!
DON'T!

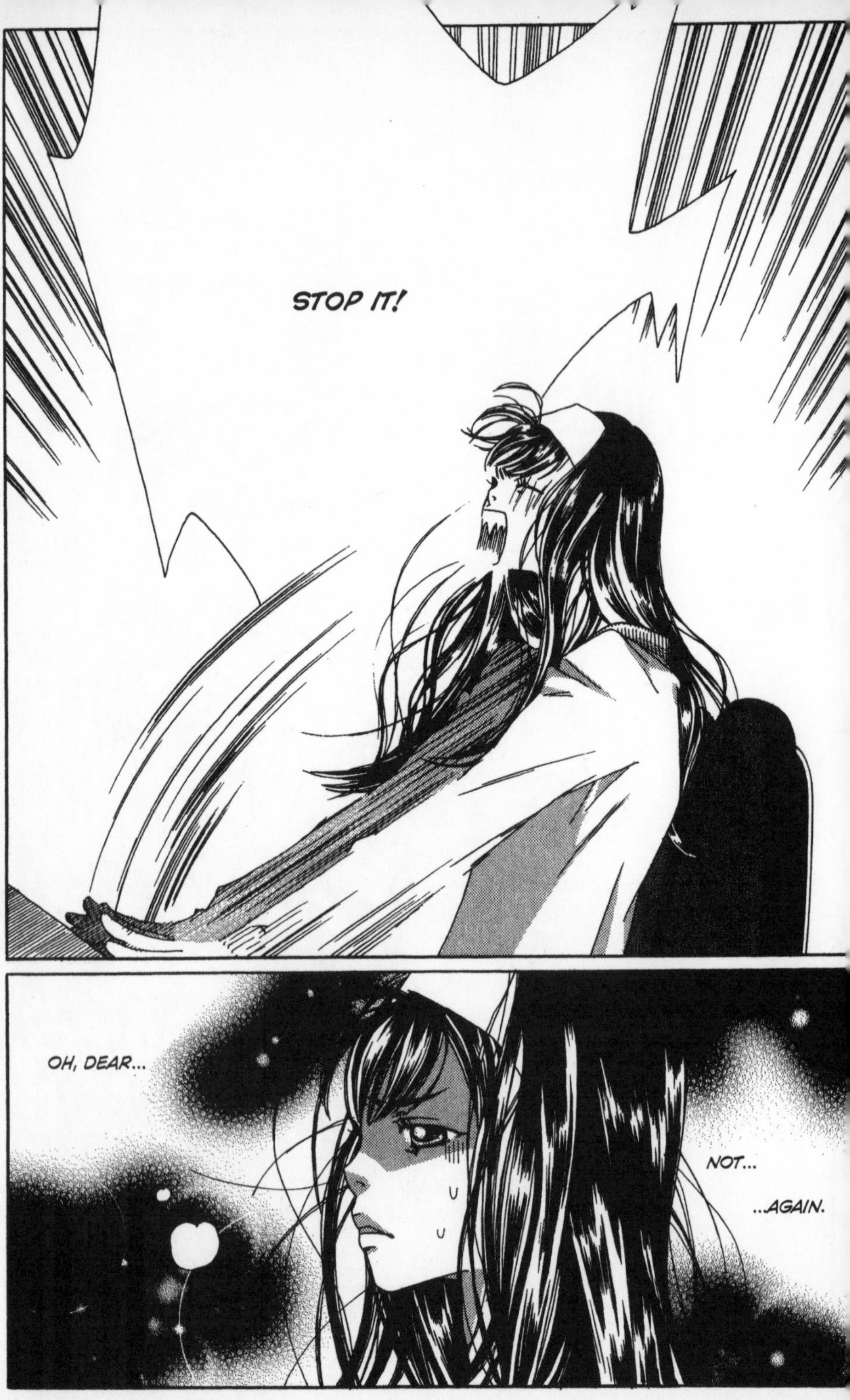
STOP IT!
OH, DEAR...
NOT...
...AGAIN.

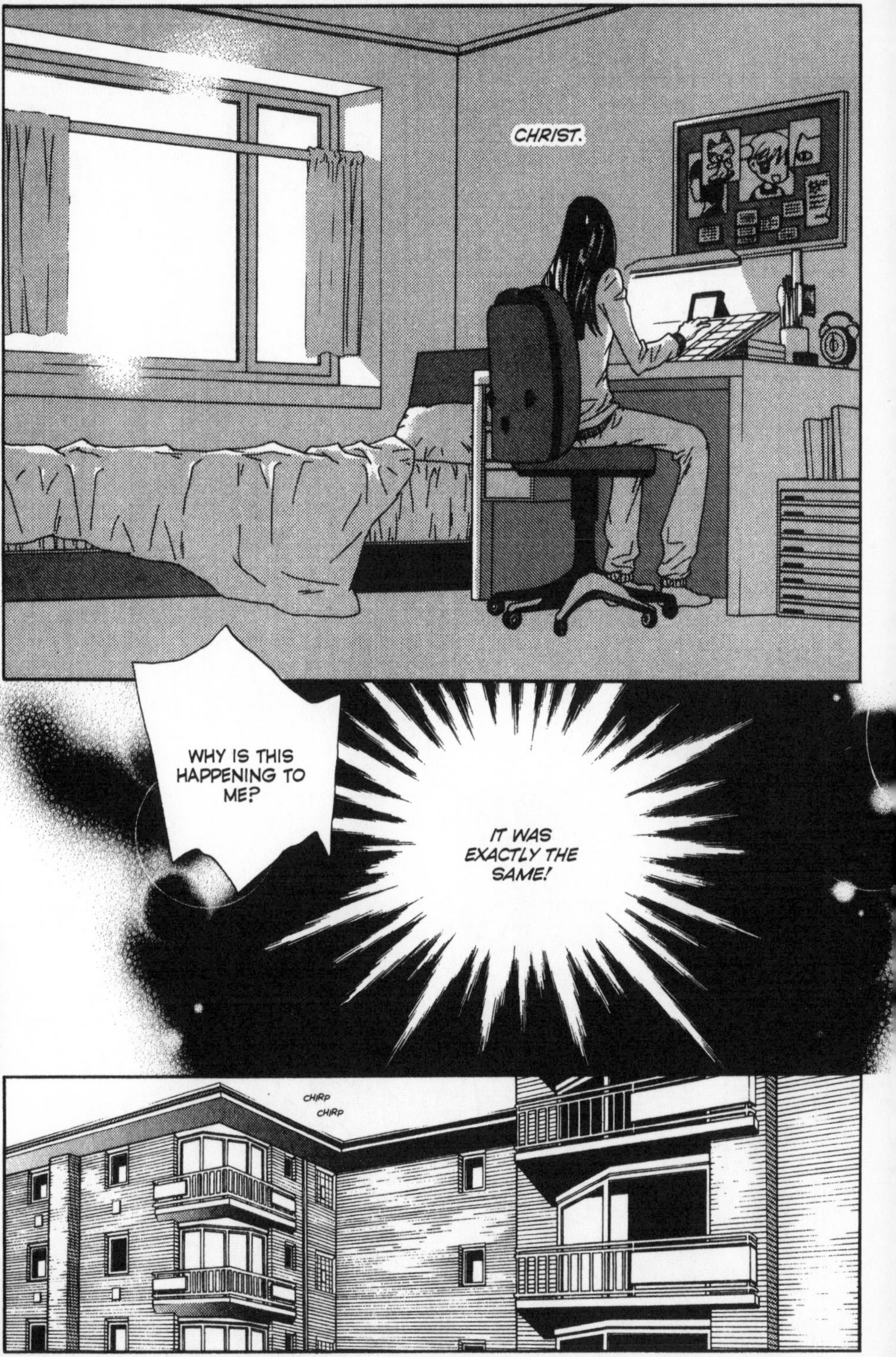
CHRIST.
WHY IS THIS HAPPENING TO ME?
IT WAS EXACTLY THE SAME!
CHIRP
CHIRP

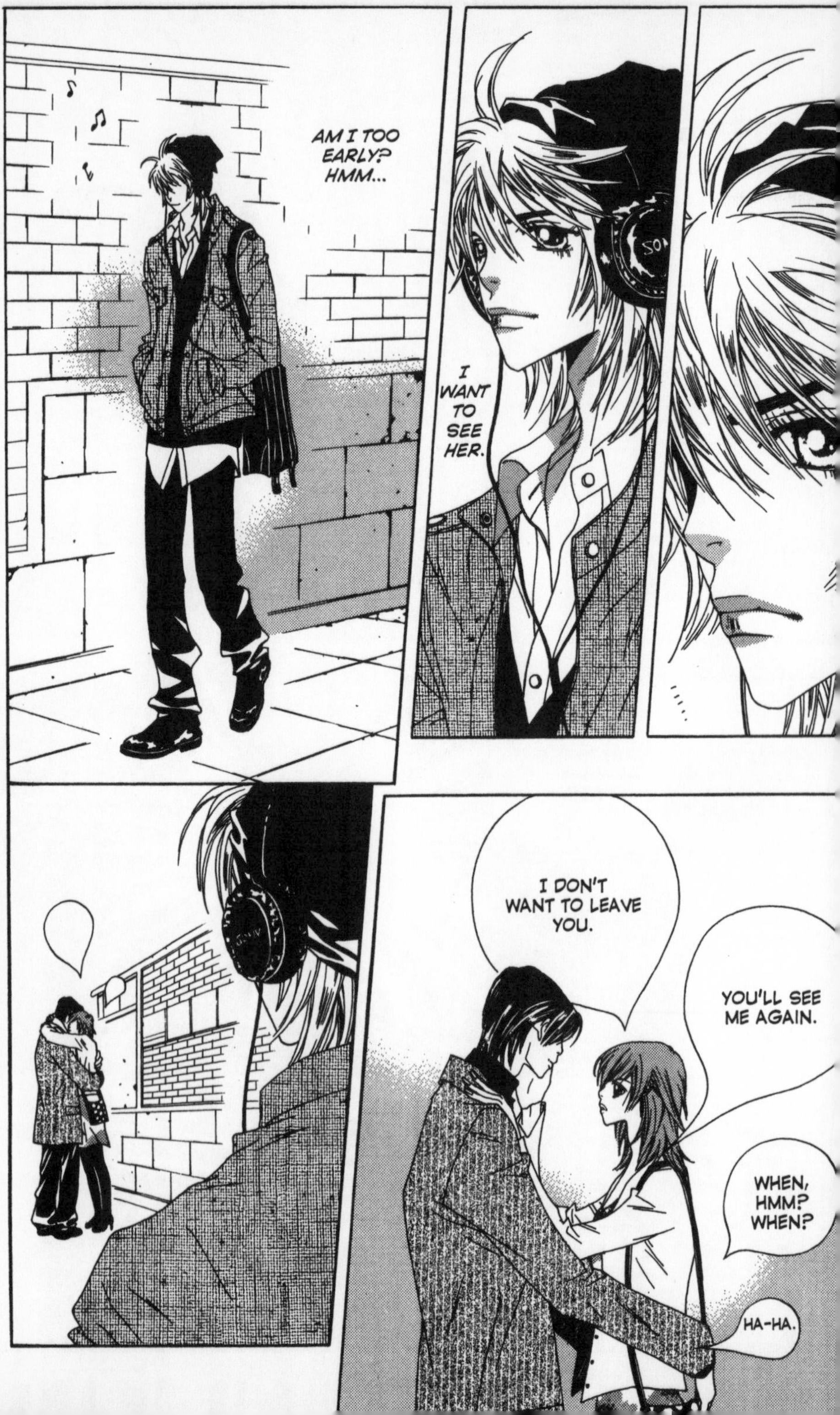
AM I TOO EARLY? HMM...
I WANT TO SEE HER.
I DON'T WANT TO LEAVE YOU.
YOU'LL SEE ME AGAIN.
WHEN, HMM? WHEN?
HA-HA.

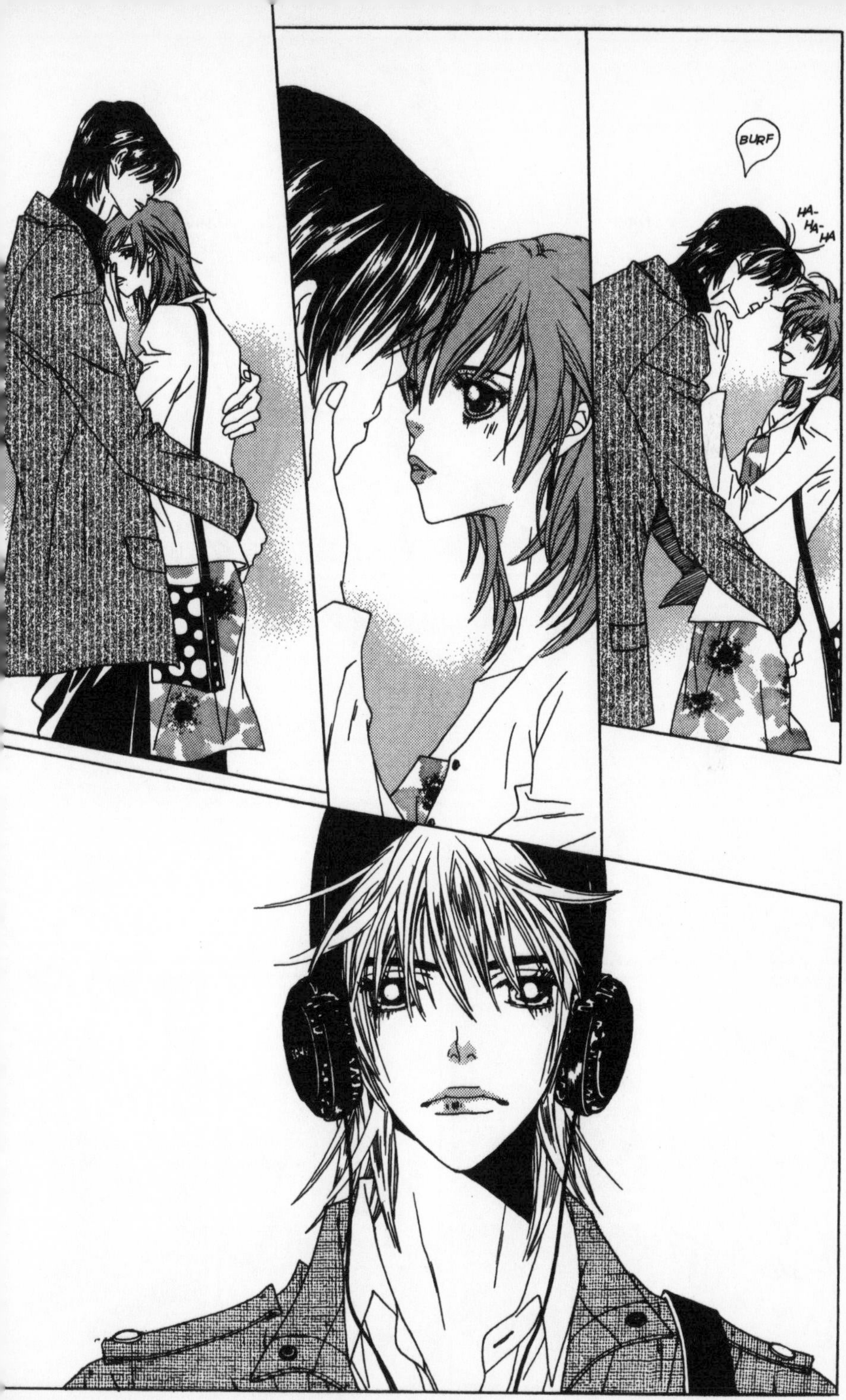
BURF
HA-HA-HA

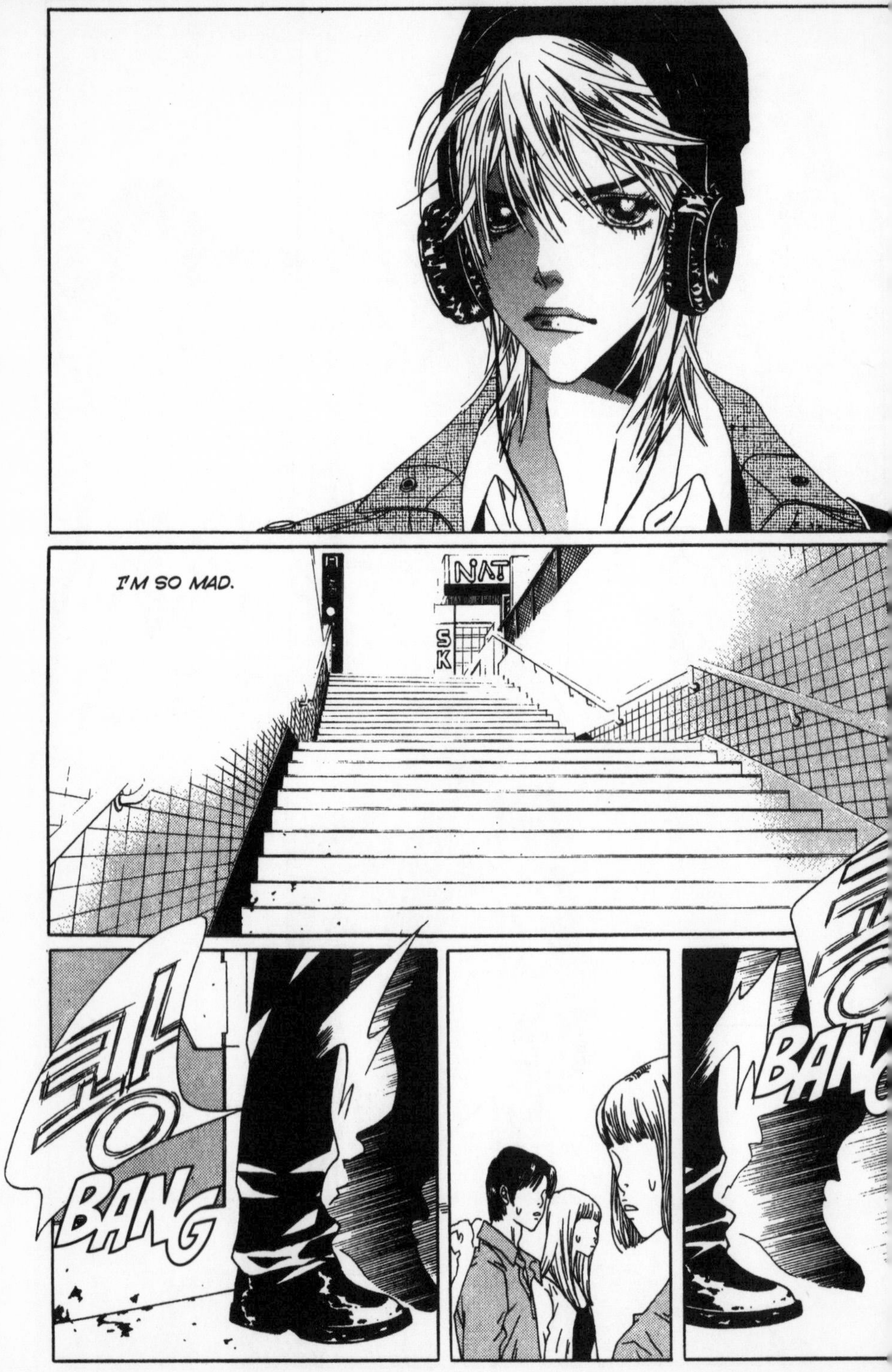
I'M SO MAD.
BANG
BAN

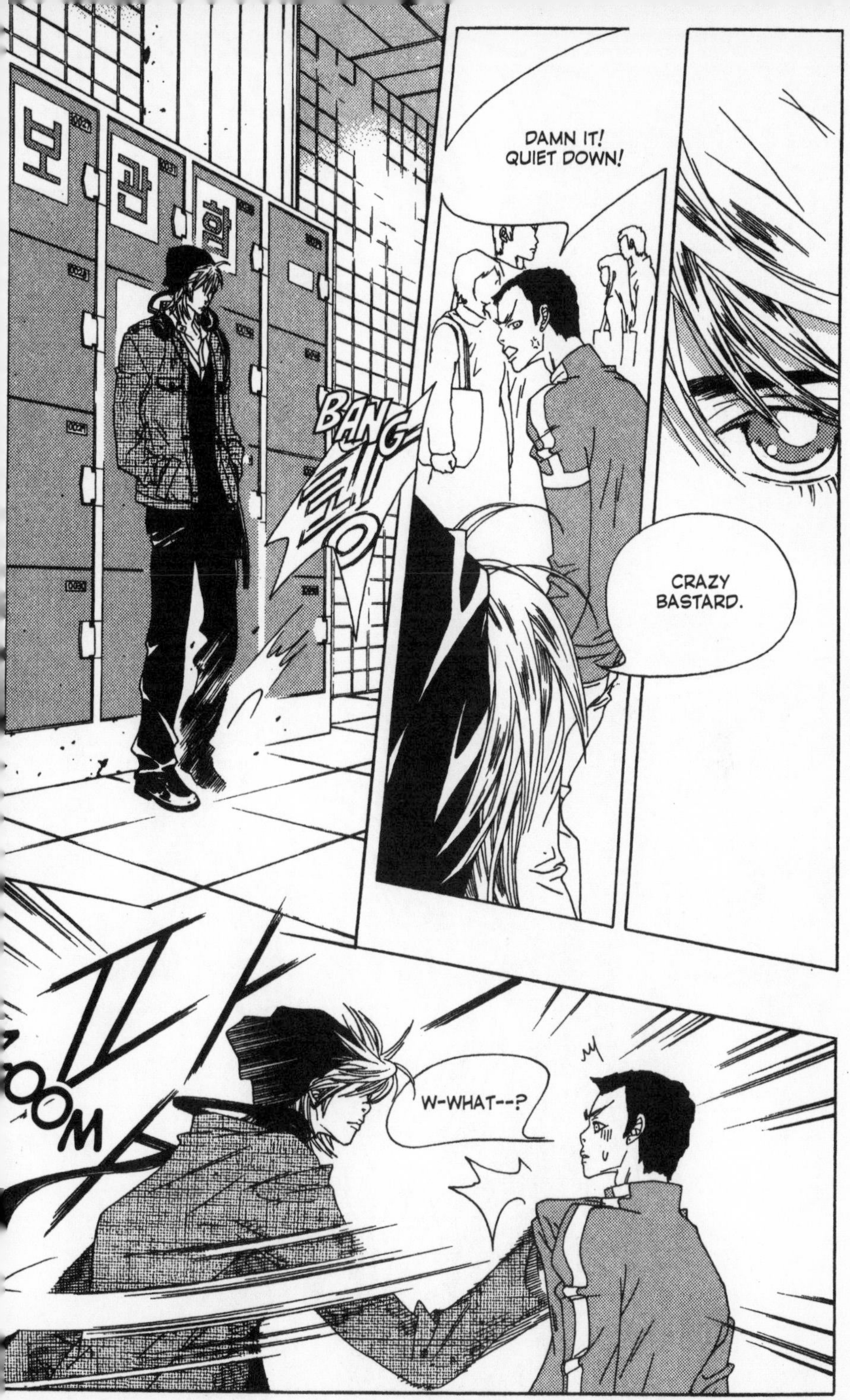
보관함
BANG
DAMN IT! QUIET DOWN!
CRAZY BASTARD.
W-WHAT--?

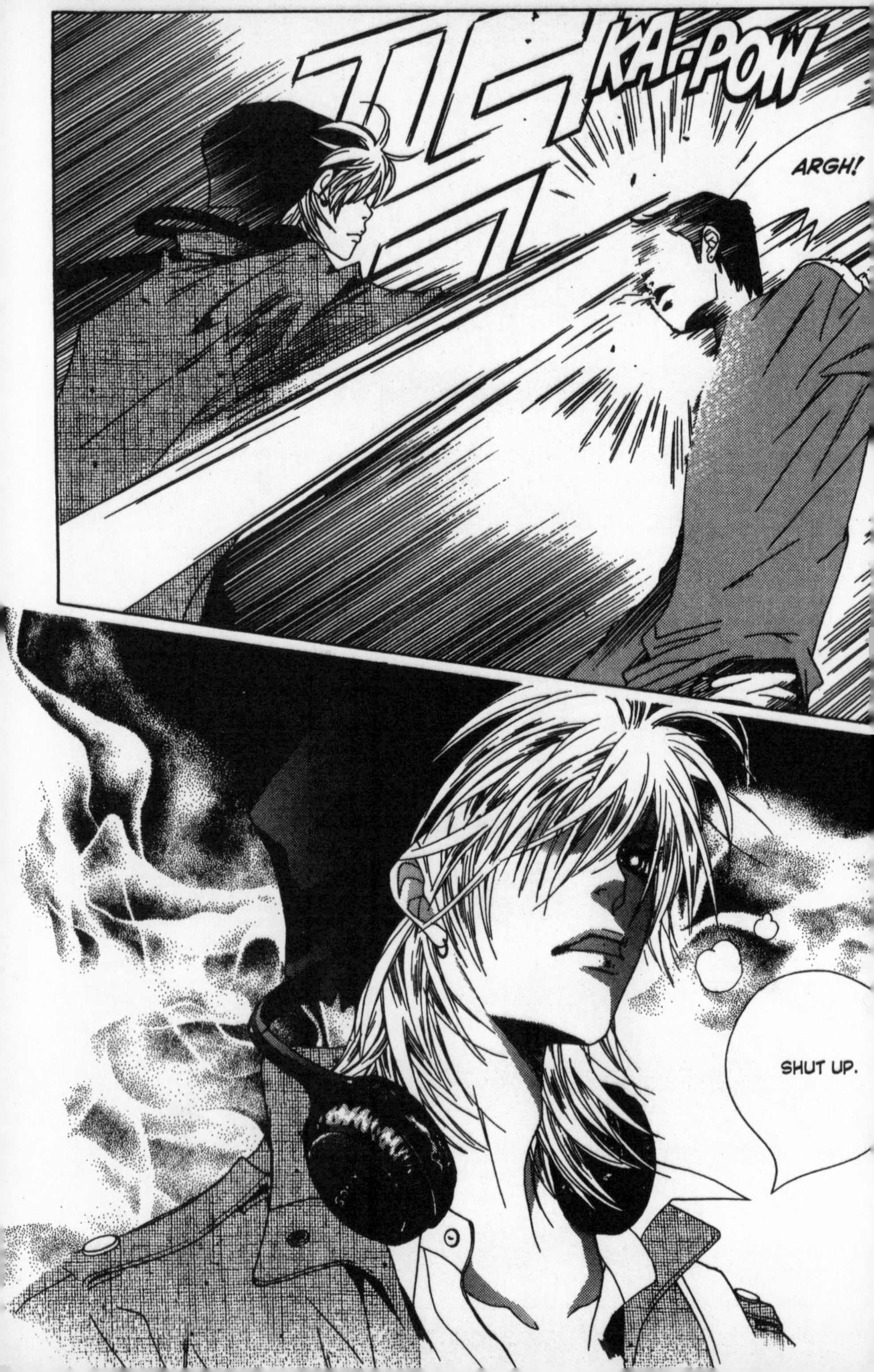
KA-POW
ARGH!
SHUT UP.

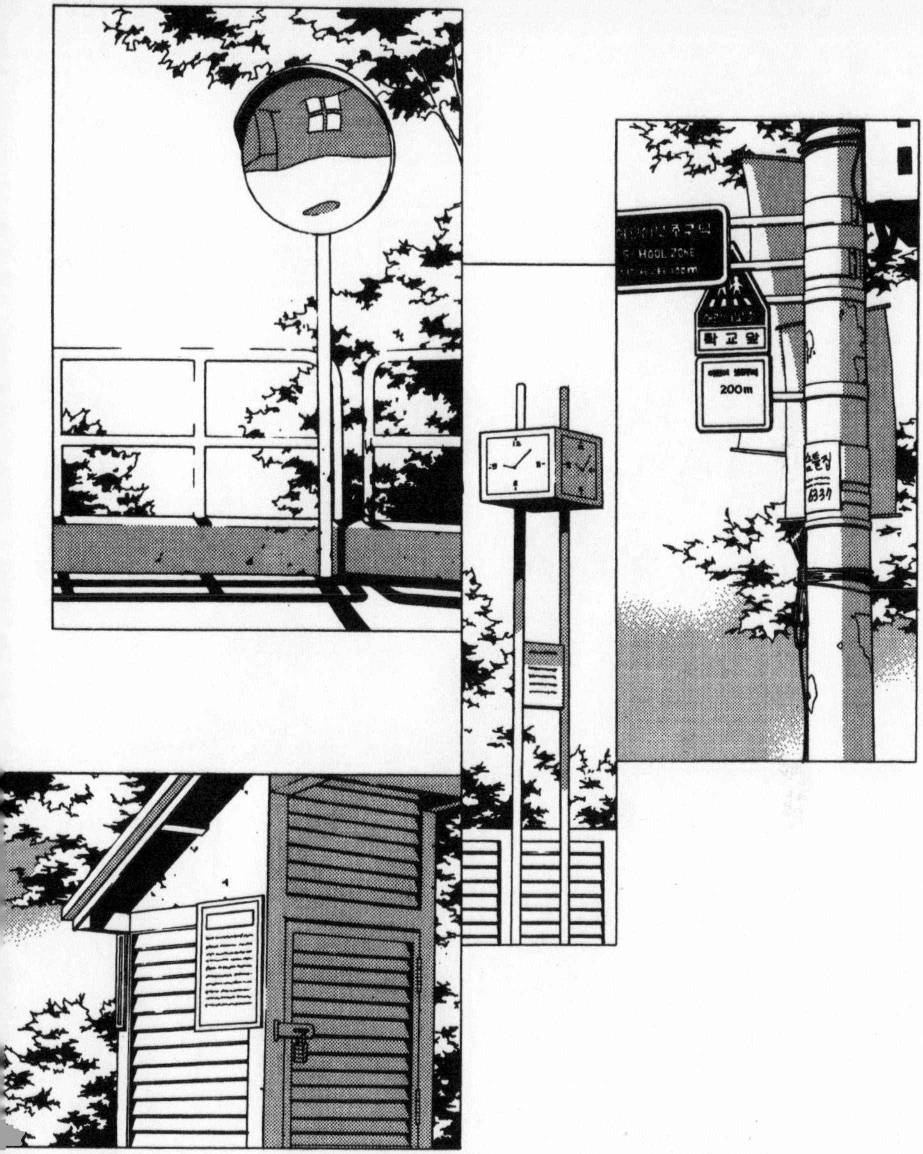
학교앞
200m
6337

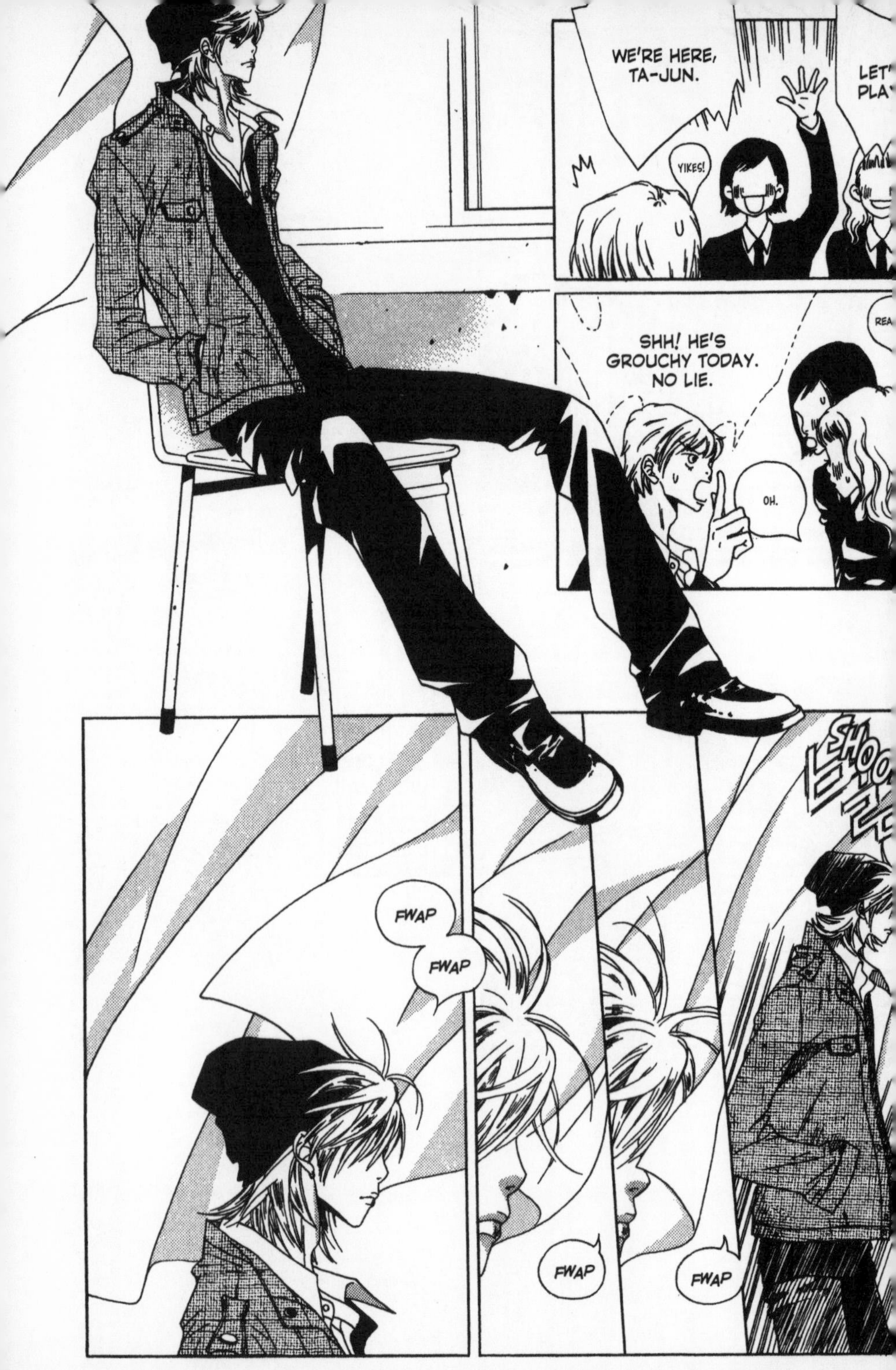
WE'RE HERE, TA-JUN.
YIKES!
SHH! HE'S GROUCHY TODAY. NO LIE.
OH.
FWAP
FWAP
FWAP
FWAP

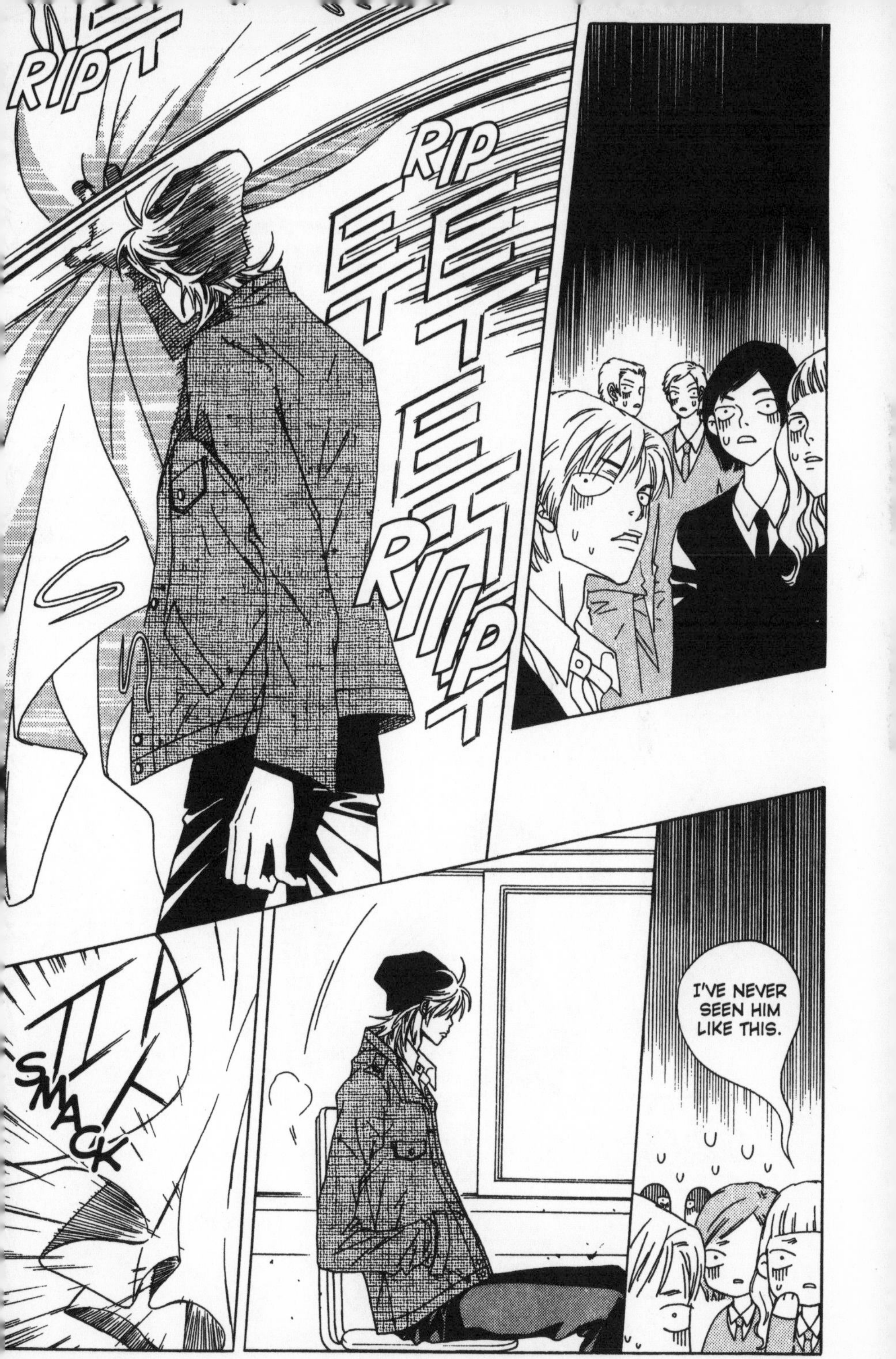
RIP
RIP
RIIIP
SMACK
I'VE NEVER SEEN HIM LIKE THIS.

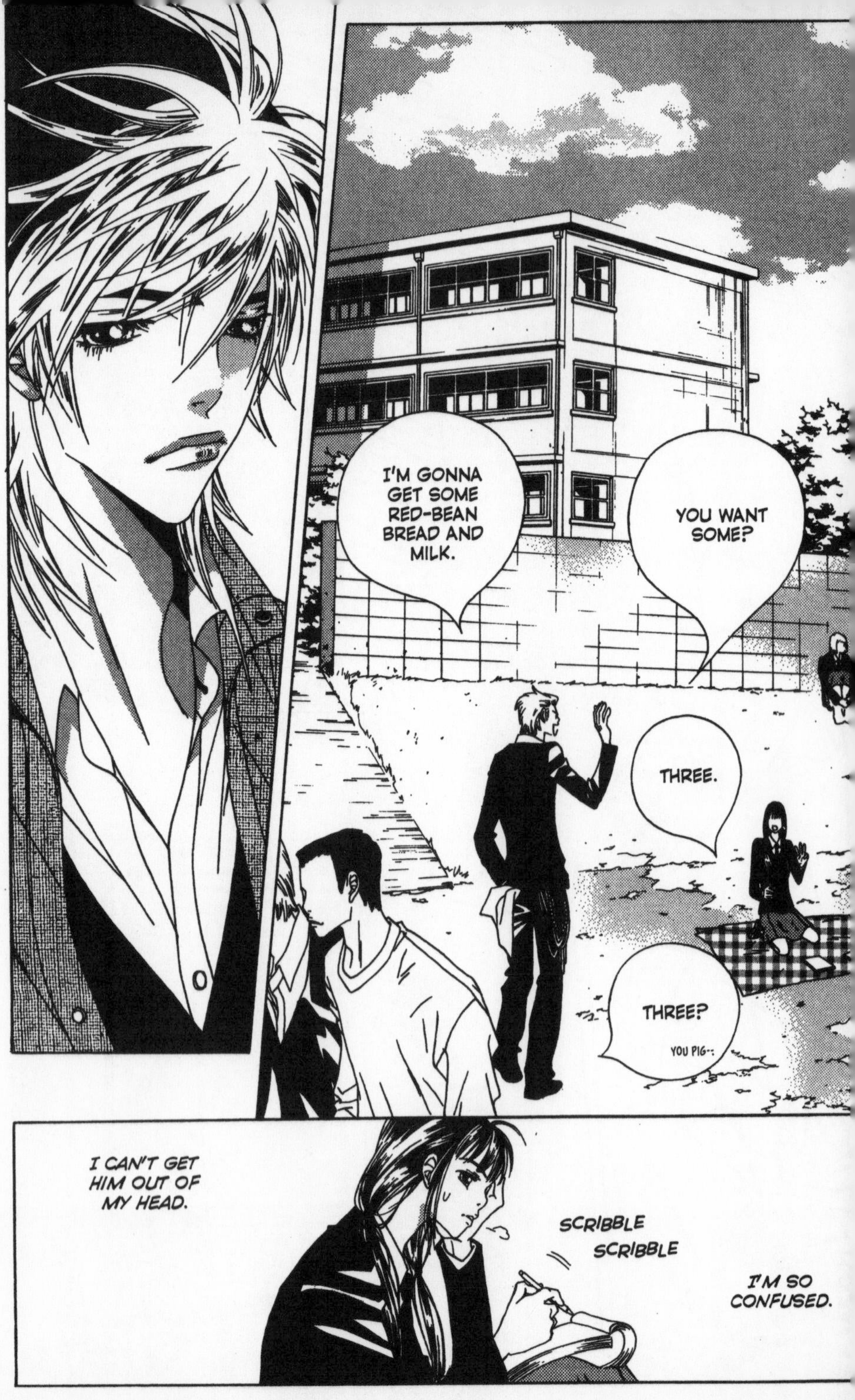
I'M GONNA GET SOME RED-BEAN BREAD AND MILK.
YOU WANT SOME?
THREE.
THREE?
YOU PIG--
I CAN'T GET HIM OUT OF MY HEAD.
SCRIBBLE SCRIBBLE
I'M SO CONFUSED.

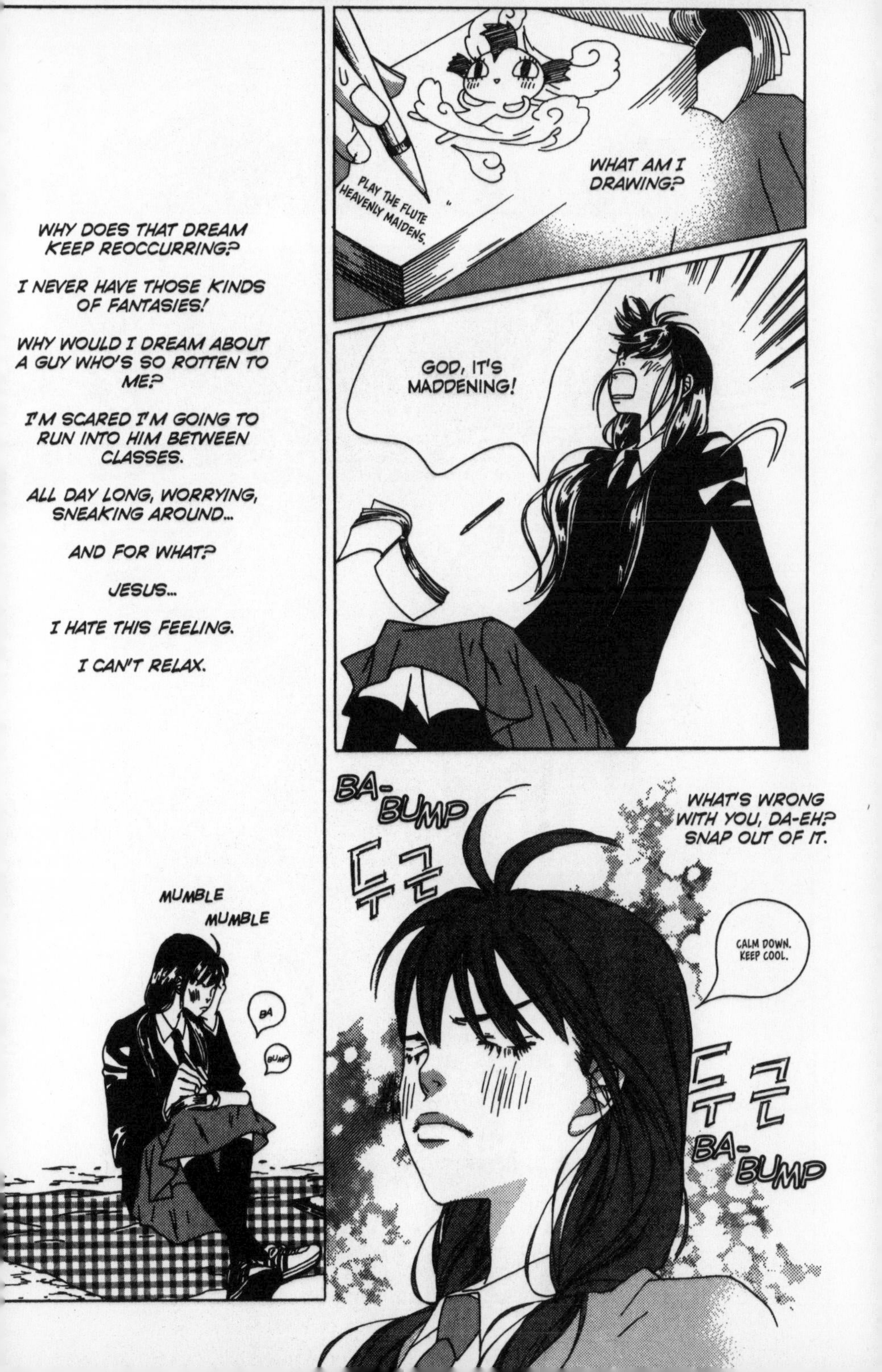
WHY DOES THAT DREAM KEEP REOCCURRING?
I NEVER HAVE THOSE KINDS OF FANTASIES!
WHY WOULD I DREAM ABOUT A GUY WHO'S SO ROTTEN TO ME?
I'M SCARED I'M GOING TO RUN INTO HIM BETWEEN CLASSES.
ALL DAY LONG, WORRYING, SNEAKING AROUND...
AND FOR WHAT?
JESUS...
I HATE THIS FEELING.
I CAN'T RELAX.
MUMBLE MUMBLE
BA
BUMP
PLAY THE FLUTE HEAVENLY MAIDENS.
WHAT AM I DRAWING?
GOD, IT'S MADDENING!
BA-BUMP
두근
WHAT'S WRONG WITH YOU, DA-EH? SNAP OUT OF IT.
CALM DOWN. KEEP COOL.
두근
BA-BUMP

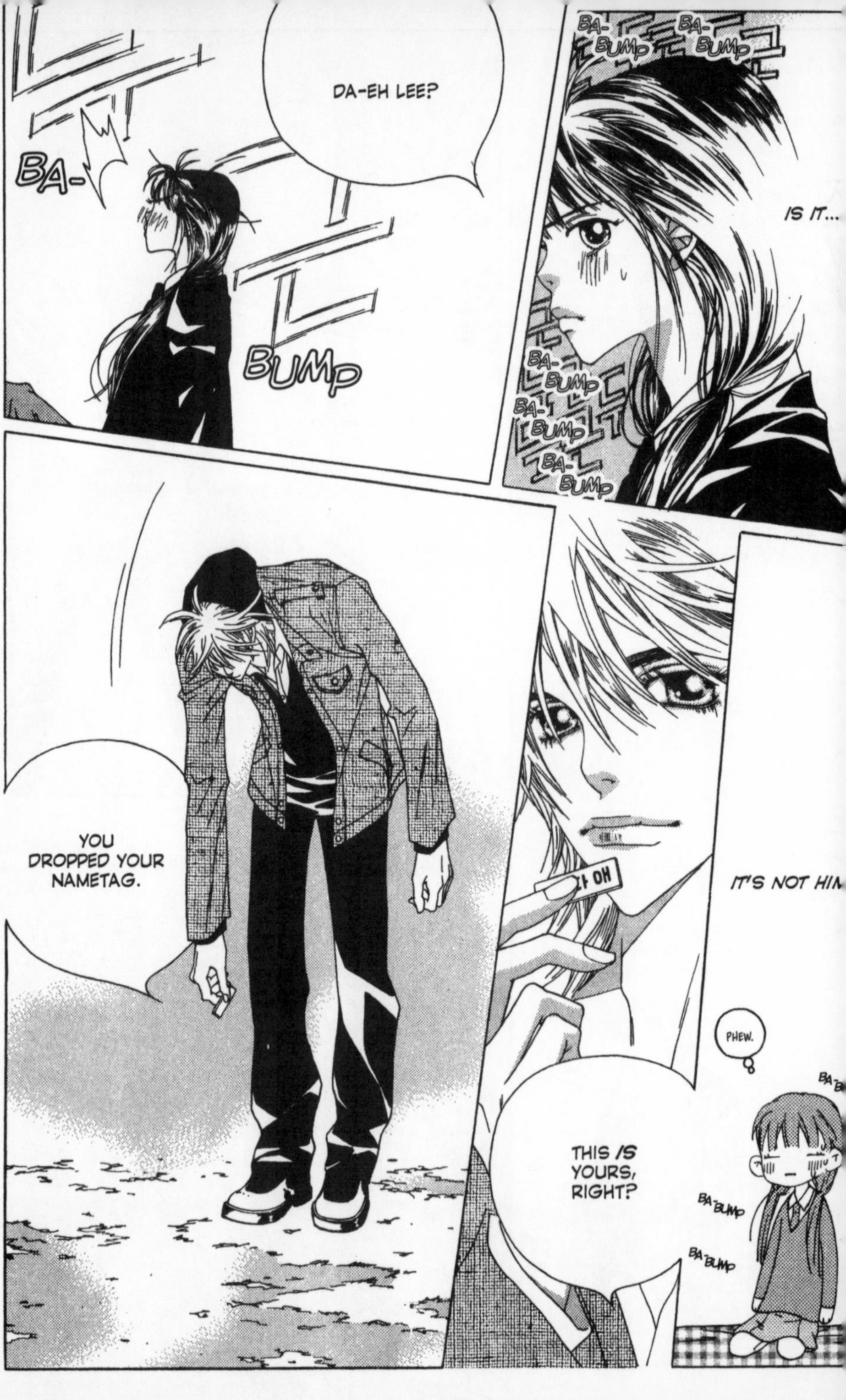
BA-
BUMP
DA-EH LEE?
BA-BUMP BA-BUMP
IS IT...
BA-BUMP BA-BUMP BA-BUMP
YOU DROPPED YOUR NAMETAG.
THIS IS YOURS, RIGHT?
IT'S NOT HIM
PHEW.
BA-BUMP
BA-BUMP

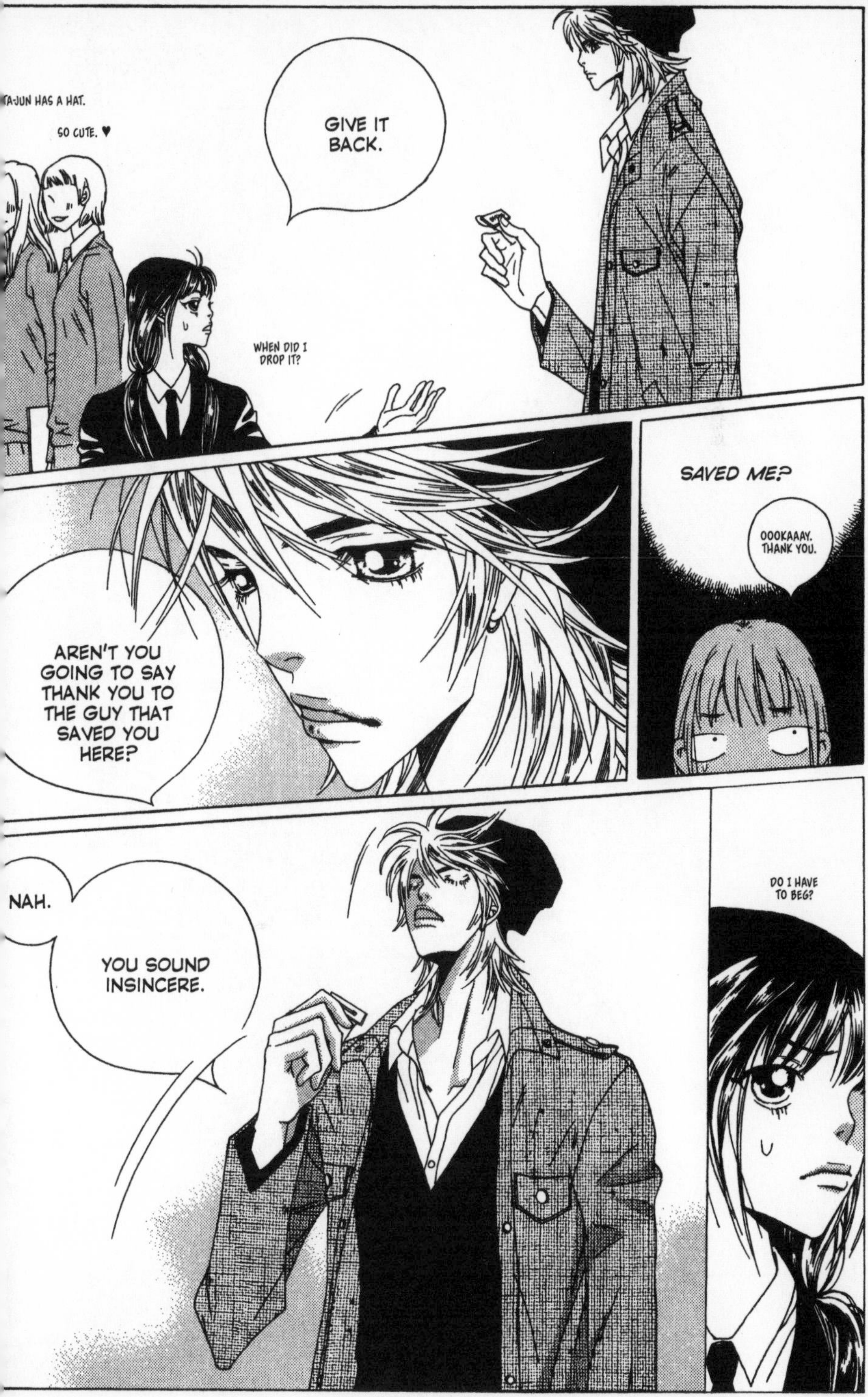
TA-JUN HAS A HAT.
SO CUTE. ♥
GIVE IT BACK.
WHEN DID I DROP IT?
AREN'T YOU GOING TO SAY THANK YOU TO THE GUY THAT SAVED YOU HERE?
SAVED ME?
OOOKAAAY. THANK YOU.
NAH.
YOU SOUND INSINCERE.
DO I HAVE TO BEG?

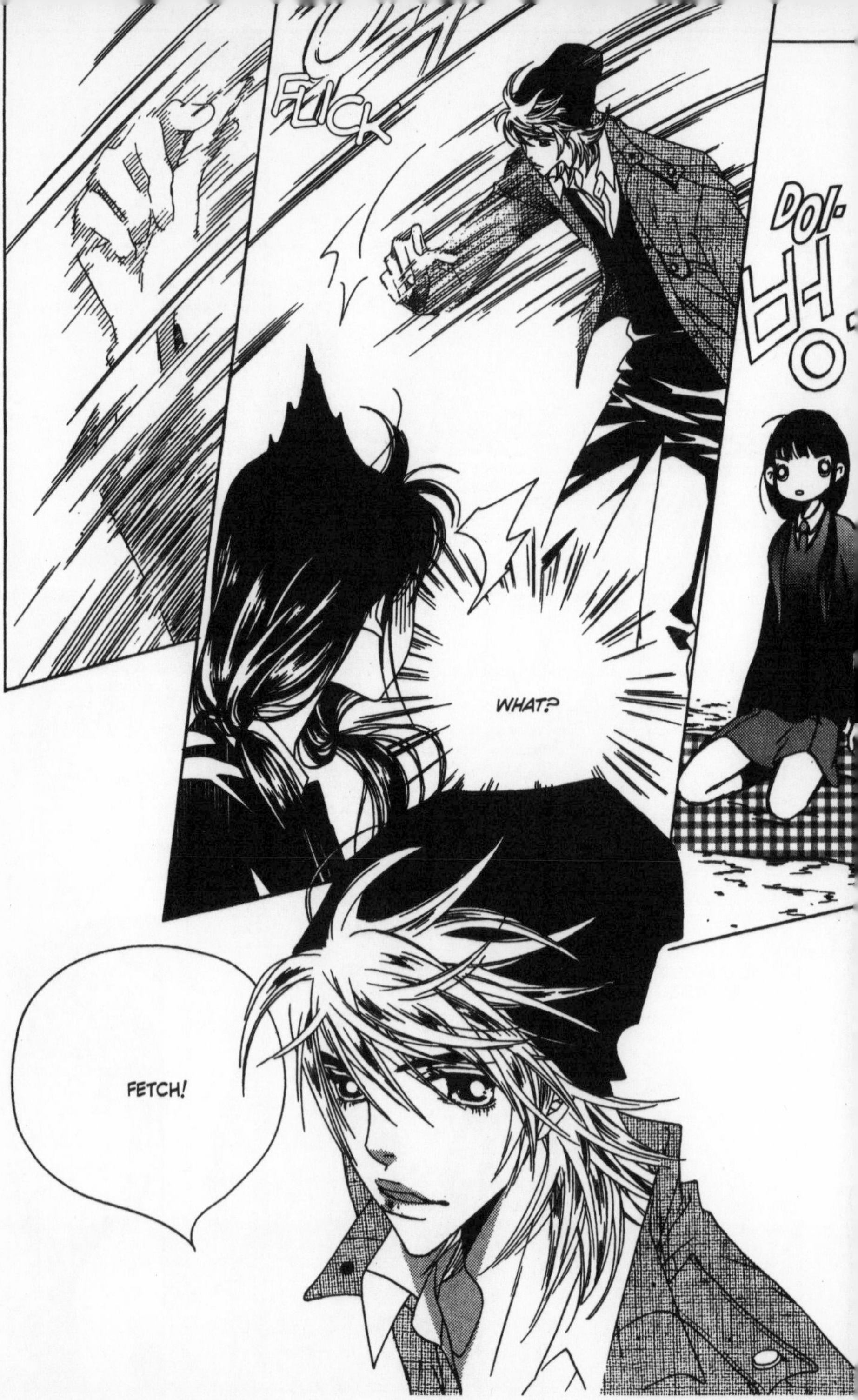
FLICK
DOI-
WHAT?
FETCH!

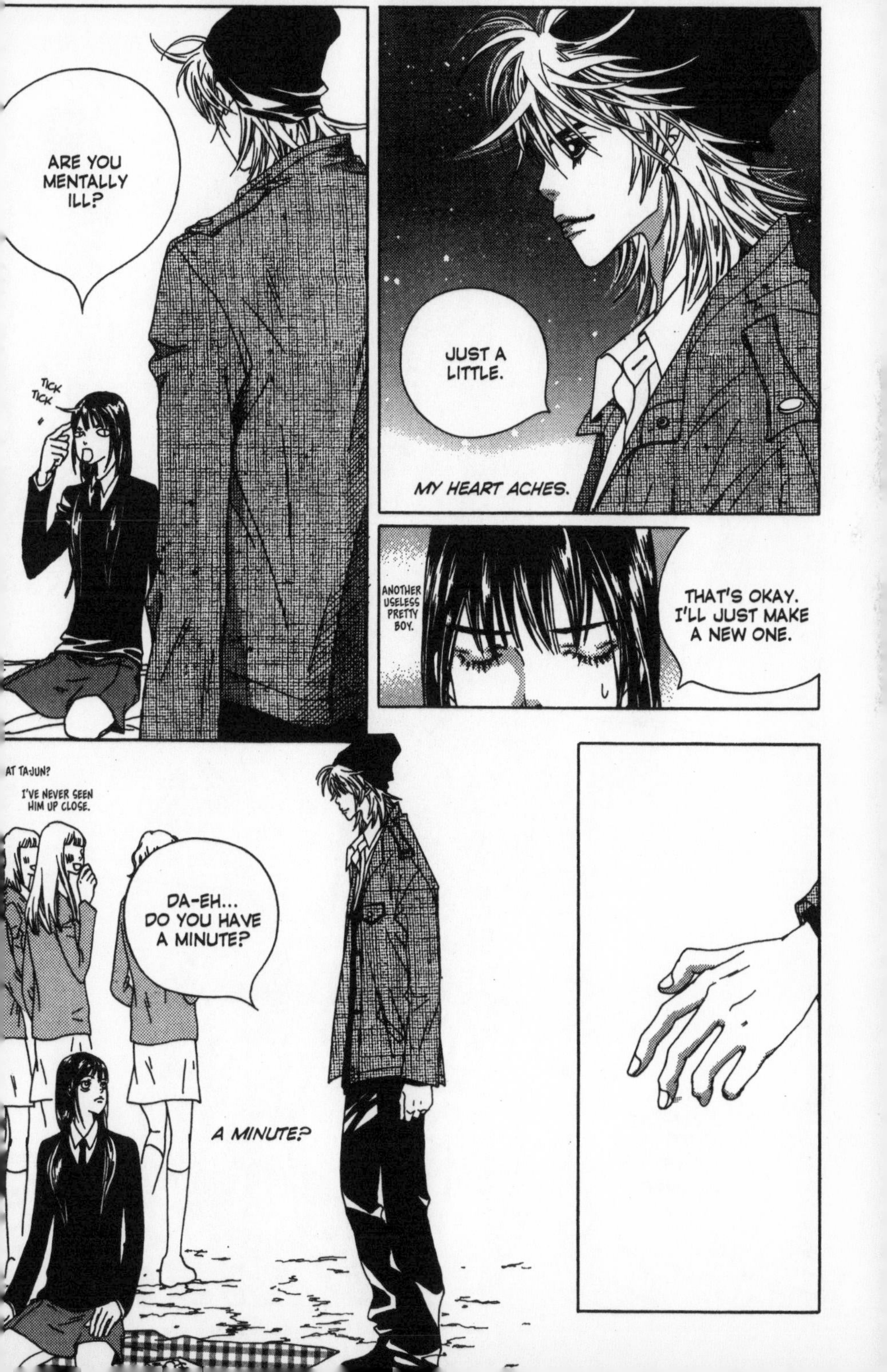
ARE YOU MENTALLY ILL?
TICK TICK
JUST A LITTLE.
MY HEART ACHES.
ANOTHER USELESS PRETTY BOY.
THAT'S OKAY. I'LL JUST MAKE A NEW ONE.
AT TA-JUN?
I'VE NEVER SEEN HIM UP CLOSE.
DA-EH... DO YOU HAVE A MINUTE?
A MINUTE?

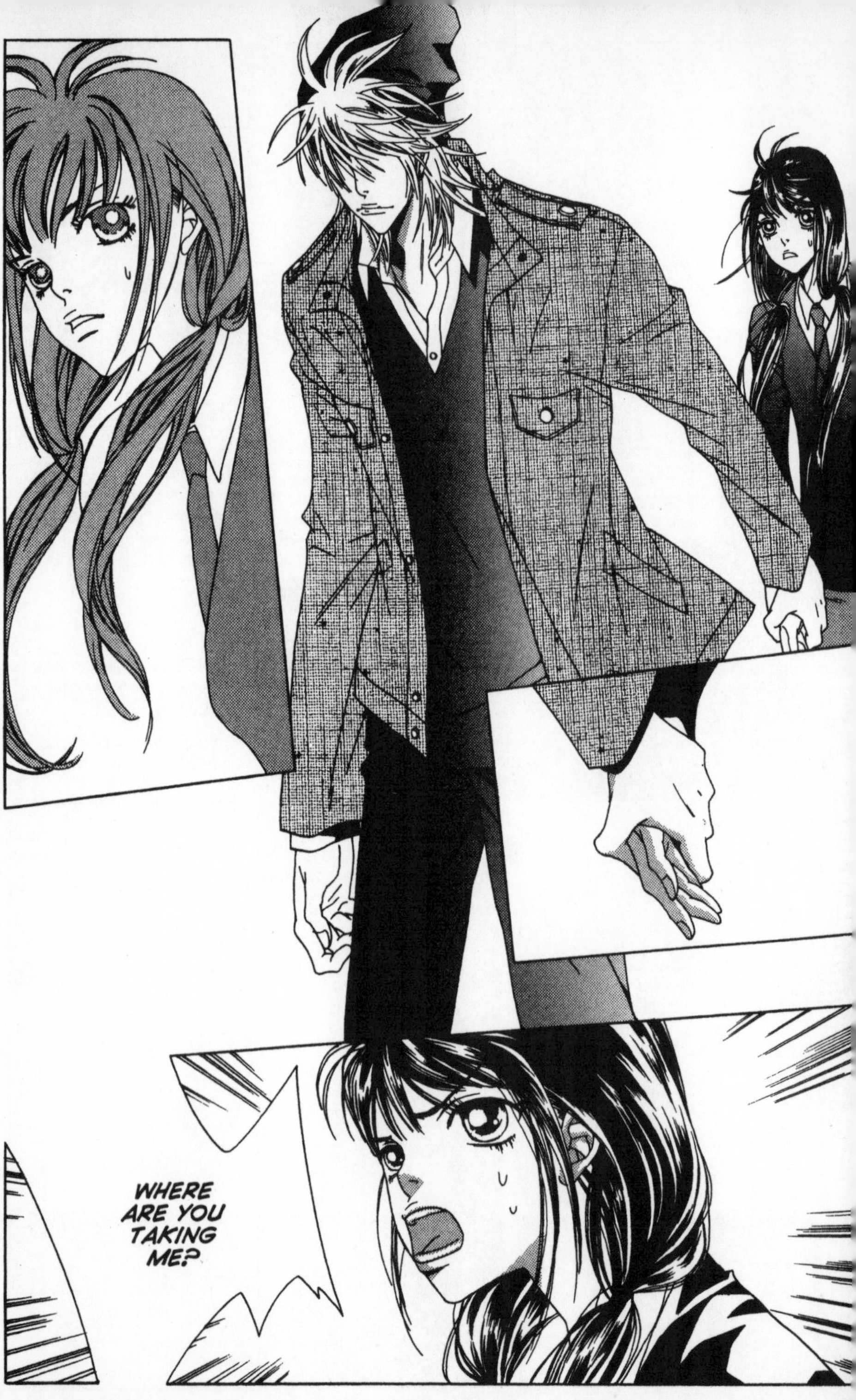
WHERE ARE YOU TAKING ME?

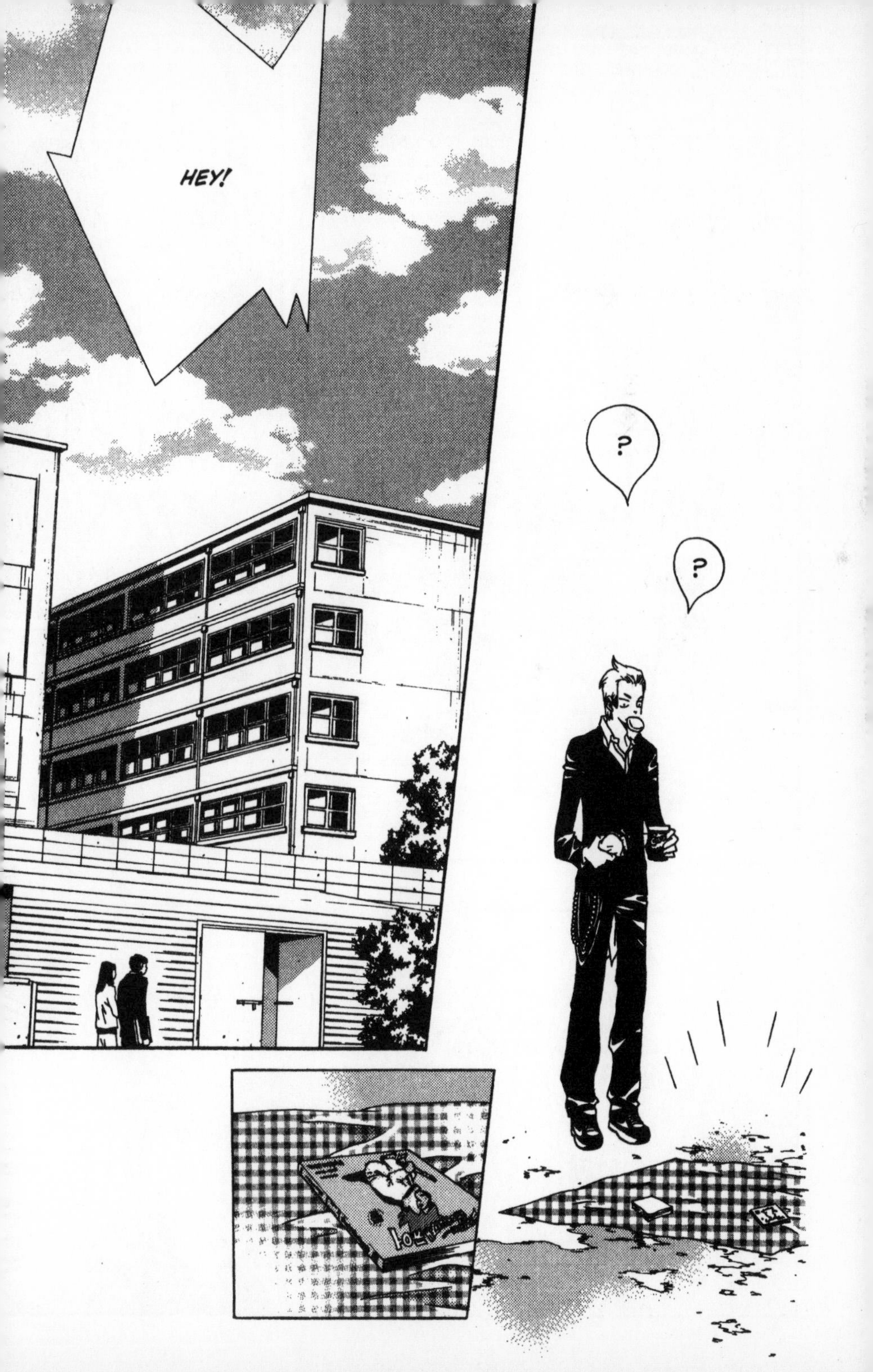
HEY!
?
?

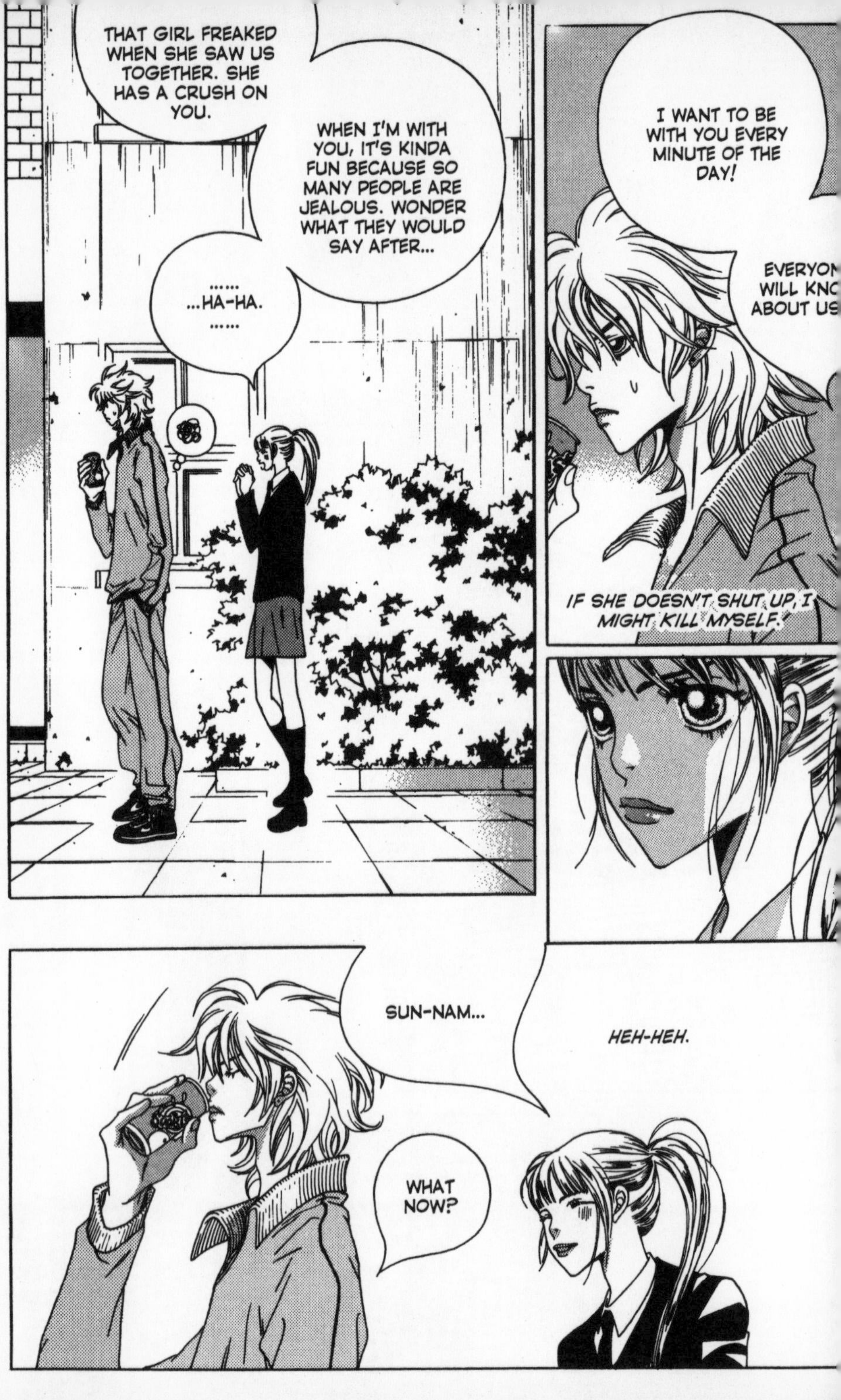
THAT GIRL FREAKED WHEN SHE SAW US TOGETHER. SHE HAS A CRUSH ON YOU.
WHEN I'M WITH YOU, IT'S KINDA FUN BECAUSE SO MANY PEOPLE ARE JEALOUS. WONDER WHAT THEY WOULD SAY AFTER...
....HA-HA. ......
I WANT TO BE WITH YOU EVERY MINUTE OF THE DAY!
EVERYON WILL KNO ABOUT US
IF SHE DOESN'T SHUT UP, I MIGHT KILL MYSELF.
SUN-NAM...
HEH-HEH.
WHAT NOW?

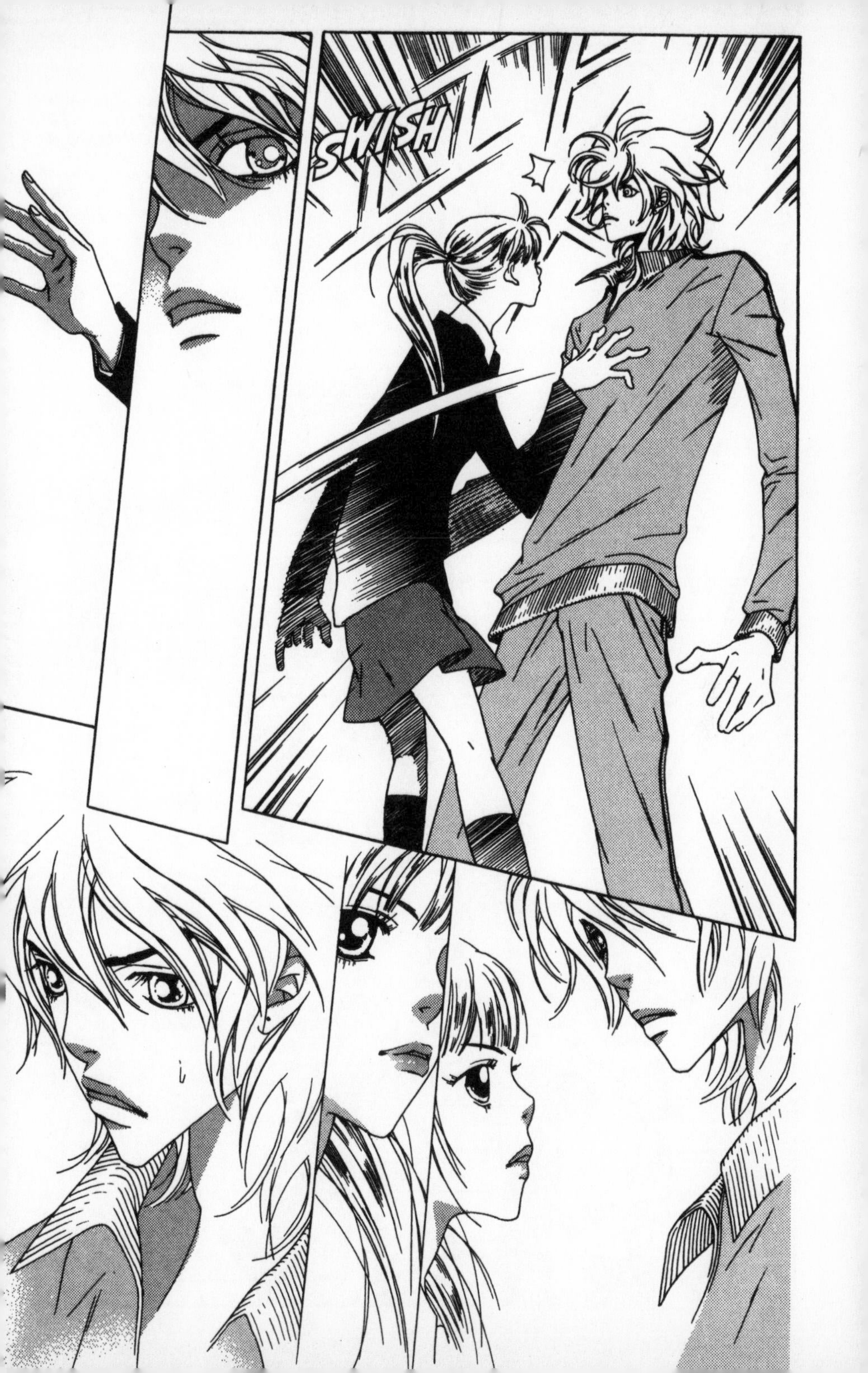
SWISH

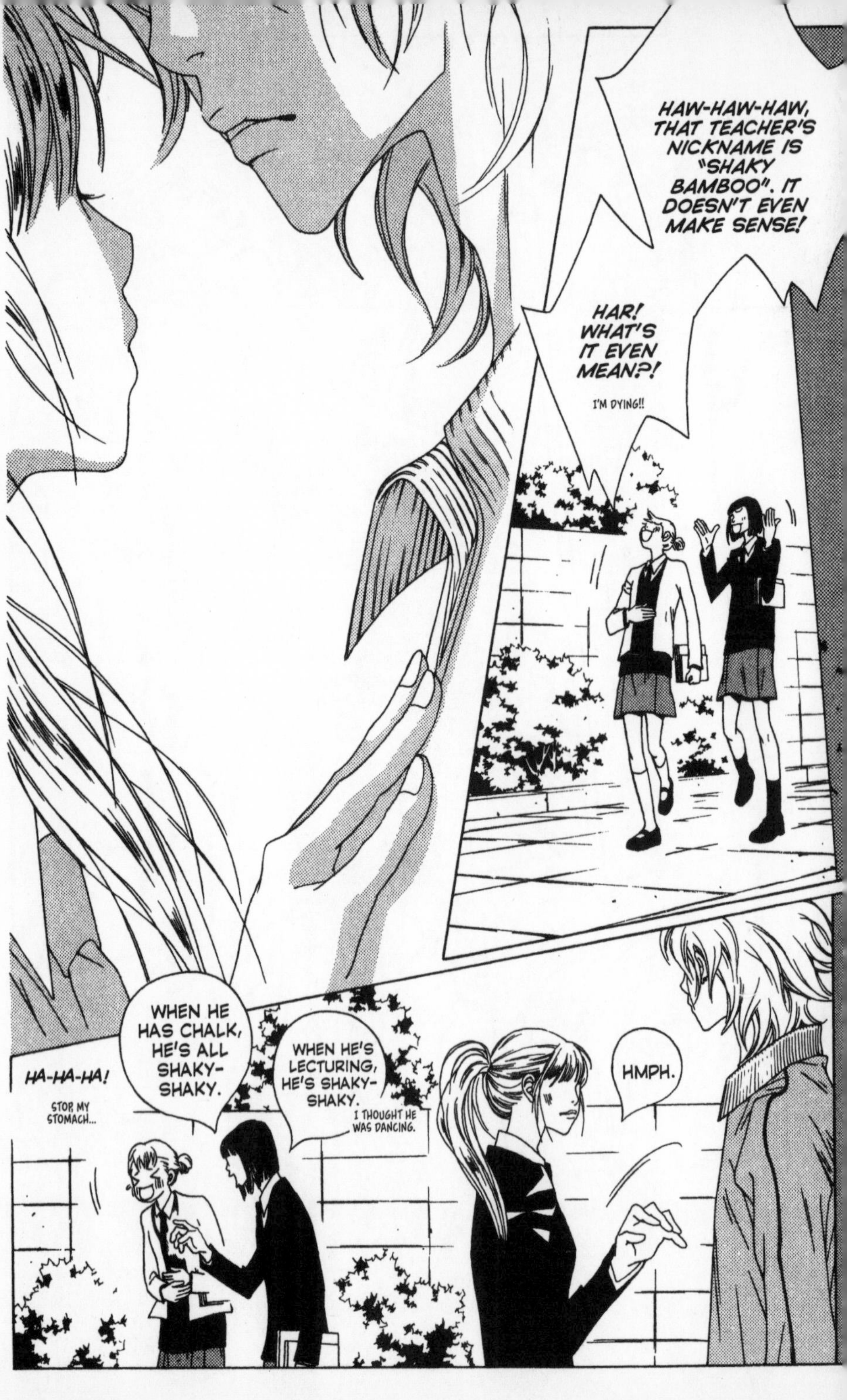
HAW-HAW-HAW, THAT TEACHER'S NICKNAME IS "SHAKY BAMBOO". IT DOESN'T EVEN MAKE SENSE!
HAR! WHAT'S IT EVEN MEAN?!
I'M DYING!!
HA-HA-HA!
STOP MY STOMACH...
WHEN HE HAS CHALK, HE'S ALL SHAKY-SHAKY.
WHEN HE'S LECTURING, HE'S SHAKY-SHAKY.
I THOUGHT HE WAS DANCING.
HMPH.

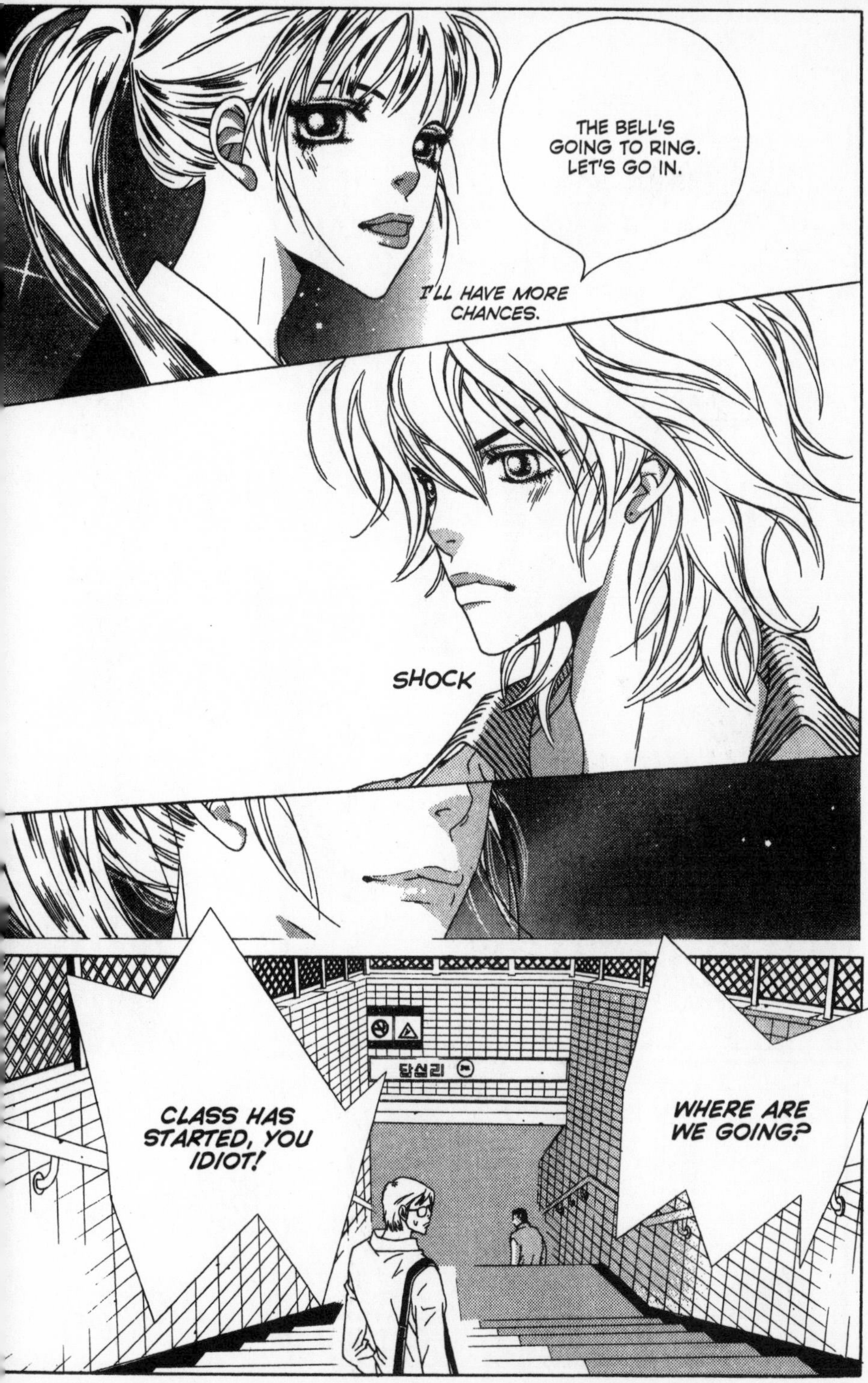
THE BELL'S GOING TO RING. LET'S GO IN.
I'LL HAVE MORE CHANCES.
SHOCK
답십리
CLASS HAS STARTED, YOU IDIOT!
WHERE ARE WE GOING?

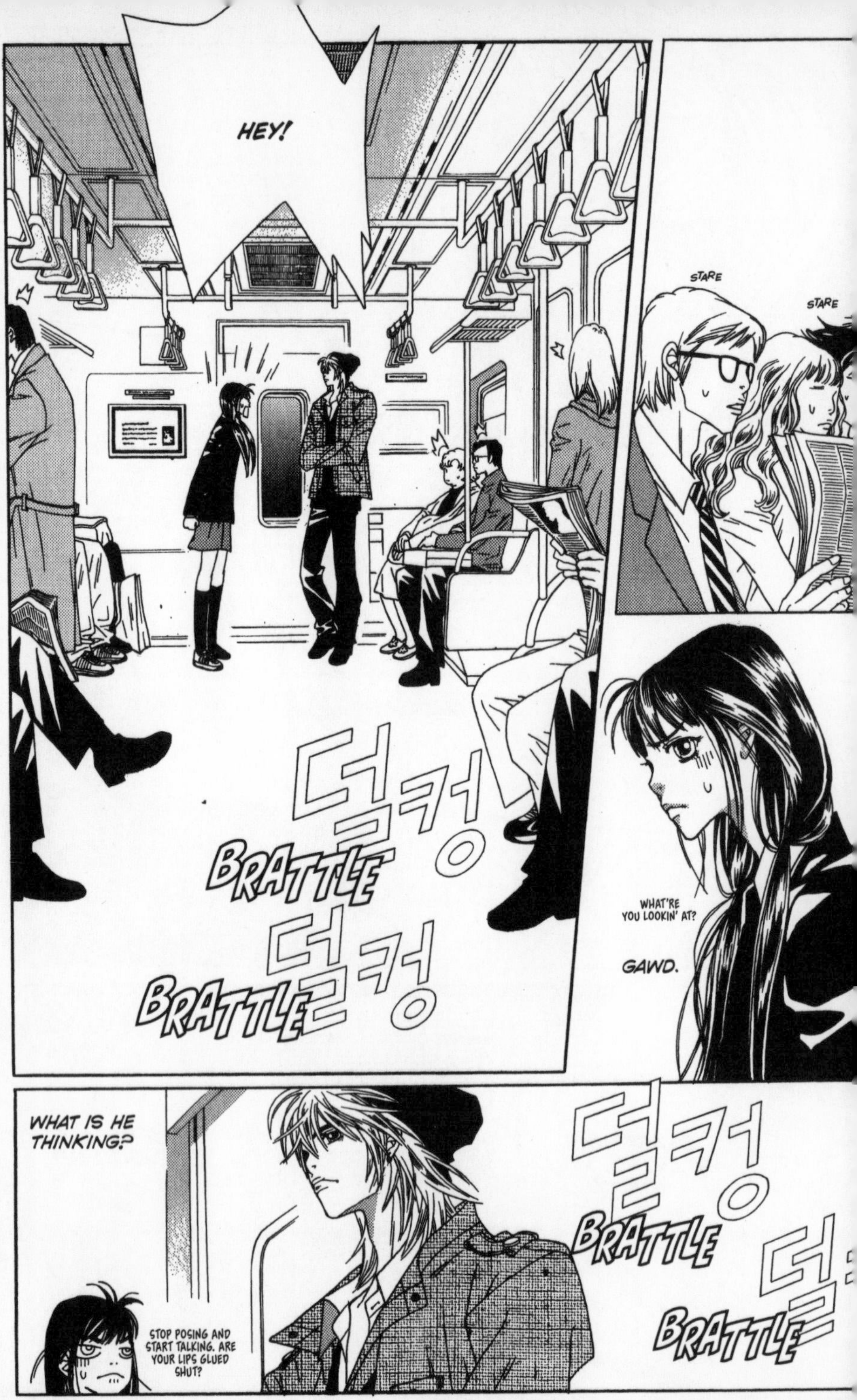
HEY!
덜컹
BRATTLE
덜컹
BRATTLE
STARE
STARE
WHAT'RE YOU LOOKIN' AT?
GAWD.
WHAT IS HE THINKING?
STOP POSING AND START TALKING. ARE YOUR LIPS GLUED SHUT?
덜컹
BRATTLE
덜
BRATTLE

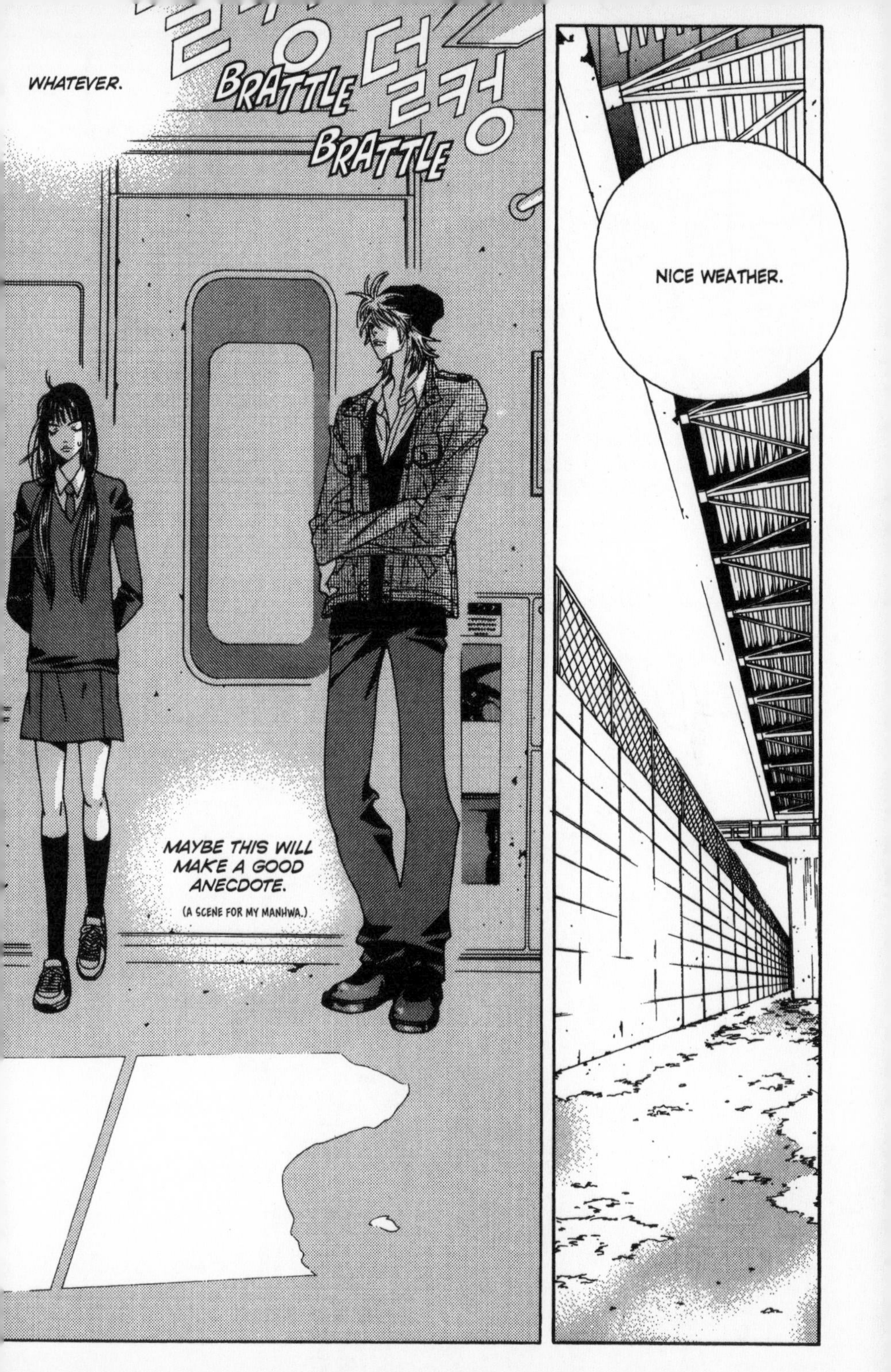
WHATEVER.
BRATTLE 덜컹
BRATTLE
MAYBE THIS WILL MAKE A GOOD ANECDOTE.
(A SCENE FOR MY MANHWA.)
NICE WEATHER.

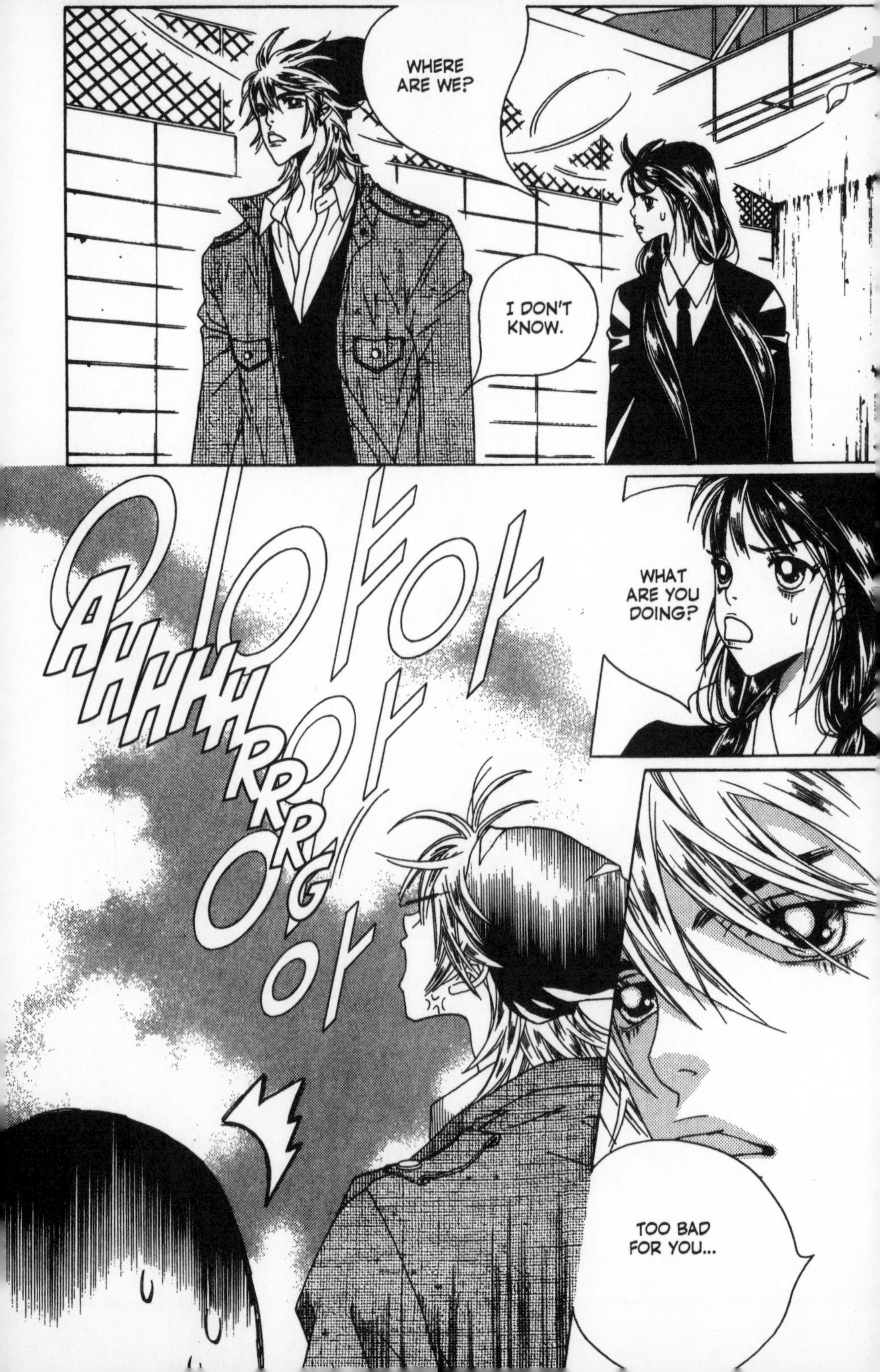
WHERE ARE WE?
I DON'T KNOW.
AHHHHRRRG
WHAT ARE YOU DOING?
TOO BAD FOR YOU...

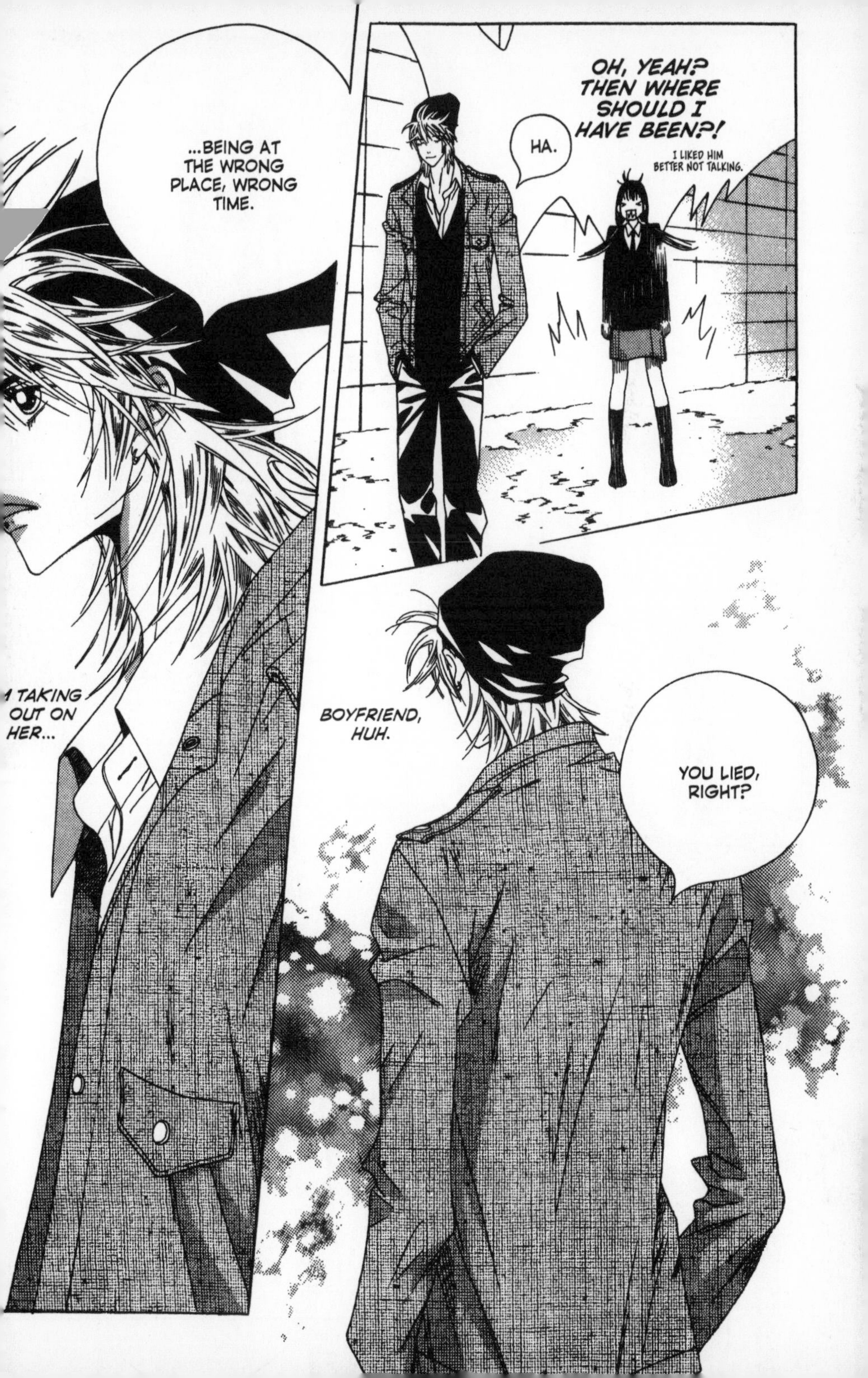
...BEING AT THE WRONG PLACE, WRONG TIME.
TAKING OUT ON HER...
OH, YEAH? THEN WHERE SHOULD I HAVE BEEN?!
HA.
I LIKED HIM BETTER NOT TALKING.
BOYFRIEND, HUH.
YOU LIED, RIGHT?

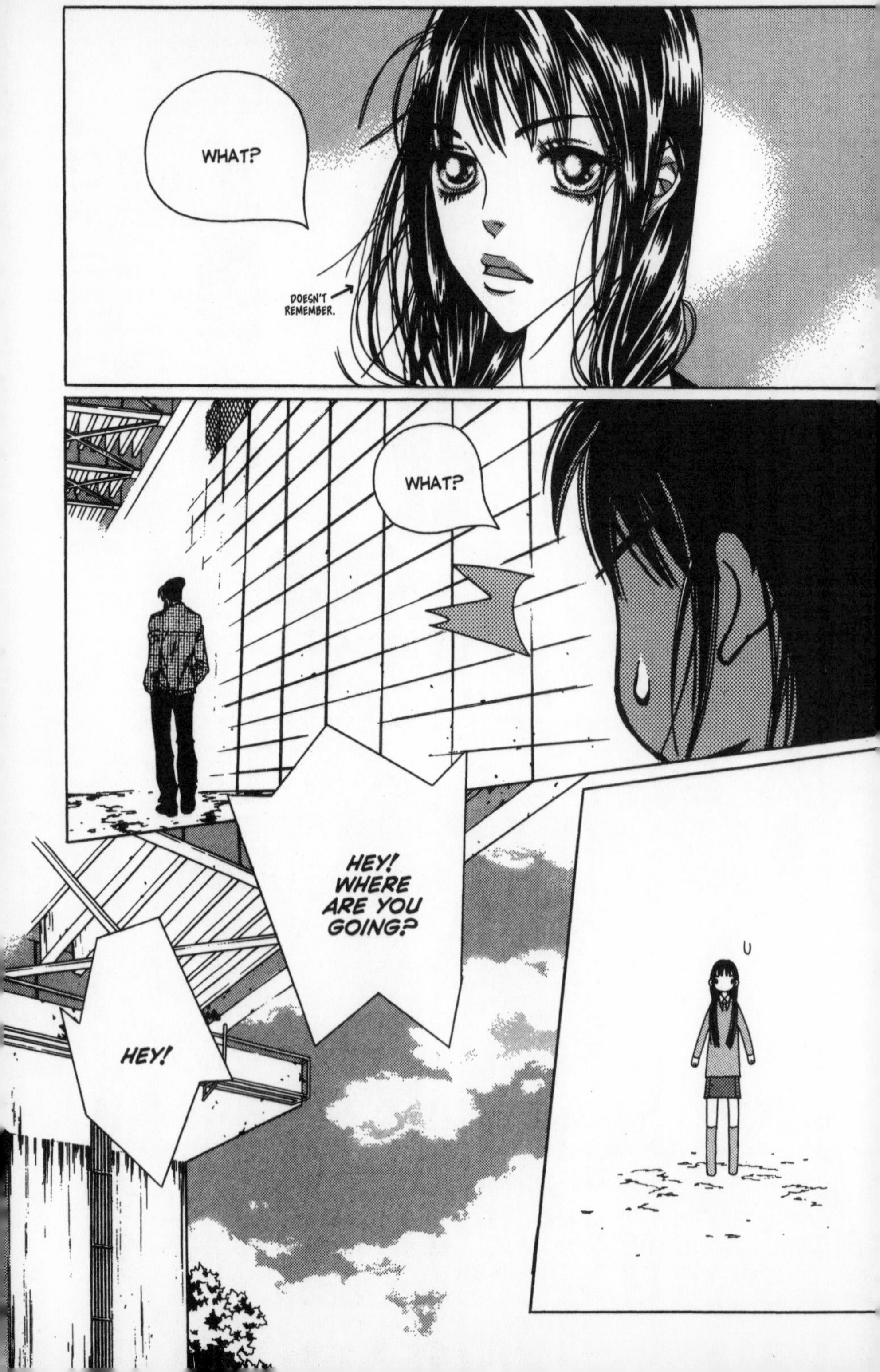
WHAT?
DOESN'T REMEMBER.
WHAT?
HEY! WHERE ARE YOU GOING?
HEY!

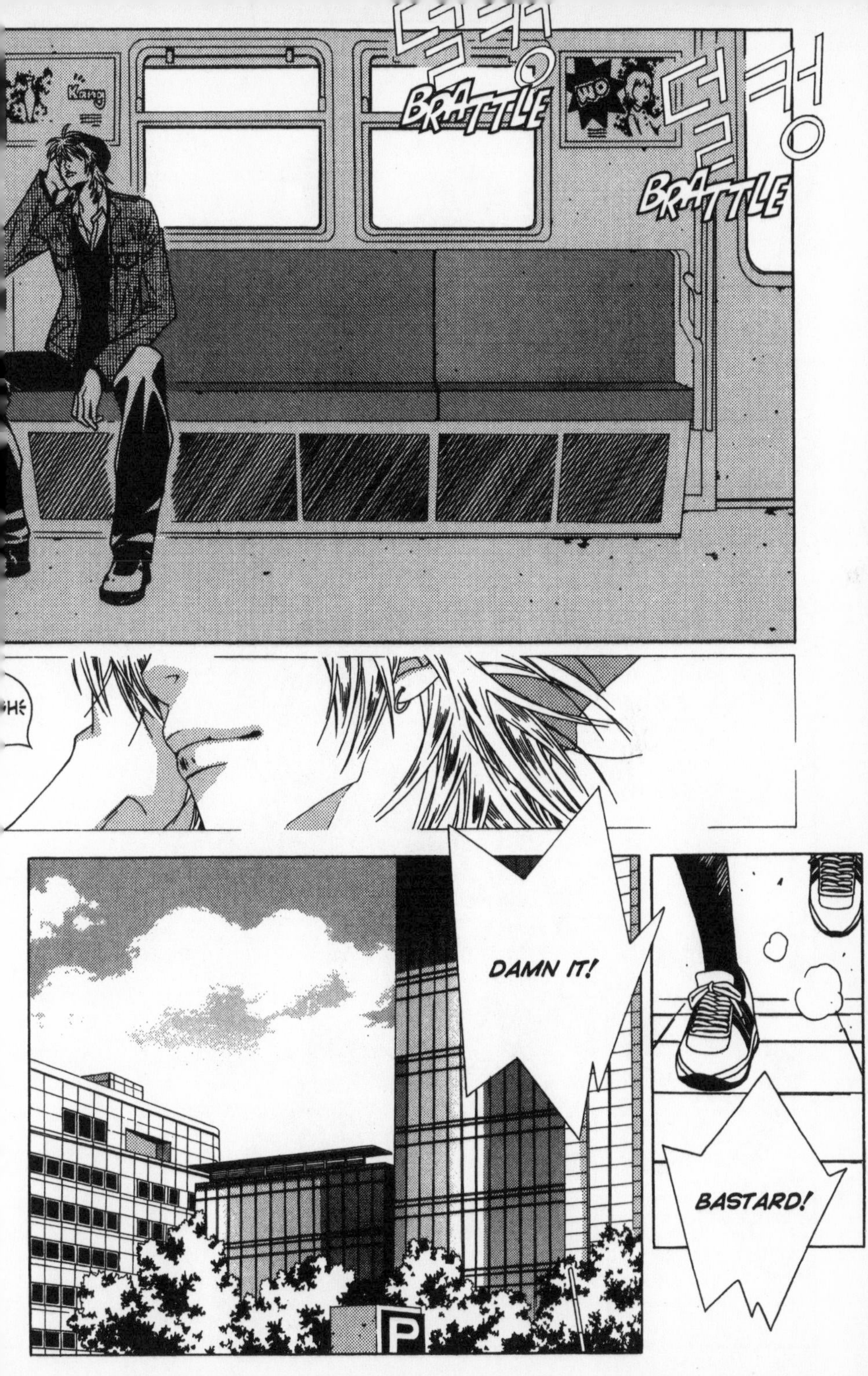
덜컹
BRATTLE
덜컹
BRATTLE
DAMN IT!
BASTARD!

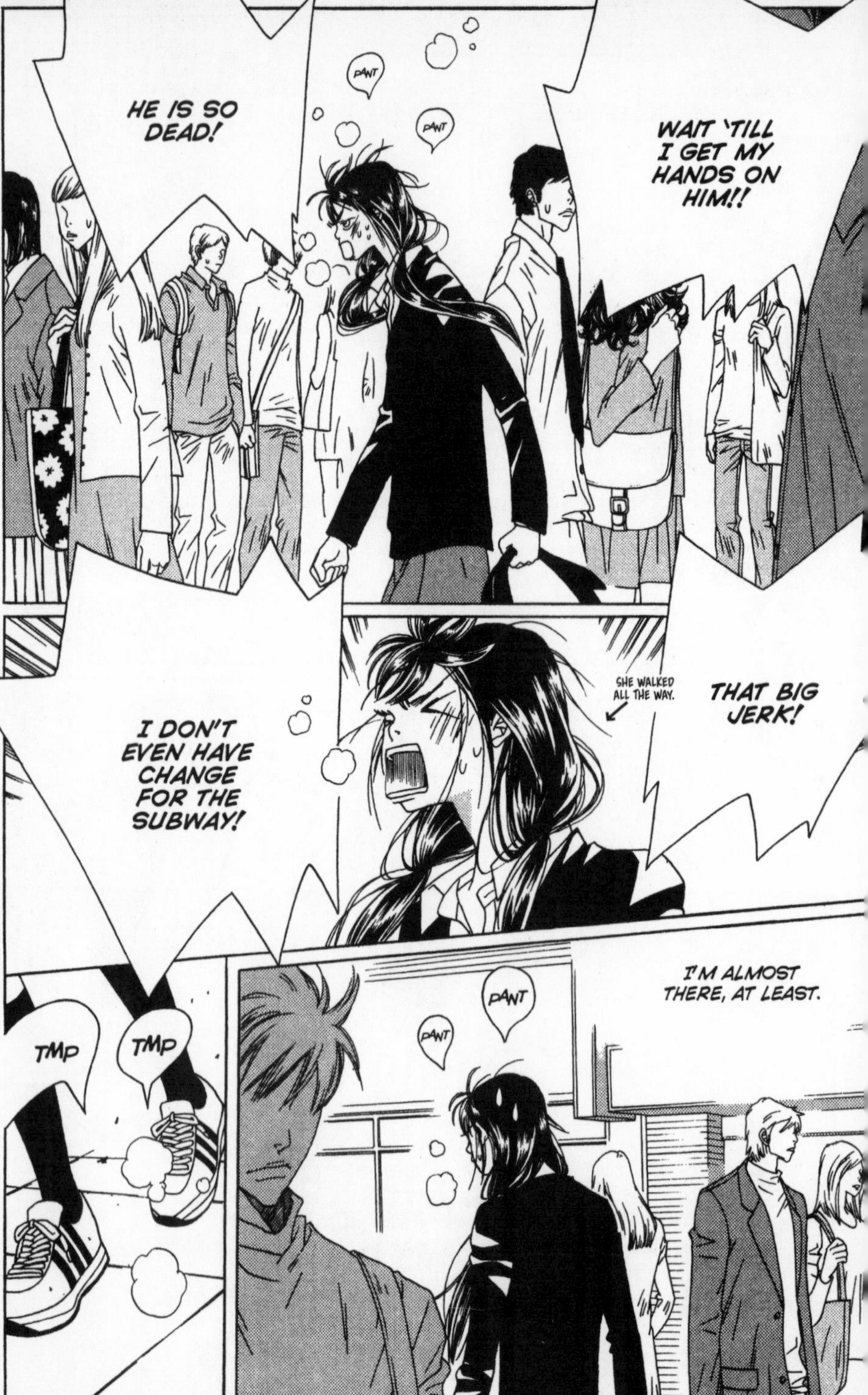
HE IS SO DEAD!
PANT
PANT
WAIT 'TILL I GET MY HANDS ON HIM!!
I DON'T EVEN HAVE CHANGE FOR THE SUBWAY!
SHE WALKED ALL THE WAY.
THAT BIG JERK!
TMP
TMP
PANT
PANT
I'M ALMOST THERE, AT LEAST.

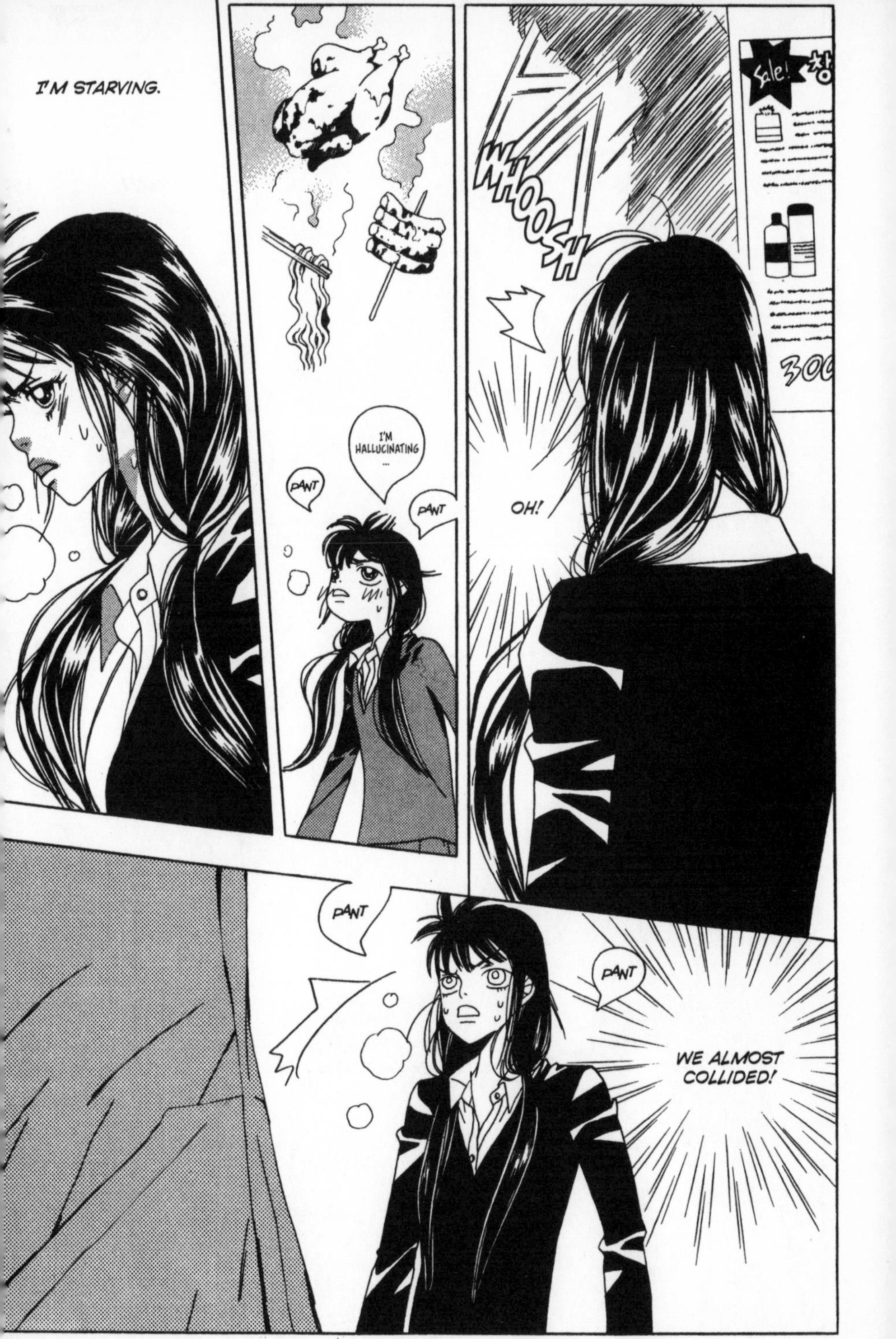
I'M STARVING.
PANT
I'M HALLUCINATING ...
PANT
WHOOSH
Sale!
OH!
PANT
PANT
WE ALMOST COLLIDED!

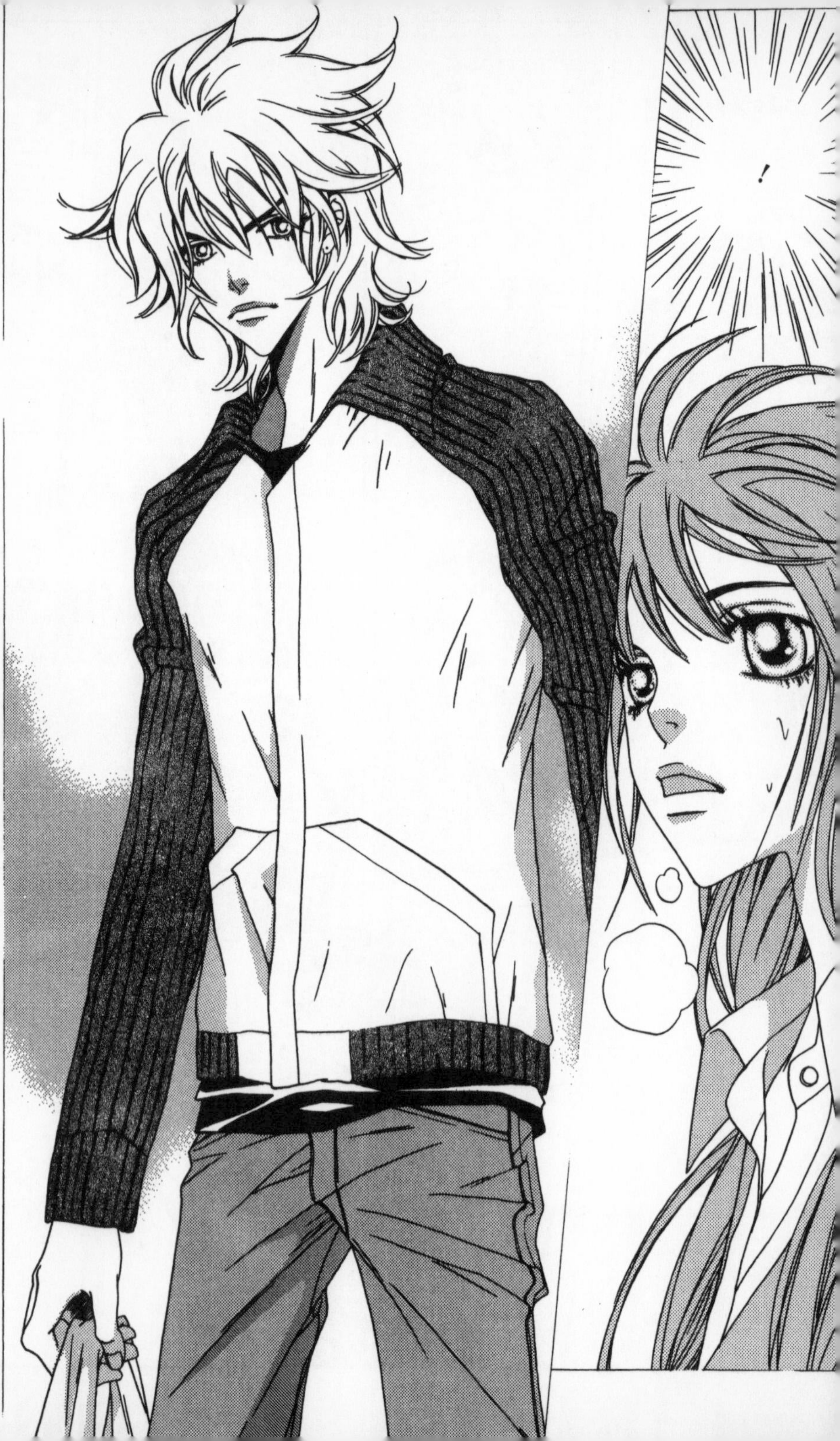
!

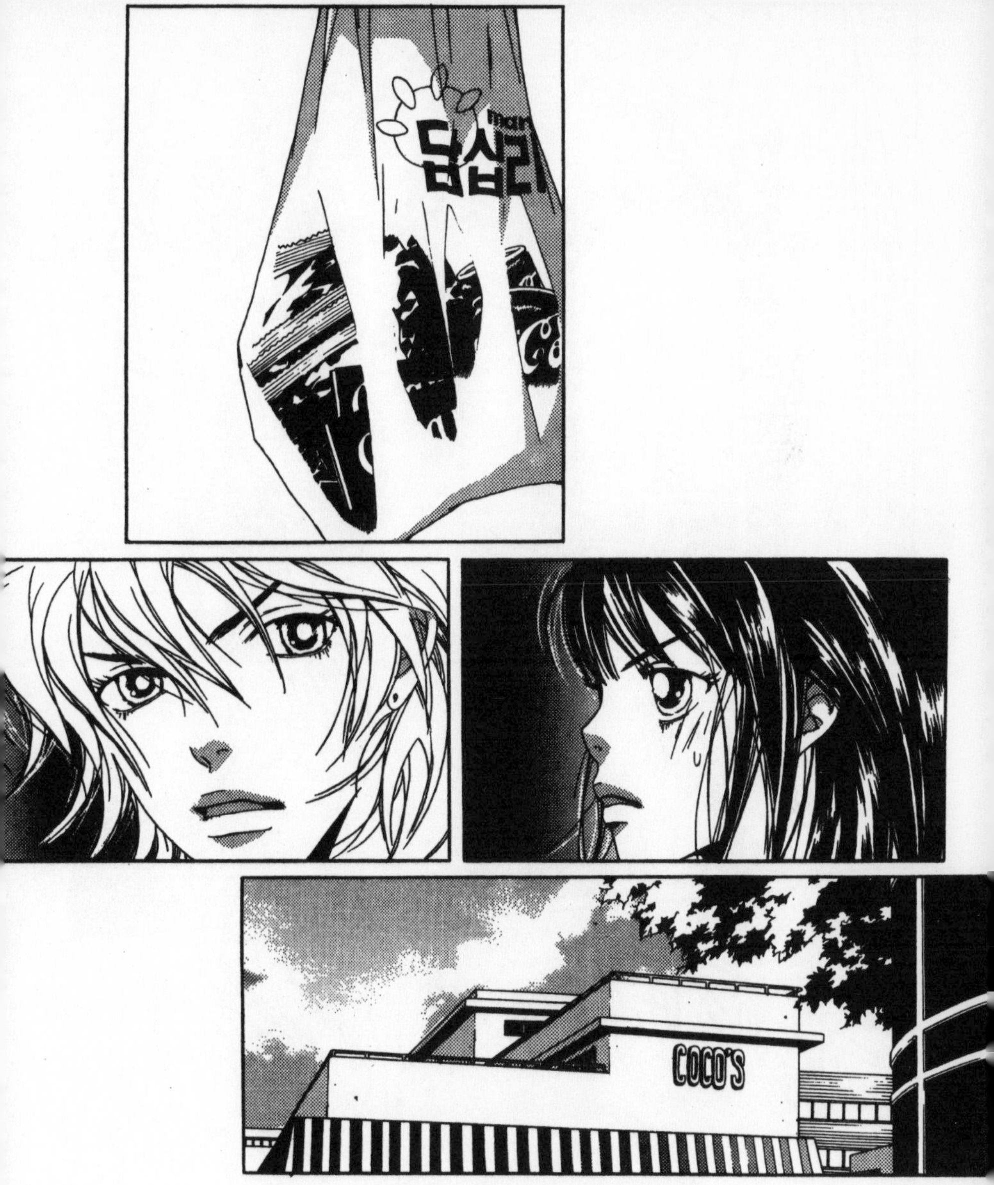
답십리
COCO'S

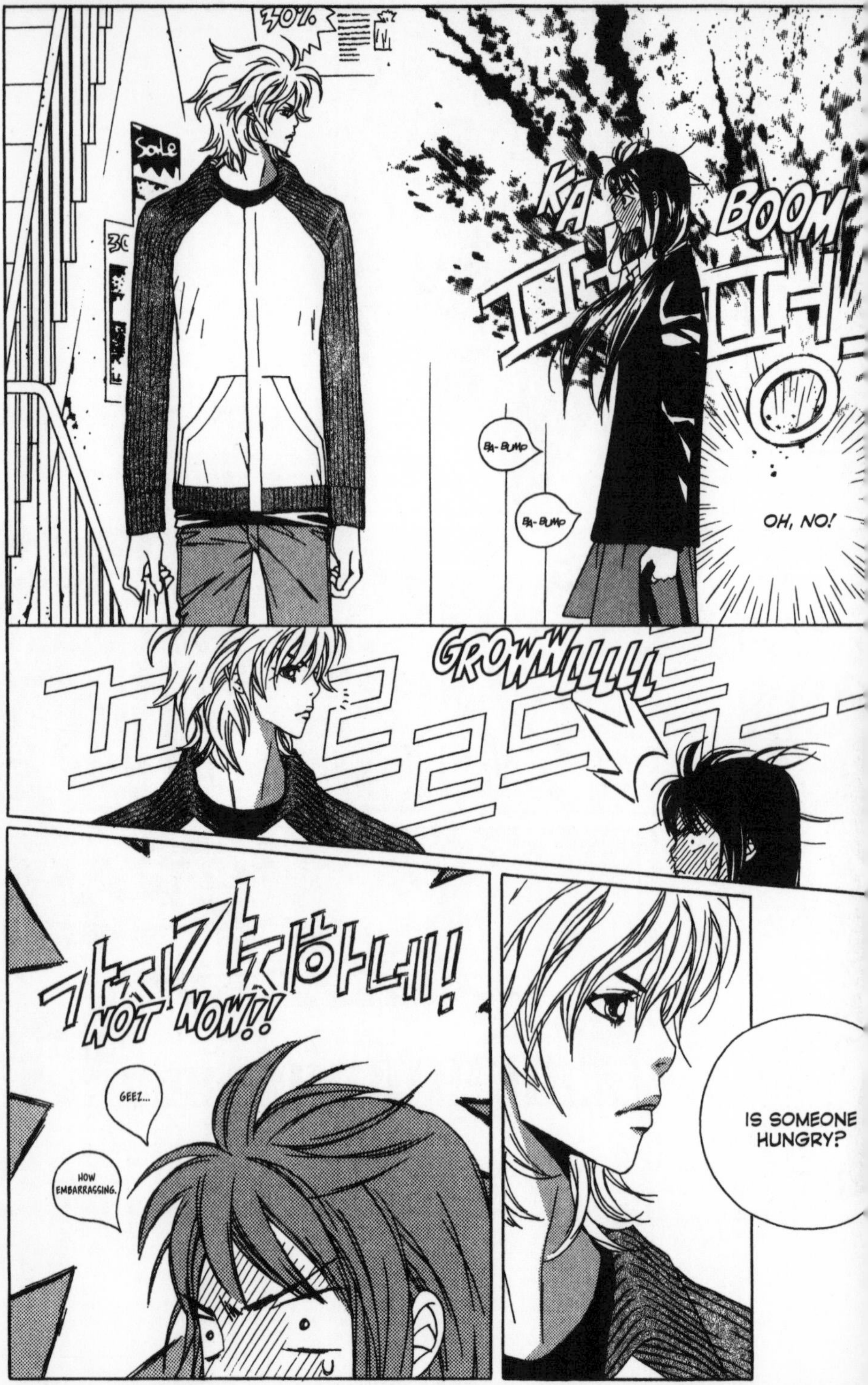
KA BOOM
BA-BUMP
BA-BUMP
OH, NO!
GROWWLLLLL
가지가지하네!
NOT NOW!?!
GEEZ...
HOW EMBARRASSING.
IS SOMEONE HUNGRY?

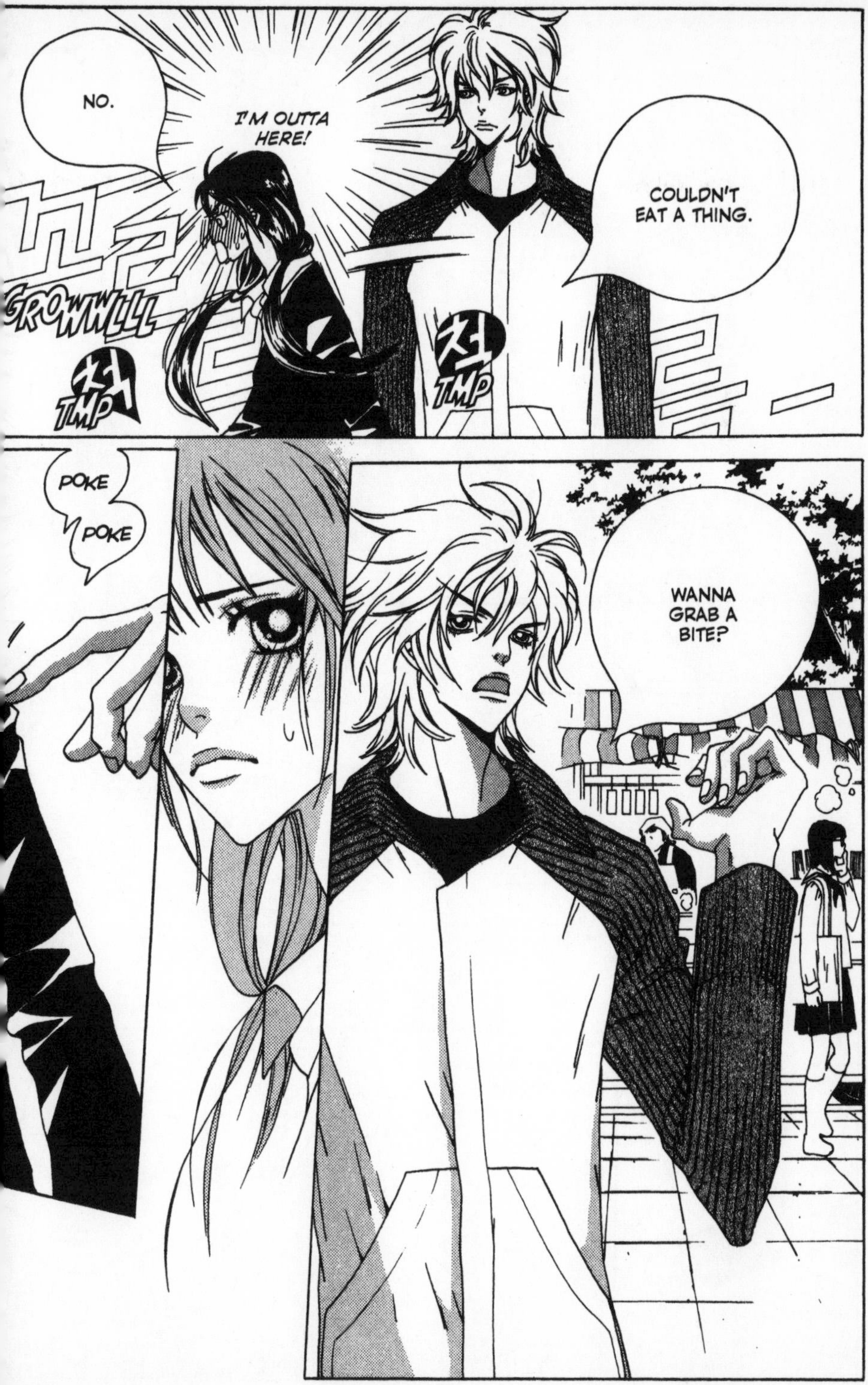
NO.
I'M OUTTA HERE!
GROWWLLL
TMP
TMP
COULDN'T EAT A THING.
POKE POKE
WANNA GRAB A BITE?

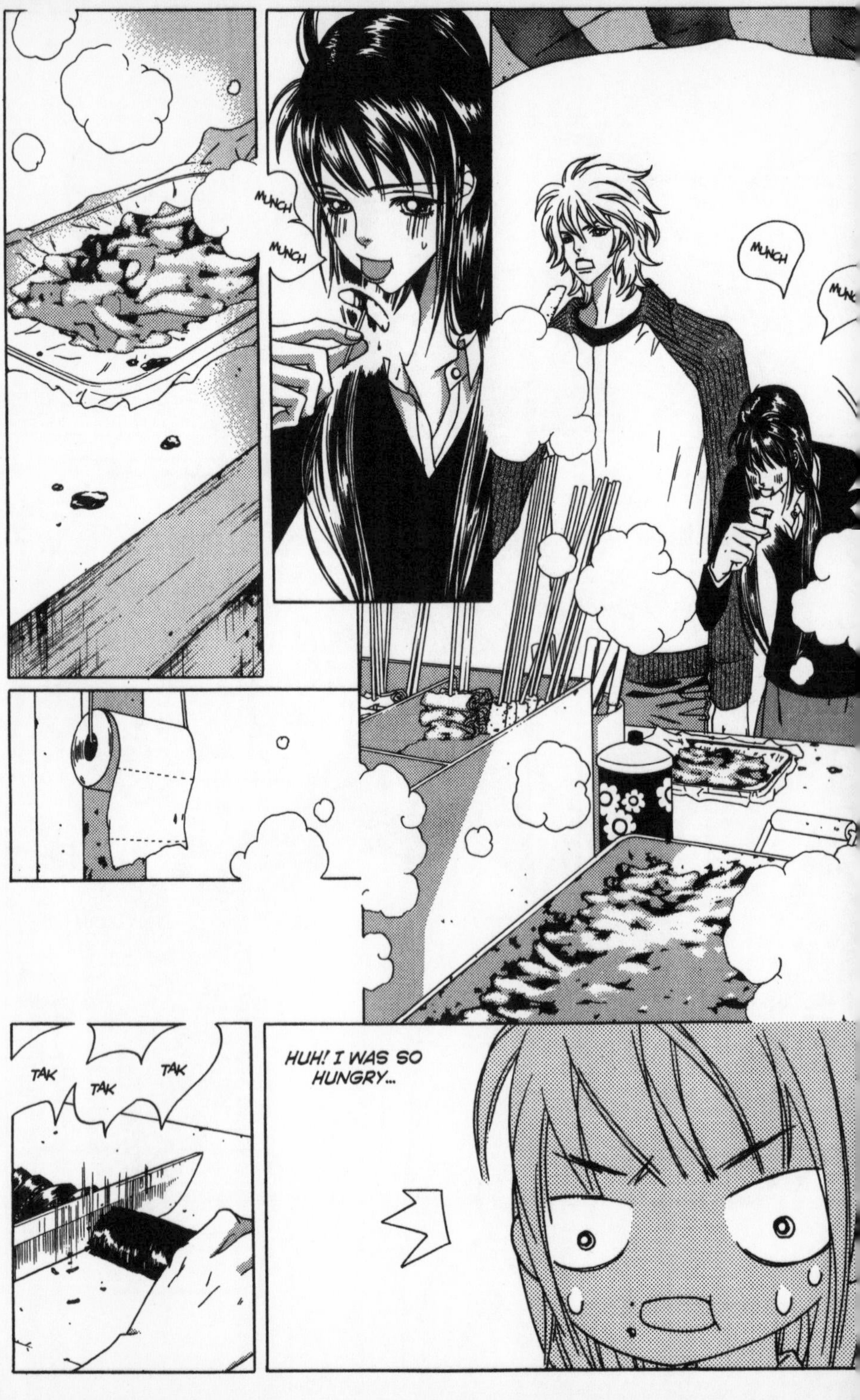
MUNCH
MUNCH
MUNCH
TAK
TAK
TAK
HUH! I WAS SO HUNGRY...

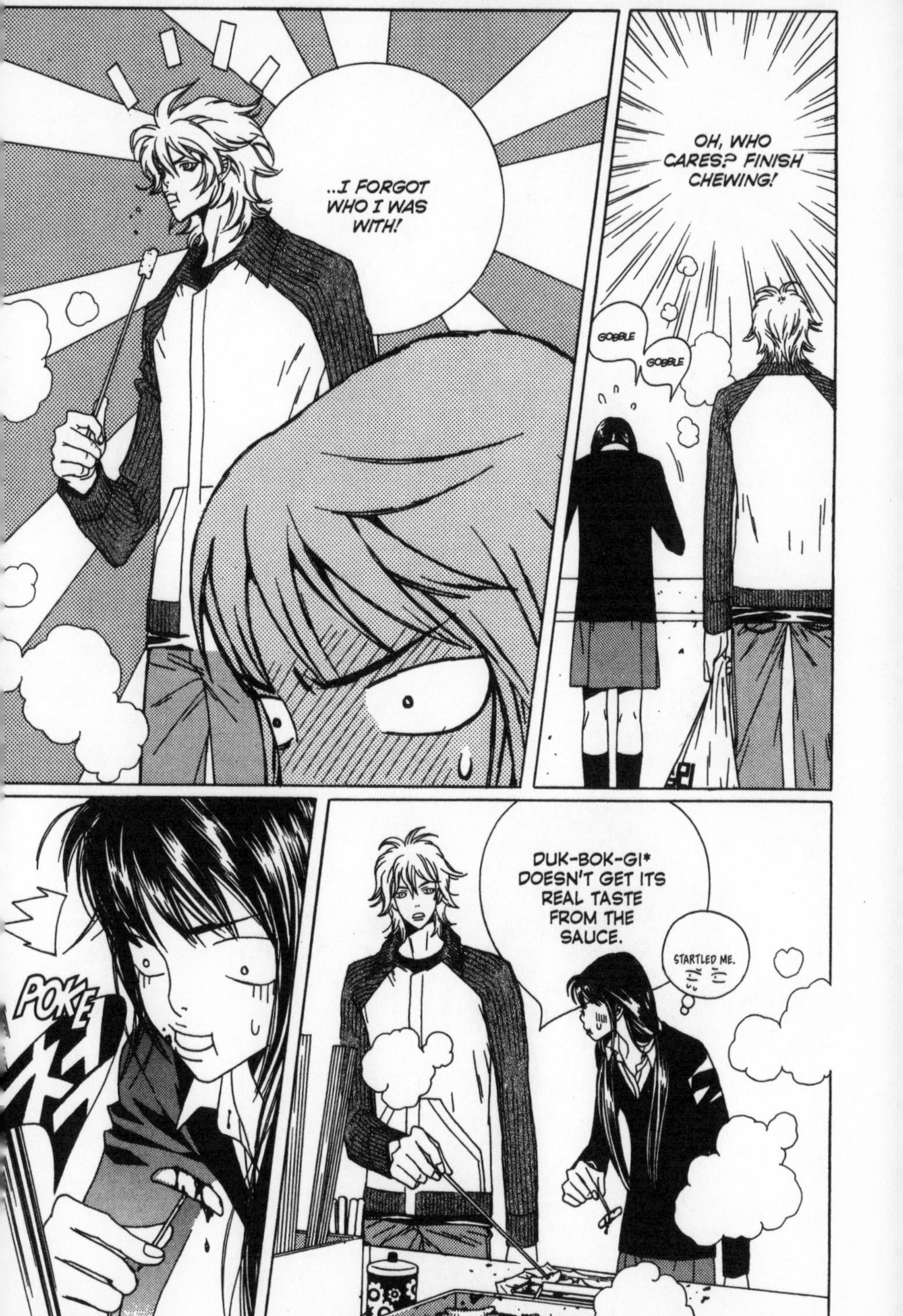
..I FORGOT WHO I WAS WITH!
OH, WHO CARES? FINISH CHEWING!
GOBBLE
GOBBLE
POKE
DUK-BOK-GI* DOESN'T GET ITS REAL TASTE FROM THE SAUCE.
STARTLED ME.

*DUK-BOK-GI : RICE CAKES COOKED IN SPICY SAUCE.

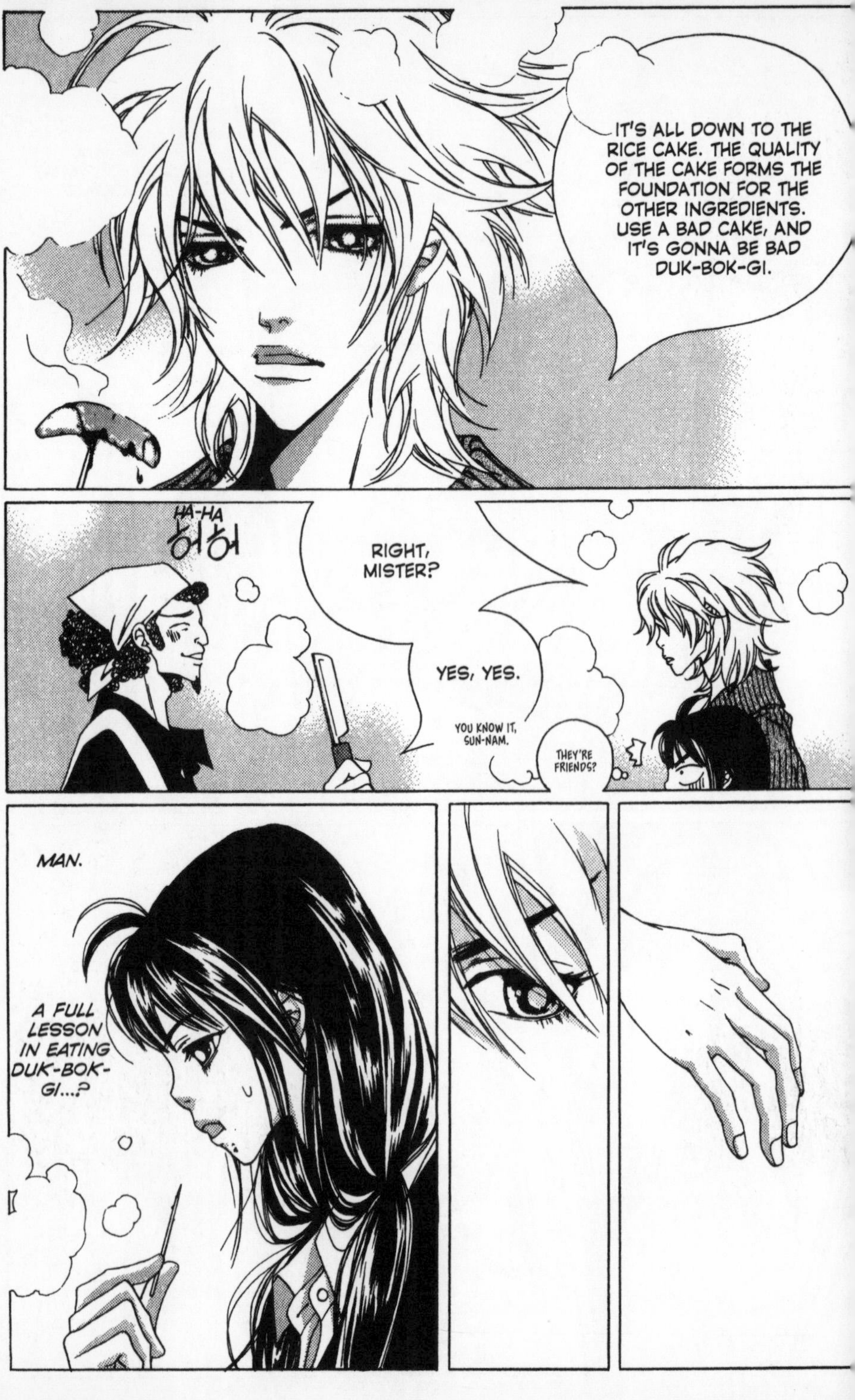
IT'S ALL DOWN TO THE RICE CAKE. THE QUALITY OF THE CAKE FORMS THE FOUNDATION FOR THE OTHER INGREDIENTS. USE A BAD CAKE, AND IT'S GONNA BE BAD DUK-BOK-GI.
HA-HA
허허
RIGHT, MISTER?
YES, YES.
YOU KNOW IT, SUN-NAM.
THEY'RE FRIENDS?
MAN.
A FULL LESSON IN EATING DUK-BOK-GI...?

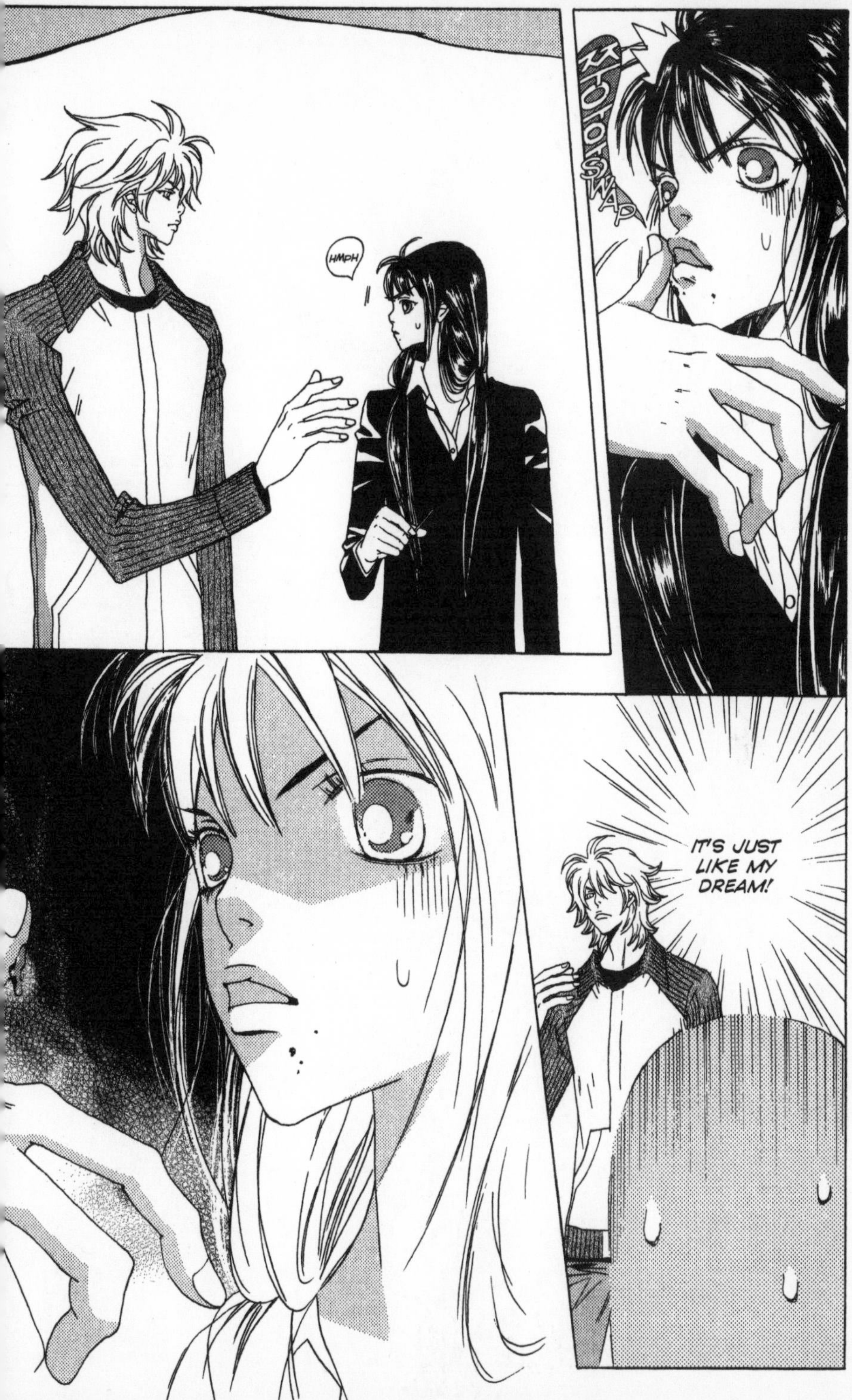
HMPH
SWAP
IT'S JUST LIKE MY DREAM!

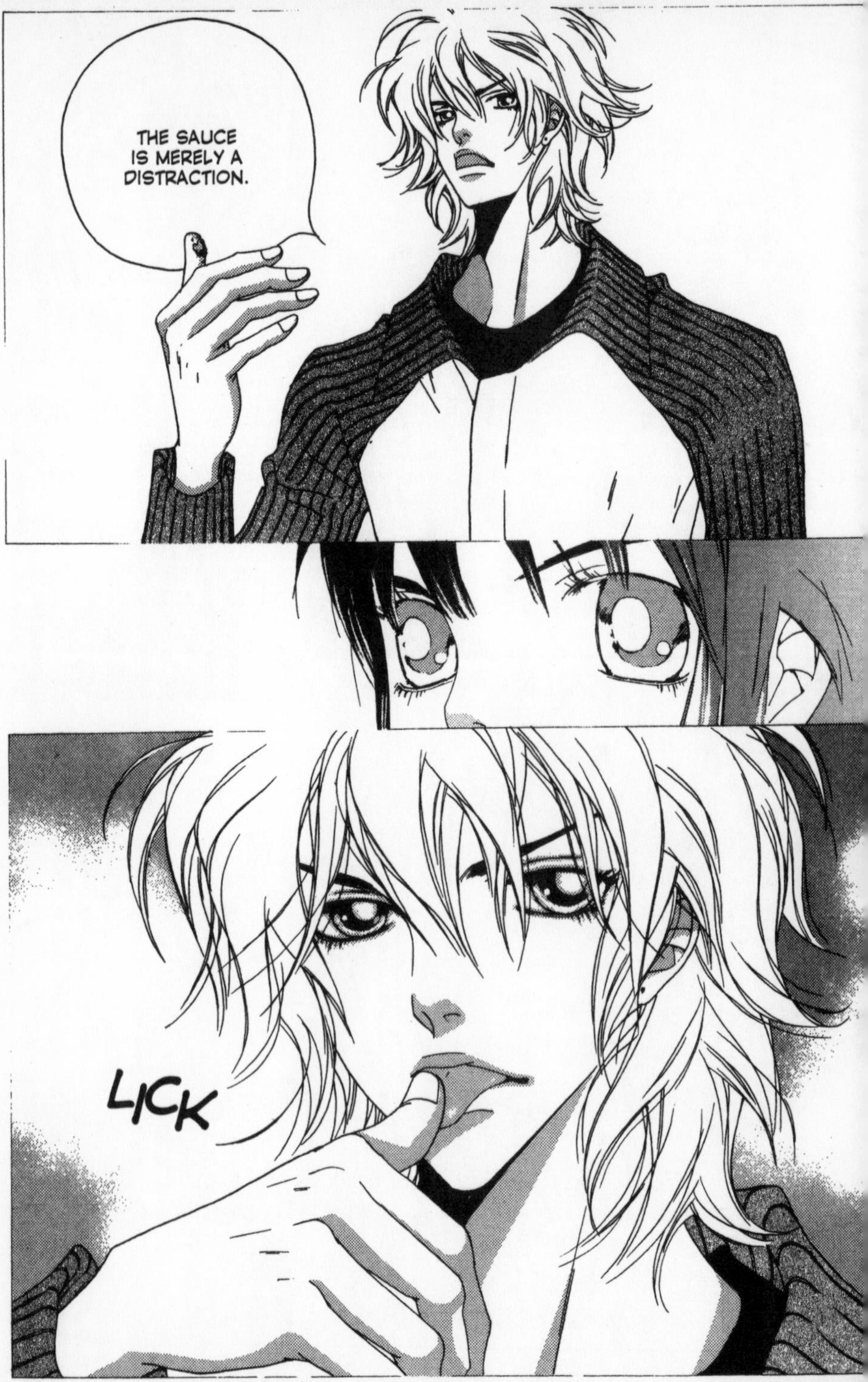
THE SAUCE IS MERELY A DISTRACTION.
LICK

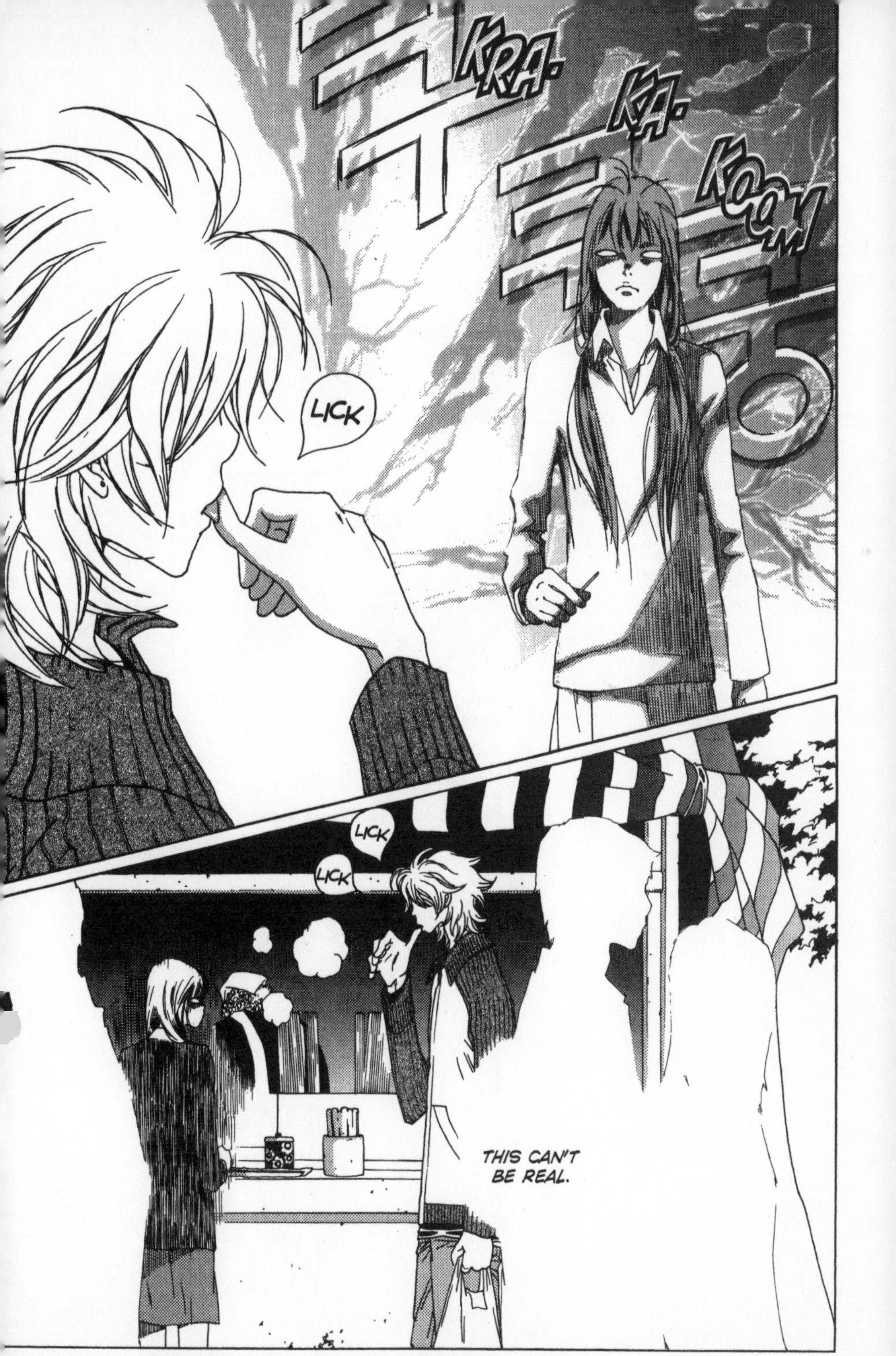
KRA-
KA-
KOOM!
LICK
LICK
LICK
THIS CAN'T BE REAL.

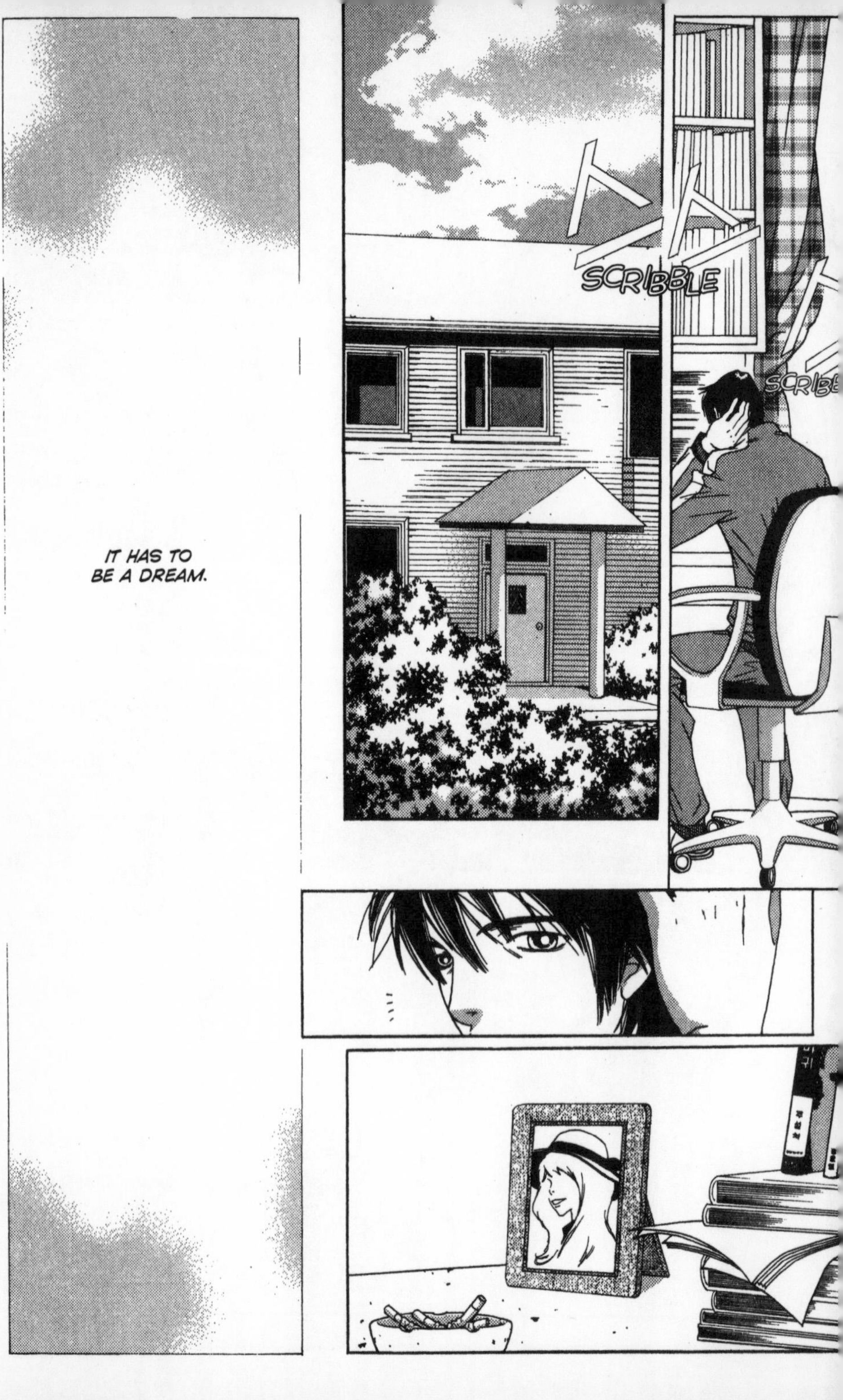
IT HAS TO
BE A DREAM.
SCRIBBLE

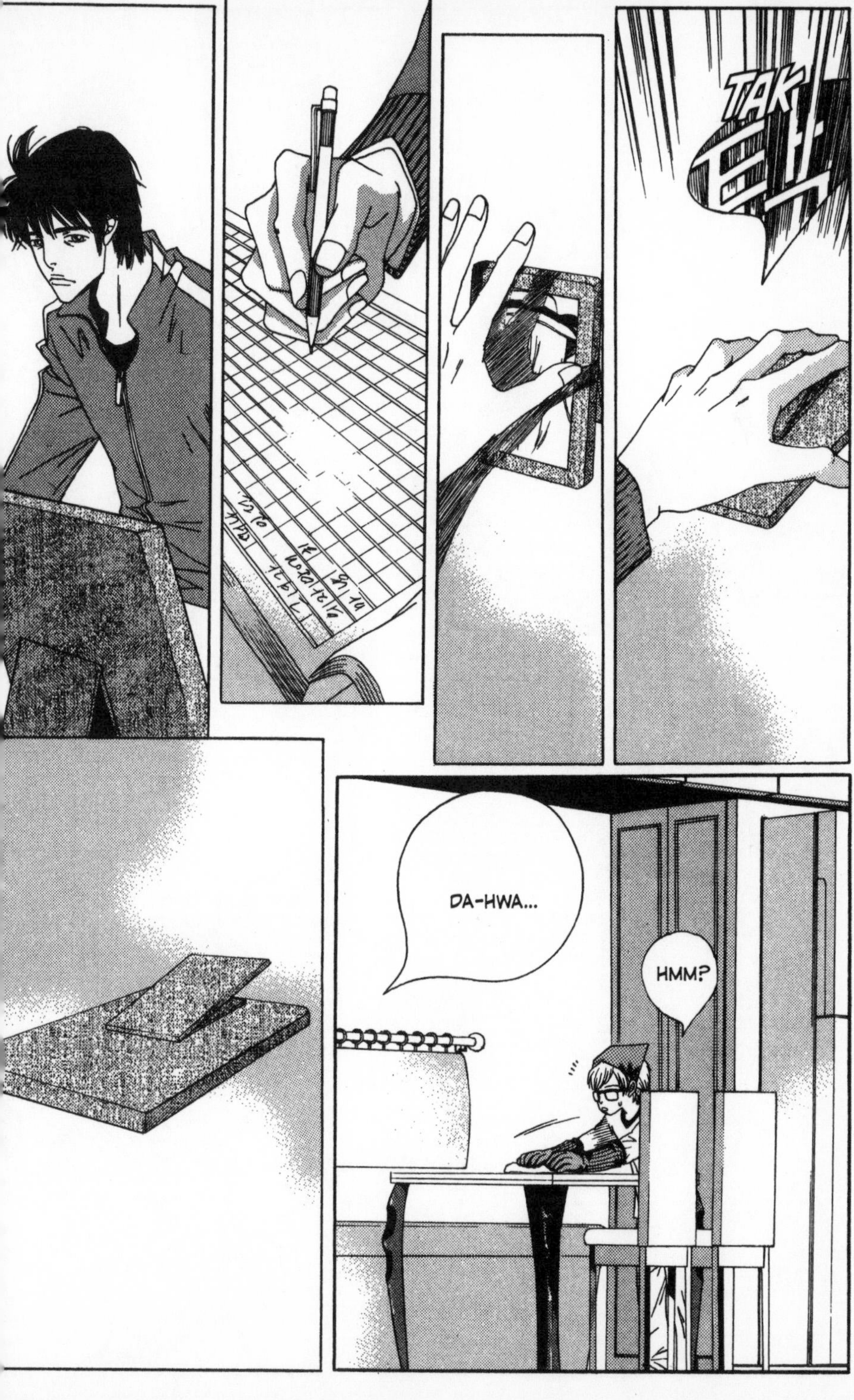
TAK
DA-HWA...
HMM?

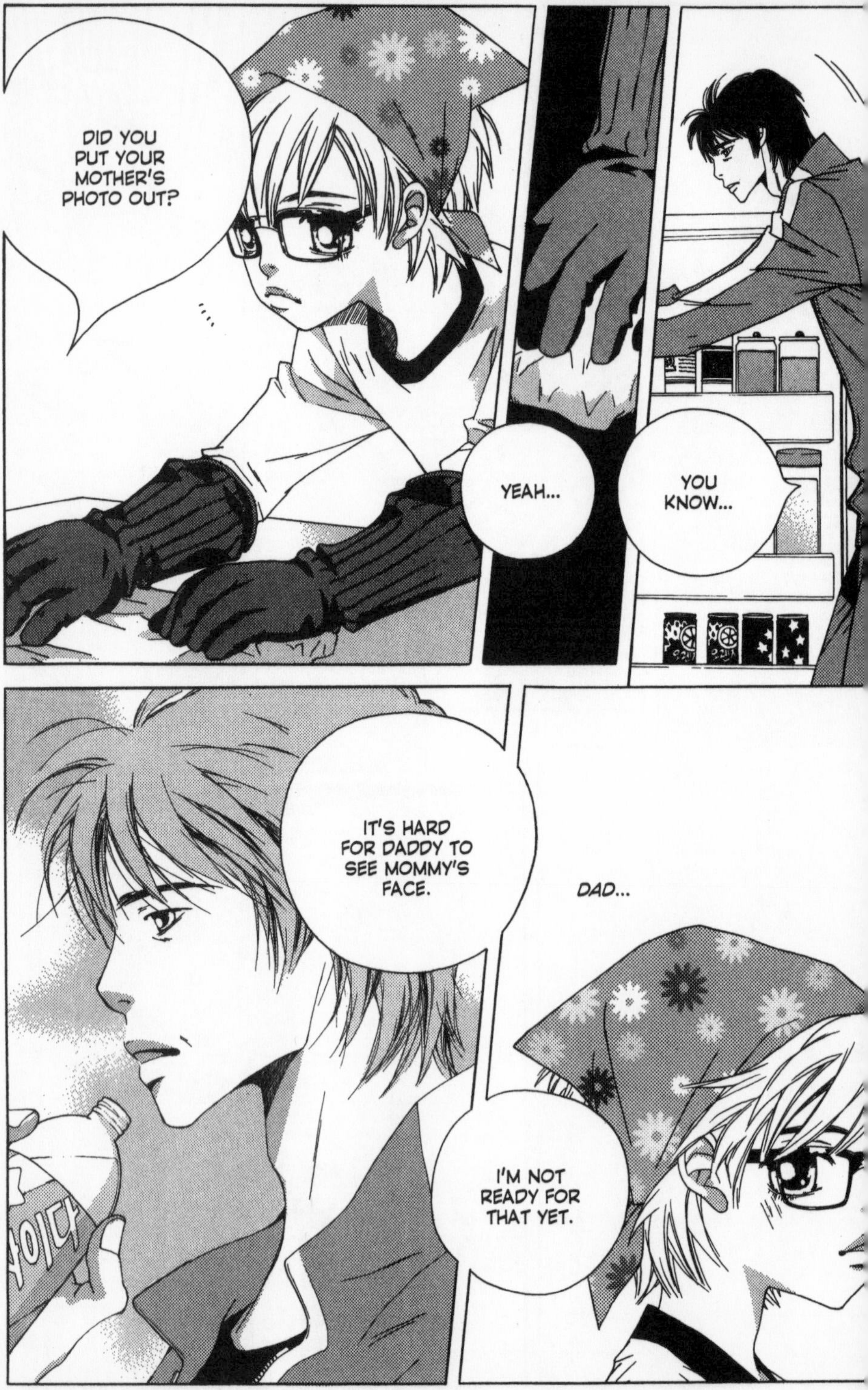

DID YOU PUT YOUR MOTHER'S PHOTO OUT?
....
YEAH...
YOU KNOW...
IT'S HARD FOR DADDY TO SEE MOMMY'S FACE.
I'M NOT READY FOR THAT YET.
DAD...

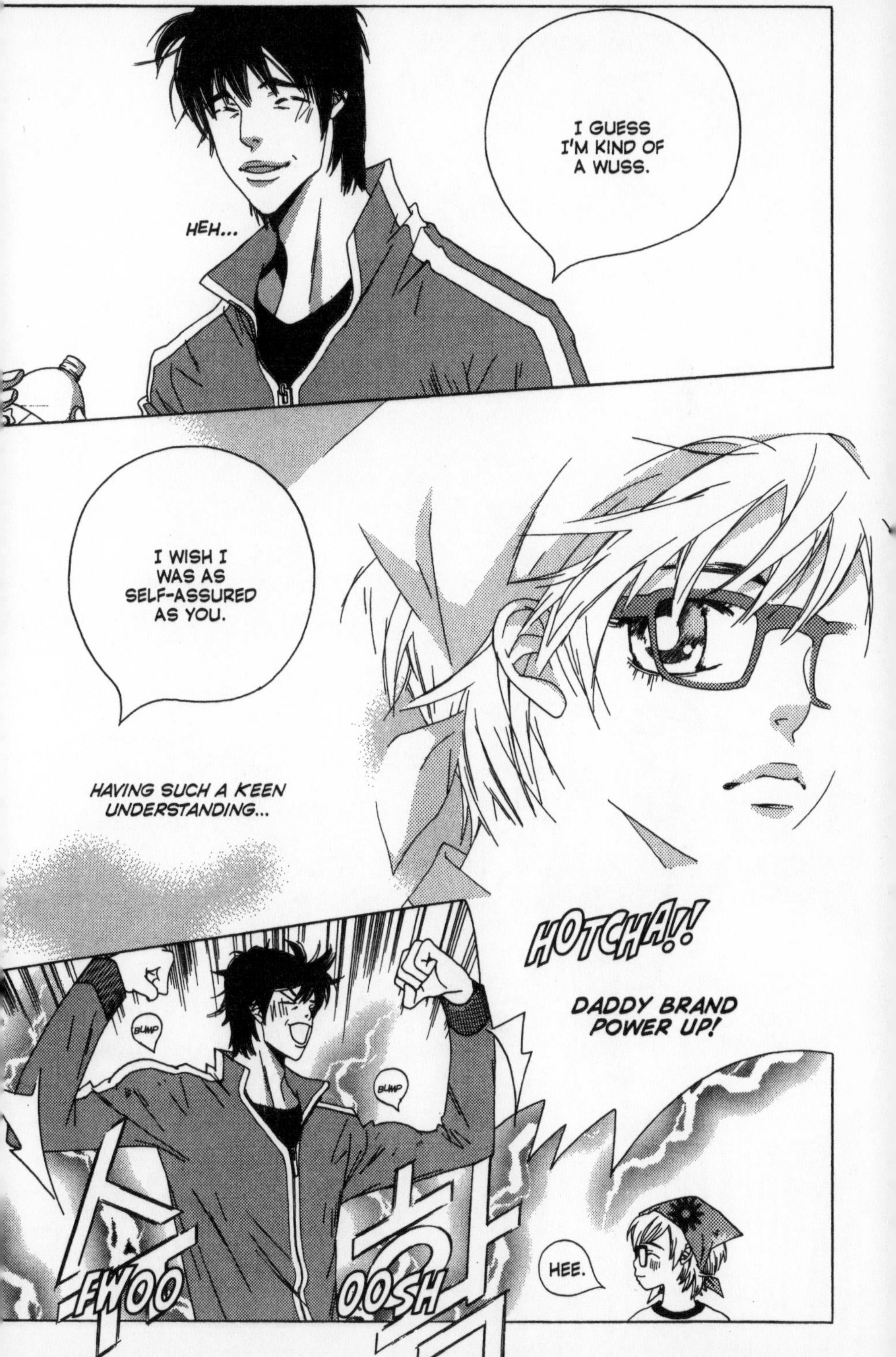
HEH...
I GUESS I'M KIND OF A WUSS.
I WISH I WAS AS SELF-ASSURED AS YOU.
HAVING SUCH A KEEN UNDERSTANDING...
HOTCHA!!
DADDY BRAND POWER UP!
BUMP
BUMP
FWOO
OOSH
HEE.

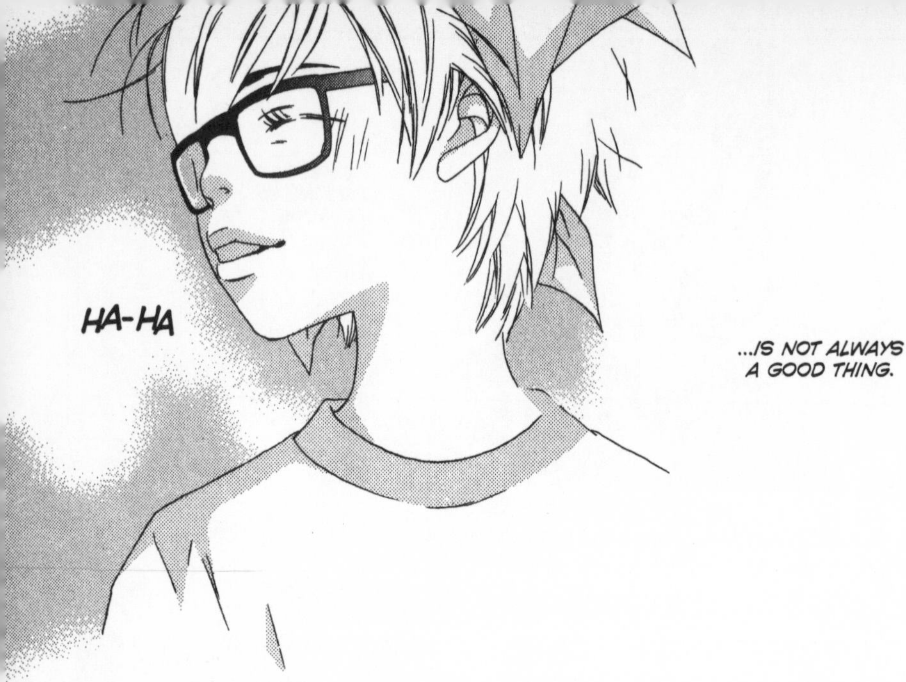
HA-HA
...IS NOT ALWAYS A GOOD THING.

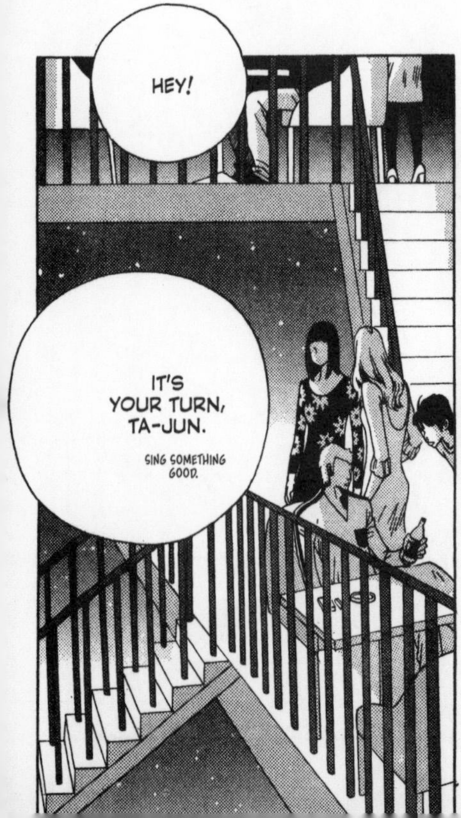
HEY!
IT'S YOUR TURN, TA-JUN.
SING SOMETHING GOOD.

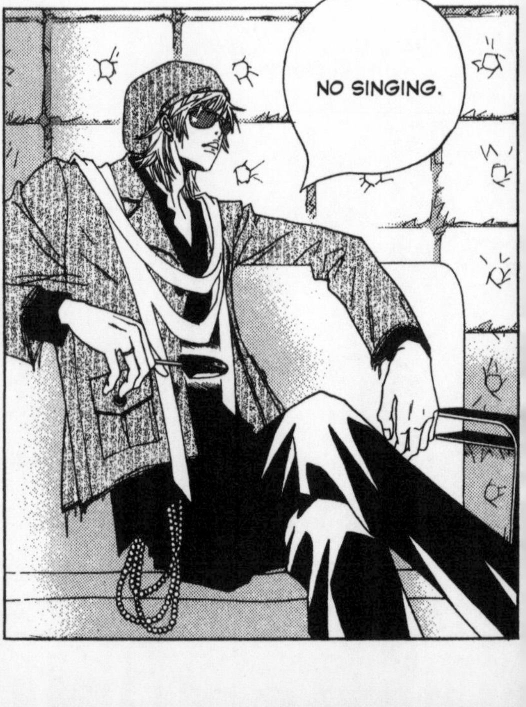
NO SINGING.

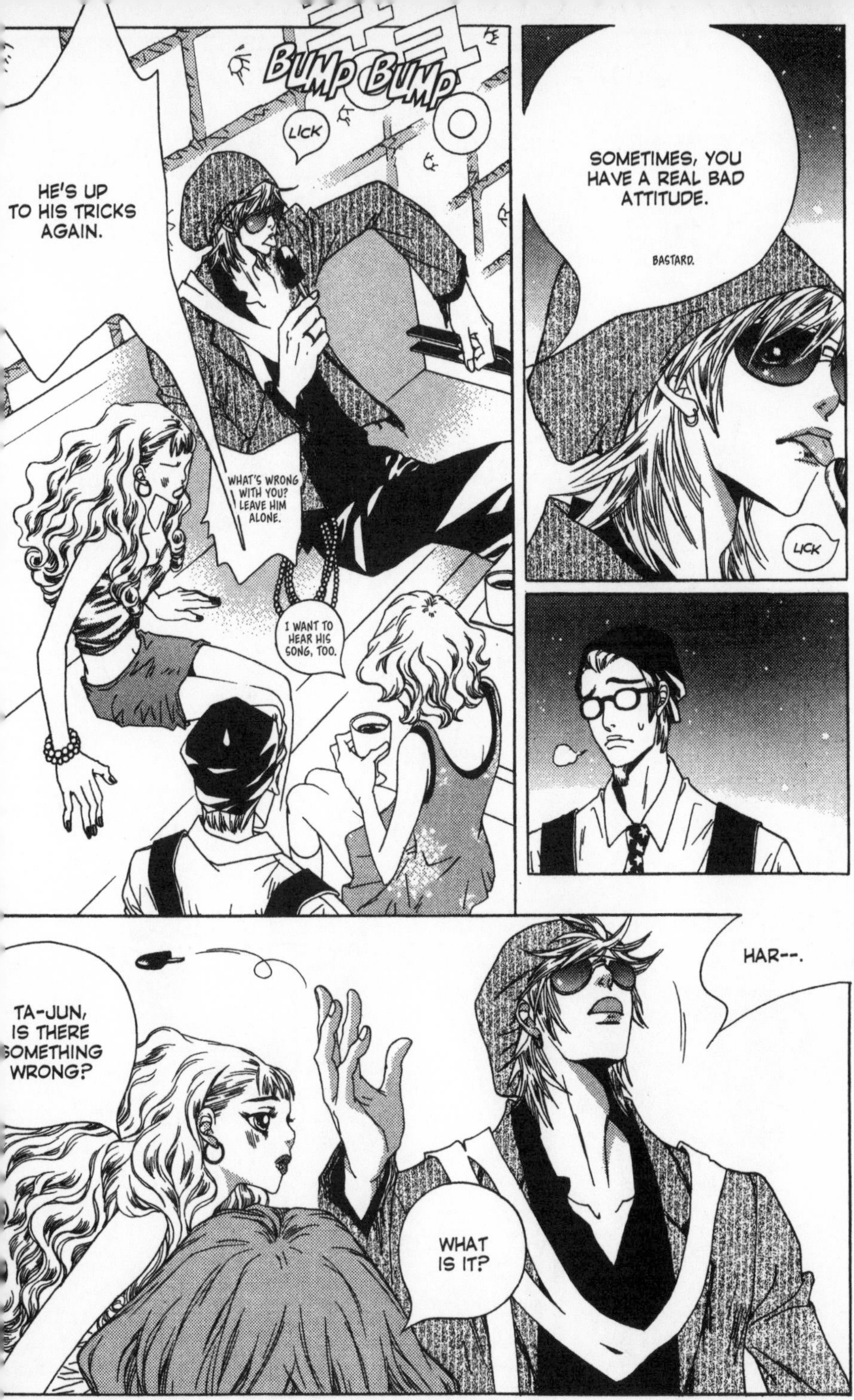
HE'S UP TO HIS TRICKS AGAIN.
BUMP BUMP
LICK
WHAT'S WRONG WITH YOU? LEAVE HIM ALONE.
I WANT TO HEAR HIS SONG, TOO.
SOMETIMES, YOU HAVE A REAL BAD ATTITUDE.
BASTARD.
LICK
TA-JUN, IS THERE SOMETHING WRONG?
WHAT IS IT?
HAR--.

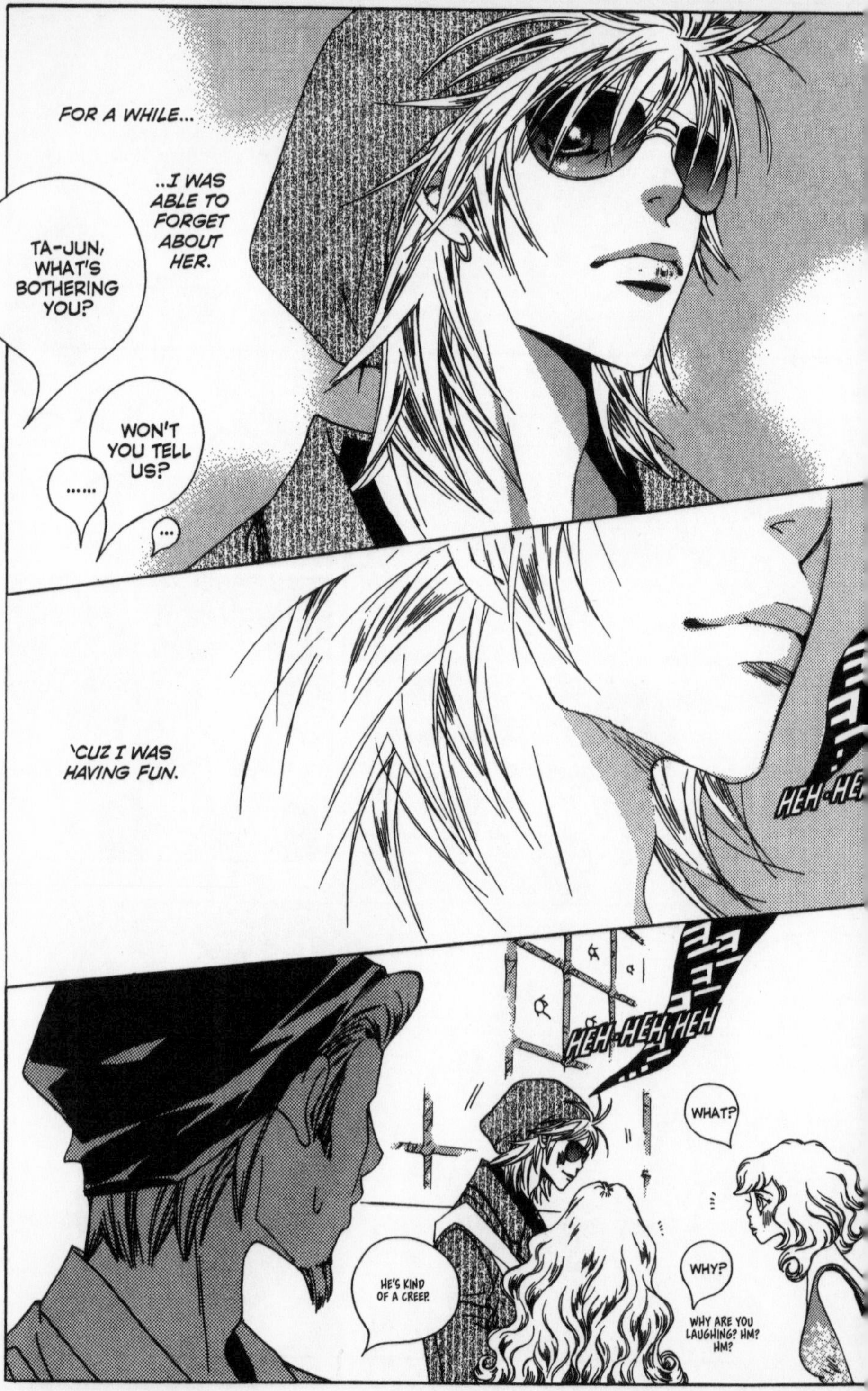
FOR A WHILE...
TA-JUN, WHAT'S BOTHERING YOU?
...I WAS ABLE TO FORGET ABOUT HER.
WON'T YOU TELL US?
......
...
'CUZ I WAS HAVING FUN.
HEH-HE
HEH-HEH-HEH
WHAT?
HE'S KIND OF A CREEP.
WHY?
WHY ARE YOU LAUGHING? HM? HM?

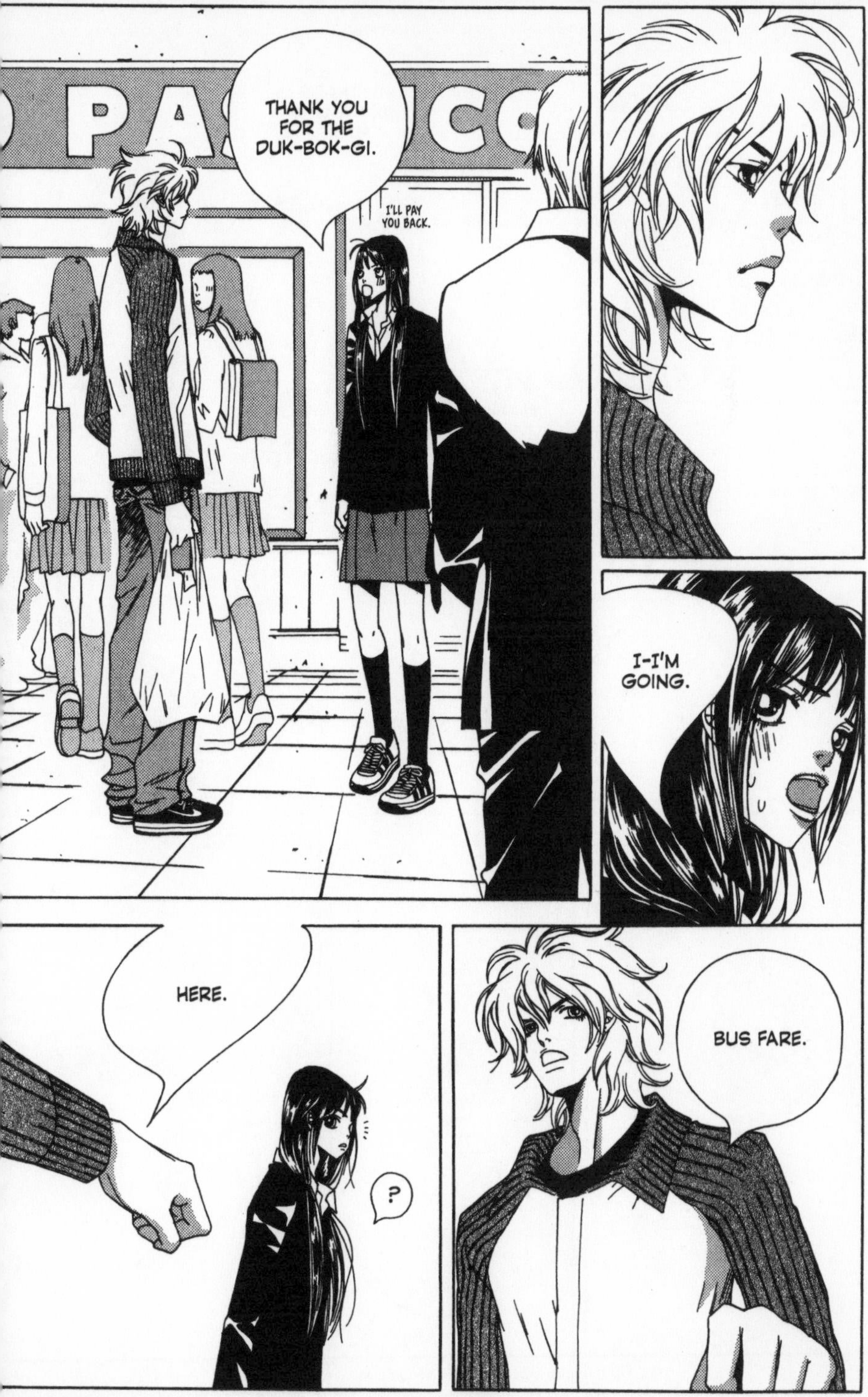
THANK YOU FOR THE DUK-BOK-GI.
I'LL PAY YOU BACK.
I-I'M GOING.
HERE.
?
BUS FARE.

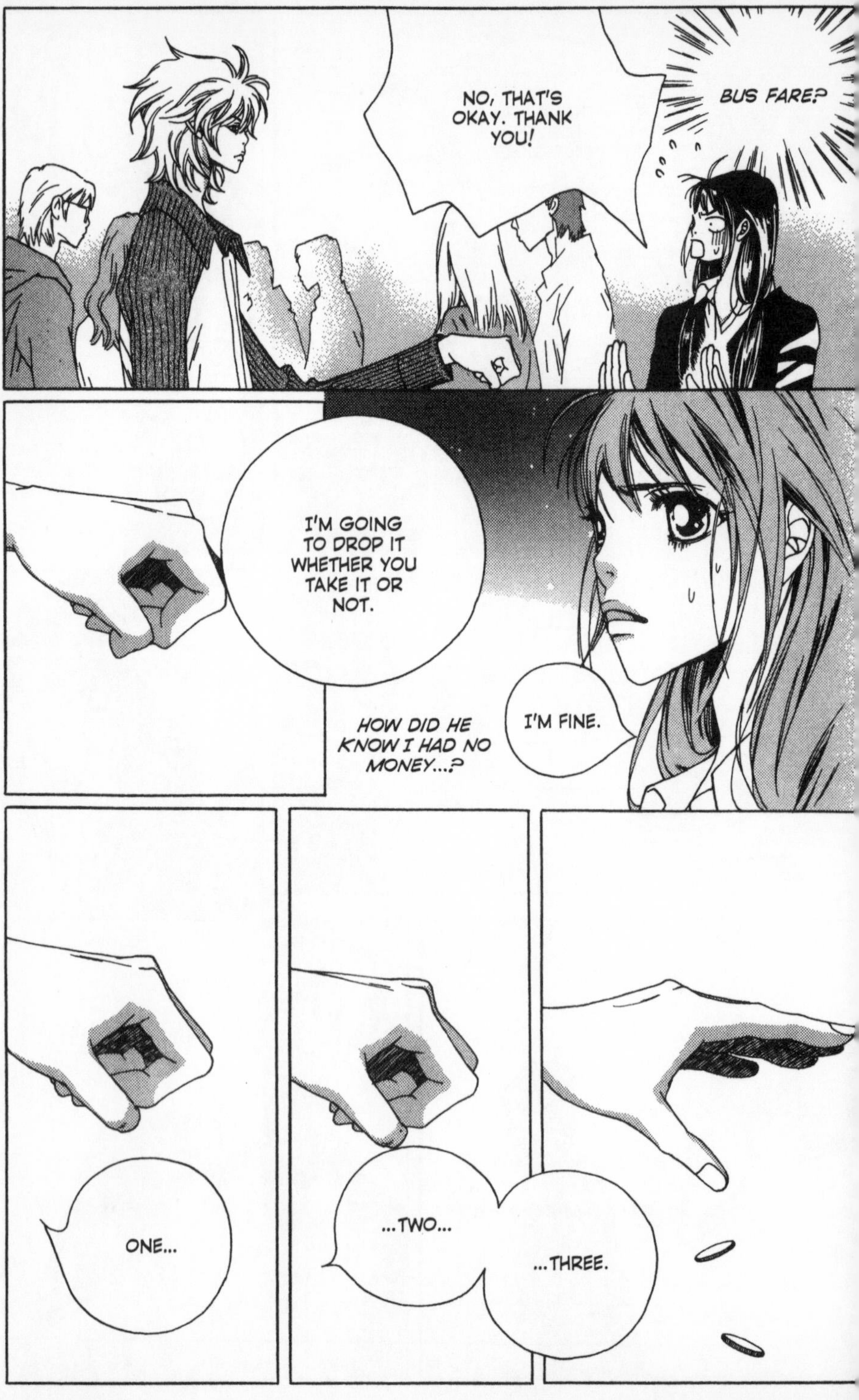
NO, THAT'S OKAY. THANK YOU!
BUS FARE?
I'M GOING TO DROP IT WHETHER YOU TAKE IT OR NOT.
HOW DID HE KNOW I HAD NO MONEY...?
I'M FINE.
ONE...
...TWO...
...THREE.

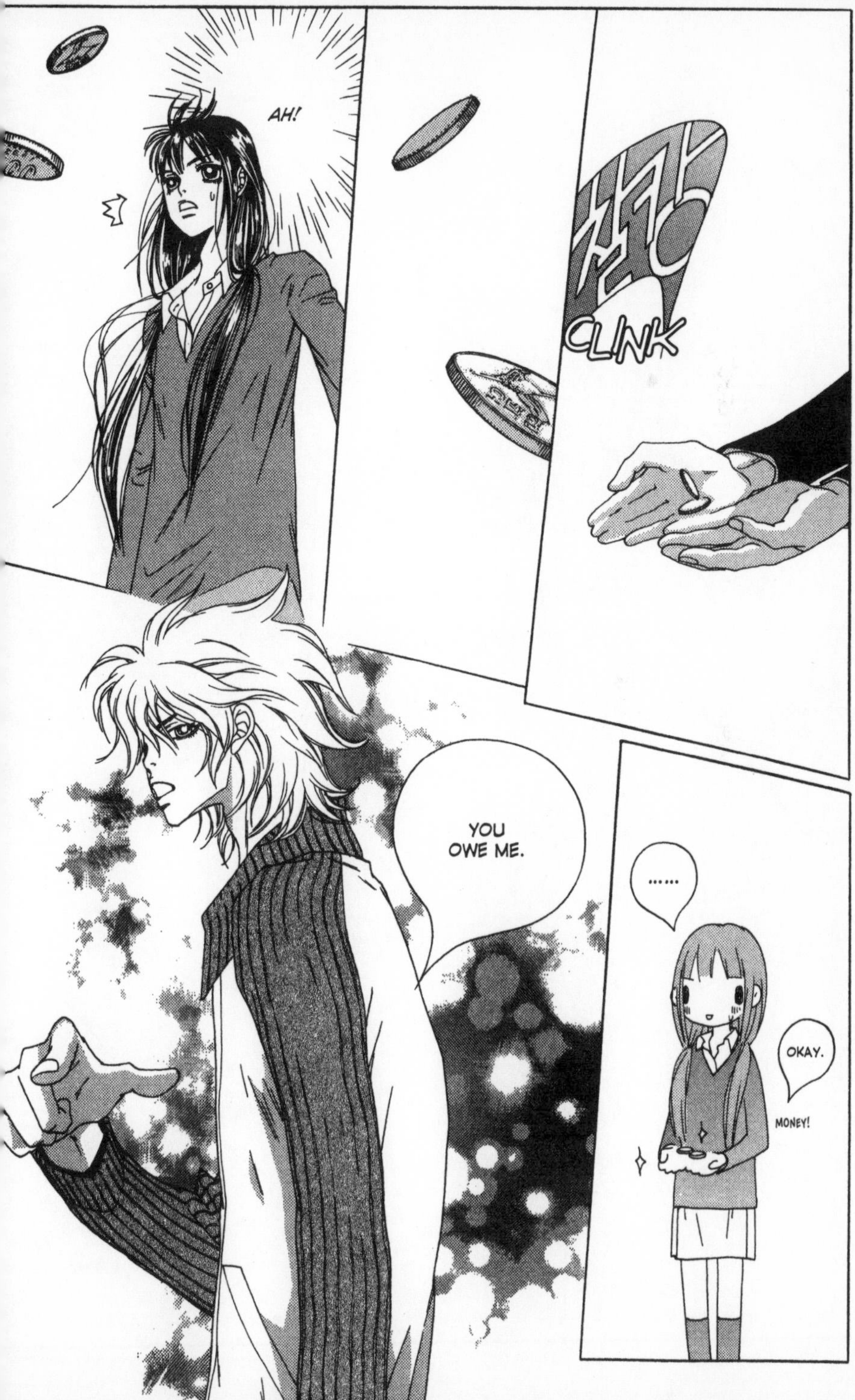
AH!
CLINK
YOU OWE ME.
……
OKAY.
MONEY!

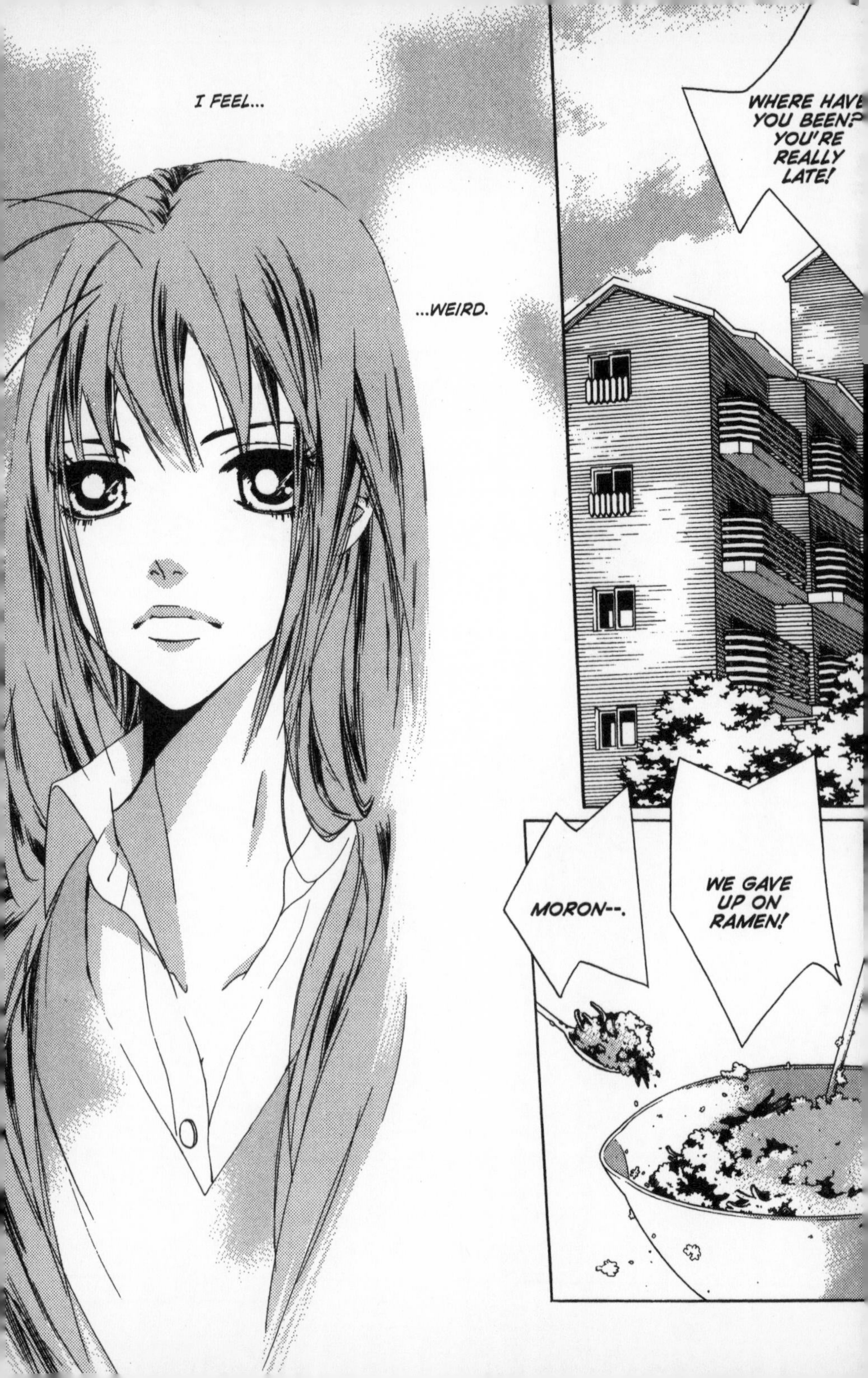
I FEEL...
...WEIRD.
WHERE HAVE YOU BEEN? YOU'RE REALLY LATE!
MORON--.
WE GAVE UP ON RAMEN!

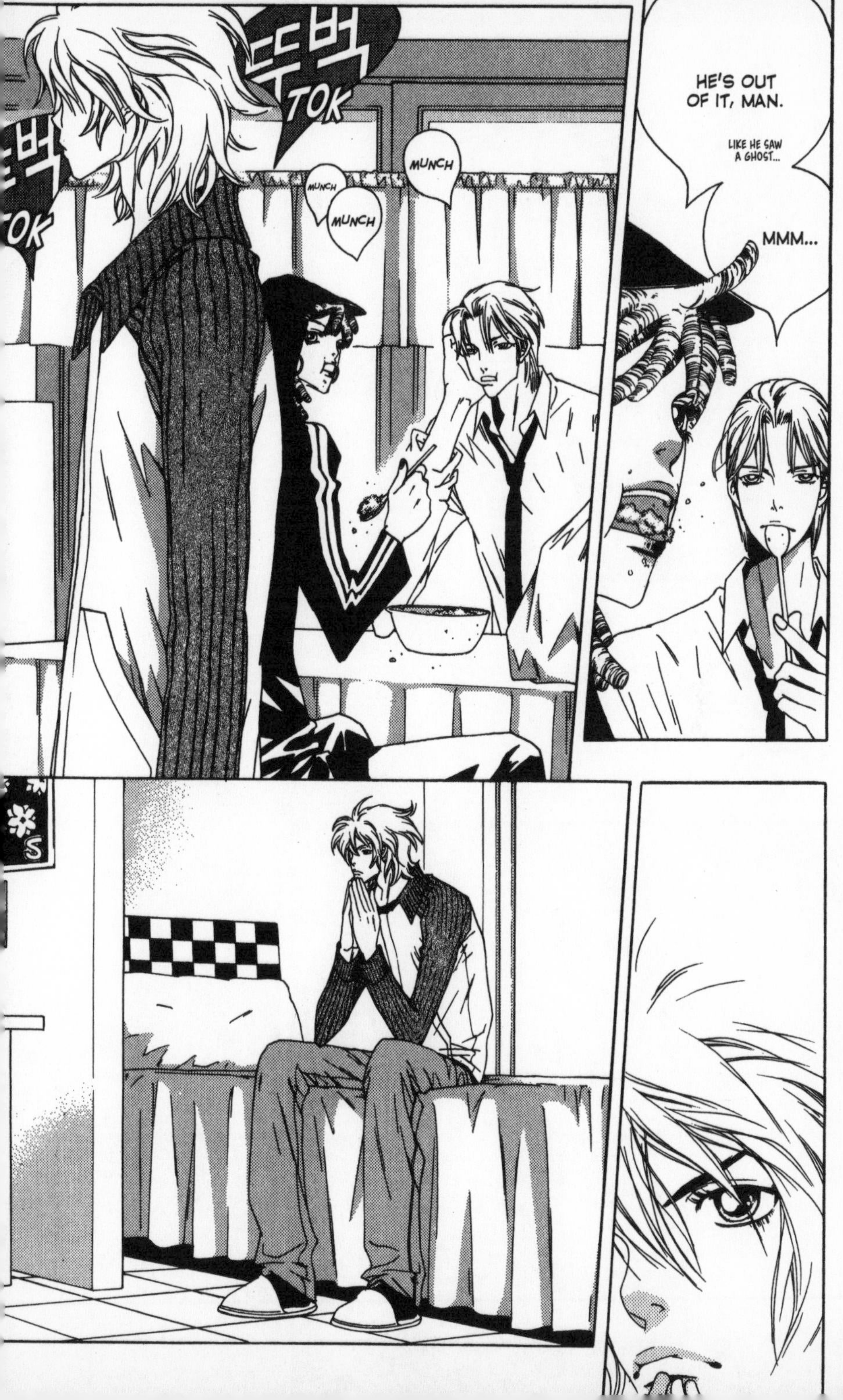
뚜벅
TOK
TOK
MUNCH
MUNCH
MUNCH
HE'S OUT OF IT, MAN.
LIKE HE SAW A GHOST...
MMM...

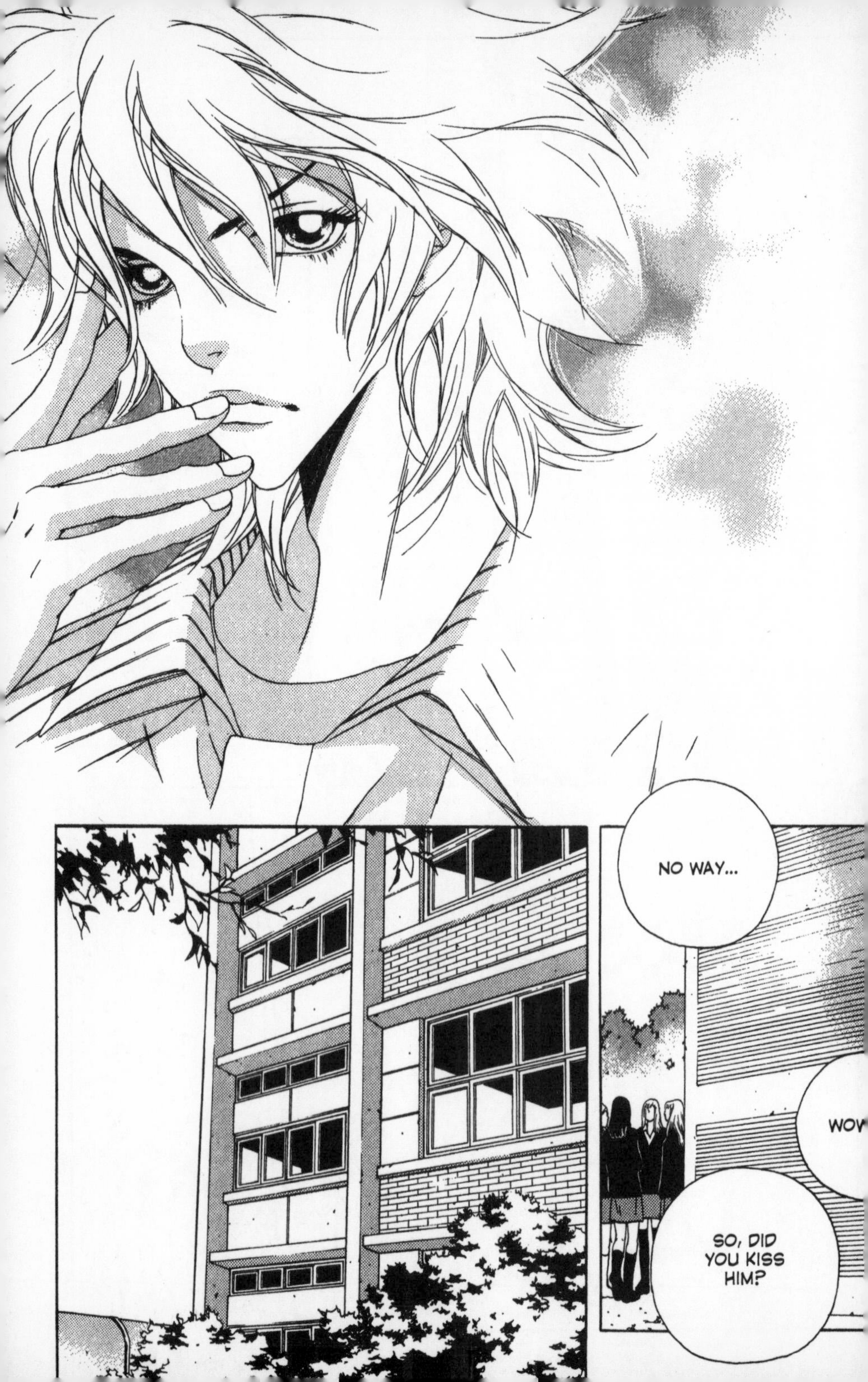
NO WAY...
SO, DID YOU KISS HIM?

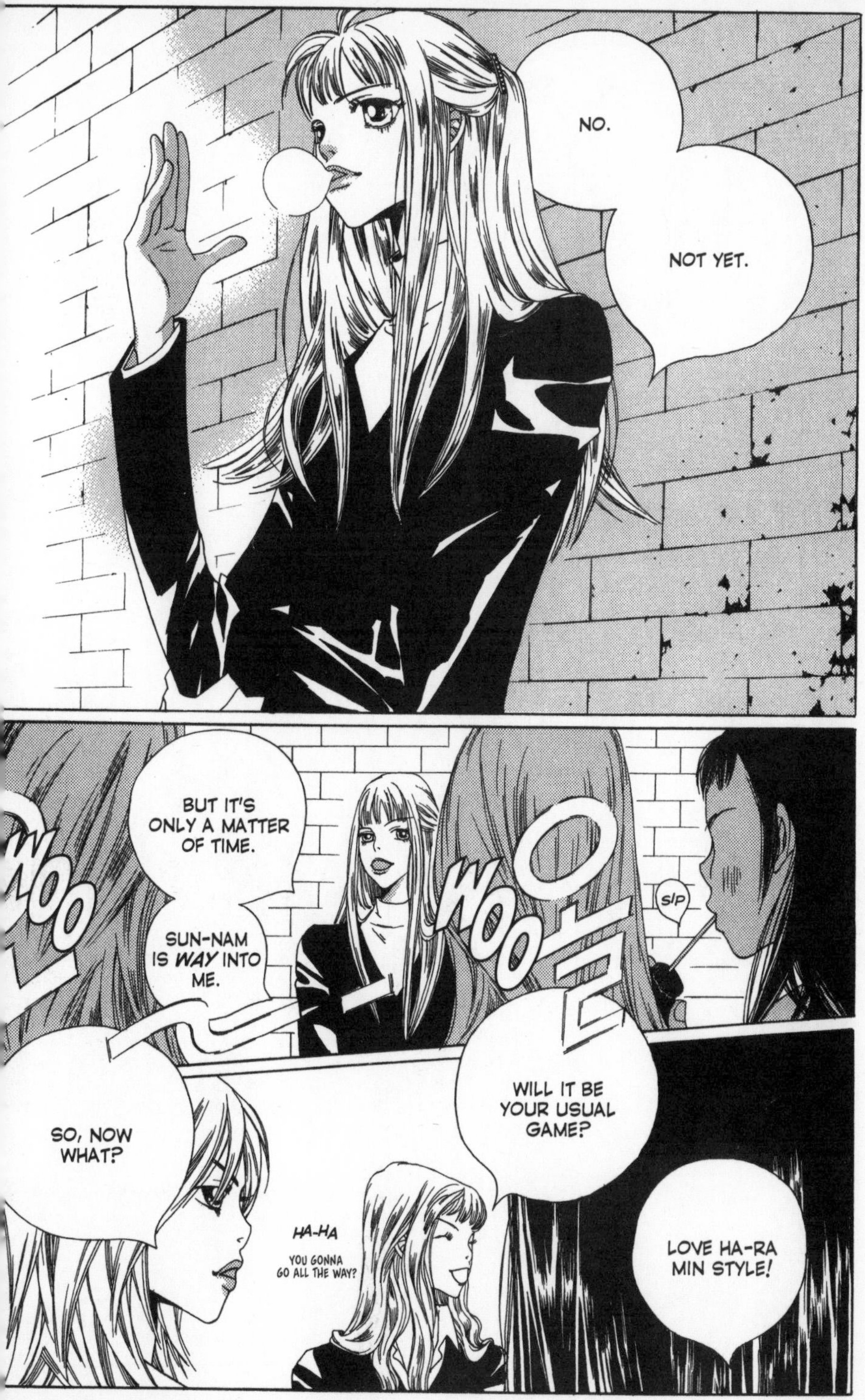
NO.
NOT YET.
WOO
BUT IT'S ONLY A MATTER OF TIME.
SUN-NAM IS *WAY* INTO ME.
WOO
SIP
SO, NOW WHAT?
HA-HA
YOU GONNA GO ALL THE WAY?
WILL IT BE YOUR USUAL GAME?
LOVE HA-RA MIN STYLE!

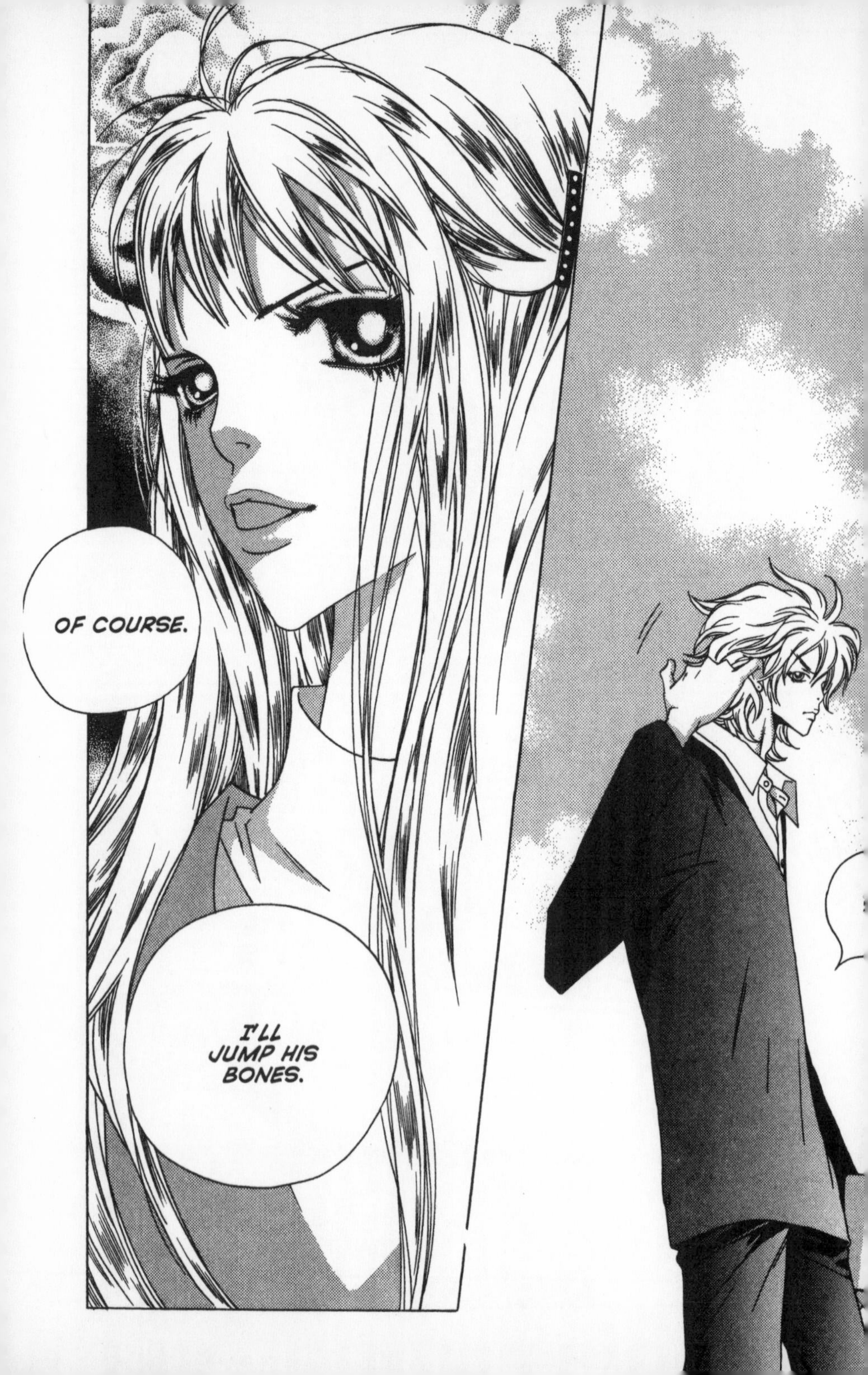
OF COURSE.
I'LL JUMP HIS BONES.

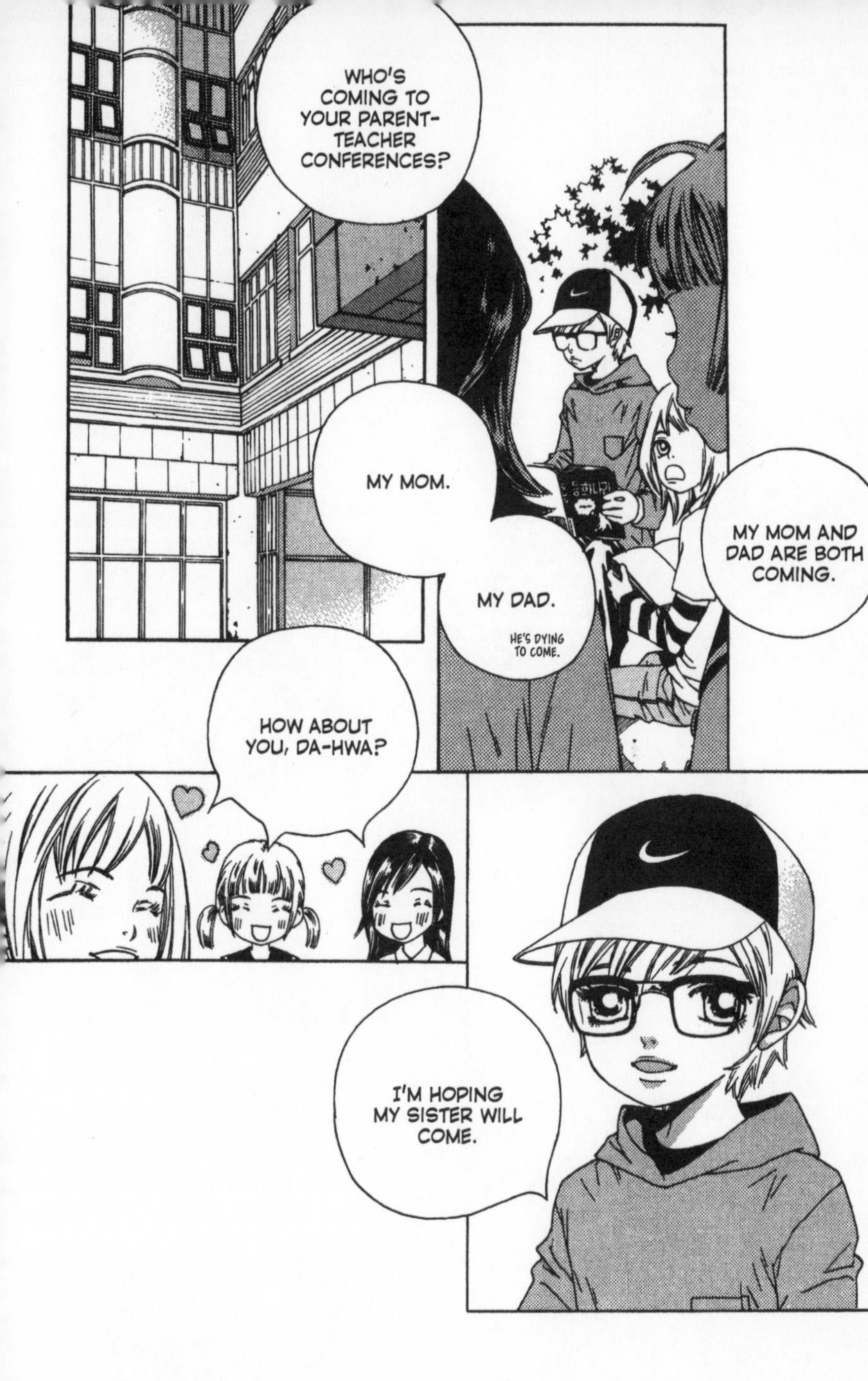
WHO'S COMING TO YOUR PARENT-TEACHER CONFERENCES?
MY MOM.
MY DAD.
HE'S DYING TO COME.
MY MOM AND DAD ARE BOTH COMING.
HOW ABOUT YOU, DA-HWA?
I'M HOPING MY SISTER WILL COME.

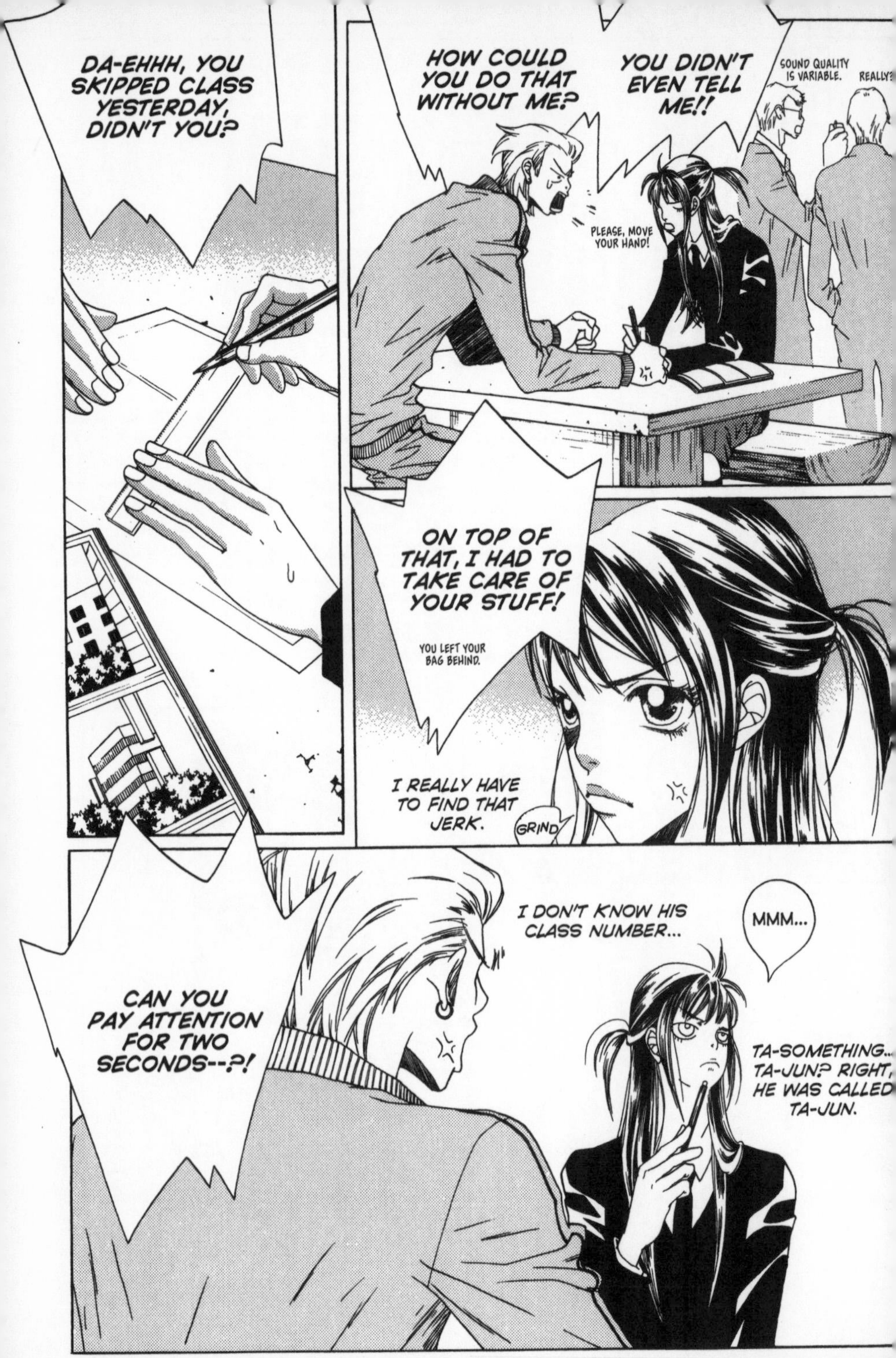
DA-EHHH, YOU SKIPPED CLASS YESTERDAY, DIDN'T YOU?
HOW COULD YOU DO THAT WITHOUT ME?
YOU DIDN'T EVEN TELL ME!!
PLEASE, MOVE YOUR HAND!
SOUND QUALITY IS VARIABLE.
REALLY?
ON TOP OF THAT, I HAD TO TAKE CARE OF YOUR STUFF!
YOU LEFT YOUR BAG BEHIND.
I REALLY HAVE TO FIND THAT JERK.
GRIND
CAN YOU PAY ATTENTION FOR TWO SECONDS--?!
I DON'T KNOW HIS CLASS NUMBER...
MMM...
TA-SOMETHING... TA-JUN? RIGHT, HE WAS CALLED TA-JUN.

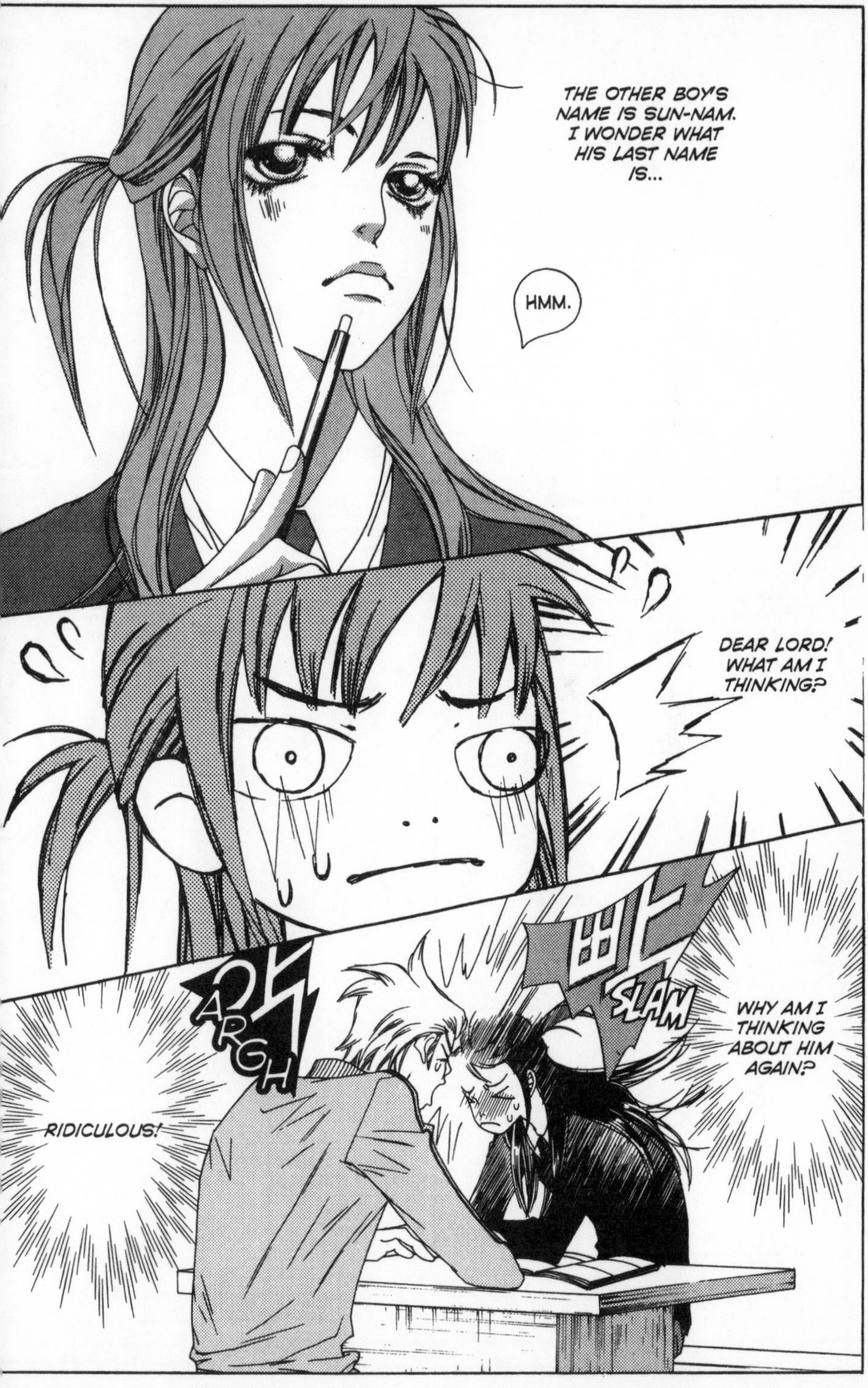
THE OTHER BOY'S NAME IS SUN-NAM. I WONDER WHAT HIS LAST NAME IS...
HMM.
DEAR LORD! WHAT AM I THINKING?
ARGH
SLAM
WHY AM I THINKING ABOUT HIM AGAIN?
RIDICULOUS!

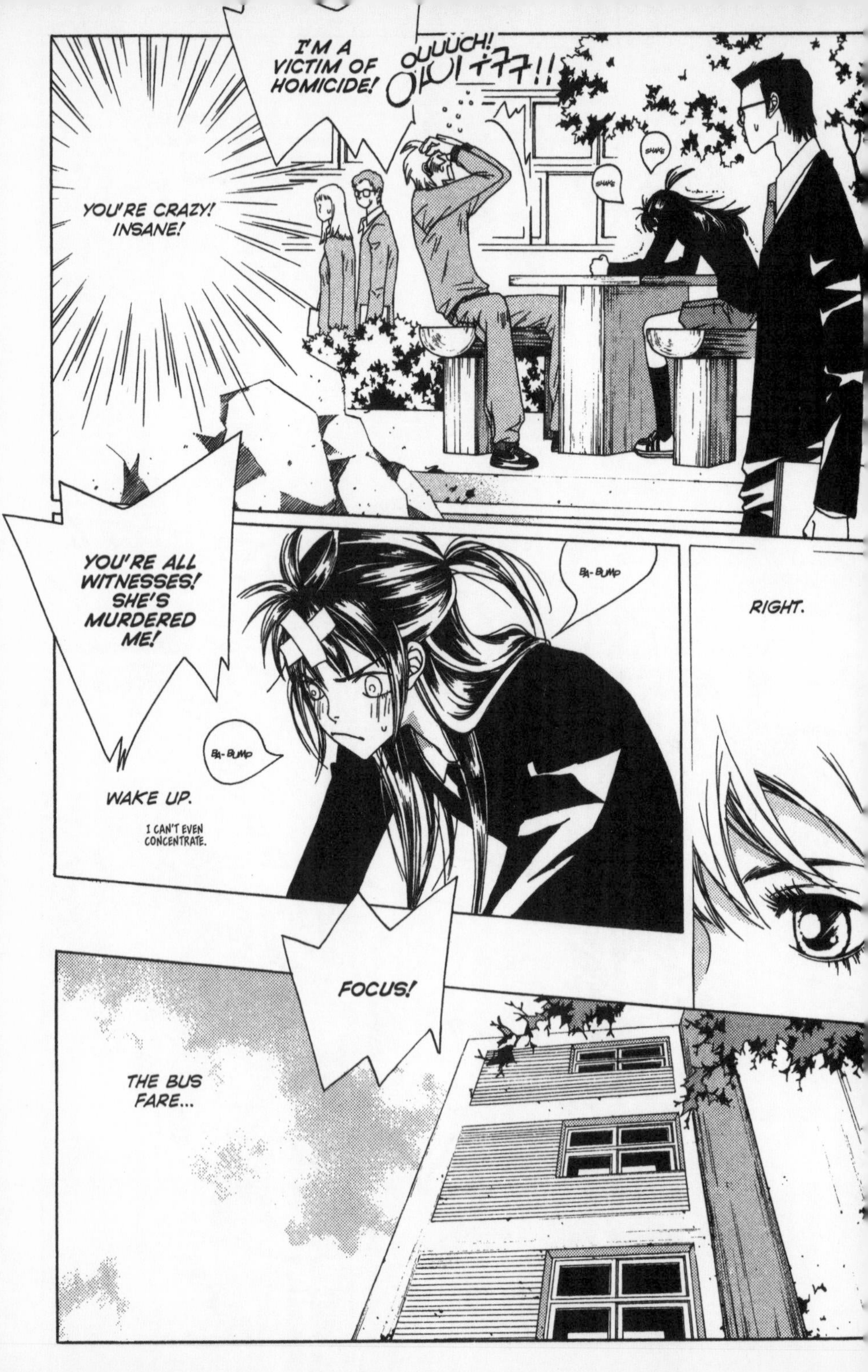
I'M A VICTIM OF HOMICIDE!
OUUUCH!
SHAKE
SHAKE
YOU'RE CRAZY! INSANE!
YOU'RE ALL WITNESSES! SHE'S MURDERED ME!
BA-BUMP
BA-BUMP
WAKE UP.
I CAN'T EVEN CONCENTRATE.
RIGHT.
FOCUS!
THE BUS FARE...

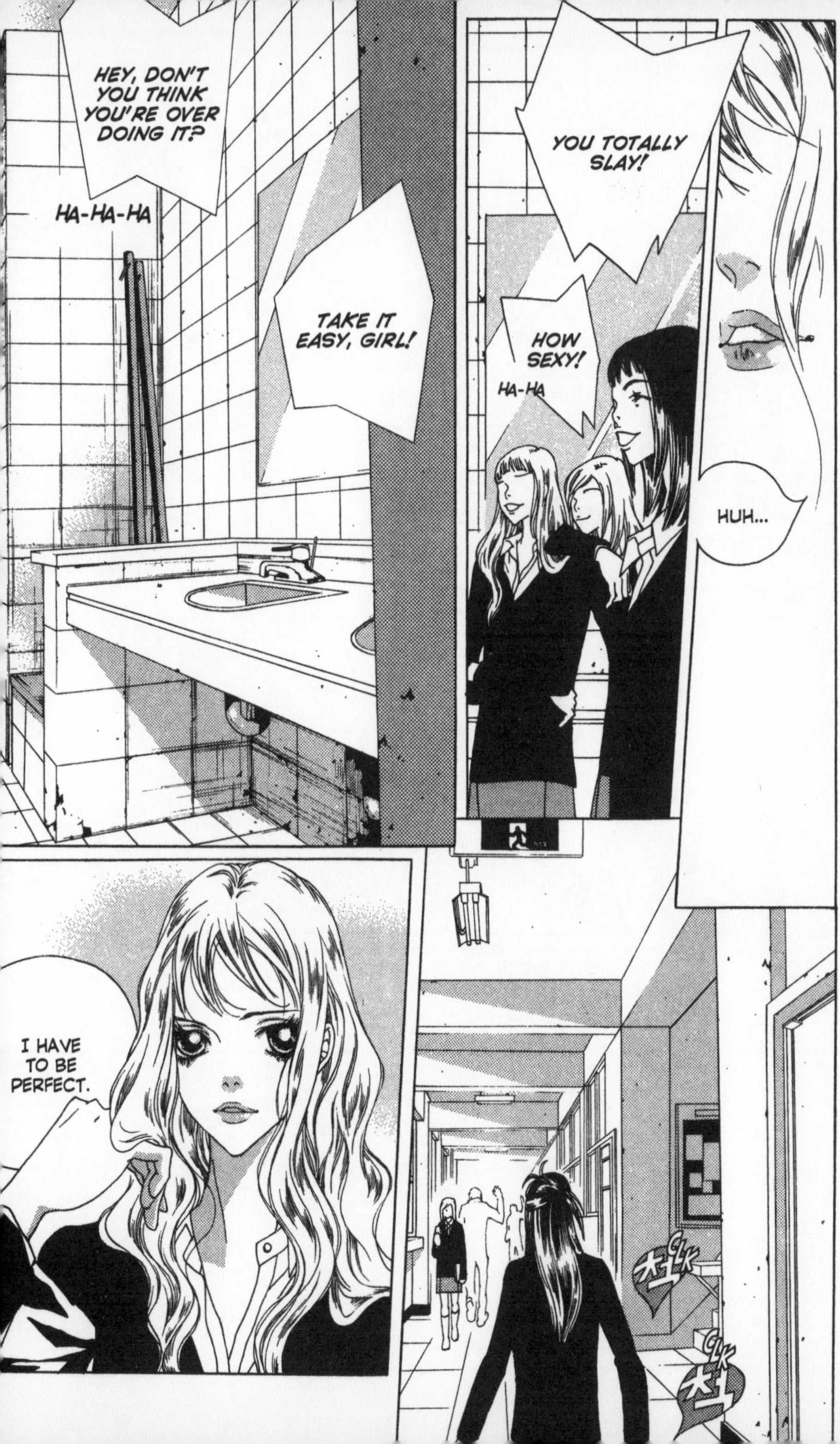
HEY, DON'T YOU THINK YOU'RE OVER DOING IT?
HA-HA-HA
TAKE IT EASY, GIRL!
YOU TOTALLY SLAY!
HOW SEXY!
HA-HA
HUH...
I HAVE TO BE PERFECT.
CLK
CLK

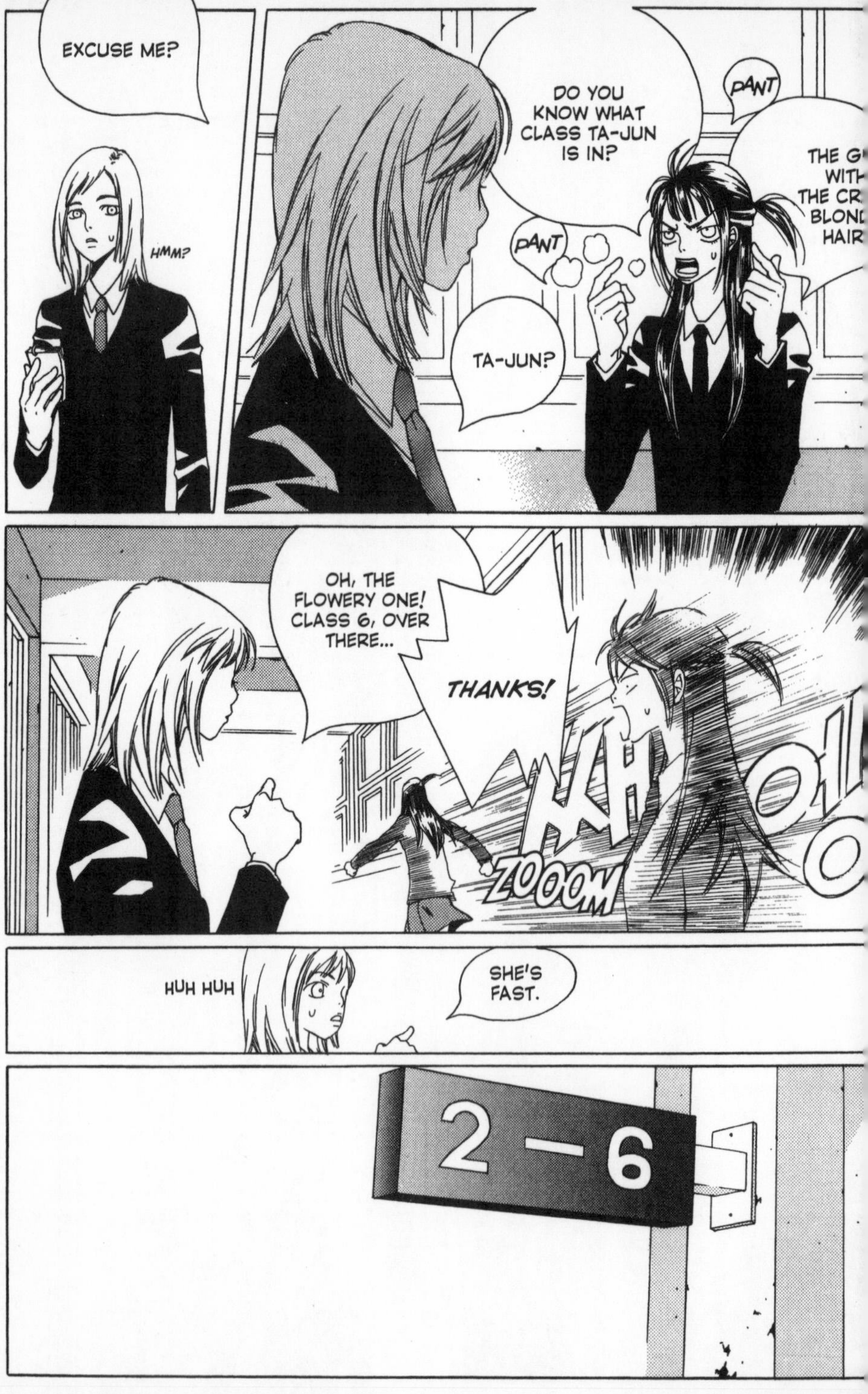
EXCUSE ME?
HMM?
DO YOU KNOW WHAT CLASS TA-JUN IS IN?
PANT
THE G WITH THE CR BLOND HAIR
PANT
TA-JUN?
OH, THE FLOWERY ONE! CLASS 6, OVER THERE...
THANKS!
ZOOOM
HUH HUH
SHE'S FAST.
2 - 6

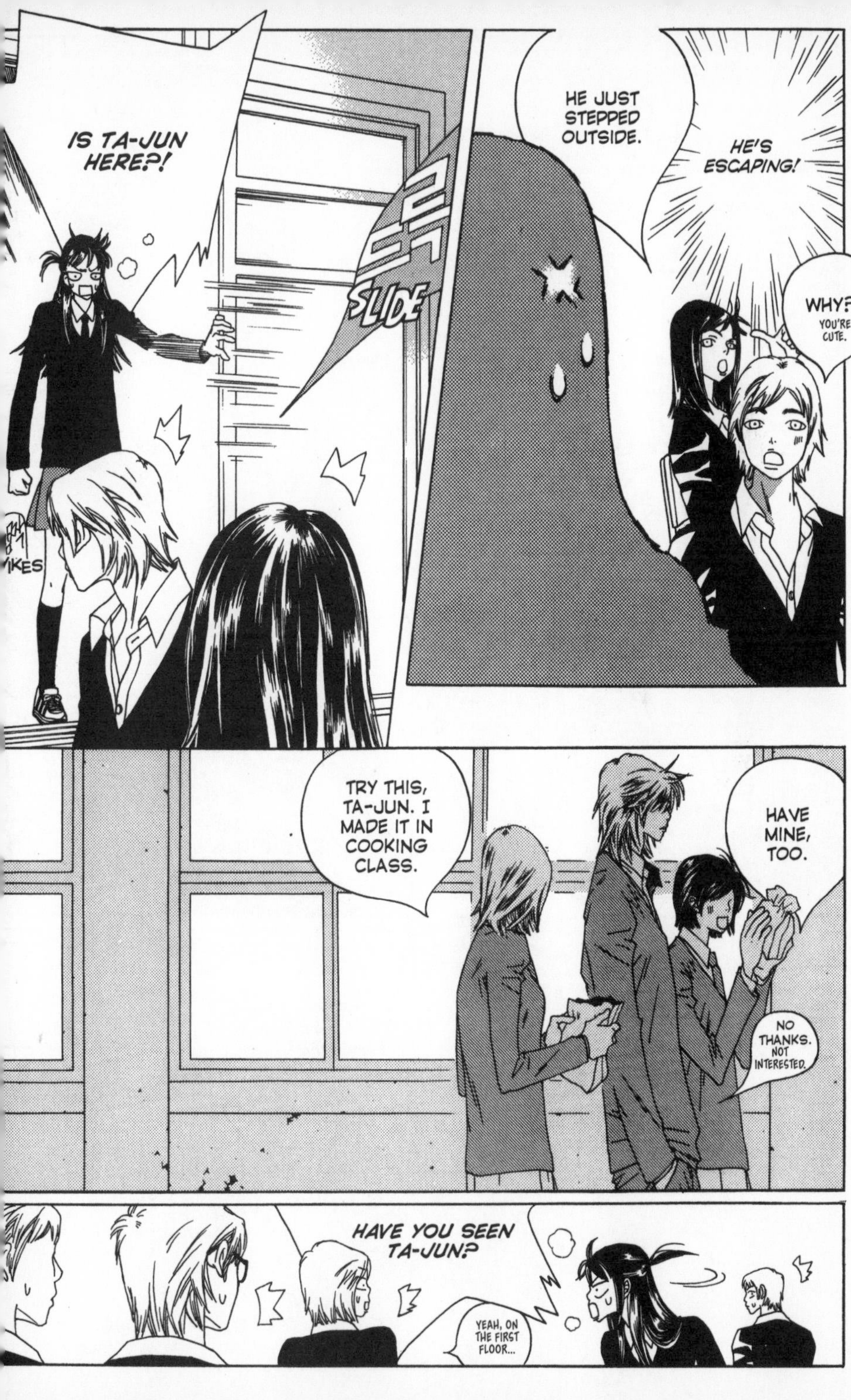
IS TA-JUN HERE?!
SLIDE
YIKES
HE JUST STEPPED OUTSIDE.
HE'S ESCAPING!
WHY?
YOU'RE CUTE.
TRY THIS, TA-JUN. I MADE IT IN COOKING CLASS.
HAVE MINE, TOO.
NO THANKS. NOT INTERESTED.
HAVE YOU SEEN TA-JUN?
YEAH, ON THE FIRST FLOOR...

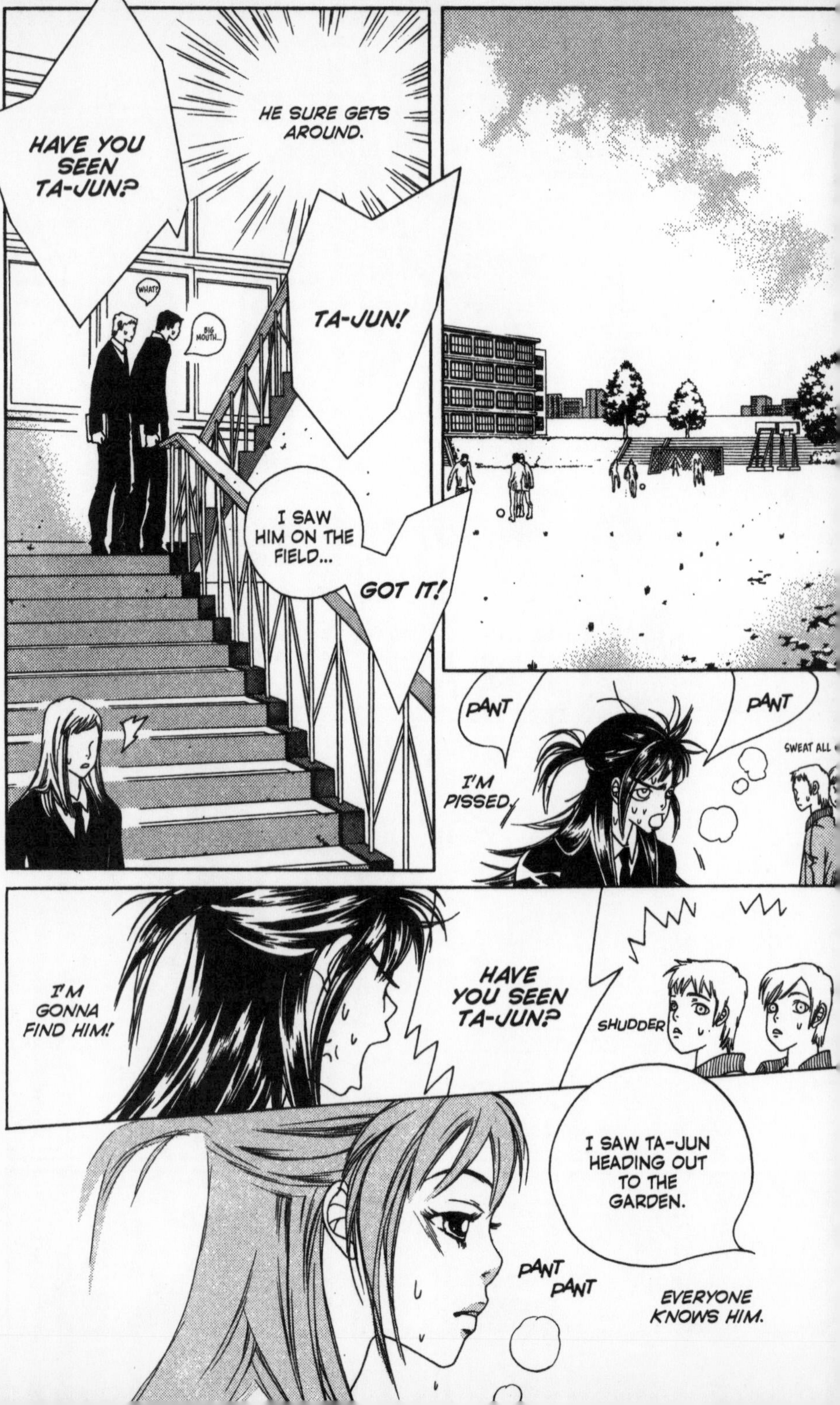
HAVE YOU SEEN TA-JUN?
HE SURE GETS AROUND.
WHAT?
BIG MOUTH...
TA-JUN!
I SAW HIM ON THE FIELD...
GOT IT!
PANT
I'M PISSED
PANT
SWEAT ALL
I'M GONNA FIND HIM!
HAVE YOU SEEN TA-JUN?
SHUDDER
I SAW TA-JUN HEADING OUT TO THE GARDEN.
PANT PANT
EVERYONE KNOWS HIM.

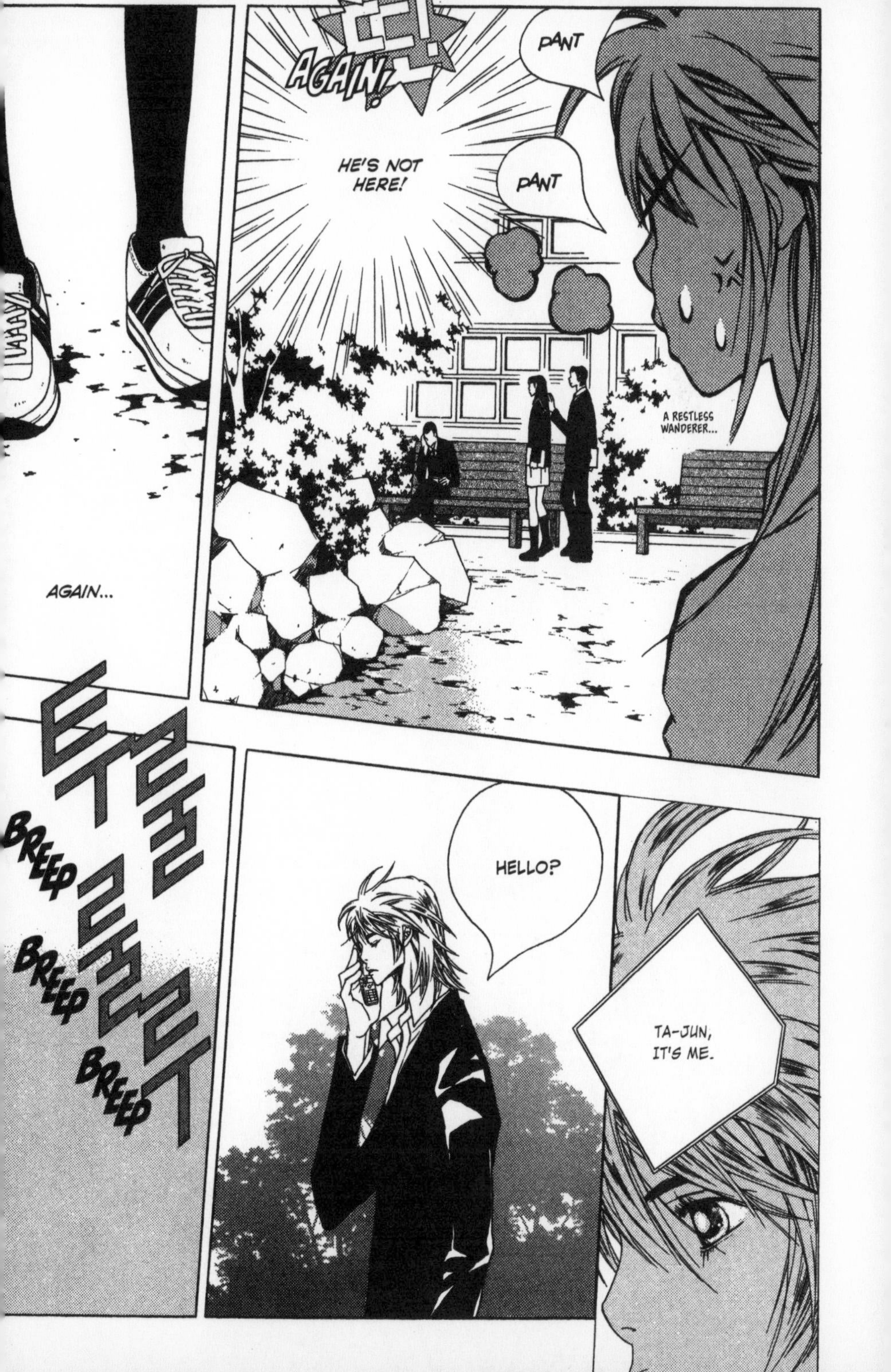
AGAIN...
AGAIN!
PANT
HE'S NOT HERE!
PANT
A RESTLESS WANDERER...
BREEP
BREEP
BREEP
HELLO?
TA-JUN, IT'S ME.

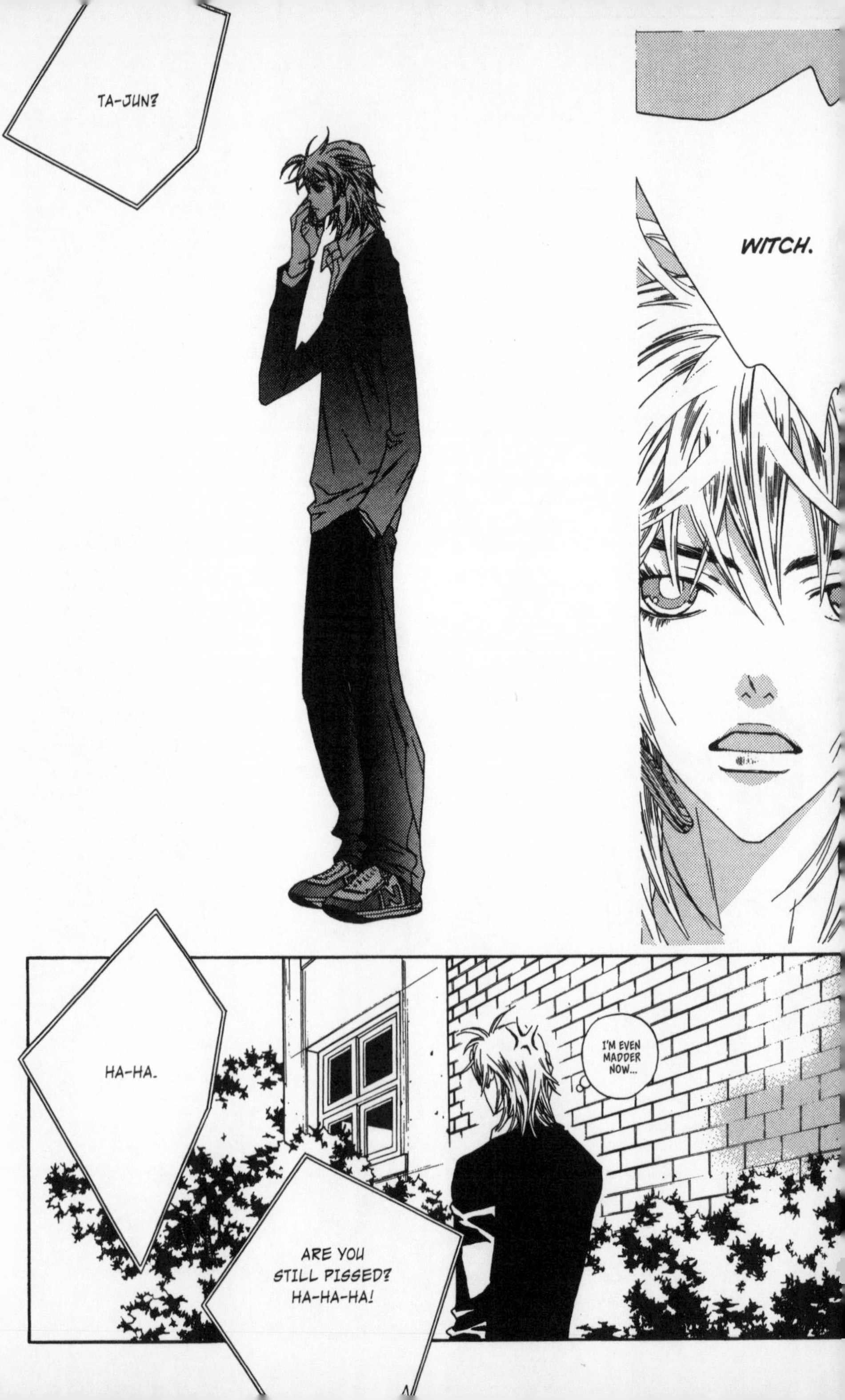
TA-JUN?
WITCH.
HA-HA.
ARE YOU STILL PISSED? HA-HA-HA!
I'M EVEN MADDER NOW...

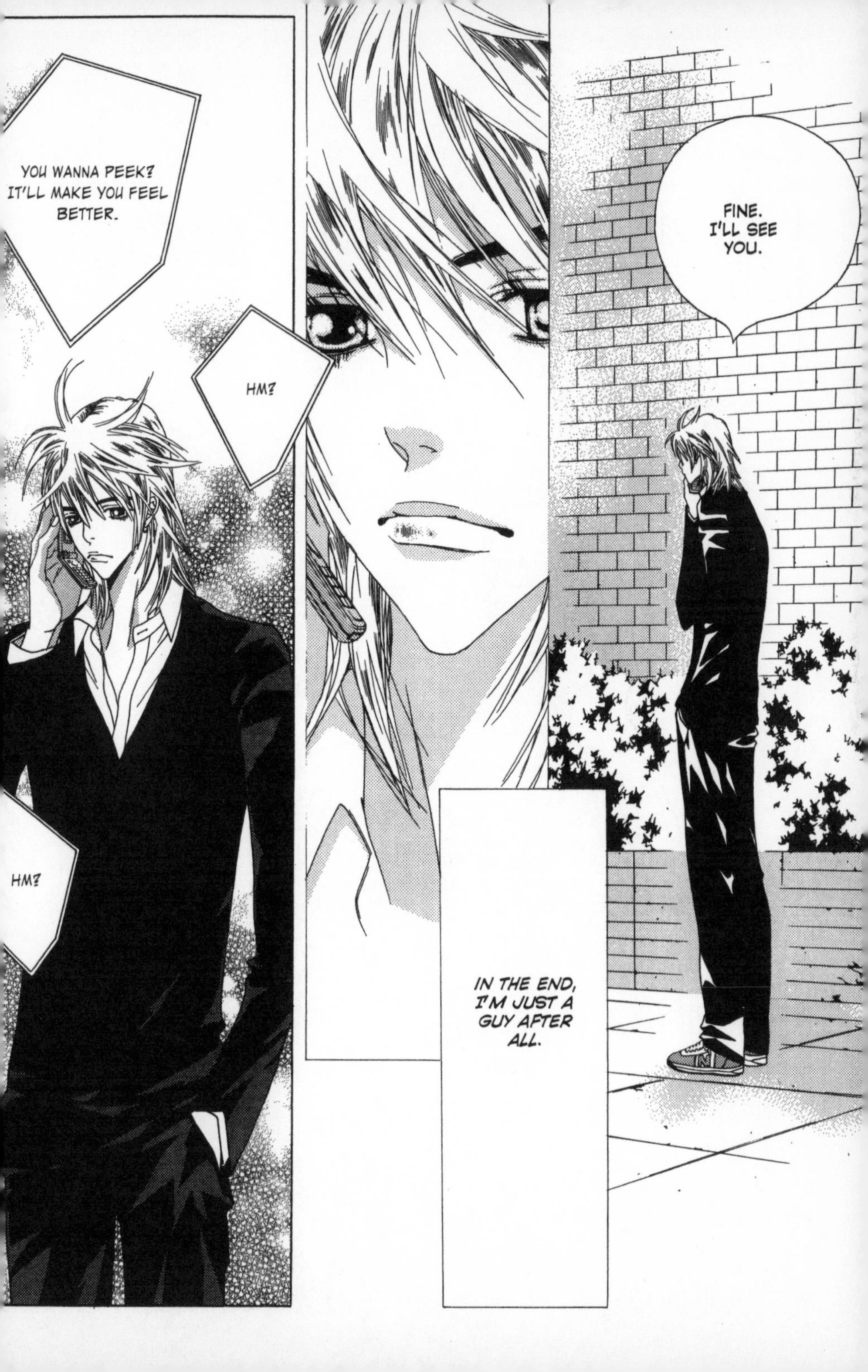
YOU WANNA PEEK? IT'LL MAKE YOU FEEL BETTER.
HM?
HM?
FINE. I'LL SEE YOU.
IN THE END, I'M JUST A GUY AFTER ALL.

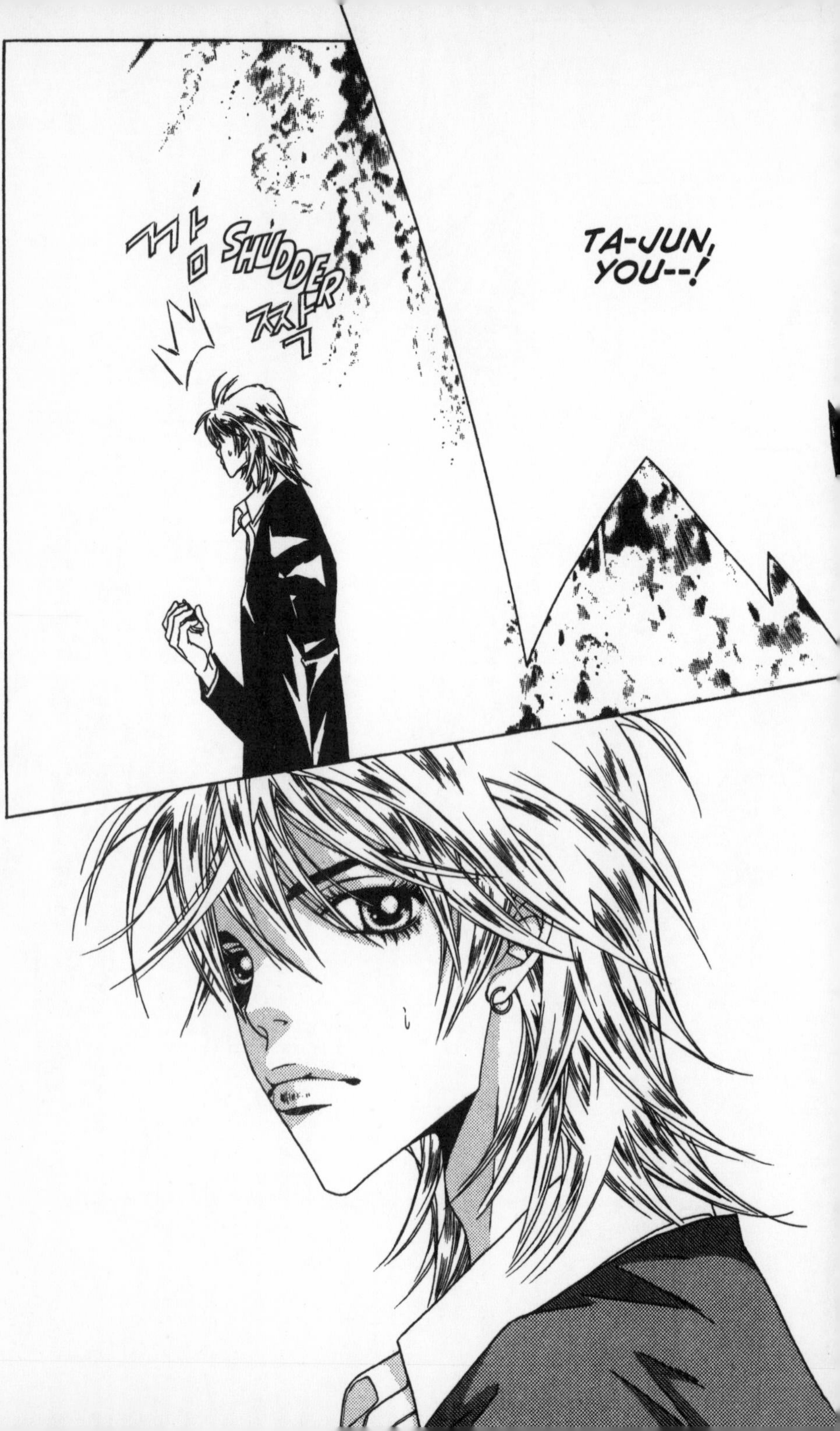
SHUDDER
TA-JUN, YOU--!

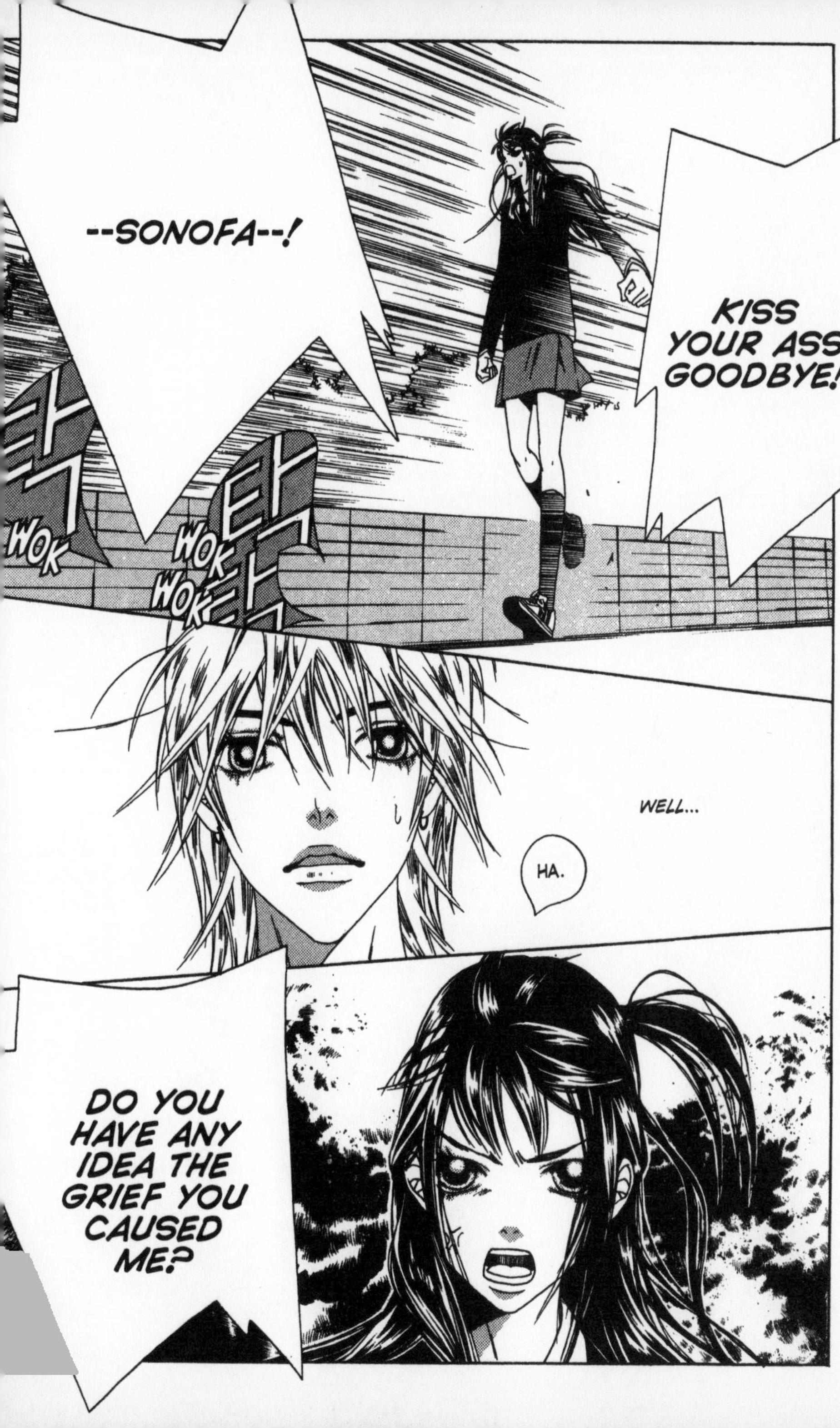
--SONOFA--!
WOK
WOK
WOK
KISS YOUR ASS GOODBYE!
WELL...
HA.
DO YOU HAVE ANY IDEA THE GRIEF YOU CAUSED ME?

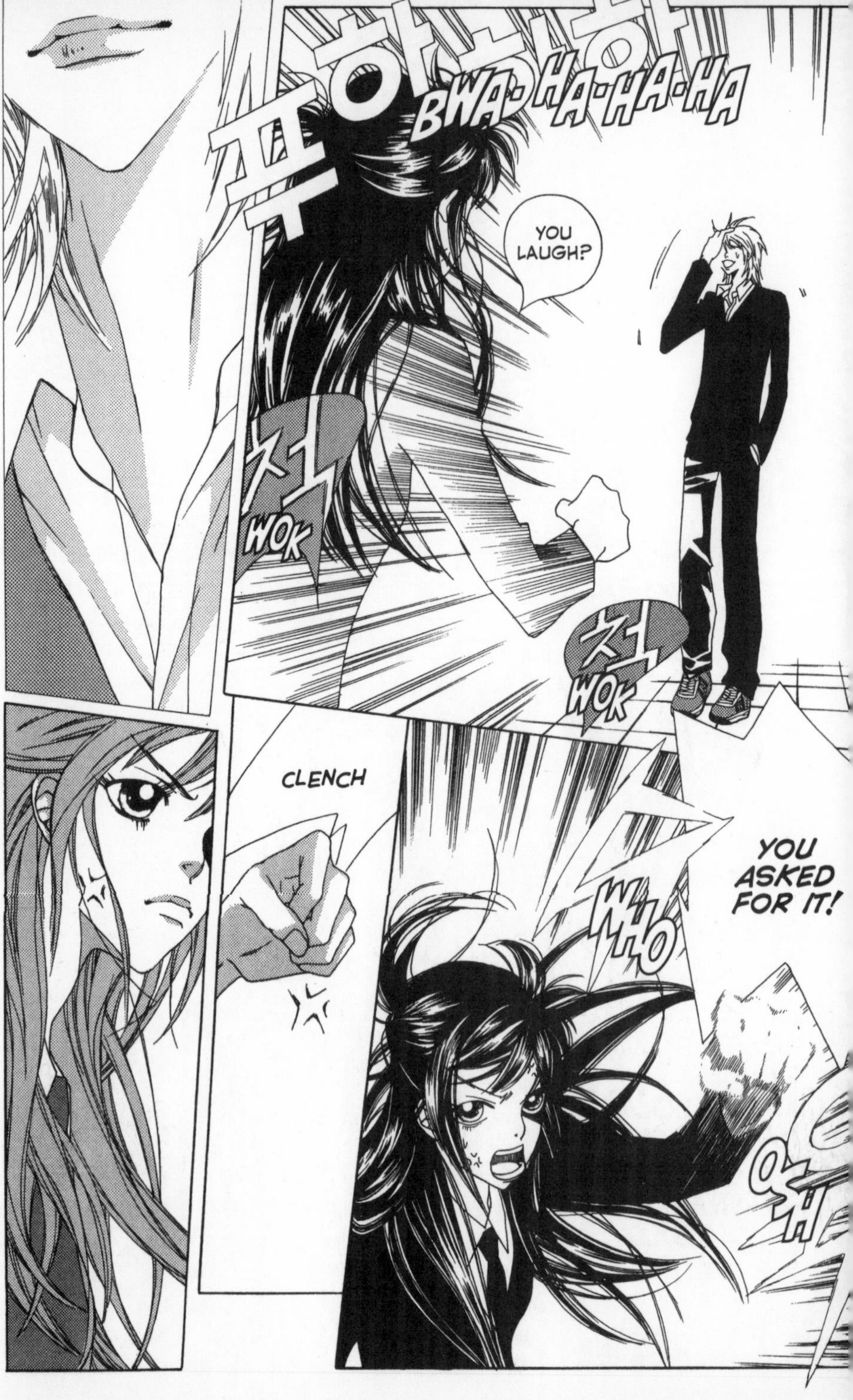
푸하하하
BWA-HA-HA-HA
YOU LAUGH?
WOK
WOK
CLENCH
WHO
YOU ASKED FOR IT!
OSH

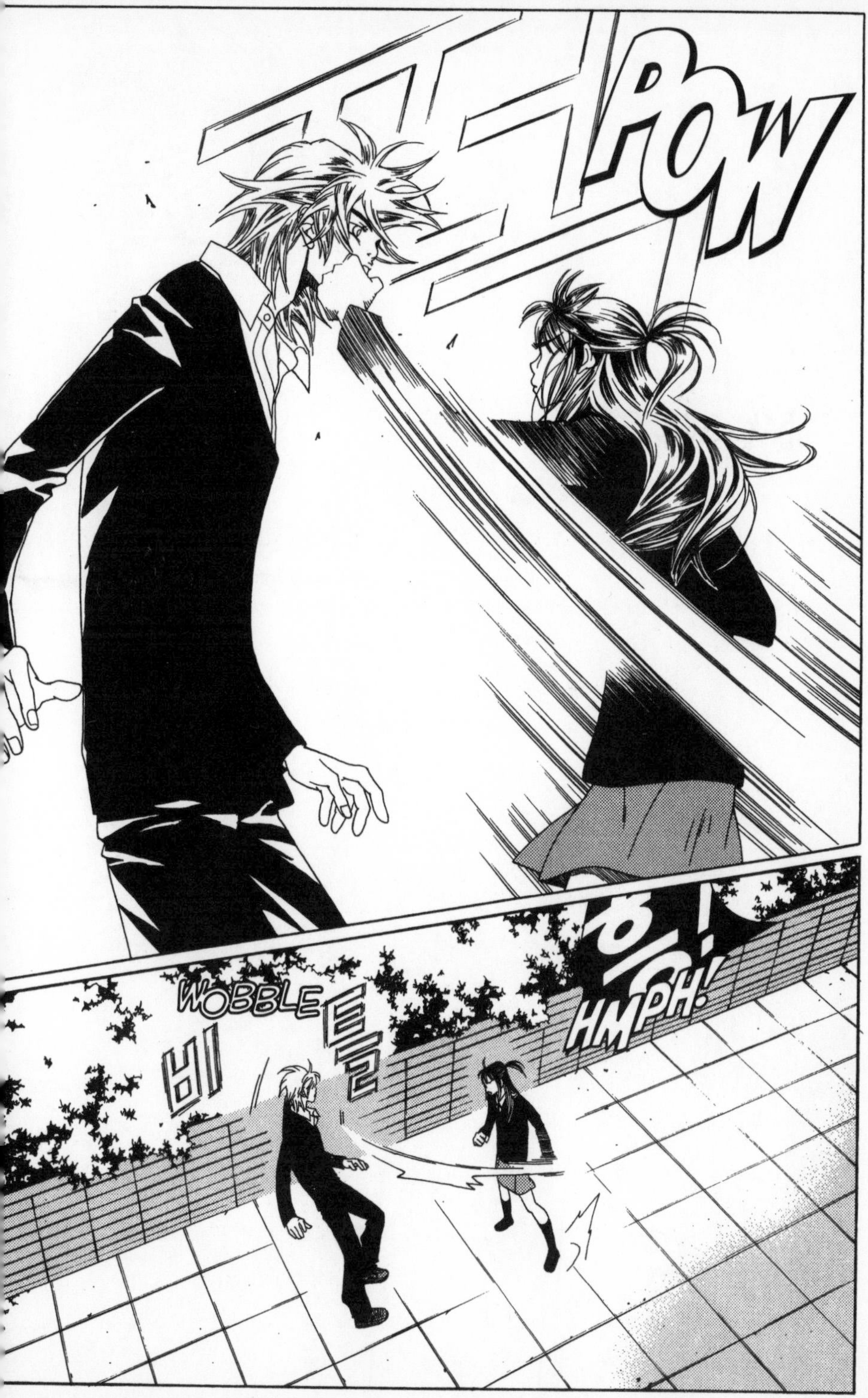
POW
흥!
HMPH!
WOBBLE
비틀

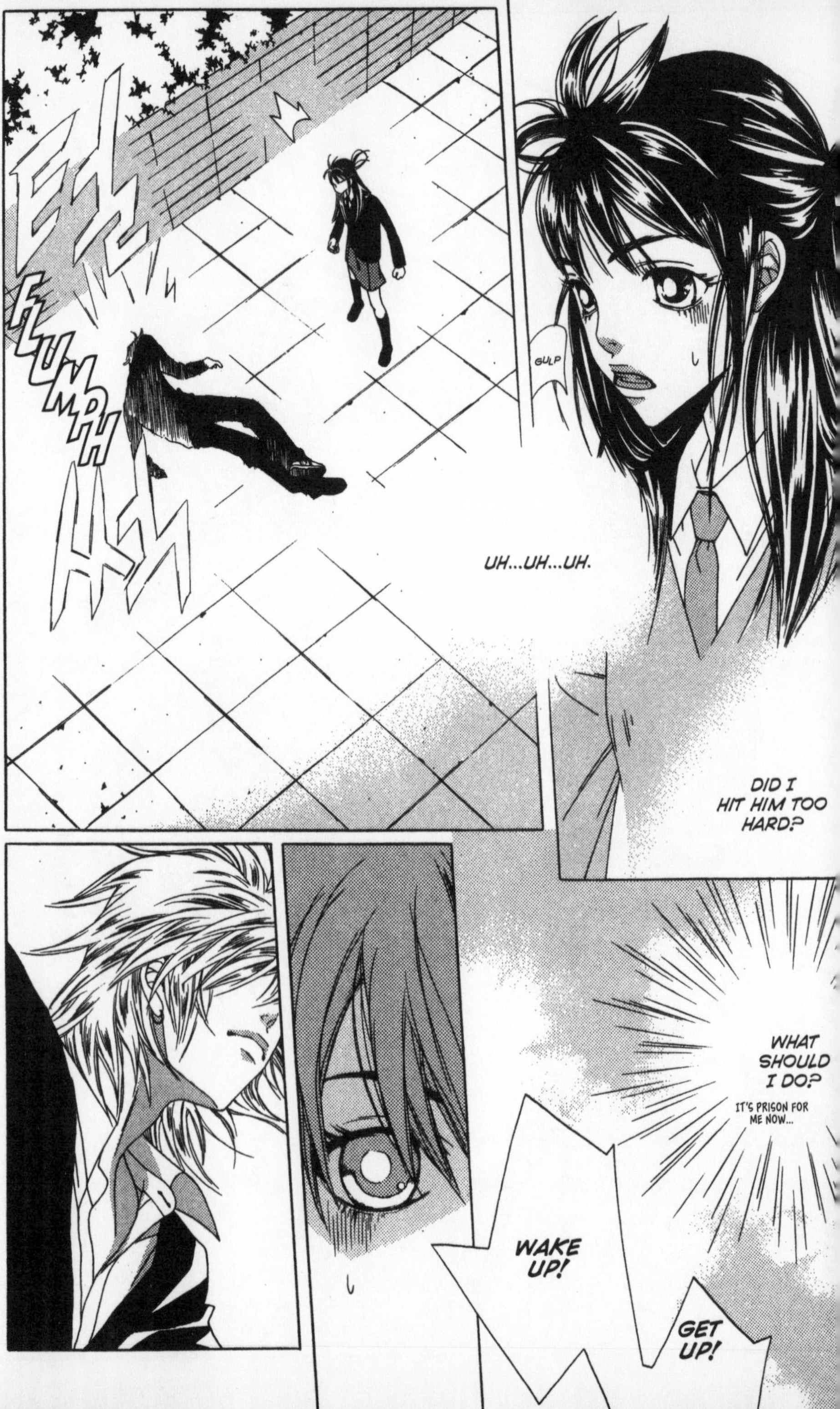
FLUMPH
GULP
UH...UH...UH.
DID I HIT HIM TOO HARD?
WHAT SHOULD I DO?
IT'S PRISON FOR ME NOW...
WAKE UP!
GET UP!

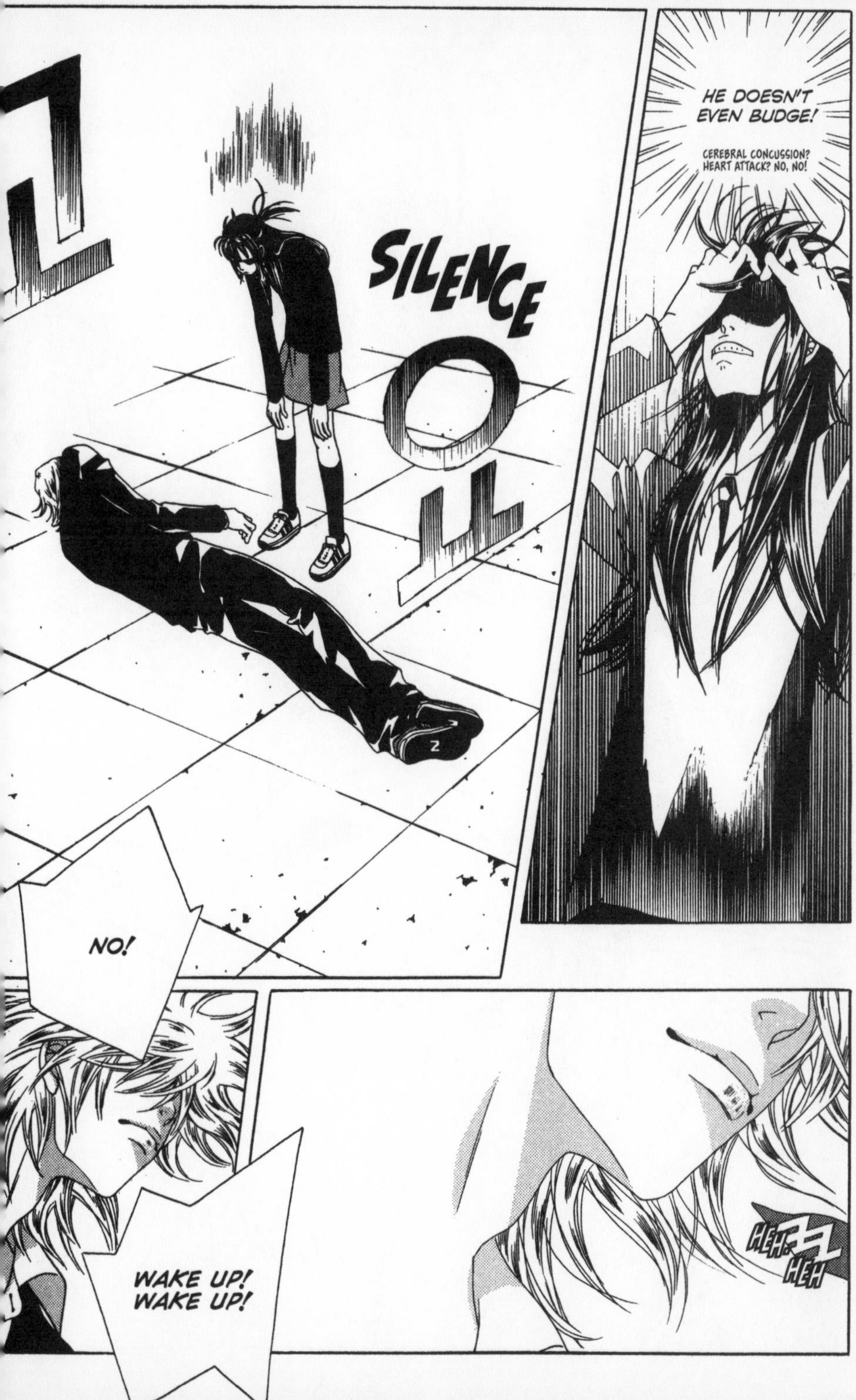
SILENCE
HE DOESN'T EVEN BUDGE!
CEREBRAL CONCUSSION? HEART ATTACK? NO, NO!
NO!
WAKE UP! WAKE UP!
HEH HEH

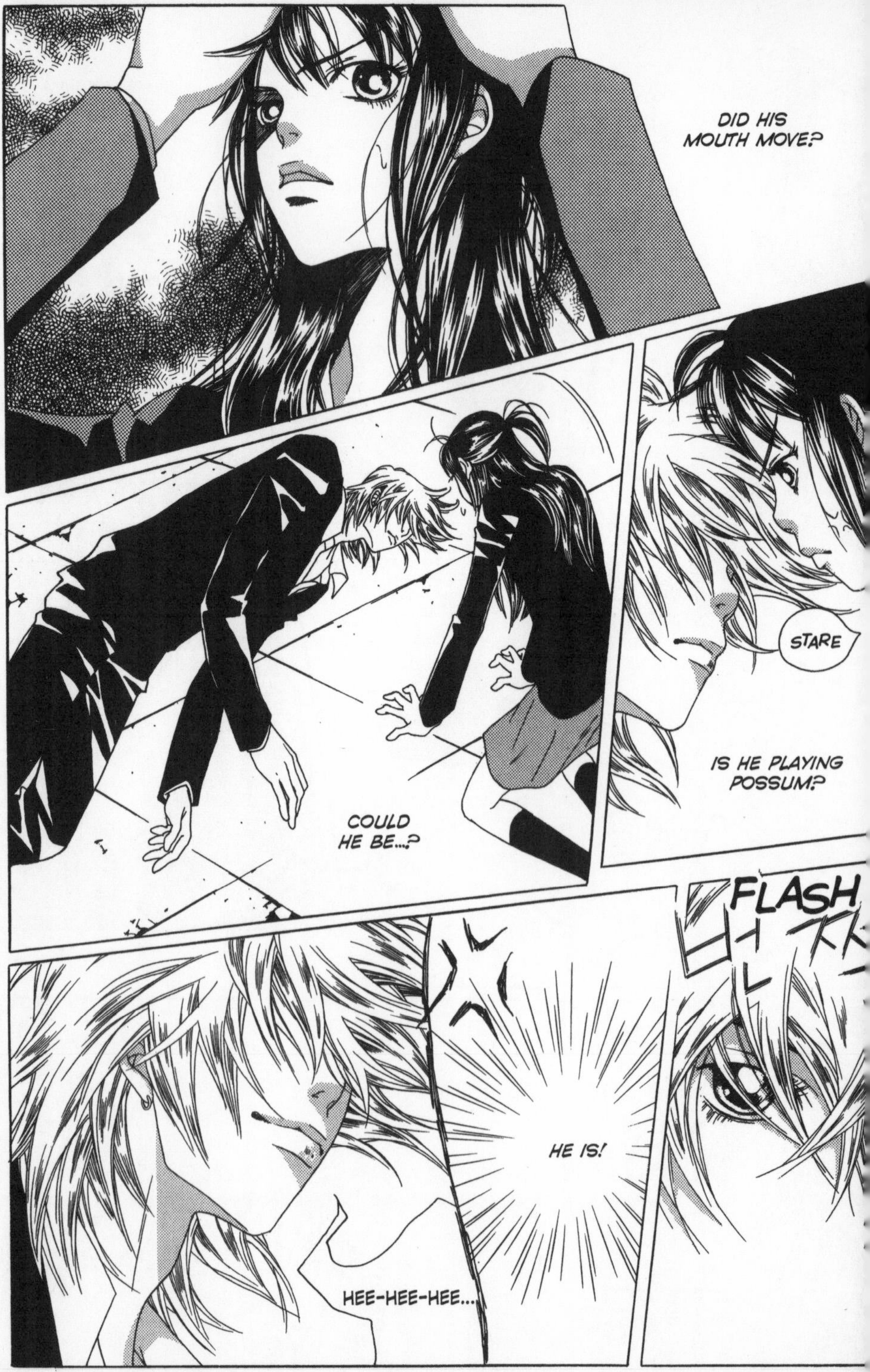
DID HIS
MOUTH MOVE?
COULD
HE BE...?
STARE
IS HE PLAYING
POSSUM?
HEE-HEE-HEE...
HE IS!
FLASH

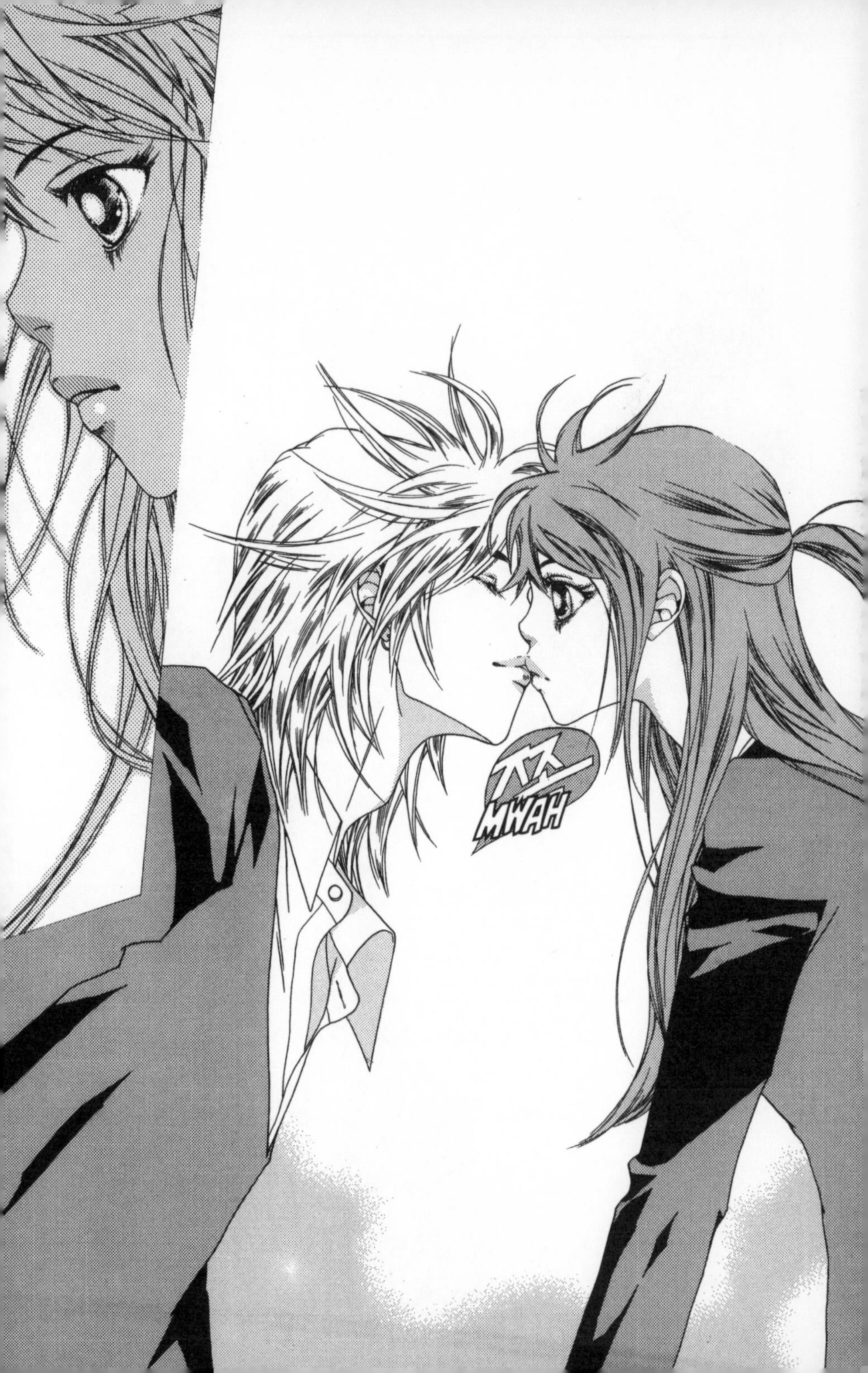
MWAH

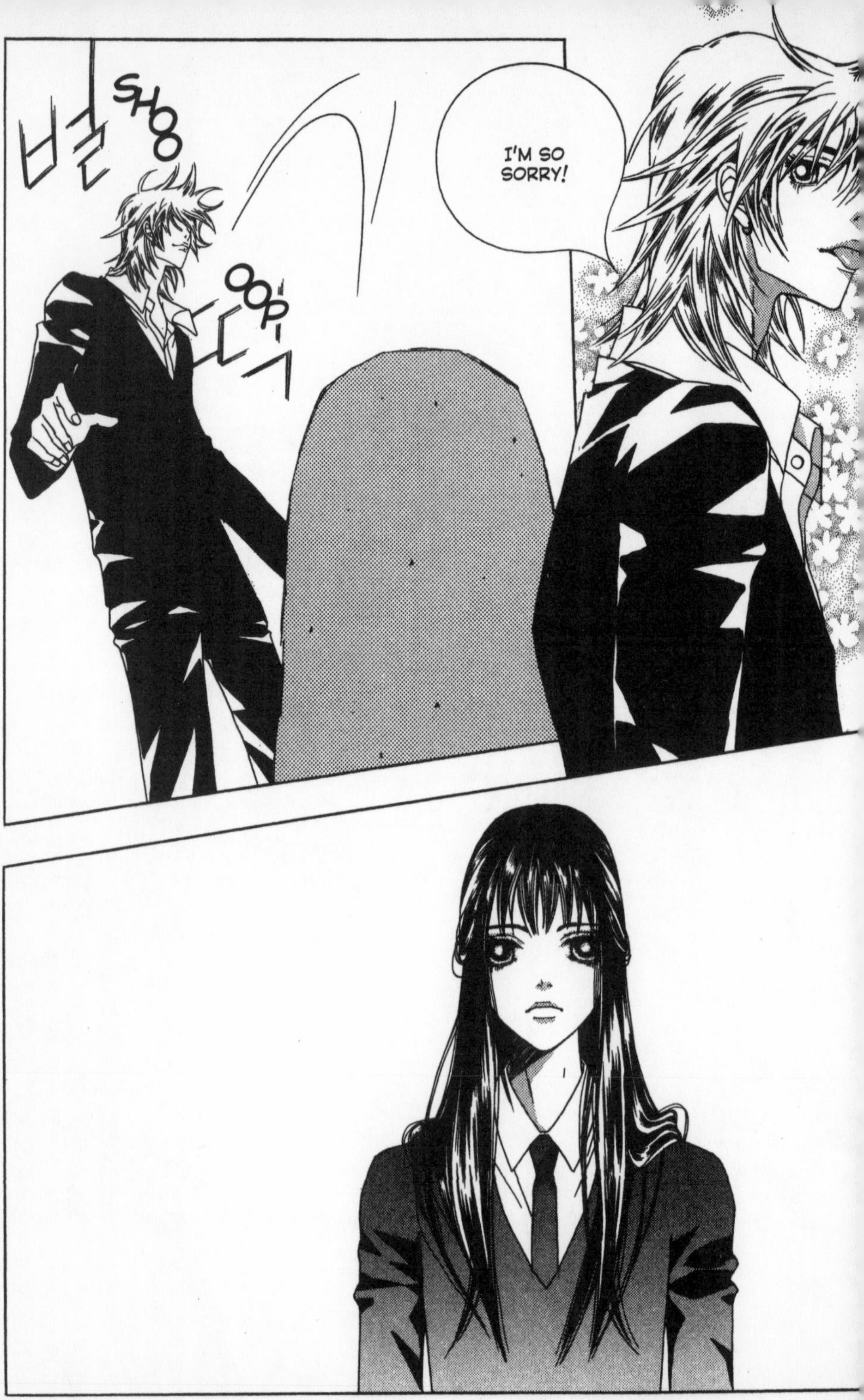
SHOO
OOP!
I'M SO SORRY!

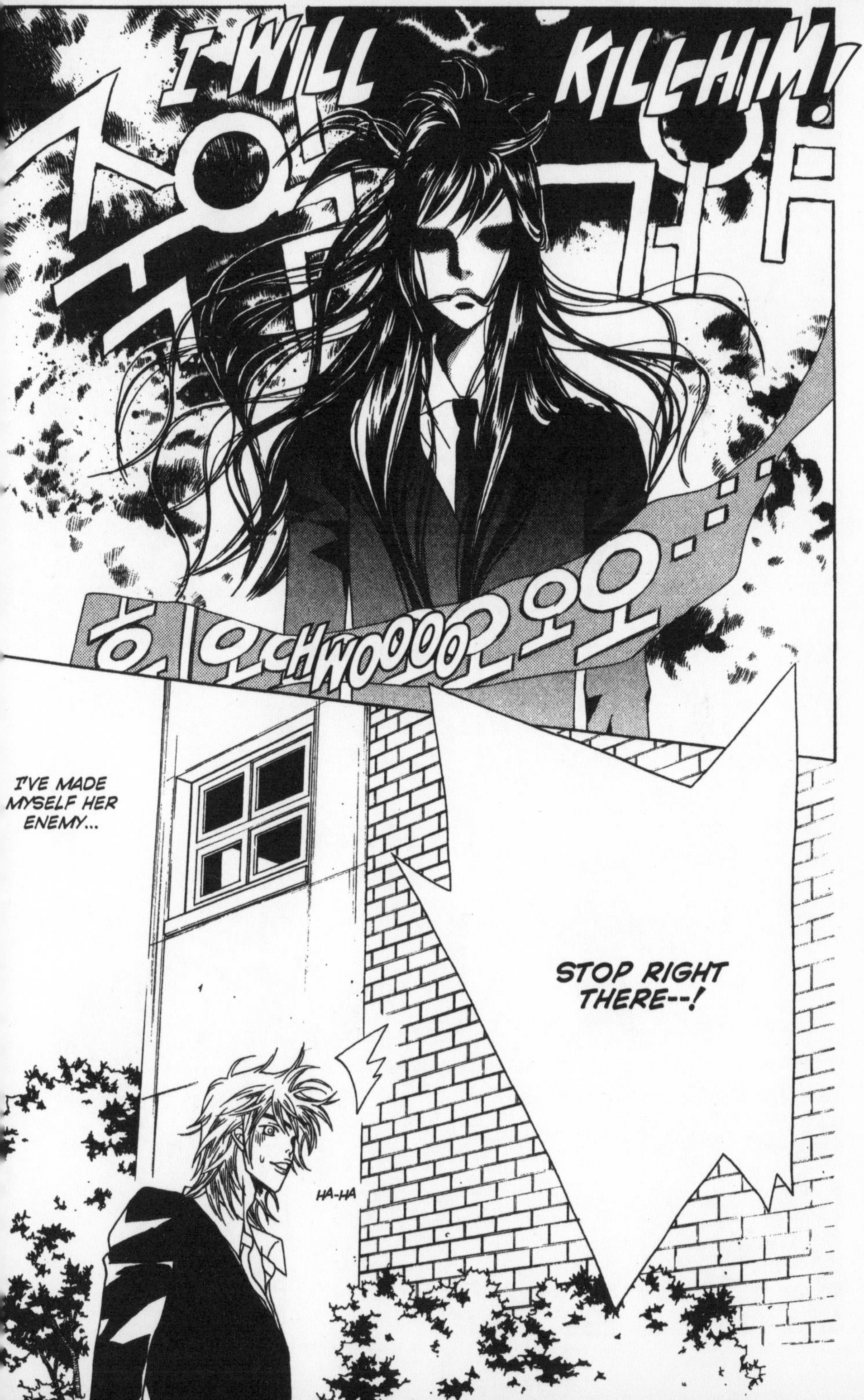
I WILL KILL-HIM!
CHWOOOO
I'VE MADE MYSELF HER ENEMY...
STOP RIGHT THERE--!
HA-HA

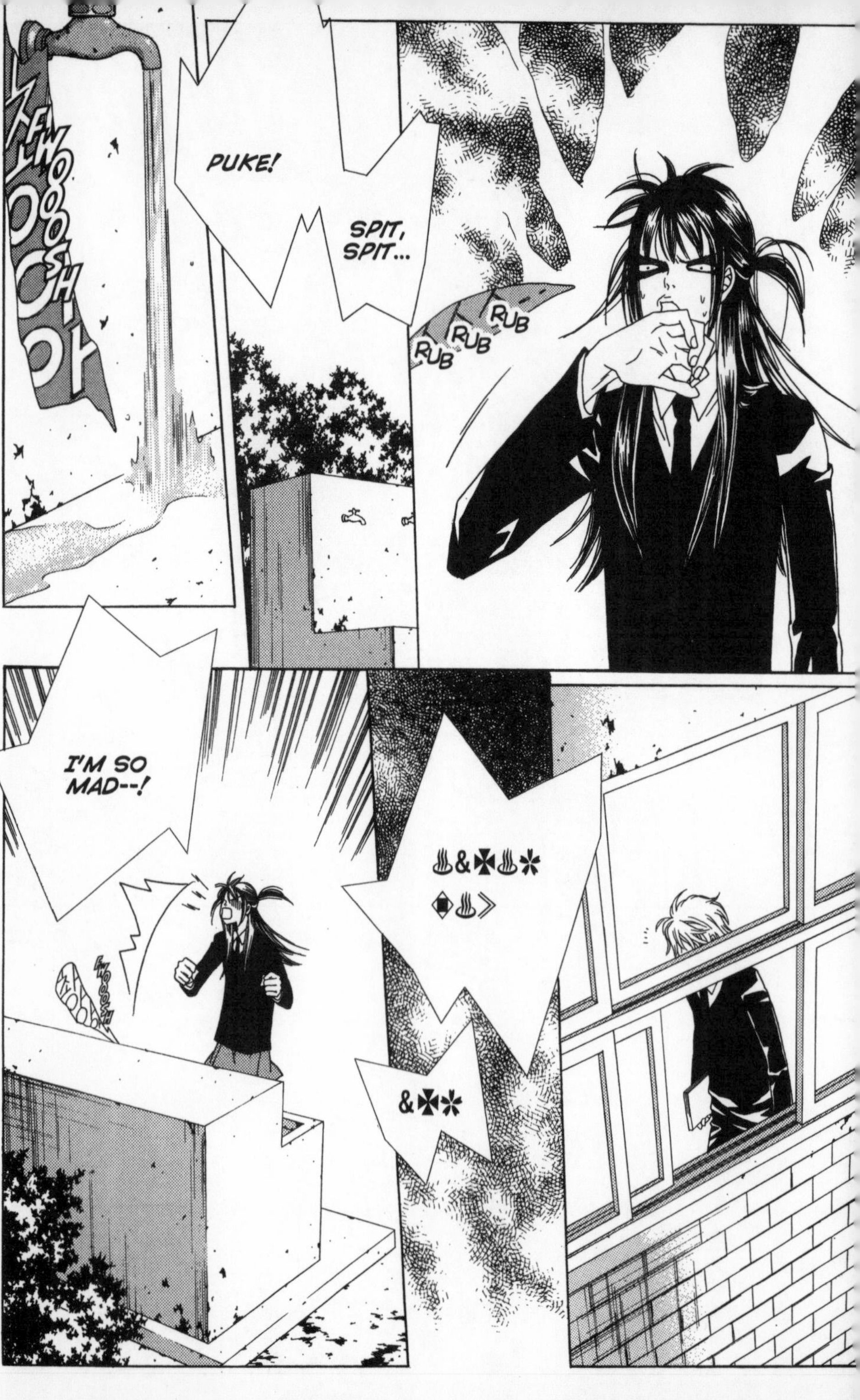
FWOOOOSH
PUKE!
SPIT, SPIT...
RUB RUB RUB
I'M SO MAD--!
FWOOOSH

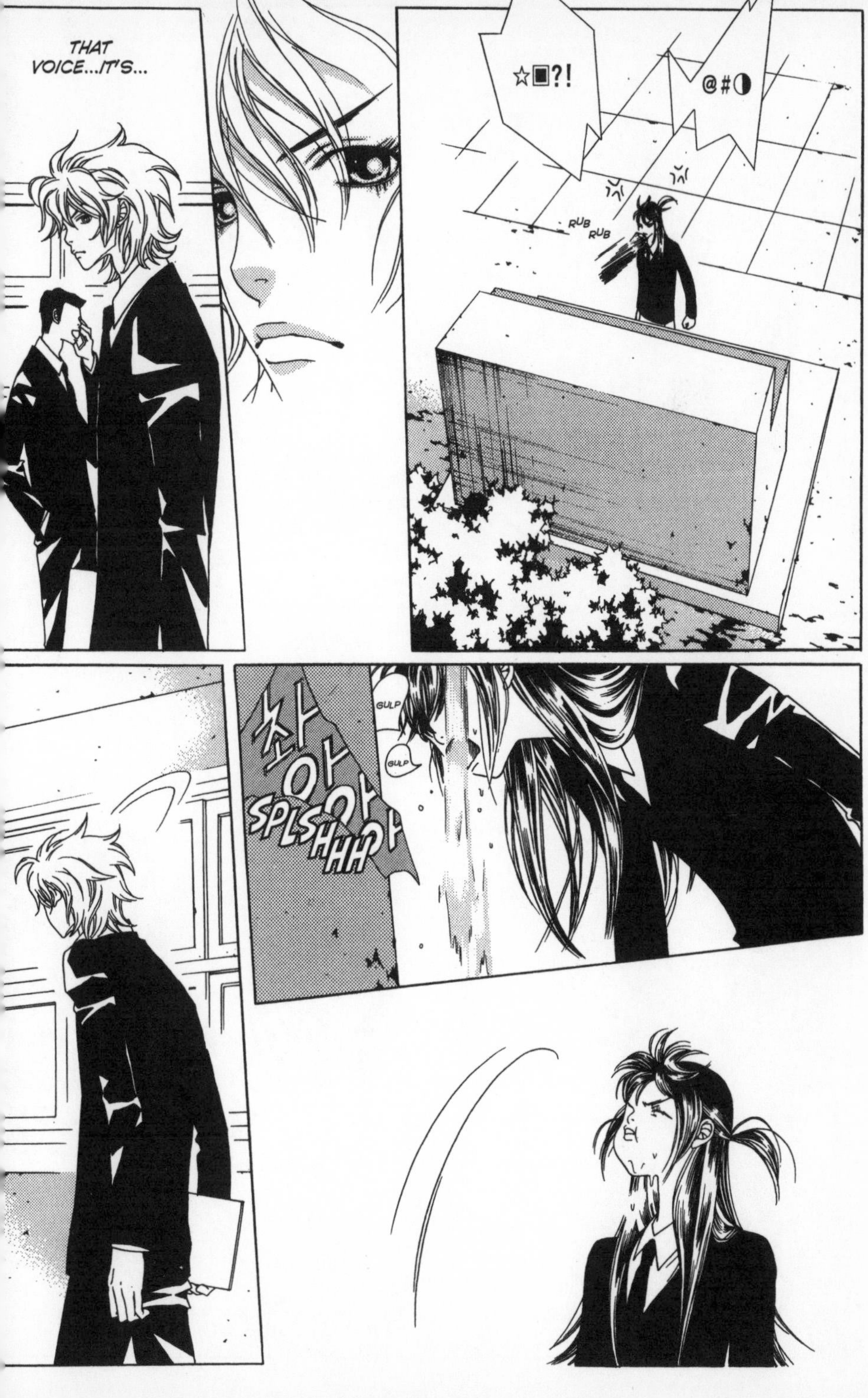
THAT VOICE...IT'S...
☆■?!
@#◐
RUB RUB
촤아아아
SPLSHHHH
GULP
GULP

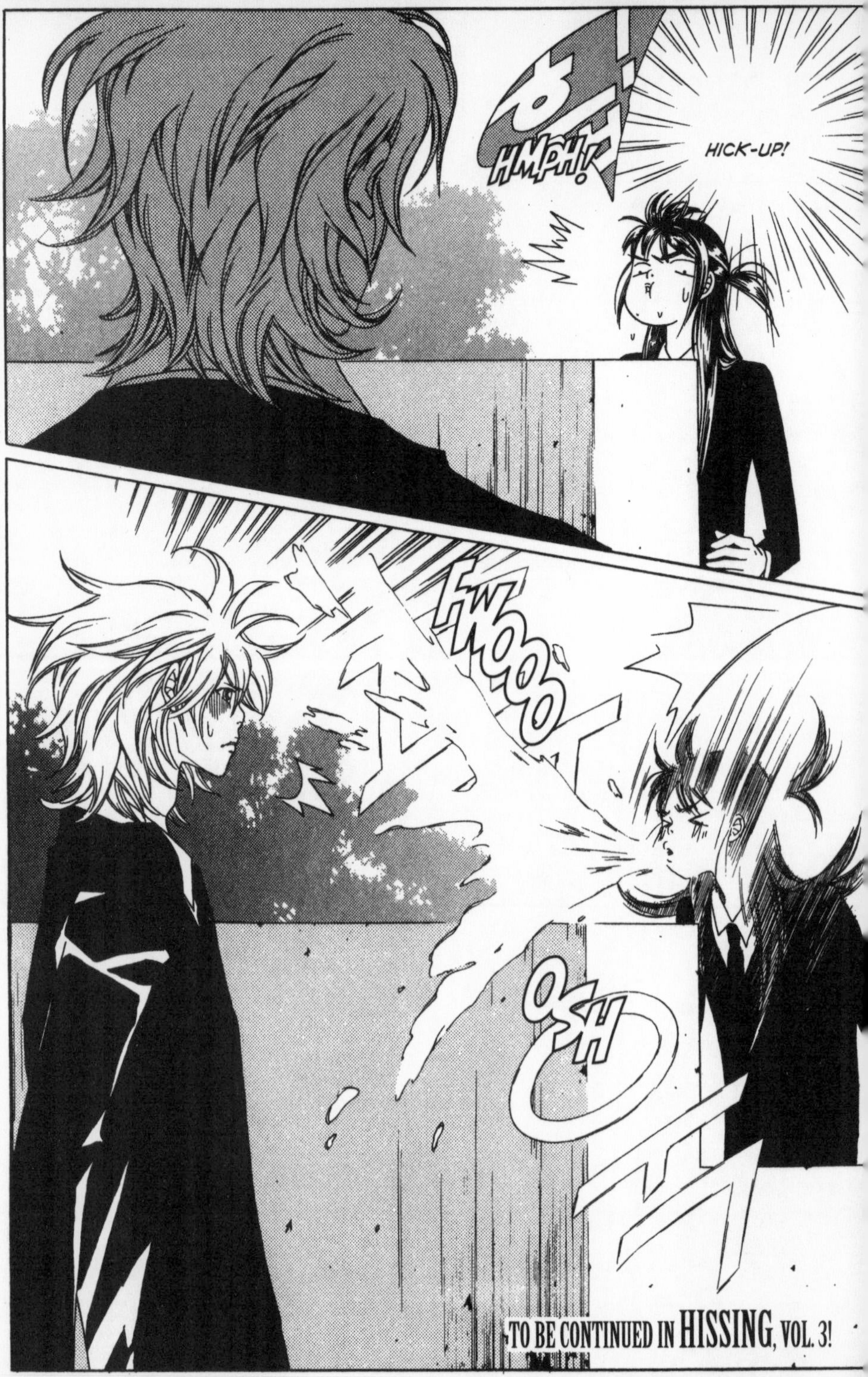
HMPH!
HICK-UP!
FWOOOO
OSH
TO BE CONTINUED IN HISSING, VOL. 3!

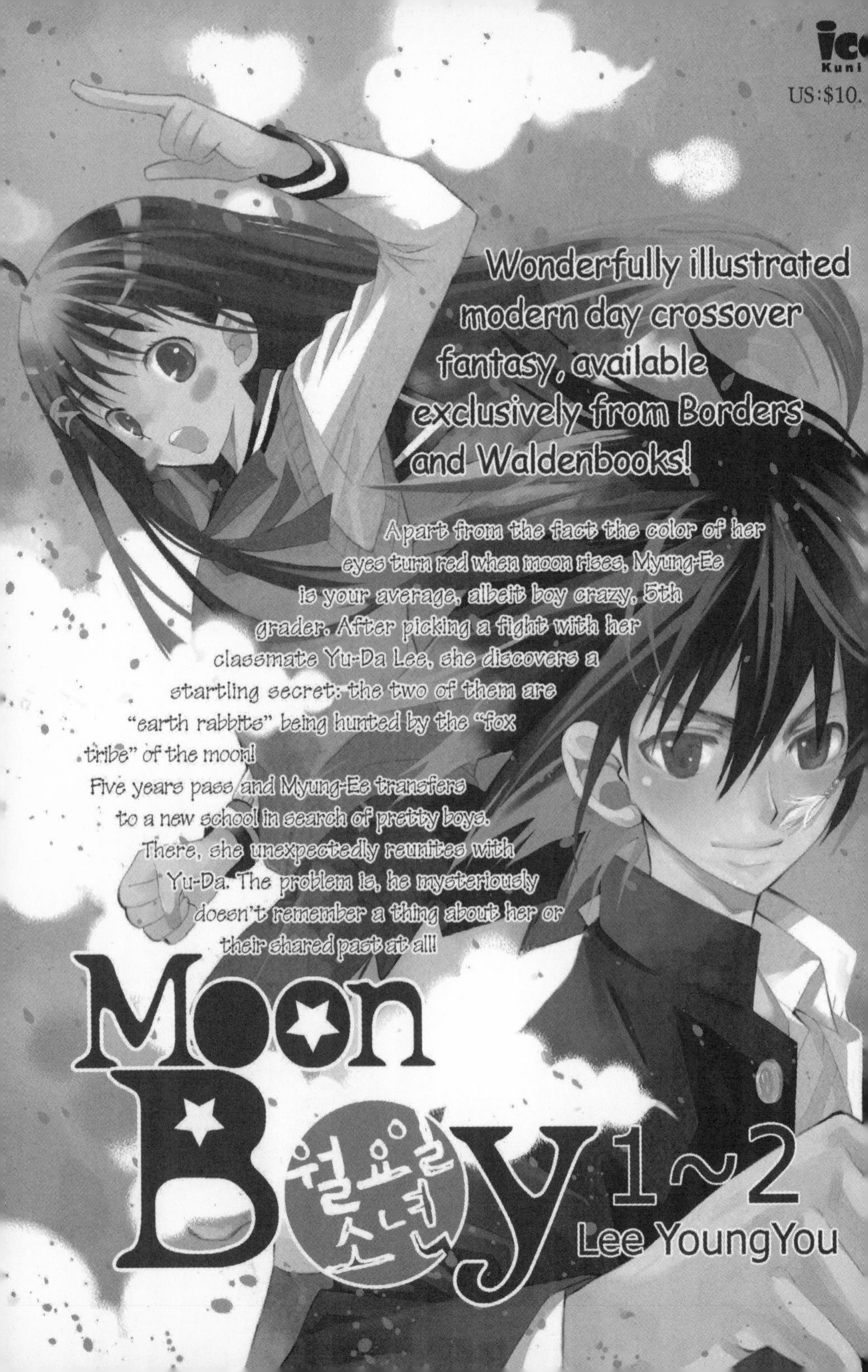

US:$10.
Wonderfully illustrated modern day crossover fantasy, available exclusively from Borders and Waldenbooks!
Apart from the fact the color of her eyes turn red when moon rises, Myung-Ee is your average, albeit boy crazy, 5th grader. After picking a fight with her classmate Yu-Da Lee, she discovers a startling secret: the two of them are "earth rabbits" being hunted by the "fox tribe" of the moon!
Five years pass and Myung-Ee transfers to a new school in search of pretty boys. There, she unexpectedly reunites with Yu-Da. The problem is, he mysteriously doesn't remember a thing about her or their shared past at all!
Moon Boy
월요일 소년
1~2
Lee YoungYou

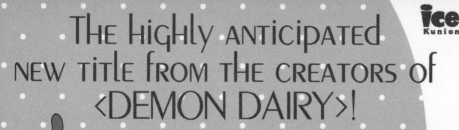

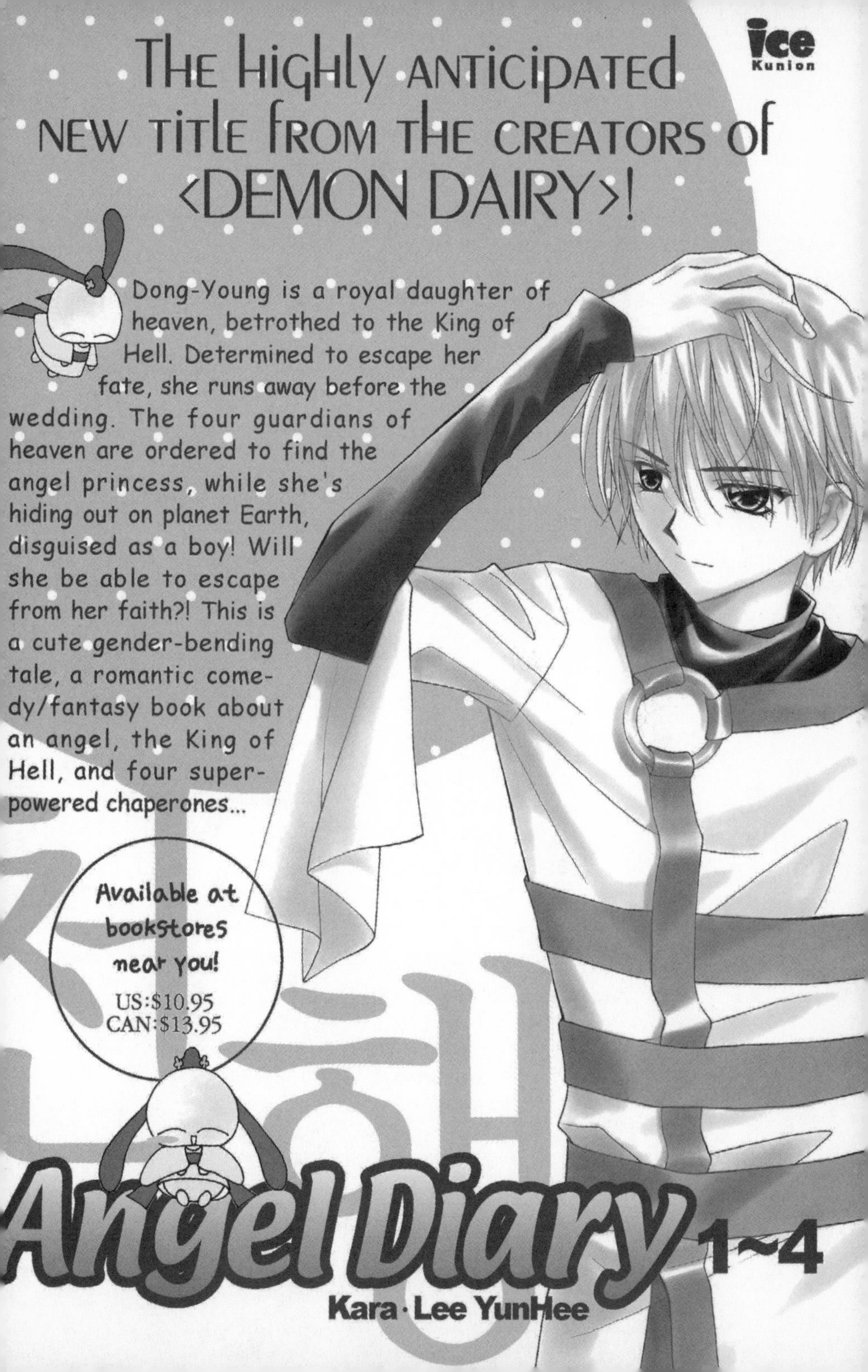

THE highly ANTICIPATED NEW TITLE FROM THE CREATORS of <DEMON DAIRY>!

Dong-Young is a royal daughter of heaven, betrothed to the King of Hell. Determined to escape her fate, she runs away before the wedding. The four guardians of heaven are ordered to find the angel princess, while she's hiding out on planet Earth, disguised as a boy! Will she be able to escape from her faith?! This is a cute gender-bending tale, a romantic comedy/fantasy book about an angel, the King of Hell, and four super-powered chaperones...

Available at bookstores near you!

US:$10.95
CAN:$13.95

Angel Diary 1~4

Kara·Lee YunHee

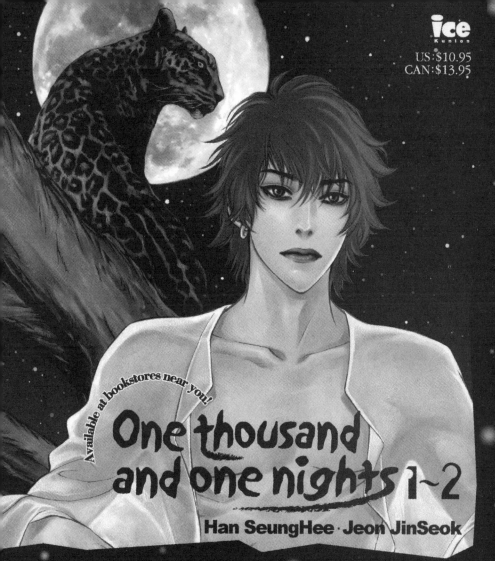

ice
Kunlon

US:$10.95
CAN:$13.95

Available at bookstores near you!

One thousand and one nights 1~2

Han SeungHee · Jeon JinSeok

Totally new Arabian nights, where Shahrazad is a guy!

Everyone knows the story of Shahrazad and her wonderful tales in the Arabian Nights. For one thousand and one nights, the stories that she created entertained the mad Sultan and eventually saved her life. In this version, our Shahrazad is a guy who wanted to save his sister from the mad Sultan by disguising himself as a woman. When he puts his life on the line, what kind of strange and wacky stories would he tell? This new twist on one of the greatest classical tales, Arabian Nights, might just keep you awake for another <one thousand and one nights>.

Danbi Original

Story and art by EunYoung Kang

Translation June Um · HyeYoung Im
English Adaptation Jamie S. Rich
Touch-up and Lettering Terri Delgado · Marshall Dillon
Graphic Design EunKyung Kim

ICE Kunion

English Adaptation Editor HyeYoung Im · J. Torres
Managing Editor Marshall Dillon
Marketing Manager Erik Ko
Senior Editor JuYoun Lee
Editorial Director MoonJung Kim
Managing Director Jackie Lee
Publisher and C.E.O. JaeKook Chun

Hissing © 2006 EunYoung Kang
First published in Korea in 2004 by SEOUL CULTURAL PUBLISHERS, Inc.
English text translation rights arranged by SEOUL CULTURAL PUBLISHERS, Inc.
English text © 2006 ICE KUNION

Published by ICE Kunion.
SIGONGSA 2F Yeil Bldg. 1619-4, Seocho-dong, Seocho-gu, Seoul, 137-878, Korea

ISBN : 89-527-4495-0

First printing, September 2006
10 9 8 7 6 5 4 3 2 1
Printed in Canada

www.icekunion.com/www.koreanmanhwa.com